Relationship
Marketing

OXFORD

UNIVERSITY PRESS

Great Clarendon Street, Oxford OX2 6DP

Oxford University Press is a department of the University of Oxford.
It furthers the University's objective of excellence in research, scholarship,
and education by publishing worldwide in

Oxford New York

Auckland Cape Town Dar es Salaam Hong Kong Karachi
Kuala Lumpur Madrid Melbourne Mexico City Nairobi
New Delhi Shanghai Taipei Toronto

With offices in

Argentina Austria Brazil Chile Czech Republic France Greece
Guatemala Hungary Italy Japan Poland Portugal Singapore
South Korea Switzerland Thailand Turkey Ukraine Vietnam

Oxford is a registered trade mark of Oxford University Press
in the UK and in certain other countries

Published in the United States
by Oxford University Press Inc., New York

© Mark Godson 2009

The moral rights of the author have been asserted
Database right Oxford University Press (maker)

First published 2009

British Library Cataloguing in Publication Data

Data available

Library of Congress Cataloging in Publication Data

Data available

Typeset by Graphicraft Limited, Hong Kong
Printed in Great Britain by
Ashford Colour Press Ltd, Gosport, Hampshire

ISBN 978–0–19–921156–2

3 5 7 9 10 8 6 4 2

Relationship
Marketing

Mark Godson

OXFORD
UNIVERSITY PRESS

Preface

This book has been written as an introduction to the broad and sometimes controversial subject of relationship marketing (RM). I first became acquainted with the subject of RM when studying for an MBA in the early 1990s. At that time, I was working as a New Product Development Manager within the Marketing Department of a market leading industrial products manufacturer. I have to confess that despite an academic background in marketing, I had often struggled to apply many of the principles of 'traditional' marketing theory to my own experiences and I had become a little sceptical about the subject. In RM, however, I found something that I could directly relate to and my enthusiasm for marketing as a subject was rekindled.

Several years later, however, when I set out to teach relationship marketing myself on a newly validated Postgraduate Masters programme at university, I was faced with something of a dilemma—what books should I use as core texts? As you shall see, RM is a broad subject covering areas from services marketing, industrial network marketing, retention marketing, database enabled customer relationship management (CRM), public relations, supply chain marketing—even aspects of human resource management! This diversity meant that not only was it difficult to apply hard-and-fast rules to RM, the subject could be approached from a number of different directions. Furthermore, the interpretation and application of RM could be unique to any particular organization depending on their own particular set of circumstances.

As a result, I used a variety of texts and published papers when putting my course together and combined this with my own experiences as a practising manager of over 25 years. It quickly became apparent that my students (all practising managers themselves on a part-time Masters degree) bought into the concepts and ideals just as enthusiastically as I had done, and were able to relate these to their own organizations. Some of them (particularly those working in not-for-profit organizations such as local authorities) admitted that this was the first time that a 'marketing' subject had had much relevance for them. But although I changed and adapted the course reading list over the years, it remained very diverse and lacked core texts which covered the entire subject area.

When it came to putting together a RM module for undergraduates, I decided to write this book to bring together the key principles of the subject and contextualize them through examples, real life cases, discussions, and debates. Given the propensity for individual interpretation and application around the subject, the book is designed to stimulate thought, reflection, and considered application around these principles, rather than provide a bolt-on tool box approach. The discussion questions incorporated into each case study and at the end of each chapter are all designed to this end and can be used in class, to stimulate debate, or in private study to stimulate reflection and further research.

It is not the intention of this book to dismiss 'traditional' marketing theory. Instead, it is intended to build upon the marketing knowledge already possessed by the reader and integrate this with the constellation of variables that can constitute RM. Although the book is predominantly aimed at undergraduate students, it can also be used by postgraduates who require a straightforward overview of the subject and by practitioners who are seeking to adopt a marketing strategy based around the specific requirements of their own organization.

The book broadly follows the four areas generalized in Morgan and Hunt's (1994) 'commitment–trust' theory of relationship marketing (*buyer partnerships*, *supplier partnerships*, *lateral partnerships*, and *internal partnerships*). However, in order to give the subject context and application the book has been presented in four basic sections:

- *Identification*—of what constitutes RM and where and to what extent it might be applicable.

- *Investigation and Interpretation (customer relationships)*—recognizing that customer relationships will be of first and foremost importance from a marketing point of view and exploring how these might work in practice.

- *Investigation and Interpretation (other relationships)*—the quality of relationships in the other three broad areas (supplier, lateral, and internal) which can impact upon how effectively an organization can serve its markets.

- *Implications*—of where this leaves organizations considering adopting the principles of RM and also in terms of where this might lead marketing as an area of academic study.

By adopting a broad base, I have attempted to provide a platform from which readers can identify areas of greater interest or relevance in order to pursue further reading or research, and the references and further reading sections given at the end of each chapter are intended to encourage the reader in this direction.

Throughout the book I have attempted to show how the principles of relationship marketing might apply (or not apply) in particular situations. Inevitably the use of contemporary cases and examples can lead to differences in interpretation and opinion and hence academic debate. Additionally, in a dynamic world things are constantly changing and I would therefore welcome any observations or suggestions which would help me to correct, update, or otherwise improve the text. To this end I would also be pleased to enter into further discussion with any reader who wishes to contact me.

Mark Godson
December 2008

Acknowledgements

The author would like to thank the following individuals, without whose input this book would not have been possible:

- Colin Gilligan for his guidance, support, and contributions;
- Peter Rudolph and Nick Hawkins for their contributions to Chapters 8 and 11;
- Nicki Sneath, Sacha Cook, and Helen Cook at Oxford University Press for their unflinching support and assistance in the writing process;
- Sue Hilditch for endless hours of proofreading and the production of figures and diagrams;
- all of the reviewers whose comments and suggestions were invaluable in helping to improve the text;
- Andy Cropper for his moral support.

Thank you all.

Mark Godson
July 2008

Dedicated to Nancy and Derek

And to the memory of Harry Hilditch (1934–2006)

Brief Contents

Detailed Contents

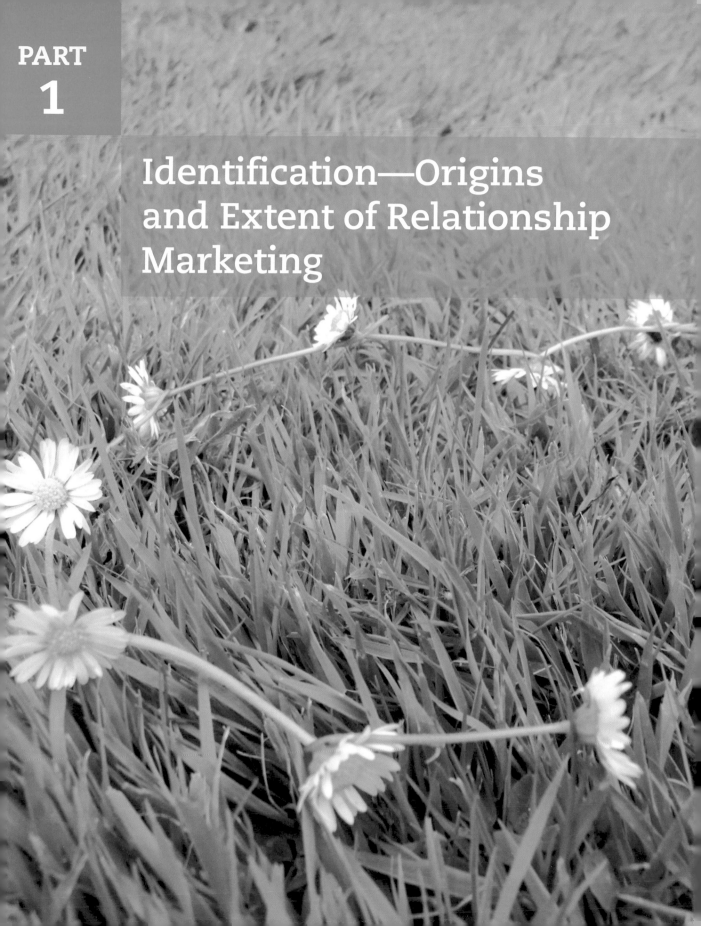

PART 1

Identification—Origins and Extent of Relationship Marketing

Background and Theory

Chapter Outline

Learning Outcomes

After reading this chapter you should be able to:

- understand the context of relationships and marketing;
- recognize the difference between 'traditional' transaction-based marketing and relationship marketing;
- acknowledge the potential limitations of traditional marketing theory;
- relate to the underlying principles of relationship marketing;
- draw upon some models of relationship marketing;
- accept some of the criticisms levelled against relationship marketing.

Introduction—the Scope of Relationship Marketing

Over the last 10 to 15 years, an alternative approach has gained attention in marketing circles—relationship marketing (the concentration of marketing efforts and resources on developing and maintaining long term, close relationships with customers and other stakeholders). Some have argued that this represents a fundamental shift in thinking within the marketing subject area and reflects the evolving nature of customer needs and expectations. Others maintain that relationship marketing is nothing new, that it is merely a redressing of existing business to business and service marketing principles, and that it has always been adequately covered within traditional marketing theory.

Whichever perspective is taken, there is no denying that relationship marketing is a tricky area to define, as it covers a wide range of areas, including customer relationships, supply chain relationships, customer value management, retention, and loyalty. It could be considered that relationship marketing begins and ends with customers—in which case the subject might be termed customer relationship management, or CRM. However, the early proponents of relationship marketing see the concept as being much wider than just relationships with customers; they would include all the relationships which a business must manage, both internal and external, in order for it to remain competitive and meet its customers' needs effectively. This view considerably expands the simple linear view of a supplier–customer relationship and replaces it with a 'constellation' of relationships (see Figure 1.1). If this is accepted,

Figure 1.1 Linear and constellation marketing relationships

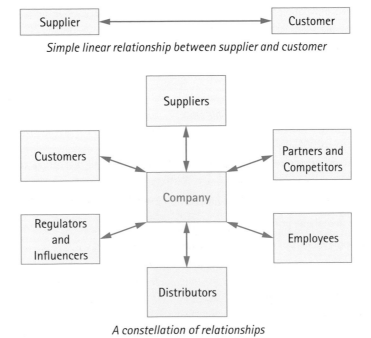

Simple linear relationship between supplier and customer

A constellation of relationships

then it makes the scope of **relationship marketing** (or RM) very broad indeed—in fact it takes it much further than the remit of the individual marketing department alone. The Opening Case illustrates how managing a variety of relationships has helped Sheffield Theatres to success.

Relationship marketing
a marketing approach which is based upon networks, interactions, and relationships

Opening Case Study with Questions

A Constellation of Relationships at Sheffield Theatres

Take a trip around the country and it soon becomes apparent that a revolution is taking place in theatre-going. The Birmingham Rep has seen a whopping 97% increase in box-office takings since 2001, and while others such as the Chichester Festival Theatre, the Bristol Old Vic, and the Liverpool Playhouse have seen more modest rises, all of them are in a decidedly better position than they were ten years ago. None more so than Sheffield Theatres (incorporating the Crucible Theatre, the Lyceum, and the Studio) where box-office takings have nearly doubled in the last decade.

Despite this resurgence, however, regional theatre-going still lags far behind cinema-going, particularly among younger audiences. In Sheffield, for instance, there are over 45 cinema screens, showing at any one time an average of 18 different films. While it is not unusual to make repeated visits to the cinema over a year, for many, a trip to the theatre is still a relatively infrequent event. The challenge for Sheffield Theatres therefore is not only to grow their market share, but also to develop this into long-term regular attendances. To this end they have pursued a number of objectives.

First, Sheffield Theatres have been busy raising the profile of their own theatre production company. For instance they have successfully drawn down a share of the £25 million cash grant made available by the Arts Council in 2001 to boost regional theatre-going. This has enabled them to employ renowned artistic directors Michael Grandage and, more latterly, Samuel West, whose ambitious programming schedules have attracted major artists such as Joseph Fiennes, Diana Rigg, Kenneth Branagh, and Derek Jacobi. Big names such as these draw big audiences and plays such as *Edward II* and *Suddenly Last Summer* have been huge sell-outs.

On top of this the Lyceum Theatre has been fully restored to all its original splendour. Designed by classic theatre architect W. G. R. Sprague, the Lyceum Theatre (his only surviving design outside London) opened in 1897, but by the 1970s had become run down and was very nearly demolished by the City Council. It was saved thanks to the efforts of the Hallamshire Historic Buildings Society, who successfully lobbied for the theatre to be given Grade 2 Star listed-building status. This saved it from the bulldozers, but it was not until the late 1980s that full restoration got under way thanks to a successful bid for funding from the European Regional Development Fund (ERDF) and funding from the City Council and local public donations. The newly restored theatre was opened to great acclaim in 1991 and now regularly attracts top theatre touring companies such as Northern Ballet, Opera North, the Royal National Theatre, and the Royal Shakespeare Company.

But this is not all. To many people, Sheffield's Crucible Theatre is synonymous with snooker, as it has been the venue for the World Snooker Championships since 1977. As well as the huge publicity the championships bring to the theatre and to the city of Sheffield, the income generated through ticket sales and television rights as well as sales in hotels, restaurants, and shops is a major boost not only to Sheffield Theatres, but also to the local economy.

In 2004, Chairman of the World Snooker Association, Sir Rodney Walker announced that other cities would be allowed to bid to host the annual championships. At just 980 seats, there was a feeling that the venue was too small. Additionally, the Crucible itself was beginning to show its age, particularly in its backstage facilities and lack of corporate entertainment areas. International interest in the sport was growing, particularly in China, and new sponsors, 888.com, were injecting large amounts of cash into the World Championships. The players themselves were generally against a move, as many of them really liked the intimacy of the Crucible and its association with the sport.

Sheffield Theatres immediately joined forces with the City Council to ensure that Sheffield's bid to retain the Snooker World Championships was successful. This involved commitment to refurbishing the Crucible Theatre and the development of a National Snooker Academy to be based at the Institute of Sport within the city. In the end, the partnership between Sheffield Theatres, the City Council, and local businesses was successful and Sheffield won the bid to host the contest for the next five years.

While Sheffield Theatres has been successful in raising its profile with touring companies, developing its own productions and retaining world snooker, it has to find a way of maintaining customer numbers. Like many theatres, it has long used direct mail as a means of keeping in touch with its customers, using a database of customers' names and addresses built up through previous ticket orders. This can be used to notify customers of forthcoming attractions. In addition the theatre has introduced a customer membership scheme called Square Circle in an attempt to develop closer relationships with its customers by enabling them to become 'part of the theatres'.

Square Circle is a tiered benefit scheme built around different levels of membership. All levels of membership attract a number of benefits including discounts on ticket prices, priority bookings, social events, talks, and tours of the theatres. Additional benefits are available depending on the level at which a customer joins. The annual fee ranges from £10 for Young Person (18–26) Membership up to £150 for Prestige Membership. Young people between the ages of 11 and 17 can join the scheme for free. The whole objective is not only to reward loyal customers but to give them a sense of ownership and involvement with the theatres and their productions.

Although theatre-going will probably never seriously rival cinema-going, the immediate future for Sheffield Theatres at least, looks bright.

Questions

1. Identify the relationships that Sheffield Theatres has had to develop in order to remain successful.
2. Should all of these be the responsibility of the marketing department?
3. How has Sheffield Theatres attracted new customers? How have they attempted to retain existing customers?
4. Do Sheffield Theatres distinguish between different types of customer?
5. How do managing non-customer relationships help Sheffield Theatres stay successful?

Sources:
'End of an era for the Crucible?' http://news.bbc.co.uk/sport accessed 22/04/05
'Snooker's future rests in Sheffield' http://news.bbc.co.uk/sport accessed 22/04/05
'Lyceum Theatre' http://www.made-in-sheffield.com accessed 14/02/07
Sheffield Theatres http://sheffieldtheatres.co.uk accessed 14/02/07

Can Relationships and Marketing be put Together?

Let's just consider relationships for a moment. We're all familiar with what the word 'relationship' means—simply put, it describes the state of affairs between two entities. Although relationships can exist between non-living objects (e.g. the relationship between the moon and the tides), we are predominantly concerned here with human relationships, with which we are surrounded; at home, at work, in our social lives, with neighbours, and indeed, with anyone with whom we come into contact, while going about our daily business. The nature and intensity of these relationships varies, but we all have them. It is impossible to have a relationship on your own. Society is thus a network of relationships—it's what makes the world go round.

So where does marketing come in? Most definitions of marketing focus on an organization's customer orientation and its ability to satisfy customer needs.

> Marketing is the management process responsible for identifying, anticipating and satisfying customer requirements profitably. (Chartered Institute of Marketing)

> Marketing is the social process by which individuals and groups obtain what they need and want through creating and exchanging products and value with others. (Philip Kotler)

> Marketing is essentially about marshalling the resources of an organization so that they meet the changing needs of the customer on whom the organization depends. (Adrian Palmer)

> The achievement of corporate goals through meeting and exceeding customer needs better than the competition. (David Jobber)

There are clearly two entities here: organizations (sellers) and customers (buyers) who, however fleetingly, interact with each other. Hence, a relationship of some sort must exist between the two. The study of RM concentrates on this area and seeks to show how the effective management of relationships can meet the organization's marketing objectives. The idea that good relationships with customers and others will lead to marketing success sounds obvious, but for many years this was not acknowledged in text book marketing theory. Instead of relationships, marketing thinkers concentrated on a more mechanical approach that could be adopted by any organization in order to put together a successful marketing strategy. This was predominantly based around the Four Ps (4Ps)—what is referred to here as 'traditional marketing theory'.

The Rise of Traditional Marketing Theory

Traditional marketing theory grew out of the onset of mass-produced consumer goods, which themselves were the result of the rapidly developing western economies of the nineteenth and twentiethth centuries. Mass production broke the direct link between customer and producer as most products went through a myriad system of supply channels to reach their end market. In mass-production-based economies, customers rarely met the people who were producing the products they bought and so relationships were not seen as being a part of marketing. Instead, companies developed brands in order to address issues of trust between buyer and seller. This is clearly illustrated by Henry Ford's standardized, black Model Ts which rolled off the production line like soldier ants. Henry had no direct relationship with his customers; if he had done, he would have offered more than just the one colour—but he did build a powerful brand name which is still a common sight on today's roads.

Direct relationships between customers and producers still existed of course—particularly in service industries (e.g. retail, travel, banking, insurance, and leisure), and in business-to-business (B2B) encounters where personal selling was hugely important and buyers and sellers met each other face to face. The recognition of 'relationships', however, was overlooked as theorists tried to come up with a marketing framework which could be applied to any commercial organization and aid the understanding and development of marketing as a business discipline.

Thus, the concept of 'traditional marketing', using a 'marketing mix' (Borden, 1964) was born. During the 1960s, American academic E. Jerome McCarthy (1960) devised the 4Ps as a simple framework in order to help businesses Produce, Price, Promote, and Place their products in a way that would make customers want to buy them (see Figure 1.2). This framework and its later descendents became the basis of what most would now consider to be traditional marketing theory.

At a time when marketing was a relatively young management subject, the 4Ps offered a simple and universal approach to marketing anything from cars to baked beans. It could even be split into four further mixes: the Promotion mix, the Price mix, the Product mix, and the Place mix. As a management tool the 4Ps thus became one of the principle bases of textbook marketing theory, as exemplified by Kotler (1967), and to this day is still widely taught.

Figure 1.2 McCarthy's 4Ps marketing mix framework

Product	What the customer buys including all aspects of the individual product or service such as design, features, accessories, performance, installation, instructions, guarantees, packaging, and branding.
Price	What the customer is charged for the product or service, including all aspects of pricing strategy, discounting, etc.
Promotion	How the customer is contacted, including all aspects of marketing communications such as advertising, public relations, and personal selling, as well as sales promotions.
Place	How and where the customer buys, including all aspects of distribution channels, physical logistics of getting the product to the customer and location decisions (e.g. direct or online supply, use of intermediaries, etc.)

However, critics of the 4Ps framework have pointed out that its usefulness is limited to consumer products and that it falls down when applied to the marketing of services or B2B marketing. It does not, for instance, explain why a customer might continue to use the same hairdresser or car mechanic year after year, even when rivals come along who are cheaper (price), more modern (product), more convenient (place), or heavily advertised (promotion). The fact that the hairdresser knows the customer, greets them by name, asks about their family and so on means that the total experience is enhanced beyond the simple mechanics of the 4Ps.

Likewise, in B2B marketing the 4Ps cannot explain why a company with a better product or lower price might still lose out to a competitor whose Managing Director plays golf with the Managing Director of the buying company. In other words the 4Ps is not much good at dealing with relationships in marketing. Of the 4Ps only Promotion represents any form of relationship with the customer as it involves communicating with the customer. However much of this is one-way communication, particularly in consumer marketing. While companies can communicate with their customers through advertising, it is not possible for customers to talk back to an advert and therefore no relationship is formed.

The obvious exception under promotion is personal selling, where two-way communication takes place and relationships between buyer and seller are important; it is no coincidence that personal selling is widely used in B2B marketing. As we shall see, B2B marketing was one of the major influences in the development of RM theory.

Doubts Cast on Traditional Marketing Theory

Throughout the 1980s and 90s, traditional-based thinking came under increasing criticism. By the late 1990s there was talk of the decline and even death of marketing as a subject (Brady and Davis, 1993; Doyle, 1995; Kashani, 1996; Gordon, 1998). While this might seem a little overdramatic, there is no doubt that for many, a rethink was needed, as even the Chartered Institute of Marketing admitted that: 'the old ways of marketing have become increasingly expensive, wasteful and inefficient'.

So why, after so many years, was traditional marketing suddenly in the spotlight amid claims that it was failing? Basically, there were four main strands: changing market dynamics; an inflexible 'tool box approach'; the narrow scope of traditional marketing and the stagnation of marketing as a subject area.

Changing Market Dynamics

One of the biggest criticisms of traditional marketing theory was that it was of its time and place, that being 1960s America. This was an affluent market characterized by mass consumerism, served by mass distribution channels and fuelled by mass media. On the back of traditional marketing theory, organizations such as Proctor & Gamble, General Motors, Marlboro, and McDonalds grew and prospered.

There was no shortage of customers who respected their brand names and were receptive to their advertising. The relative strength of suppliers meant that marketing theory tended to be designed from their point of view, rather than from the customers. As Baker (2000) puts it, the traditional 4Ps approach views customers as people *to* whom something is done, as opposed to people *for* whom something is done.

An example of this change in customer attitudes can be seen in the dilution of branding. Once a mainstay of 4Ps marketing (P for Product) branding has become less effective in some areas and has struggled to justify its high budget. Supermarkets' own brands have eroded the dominance of manufacturer brands to the extent that many big manufacturers such as Heinz have begun making supermarket own-brand products as well as their own. Even respected brands such as Marks & Spencer, McDonalds and British Airways can no longer rely on customers just because of their name. At the same time, as Egan (2004) points out, branding has become less concerned with building trust (which was the original objective of brands) but is simply being used as a market segmentation tool, with no real benefit for the customer. See Minicase 1, Do Customers Still Relate to GM's Brands?

Minicase 1

Do Customers Still Relate to GM's Brands?

Few consumer product sectors have relied on branding less than the car industry. Iconic brands such as Mercedes-Benz, BMW, Ferrari, and Bentley evoke feelings amongst their followers that are both passionate and intense. Even those more mundane brands such as Toyota, Citroen, Volvo, and Volkswagen enjoy an identity (some might even say, a personality!) with which customers can associate, be it reliability, innovative design, safety, or solidity. Companies owning all of these brands protect them fiercely and ensure that the values for which they stand are maintained. They are right to do so as the automobile industry is littered with examples of brands that have lost their way—often with dire consequences for their owners and employees.

In the late 1960s, for instance, the UK car market was dominated by British Leyland Motor Corporation (BLMC), a giant conglomerate formed by the mergers of numerous smaller motor groups and incorporating no less than ten separate brand names. The problem was that while these proud names had once stood for individuality, BMLC had diluted them by attaching them all to the same cars. Thus, the original Mini was available as either a Morris Mini Minor or an Austin 7 (same car, different badge). Even more incredibly, the group's mid-range cars could be had with either an Austin, Morris, MG, Riley, Wolseley, or Vanden Plas badge—each car differing only in the shape of the radiator, the internal trim, and some engine options. The public could see through the policy and was not impressed. BLMC lost out to rivals such as Ford and eventually the entire group disappeared.

BLMC is often hailed as an example of 'badge engineering' at its worst, but in recent years General Motors (GM), the world's biggest car manufacturer, has found itself going down a similar path. Like BLMC, GM is made up of a number of separate brands which once existed as companies in their own right. Unlike BLMC, however, GM strove hard to maintain the individual values of each brand and use these to delineate its market segments. Opulent Cadillacs were designed for a wealthy, older market, while Buicks with their sensible, quality designs traditionally targeted professional people such as lawyers and doctors. Oldsmobile, GM's oldest brand, was known for its innovation and design excellence, appealing to more technically minded customers. Pontiacs, on the other hand, with their racy styling and tuned engines, had always attracted those looking for something sportier. Finally, Chevrolet, GM's bread-and-butter brand, offered solid, hard-working, value-for-money transport for the 'average working Joe'.

The problem was that GM started to let these brand values slip, with the result that many of the models became indistinguishable from one another. Like BLMC in Britain, the cars used many of the same components and often only differed in the badge they wore. Instead of meeting customer needs, it seemed as if they were just there so that GM could claim that it covered all of the market segments. The American car-buying public began to desert GM and the company's profits and market share started to slide.

In 2001 GM axed the Oldsmobile brand and concentrated on a new brand, Saturn, which was positioned to compete with Japanese rivals such as Honda and Toyota. Saturn differed from GM's other brands in that the company attempted to develop a relationship between the brand and its customers through owners' club rallies, social events, insurance and travel services. However, although Saturn has been a success, GM's other brands are still struggling. Buick and Pontiac look particularly vulnerable as we go into the future as they are becoming increasingly squeezed between Chevrolet and Cadillac, who between them appear effectively to meet the needs of most market segments.

Questions

1. What is wrong with 'badge engineering'?

2. How has BMW made a success of the Mini brand, where BLMC failed?

3. What do customers relate to in a brand?

Sources:
GM General Motors http://www.gm.com/company/corp-info/history accessed 14/02/07
'GM warns it may phase out brands' http://bbc.co.uk/1/hi/business accessed 24/03/05

As customers have become more sophisticated, successful brands are those which add value by adapting to customer lifestyles (e.g. Mini, Nike, Gap) and have thus developed a positive *relationship* (see Chapter 4).

At the same time, the new breed of customers is less likely to take adverts at face value. Instead of absorbing mass, one-way communication, customers now expect to be listened to as individuals. In short, customers today are more demanding and less accepting in what has become an age of intensified, global competition. All of this means that what worked in 1960s America, when the 4Ps were developed, is not necessarily going to work in different markets today (Grönroos, 2007).

Inflexible 'Tool-box' Approach

The second reason why traditional 4Ps-based marketing has come under fire is to do with its 'prescriptive', 'tool-box' approach (Grönroos, 2007). The idea that a marketing strategy can be developed for any organization, simply by manipulating four basic variables looks great on paper, as it is neat, memorable, and relatively easy to apply (what marketing student does not know about the 4Ps?). It takes a formulaic, scientific approach which is a little similar to tuning a car engine for maximum performance.

This is fine to an extent, but customers are not car engines. As pointed out earlier, the simple 4Ps approach lacks the human, relational touch which often drives (or holds back) business. To answer some of these criticisms, McCarthy's framework has been adapted and modified many times over the years. Some of the more notable adaptations have been the 7Ps (Booms and Bitner, 1981), which acknowledged the importance of *people*; the 15Ps (Baumgartner, 1991), and even the 4Cs (Lauterborn, 1990), which tried to turn the 4Ps from being producer-oriented to being customer-oriented. (See Figure 1.3.) However, the basic idea of the framework mix remained.

Whichever mix is adopted we still end up with a 'tool-box' or 'magic formula' approach which is prescriptive rather than diagnostic. In other words it follows rather than leads. Proponents of the relationship approach assert that a whole new way of thinking about marketing is required (e.g. Gummesson, 1987, Grönroos, 1997).

Narrow Scope of Traditional Marketing

We have already noted that traditional 4Ps-based thinking does not sit particularly well with services marketing and industrial marketing where personal relationships and networking are often more important. This in itself gives the 4Ps a narrow focus. However, Gummesson (2002) also points out that it is unsafe to assume that the 'one size fits all approach' of traditional marketing will fare any better in consumer (B2C) markets. One reason is because many so-called B2C organizations often find themselves serving consumer and industrial markets at the same time.

For instance, Heinz Baked Beans are very much a consumer product and can be marketed to consumers using the 4Ps approach; but to sell to consumers, Heinz first has to sell to supermarkets, which technically speaking is a B2B relationship. Do they need a different mix for the supermarket buyers than they do for final customers?

Figure 1.3 Adaptations of the 4Ps

7Ps	Product; Price; Promotion; Place; People; Physical Evidence; Process
15Ps	Product/service; Price; Promotion; Place; People; Politics; Public Relations; Probe; Partition; Prioritize; Position; Profit; Plan; Performance; Positive implementations
4Cs	Customer needs and wants; Cost to the user; Communication; Convenience

Furthermore, Heinz might also sell its products in bulk to caterers, hotels, hospitals, etc. This would very definitely be classed as B2B marketing. This potential duality of types of market requires a flexible approach which the prescriptive 4Ps alone cannot always give. The acknowledgement that there are different types of customer, each of whom might need a different approach, is one of the cornerstones of RM. See Minicase 2, How Many Ways Can You Sell A Roof Window?

Minicase 2

How Many Ways Can You Sell A Roof Window?

Since 1996 the average price of a house in the UK has risen by over 200%. One of the consequences of this dramatic increase is that householders have embarked upon a frenzy of home improvements in order to get more out of their existing properties or to increase their value even further. At the same time, builders and developers have tried to make more efficient use out of smaller plot sizes in order to make new properties more affordable for first-time buyers.

All of this has led to an explosion in the sales of roof windows, as extra living spaces are created out of lofts and roof voids. Traditionally, the roof window market in the UK has been dominated by Velux, whose name has become synonymous with the product. However, in 1995 a new product, manufactured by Polish company Roto-Franke SA, entered the market. Branded in the UK as Skyview, the new window competed head-on with Velux.

The first thing Skyview needed was a marketing plan in order to establish the product and build up sales. However, it soon became apparent that although householders were the eventual users of the windows, a number of routes to the market existed, each of which had different requirements or expectations. In effect there were six distinct potential customers at whom Skyview could pitch their product. The market shares of these are shown below.

Figure 1.4 Routes to the market

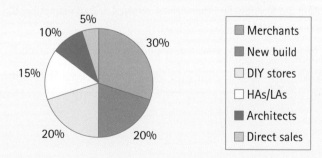

Builders merchants such as Jewson, Wickes, and Travis Perkins made up the biggest customer group. They sold on to jobbing builders who were typically employed by householders to do small building and conversion jobs. The merchants' primary concern was speed of delivery as they did not want to stock a huge range of different sizes themselves, but wanted to be able to offer a big range to their own customers. Merchants also required assistance in promoting the window through things such as display stands, installation videos, and branded catalogues.

The new-build sector consisted of large housebuilders such as Barratt, Bellway, and Persimmon. They bought in bulk direct from the supplier and their primary concern was the product itself, as its quality would reflect upon their own reputation as new housebuilders. These customers also required a keen price, particularly as they were buying in bulk.

The DIY superstores (B & Q, Homebase, Focus, etc.) also formed an important customer group. They sold directly on to householders who had elected to fit the windows themselves. Their chief requirement was low prices, along with heavy promotion in order to make the windows easier for them to sell on.

Housing associations (HAs) and Local Authorities (LAs) also formed an important customer group. They tended to buy in bulk for large social housing projects. Their concerns were low prices first, then product specification. This differed from architects who made up the fifth customer group. They demanded a very high specification which met their own design standards and they also expected expensive promotional items such as computer-aided design (CAD) packages to help them incorporate the roof window into their own specifications.

Finally, there was a small group of customers who were using the windows for themselves and chose to buy direct from the manufacturer. Price was unimportant to them as long as they found the right product and this usually meant something a bit out of the ordinary such as frosted or coloured glass or non-standard sizes.

Velux comfortably covered all of these customer types, but if Skyview wanted to follow suit, it was clear that they would need a completely different marketing mix for each customer type.

Questions

1. How might a marketing mix using the 4Ps differ between selling to new housebuilders and to builders merchants?

2. To what extent did Skyview find themselves involved in B2B marketing, B2C marketing, and service marketing?

3. What part might relationships play in developing some of these markets?

Source: Jeld Wen UK Ltd

Additionally, many *product*-based organizations also get involved in *service* marketing, usually in the form of training, installation, product guarantees, and back-up service. These peripheral service areas, which are often crucial to the sale of the product (and to the sale of *future products*) tend to be sidelined by a traditional marketing mix approach (Gummesson, 2002). Furthermore there are now a whole range of organizations requiring marketing skills, for whom the marketing mix approach appears inapplicable. Think about charities, football clubs, universities, political parties, hospitals, police authorities, and government agencies such as the tax office. All of them use marketing, but is it possible to apply 4Ps thinking to any of them?

The mention above of *future* product sales is of special significance here as this is another area where many have asserted that the marketing mix approach falls short. Traditional mass marketing tends to concentrate on making a sale by offering the best product at the best price in the best way and with the most effective promotion. Once the sale is made the job is done and the process starts all over again. This is known as **transaction marketing** where all of the marketing resources are brought to bear to ensure that the initial transaction takes place. No distinction is made between repeat custom and new transactions. Not only is this approach potentially wasteful, it marginalizes the value of building up a loyal bank of customers over a long period of time and once again highlights the narrow scope of traditional marketing theory.

Transaction marketing focuses on making a sale rather than on the ongoing retention of customers

Stagnation of Marketing as a Subject Area

The final reason why traditional marketing has been criticized is because it has not moved on (Gummesson, 1987). Simply adding more tools to the box, from 4Ps to 7Ps to 15Ps, etc. cannot disguise what some have claimed is a lack of innovation in the marketing field. While other areas, such as operations or financial management have moved on with things like just in time (JIT), total quality management (TQM), activity-based costing (ABC), and business process re-engineering (BPRE), all of which focus on core processes, marketing has just 'tinkered around with the components' (Doyle, 1995).

To compound the problem, research by Denison and McDonald (1995) suggested that within many organizations the marketing department suffered from poor image, complacency and poor integration with the rest of the organization—particularly 'where marketing had allowed itself to become merely a sales support function'. This has led to what Denison and McDonald call a cultural division between marketing and other parts of the organization. In practice this is a problem because in an age of empowered consumers, intense competition, and rapidly evolving technology, marketing cannot afford to be isolated. It needs to be a philosophy that runs right through the organization to ensure that it is customer-focused in everything that it does.

For this reason, the traditional stand-alone marketing department is unlikely to be able to manage. Denison and McDonald (1995) have noted that successful organizations have seen a reduction in the size of their traditional marketing departments. Proctor & Gamble, for instance, have dispensed with their central marketing function, preferring to spread their marketing efforts throughout the company in smaller business units. What remains of central marketing departments tends to concentrate on operational aspects of marketing rather than strategic. Thus, marketing is being forced to change, whether or not it wants to (Kashani, 1996).

The Rise of Relationship Marketing

The notion of RM did not arrive overnight. Rather, it was the result of the development of a number of separate management areas that were the subject of interest to marketing academics These are shown in Figure 1.5 and are summarized below. Some of the interest being shown in these separate areas resulted from the perceived failure of traditional marketing to offer plausible explanations (e.g. Grönroos's work on service marketing) and some of it developed independently (e.g. the analysis of networks in business marketing). However, directly or indirectly, each of these areas revolved largely around the management of relationships.

Main Influencers of Relationship Marketing

Marketing of Services. Looking at mainstream marketing text books from the 1960s, 70s, or 80s, one might be forgiven for thinking that services were of secondary importance to the manufacture of products. Where the marketing of services was considered, it was usually tacked on as a separate chapter. However, it soon became clear that this emphasis on the marketing of products did not reflect reality. For instance, in the UK today, services make up 73% of total GDP (Bank of England Statistics, 2006), a proportion not dissimilar to other developed economies in Europe, North America, and Australasia.

As a result, studies into the marketing of services began to grow as a separate subject area and by default, the recognition of the role relationships played in the delivery of services. Indeed, the whole term 'relationship marketing' was first used by Berry

Figure 1.5 The main influencers of relationship marketing

(1981) when writing about the marketing of services. Some took this concept of RM in services further and applied it to products as well (Grönroos, 2007). The argument was that even manufacturers of products have to get involved in some element of service (e.g. delivery, installation, usage instructions, invoicing, and after-sales service). The marketing of services thus provided a large underpinning to RM theory.

Customer Service Quality. Additionally, it was acknowledged by some that in many cases it was not the core product or service which determined customer satisfaction, but the quality of the peripheral service elements. If we buy a computer today we are buying much more than just the product; we will base our purchase on how good the back-up service is as well.

    Parasuraman *et al.* (1988) developed the theory around service quality with their technique, *SERVQUAL*, while Jan Carlzon (1987) talked about 'moments of truth'—the quality of each contact that a customer had with his company, no matter how small. Once again, the importance of customer relationships was underlined. Furthermore, the interest in service quality led to studies of *internal marketing*, as the vital role played by employees in overall customer satisfaction became clear. This in turn became another important part of RM.

> **Customer service quality**
> concentration on the customer's overall experience rather than the transaction at hand

Customer Retention Studies. While some were concentrating on service quality and overall performance, others were exploring the implications of this in terms of long-term customer retention. If it is true that 'it takes on average five times as much time, money and effort to gain a new customer as it does to retain an existing one' (Tom Peters, 1988) then many marketers are wasting their resources by constantly chasing new customers instead of looking after present ones. Consultants Peppers and Rogers (2004) and academics Reichheld and Sasser (1990) have undertaken much research to explore the value of long-term customer retention and the link between customer satisfaction and retention. We will look at this in greater depth in Chapter 3, but the acceptance of customer retention over customer acquisition has become a major part of RM theory.

Industrial (B2B) Marketing. Studies in this area have played a major role in the development of RM theory. **Industrial marketing** is often presented in traditional marketing textbooks as 'organizational buying behaviour' and has taken a different route from the 4Ps approach of consumer marketing. Instead, the marketing approach here is based around a 'decision-making unit' or DMU within the organization (Webster and Wind, 1972), with many different people being involved in the purchase decision. Companies wishing to sell into industrial markets would need to understand clearly the roles of the various people within the DMU and develop relationships at each level. This is usually above the ability of a single sales person and in real life a whole network of relationships would exist between individuals within the buying company and individuals within the selling company.

> **Industrial marketing**
> whereby a business markets its products or services to another business as opposed to the end consumer (otherwise known as B2B marketing)

    In situations like these, a successful outcome for both organizations would rely less upon how well the 4Ps have been manipulated and more on the strength and nature of the relationships between individuals within both organizations. This leads us onto the study of networking, which has been another important contributor to RM theory.

Industrial networks

organizations which are inter-connected with each other through chains of relationships

Industrial Networks. Studies in this area have been led by the Industrial Marketing and Purchasing Group (IMP). Their research led to the development of the inter-action approach to help to understand and explain how networks of relationships both within and between organizations contributed to overall business effectiveness (Ford, 2002). The idea of interorganizational relationships made up of networks of smaller, individual relationships has played a huge role in the development of RM theory. Industrial (B2B) marketing and networks will be explored in greater depth in Chapter 2.

Supply Chain Management. Linked to industrial networks is the area of supply chain management. Traditionally, distribution has fallen under marketing (P for Place), but here we are talking about the whole supply chain. Depending on where an organization sits in the chain, there will be upstream suppliers and downstream distributors. However, whereas in the past, each company in the chain might have acted individually, there has been a growing appreciation that by working together, the whole supply chain can be made more effective.

As competition increases, an effective supply chain that adds value for customers will benefit all the companies in the chain. Companies such as Tesco and Toyota have been quick to recognize this and use it for competitive advantage. Indeed, it is no longer a case of individual companies competing with each other; it is now supply chain against supply chain (Christopher and Peck, 2003). The careful management of relationships within the chain has thus become another important contributor to RM. Supply chain relationships are considered in Chapter 8.

Total Quality Management (TQM) is the final big influence on the development of RM theory. Again, this is not a traditional marketing subject; it has grown out of Operations Management theory. However, there are some clear links with market-ing and, in particular, with the thinking behind RM. For instance, both TQM and RM are ultimately concerned with customer perceptions and customer satisfaction. Today's definition of quality, under TQM, moves away from simple 'conformance to specification' to something which 'meets customer requirements' (Meldrum, 1997). This entails a clear appreciation of internal marketing in order that the whole company, not just the marketing department, becomes customer-oriented.

All of these subject areas developed (and are still developing) as separate research areas in their own right, but all of them have had a strong influence on the develop-ment of RM. The underlying theme is the consideration of customer added value and satisfaction brought about through the successful management of long-term rela-tionships—both inside and outside the organization.

Nordic School

a group of Scandinavian marketing academics and practitioners who championed the philosophy of RM in the 1990s

The Nordic School

Among those who were instrumental in developing the concept of RM were Evert Gummesson at Stockholm University and Christian Grönroos at the Swedish School of Economics. In the early 1980s they established the **Nordic School**, a group of academics and marketing practitioners interested in the development of services. Indeed, if Philip Kotler (1984) can be described as the 'grandfather' of traditional marketing literature in the 1960s, then Evert Gummesson might be considered the 'grandfather' of a comprehensive RM concept in the 1990s.

It was Gummesson who brought together the various thoughts on service marketing, industrial marketing, internal marketing, customer satisfaction and retention into one encompassing concept which he outlined in his seminal paper 'The New Marketing—Developing Long-term Interactive Relationships', which was first published in 1987. As an employee with a consultancy group, he saw that even though his company seemed to ignore all aspects of traditional marketing theory, it was still very successful. He therefore began to question the validity of traditional marketing and realized that relationships were the key. As he put it, 'if the terrain differs from the map, trust the terrain, not the map'. As a result, much of RM theory is based on real-life case studies and advocates a closer relationship between industry and academia, encouraging 'research where it all happens, by reflective practitioners'. In other words it is practical and based on real business experience.

RM caught the imagination of many European companies and unsurprisingly, given the proximity of the Nordic School, many of these were Scandinavian—SAS, Ericsson, ABB, and Volvo. During the 1990s literature on RM grew rapidly and there is now a wide section of theory and research upon which to draw from all over the world. However, perceptions of RM differ and we will look at some of the different theories shortly. For now, let us stick with Gummesson. His (2002) definition of RM is simple: 'RM is marketing based on interaction within networks of relationships'. Although the main aspects of RM have long existed in industrial and services marketing, Gummesson's work propelled RM into the world of consumer goods marketing, which had hitherto been the domain of traditional marketing and the 4Ps. As we shall see, it is in this area that RM has proved to be most controversial.

The arrival of RM caused quite a stir in marketing circles because if offered a whole new way of thinking about the subject. Advocates of RM were quick to put the concept forward as an alternative to what they dubbed 'transactional marketing' (traditional, 4Ps-based marketing designed primarily to aid the selling of a product as opposed to building relationships). Others argued that RM was not a revolution and that it could be quite comfortably accommodated within traditional theory—particularly since the 4Ps had become the 7Ps, having been joined by People, Process, and Physical Evidence. Whatever one's view point (and these will be debated in depth throughout this book), there is no denying that RM brought a different set of values to marketing thinking.

Values of Relationship Marketing

According to Gummesson, the chief differentiators of RM over transactional marketing theory are as follows:

1. Long-term sustainable relationships, primarily with customers, but also with suppliers, partners, employees, and others who might affect the firm's business.
The main goal of the marketing department changes from new customer acquisition to customer retention and extending the duration of existing relationships.

For instance, the *Reader's Digest* has built a multi-billion dollar global business through targeting existing customers with products and services that fit their previous buying profile. If you have predominantly bought books on history or nature, you will be sent offers on similar products. The company can trace its customers' buying profiles back over 20 years or more. As a result, they rarely have to advertise to attract new customers and the *Reader's Digest* magazine has the highest circulation of any magazine in the world.

2. *The idea that everyone is a winner.*

The aim of RM is to create mutual value for everyone in the relationship. Thus, there are no adversarial relationships within the supply chain or other partners. The satisfaction of customers creates a win–win situation for all. This even extends to relationships with competitors.

For example, the big airlines have long had agreements with each other to offer frequent flyer incentives. The 'Flying Blue' frequent flyer club includes Aeroflot, Air France, Aero Mexico, Continental Airlines, and KLM, even though some of these companies are direct competitors. Even bitter rivals, BA and Virgin, have an agreement to share spare parts if one of their aircraft breaks down abroad. The net winner is the customer, but the airlines win as well, as they are able to maintain their service to the customer.

3. *Recognizing that all parties can be active.*

Relationships with customers are not just confined to the sales force; interactions should take place between everyone in the network including the customer. After all, if there is no interaction, then how can there be any relationship? Customer interaction is harder to achieve in consumer markets than it is in service markets where the customer is also co-producer, but it can be done.

For example, motorcycle manufacturer Harley Davidson has built a very strong relationship with its customers. The company runs local clubs or 'chapters', for owners of its bikes, where members can meet up socially. The chapters offer additional benefits such as advanced riding courses, competitive insurance deals, and travel and touring services. Chapter members are affectionately known as 'Hoggers' (from Harley Owners Group) and feel a strong sense of belonging with each other and with the company itself.

4. *Service values not 'bureaucratic legal values'.*

Bureaucratic legal values are characterized by jargon and the application rules and regulations. In these circumstances there appears to be a mechanical approach, where customers feel that they are being treated as statistics rather than human beings. This is particularly common in financial services markets (e.g. banks and insurance companies) as well as many not-for-profit and public sector organizations (such as hospitals, tax collection agencies, etc.). By contrast, RM makes the customer the focus of everything that the organization does.

Virgin Finance has made a unique selling point out of its policy of cutting out complicated financial jargon and replacing it with simple explanations that its customers can easily understand. Likewise, recent adverts from opticians Dolland & Aitchison have highlighted the human and personal touch which their customers can expect, as opposed to the 'sausage factory' approach of their larger rivals.

All in all, the proponents of RM would have it that RM is benign and harmonious. There is no room for winning at the expense of others. It therefore takes a different approach to some traditional strategic marketing theories which talk of 'outgunning' the opposition, 'flanking manoeuvres', 'head on assaults', and 'guerrilla tactics'.

Theories of Relationship Marketing

Gummesson's Challenge to Traditional Thinking

Gummesson's landmark paper in 1987 presented nine issues that challenged traditional marketing thinking (see Figure 1.6). These issues were not so much a model of

Figure 1.6 Gummesson's nine issues to challenge traditional marketing thinking

1. *'The many headed customer and the many headed seller'* acknowledged the complicated networks of relationships made up of individuals within both the selling organization and the buying organization interacting with one another.

2. *'The real customer does not always appear in the market place'* recognized that sometimes the permission or approval of an external party is required before a sale can take place, e.g. governments or shareholders.

3. *'The customer as co-producer'* reinforces the concept of a two-way, interactive relationship between customer and supplier and the part that the customer must play in order to effect a successful transaction.

4. *'Market mechanisms are controlled externally'* acknowledges that traditional marketing efforts can often be distorted or undone by existing webs of relationships such as friendships, nepotism, club memberships, etc.

5. *'Market mechanisms are brought inside the company'* raises the issue of internal buyers and sellers within an organization, where one department buys from another.

6. *'Interfunctional dependency and the part-time marketer'*—the idea that everyone in the company, not just sales and marketing personnel, plays a part in ensuring overall customer satisfaction.

7. *'Process management and the internal customer'* extends the idea of the customer-focused organization by suggesting that everyone inside the organization should treat each other as suppliers or customers within an overall process that leads to ultimate customer satisfaction.

8. *'Internal marketing'* suggests that the organization's marketing efforts should be directed not only to the external market, but internally to employees too.

9. *'Relationship quality'* reflects how the skilled handling of relationships between the buyer and the seller enhances the customer's perception of quality.

RM as they were a challenge to traditional thinking. The overall implications were that:

- networks and external non-customer relationships must be taken into account in an organization's marketing strategy;
- internal relationships should also be managed in order to meet customers' needs more closely;
- the whole organization has to be oriented towards the customer;
- the nature and extent of relationships with customers should be understood and carefully managed.

Four Partnerships Approach to Relationship Marketing

Gummesson's thinking was developed by others into a RM model consisting of four broad partnerships where exchanges take place: customer partnerships, supplier partnerships, internal partnerships, and external partnerships (see Figure 1.7).

Although on the surface not all of these partnerships appear to be relevant to traditional marketing, they form an important part of RM theory because they can impact directly upon an organization's customer orientation. In other words, these partnerships can and do affect the overall marketing effectiveness of the organization. These theories therefore take a 'constellation relationship' approach rather than a simple linear relationship between buyer and seller.

Figure 1.7 Four broad partnerships of relationship marketing

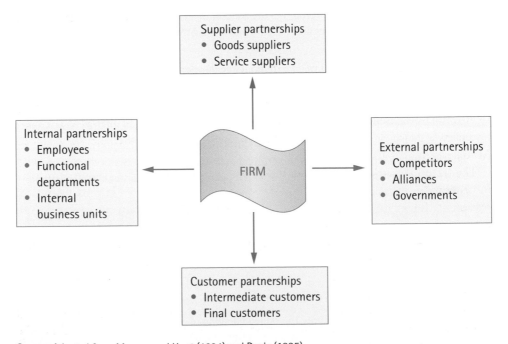

Source: Adapted from Morgan and Hunt (1994) and Doyle (1995)

Figure 1.8 The six markets model

Source: Christopher *et al.* (1991) *Relationship Marketing: Bringing Quality, Customer Service and Marketing Together.* © Elsevier. Reproduced with kind permission

The Six Markets Model

Staying within this vein is the **Six Markets Model** (Christopher *et al.*, 1991) (See Figure 1.8.)

Here, instead of talking about 'partnerships', the word 'markets' is used directly suggesting that the firm has to widen its concept of marketing. Within this model the 'customer market' appears in the middle, reflecting the fact that this is the biggest and most important market with which the firm should concentrate on developing relationships. Internal and supplier markets are similar to the partnerships already noted in the models of Doyle and Morgan and Hunt. However, the Six Markets Model introduces three different relationship 'markets'.

The 'referral market' recognizes the part that positive word-of-mouth can play in generating business for a firm. This would include recommendations from professionals, for instance a dentist recommending a particular type of toothpaste to his patients, or an estate agent recommending to her clients a good solicitor for conveyancing. It makes sense to develop good relationships with people who can recommend your products. Referrals also come from existing satisfied customers who tell their friends and acquaintances about the firm, underlying once more the importance of customer satisfaction in RM.

The 'influence market' is similar to some of the 'external partnerships' highlighted in the Morgan and Hunt and Doyle models. Influence markets might include the media, consumer groups, the government, and financiers (e.g. banks or shareholders)

Six Markets Model

proposes six key market domains, representing groups that can contribute to an organization's effectiveness

who back the firm with capital. Effective management of relationships is vital with anyone who can influence the success or otherwise of the business. This is often carried out through public relations (PR).

Finally, 'recruitment markets' refer to the firm's ability to attract and retain the right kind of employee. Organizations such as hospitals and universities will want to attract doctors and academics who are at the top of their field as this will enhance their ability to offer more to customers. At the other end of the salary scale, organizations that rely on good customer service must also attract employees who will treat their customers well. For instance, fast-food companies rely on their front-line staff to create a good customer experience. Attracting the right kind of staff here can be particularly challenging as these jobs are often seen as offering low-paid, unfulfilling jobs with few prospects.

Gummesson's 30Rs

The 30Rs

Gummesson's (2002) suggestion of '30 tangible relationships which can become part of the company's marketing planning'

Finally, Gummesson (2002) refined his original theory and came back with no less than 30 identifiable relationships which he termed the **30Rs**. (See Figure 1.9)

Figure 1.9 The 30Rs

Gummesson's 30 R's

Classic market relationships

1. Supplier–customer
2. Supplier–customer–competitor
3. Distribution channels

Special market relationships

4. Full-time marketers–part-time marketers
5. Customer–service provider
6. Many-headed customer–many-headed seller
7. Supplier–customer's customer
8. Close versus distant relationships
9. Dissatisfied customers
10. Monopoly relationships
11. Customer as 'member'
12. Electronic relationships
13. Relationships to symbols and objects
14. Non-commercial relationships
15. Green relationships
16. Law-based relationships
17. Criminal networks

Mega relationships

18. Personal and social networks
19. The real customer does not always appear in the marketplace
20. Alliances change market mechanisms
21. The knowledge relationship
22. Mega alliances change market conditions
23. Mass media relationships

Nano relationships

24. Market mechanisms are brought inside the company
25. Internal customer relationships
26. Quality relationships between operations and marketing
27. Relationships with the employee market
28. Two-dimensional matrix relationship
29. Relationship to external providers of marketing services
30. Owner–financier relationships

Source: Gummesson (2002) *Total Relationship Marketing.* © Elsevier. Reproduced with kind permission.

Gummesson split his 30Rs into four overall categories:

Classic Market Relationships are those which form the basis of all marketing and apply in some form to all organizations. Three types of relationship fall under this category:

R1: the classic dyad, the relationship between a seller and a customer, representing the basis of commercial exchange;

R2: the classic triad, the three-way relationship comprising the customer, the seller, and the seller's competitors, if competition exists within a market;

R3: the classic network, used here to represent the relationships within distribution channels.

Special Market Relationships derive from R1, the classic dyad, but require separate consideration owing to their unique characteristics. These relationships will apply to some organizations, but not to all. It can be seen that some of these (**R4, R5, R6, R7**) come straight from Gummesson's original nine issues and relate particularly to industrial and services marketing.

As a result of the explosion in Internet marketing, **R8** (close versus distant market relationships) and **R12** (electronic relationships) have become particularly significant for more and more organizations. This area will be explored in more depth in Chapter 6. Similarly **R13** (relationships to symbols and objects) reflects situations where personal contacts are not always possible (e.g. car markets with their final customers) and things such as brand and image form the basis of the relationship. This is looked at in Chapter 4.

R9 (the relationship with dissatisfied customers) and **R11** (the customer as a 'member') are very much tied up with customer retention marketing and loyalty. These are concepts which can apply across any number of marketing situations and form a hugely important part of RM. Conversely, **R10** (monopoly relationships) and **R14** (non-commercial relationships) do not usually fall within traditional marketing thinking. Examples would include bodies such as police authorities, the National Health Service, or local government. Customers have no choice but to use these bodies and pay taxes to fund them, but it is now accepted that they must deliver good customer service (as laid out in the 'customer charters' which they have adopted), or risk loss of support from local populations and possible penalties from central government.

Finally, **R15** (green relationships), **R16** (law-based relationships), and **R17** (relationships with criminal networks) all reflect the realities of doing business in a world increasingly obsessed with environmentalism, litigation, and corruption. Some have made green relationships the basis of their marketing strategy (e.g. the Body Shop and Co-op Bank), while others have struggled with poor image in this area (e.g. the US car industry). Meanwhile, every organization has to face the possibility of being sued by disgruntled customers. In some markets (e.g. medical practice) this entails a customer relationship based around lengthy disclaimers. Customers are asked to sign agreements that they will not be able to hold the company responsible if something goes wrong or that they will not seek compensation—not a great start for a close personal relationship! (See Minicase 3, The Customer's Solicitor is Always Right?) Relationships with criminal networks are an accepted part of doing business in many parts of the world, where back-handers and bribes to corrupt officials are sometimes the only way to enter a market.

Minicase 3

The Customer's Solicitor is Always Right?

Anyone using an e-mail account will have received from time to time the humorous postings from their friends regarding seemingly outrageous lawsuits brought upon companies by disgruntled customers. Such is their entertainment value, they have been given a name, 'The Stella Awards', named after 79-year-old Stella Liebeck in the USA who successfully sued McDonald's after spilling hot coffee on herself.

Other examples include Kathleen Robertson who won damages from a furniture store after falling over a child who was running around unsupervised—despite the fact that the child was her own son. Another woman was awarded over $100,000 after slipping on a drink spilled on the floor of her local restaurant. The drink was on the floor because she had just thrown it over her boyfriend during an argument. Then there is Merv Grazinski who crashed his brand new Winnebago motor home after setting the cruise control to 50 mph and going through to the back to make a sandwich. He purportedly sued Winnebago for damages, claiming that there was nothing in the vehicle's owner's manual that told him he should not do this.

Amusing though these stories are, it is likely that most of them are just urban myths. However, they do serve to illustrate that companies need to be increasingly aware of their legal responsibilities to customers. The Stella Liebeck case did actually exist and McDonald's were forced to pay damages, although not as much as some of the websites suggest, as she was found to be partly responsible herself for the mishap. In July 2000 McDonald's was sued in a joint action in the UK by over 50 customers who claimed that McDonald's served their coffee too hot. Recently, the company has had to contend further lawsuits from customers who claim that they have become obese after eating at the fast-food chain. These cases were dismissed by a court in New York.

The problem that companies have is that it only takes one successful prosecution to open the floodgates. In May 2005 the UK cigarette industry held its breath awaiting the outcome of a £500,000 case brought against Imperial Tobacco by a widow whose husband had died of lung cancer after smoking 60 a day for most of his life. She argued that at the time he took up smoking there were no warnings from the company that it could be injurious to his health, even though they had evidence to suggest that it was. In the end the court ruled against her, arguing that her late husband must have known about the risks as these were common knowledge at the time.

Nevertheless, many organizations now have had to adapt to the very real possibility of expensive litigation against them. Hospitals and medical practitioners are obvious examples, but schools and colleges have to think carefully about the activities they allow their pupils to take part in, airlines have to contend with claims for Deep Vein Thrombosis (DVT) and before the 2007 smoking ban in public places came into force in England and Wales, restaurants and pubs ran the risk of being sued by customers inhaling secondary smoke.

Questions

1. Are organizations who protect themselves against legal claims acting in an adversarial way towards customers?

2. To what extent is the threat of litigation a marketing issue for companies such as McDonald's?

3. Other than the examples shown above, which other companies might be exposed to possible future litigation for causing harm to their customers?

Sources:
http://www.avolites.org.uk/jokes/stella.htm accessed 04/01/07
BBC News: 'Court rejects tobacco test case' http://news.bbc.co.uk/1/hi/scotland/4593571.stm
    accessed 31/05/05
BBC News: 'Court dismisses McDonald's obesity case'
    http://news.bbc.co.uk/1/hi/world/americas/2685707.stm accessed 22/01/03
BBC News: McDonald's sued over 'too hot' drinks http://news.bbc.co.uk/1/hi/business/862678
    accessed 02/08/00

Mega Relationships occur at a higher level and set the conditions in which market relationships can operate. The very word 'mega' comes from the Greek word *megas* meaning great. These roughly equate to the 'external' or 'influence' markets described in other models of RM. We have already seen how Personal and Social Networks (**R18**) can completely override traditional marketing tools, particularly in industrial and international marketing and this very important area will be explored in more depth in the next chapter.

We have also seen how alliances can set the conditions for marketing exchanges. Gummesson distinguishes between two types of alliance—**R20**, comprising of alliances within the industry and **R22** (mega alliances) which are at a much higher level. Examples of industrial alliances are common, particularly in areas of product design and development and marketing. Sometimes these alliances are illegal; if, for instance, two or more firms within an industry band together to keep prices artificially high. Mega alliances on the other hand often involve whole countries—the European Union (EU) is one such example. **R19** (the real customer does not always appear in the marketplace) is a straight inclusion from Gummesson's original nine issues underpinning RM. All of these areas will be explored in more depth in Chapter 7.

R21 (the knowledge relationship) recognizes how the skills and knowledge of individual employees can impact on an organization—negatively, if that employee leaves. Similarly it refers to how organizations can become the receptacles of knowledge themselves, enabling them to compete more effectively.

Gummesson's final mega relationship is **R23** (mass media). The importance of this has long been recognized and is traditionally handled by the marketing department through public relations. However, there are examples of where higher figures than the marketing manager have affected media relationships. Gerald Ratner famously destroyed his company by announcing in an off-guard public moment that all the jewellery his shops sold was 'crap'. The press had a field day. Conversely, some industry bosses, such as Richard Branson or Alan Sugar, have developed excellent relationships with the press, through publicity stunts or television personality shows. They clearly recognize the importance of good relationships in this area.

Nano Relationships can be classed as internal relationships. Gummesson uses the word 'nano' here to signify the opposite of 'mega' relationships. The word 'nano' comes from the Greek word *nanos* meaning small. **R24, R25, R26, R27,** and **R28** relate to the internal relationships and networks described in Gummesson's earlier work. All aspects of internal relationships are covered in this book in detail in Chapter 9.

The final two relationships Gummesson describes as 'nano', **R29** (relationships with external providers of marketing services) and **R30** (owner–financier relationships) might not necessarily be classed as internal relationships. On the surface, **R29** is a classic client–supplier relationship, while **R30** could be construed as an *influence* relationship.

Criticisms of Relationship Marketing

It is easy to be whipped up in a form of euphoria over RM, with its emphasis on customer service and the ideal that everyone can be a winner. It does after all, appeal to our humanistic nature in that it involves building relationships and generally being 'nice' to one another. The subject is not, however, without its critics. These criticisms fall into three broad categories:

- what's the big deal? RM is nothing new;
- RM is too fragmented to be considered a marketing theory;
- RM sounds good on paper but doesn't work in practice.

RM is Nothing New

The first of these criticisms has arisen as a direct response to the explosion of books and theories on RM that has appeared since the late 1980s. The suggestion behind this upsurge of interest is that RM is something new and that it is a way forward for marketing. As interest has spread and more and more companies have tried to adopt the principles of RM, critics have likened this to an 'emperor's new clothes' mentality (recalling the fairy story where the emperor was tricked into believing that he was wearing the lightest and finest clothes in the land, when in fact he was naked).

As Petrov (1997) puts it:

> One would hardly argue with the logic of relationship marketing . . . however, to give this concept a history of only 13 years so would be doing a gross injustice to the contributions previous generations of marketing scholars and practitioners have made to our knowledge and understanding of the process.

Indeed, as was pointed out at the beginning of this chapter, RM is perhaps the oldest form of marketing. Additionally, many of its key tenets are based on the long-standing marketing theory and practice surrounding industrial marketing and the marketing of services. Petrov would have it that RM is simply a restating of existing marketing concepts.

RM Lacks Conciseness

This brings us on to the next criticism—that RM is too fragmented to be considered a subject in its own right. Palmer (1996) has suggested that RM has failed to position itself as a single concept, thus causing it to be interpreted in different ways. To some it begins and ends with CRM; to others it is all about developing customer loyalty, while yet others have seen it as a business philosophy that envelops the entire company. These different interpretations can clearly be seen in the myriad of different books that can be found in any business library. (It is worth noting here that this book takes the wider approach to RM, as demonstrated in the theories discussed earlier in this chapter, e.g. Gummesson, Grönroos, Christopher *et al.*, Morgan and Hunt).

RM is Easier Said than Done

The final broad criticism of RM is that it does not work in practice. Palmer (1996) suggests that it is unrealistic to expect that customers will always want a relationship with suppliers. This is especially true in the marketing of fast-moving consumer goods (FMCGs) such as baked beans and toothpaste, and consumer durables such as washing machines or hair dryers. In fact, as long as the product works properly, the customer will not expect to hear from the manufacturer or supplier. Is it therefore realistic to talk in terms of relationships when all the overtures for a relationship are coming from one party? In human terms we cannot claim to be in a relationship with someone if they don't reciprocate our advances. In fact, persistence in trying to pursue a relationship in these circumstances would be construed as 'stalking'—hardly the image a company would like to project. These issues will be covered in more depth when we look at 'Involving the Customer' in Chapter 4 and 'Customer Relationship Management (CRM)' in Chapter 5.

Palmer (2000) further points out that some B2B marketing situations are also out of bounds for RM theory because they are too highly formalized. In the UK, for instance, the rules of doing business with government departments and authorities prevent the development of close relationships. All jobs must be tendered for according to strict rules and it is illegal even to accept a free pen or calendar from a supplier, as this might be classed as a bribe.

It would appear that RM works well in some situations but less so in others and that the development of an RM strategy should be taken within the context of individual marketing situations (see, for instance, Veloutsou *et al.*, 2002 and Bund-Jackson, 1985). In other words, a blanket approach or 'one size fits all' is not possible with RM. The practical implications of this for companies wishing to adopt RM strategies are explored in Chapter 10 of this book.

Chapter Summary

As competition has increased, customers have become more demanding. As a result, companies have had to look harder at how they can better meet the expectations of their customers. This means getting to know them better, keeping them loyal, and ensuring customer satisfaction. In marketing terms this boils down to effective segmentation, product and brand development, direct marketing, marketing communications, and customer retention marketing. These all fall within the remit of the traditional marketing department as we know it.

However, this book considers the wider view that effective management of all relationships, not just those that are directly with the customer, are of importance in enabling an organization to be more effective. Taking such a wide view means that the boundaries of traditional marketing are stretched. Shouldn't the management of internal (i.e. employee relationships) fall under Human Resource Management? Shouldn't the management of supply-chain relationships fall under Operations Management? And shouldn't the management of relationships with external parties such as governments or regulatory bodies fall under the remit of the Chief Executive or Managing Director?

The answer might be yes but all of these areas can have a huge impact on the organization's marketing effectiveness. Take Scandinavian Airline Services (SAS) where Jan Carlzon realized that the attitude and demeanour of his front-line staff could add value to customers and differentiate his company (see the End of Chapter Case below). Or look at Tesco, whose careful management of the supply chain enabled them to provide customers with greater choice and value and led them to become the largest supermarket retailer in the UK. Then there is Toyota, who through industry alliances and relationships with governments and communities around the world have been enabled to break into every major car market to the extent that they are now knocking on the door of General Motors as potentially the world's biggest car producer.

The net result is that RM starts to go beyond the remit of an organization's marketing department. It starts to involve the whole company, from the top down, and it is for this reason that some have claimed that RM is a paradigm shift—a whole new way of thinking about marketing.

End of Chapter Case with Questions

Relationship Marketing Thinking Helps Turn Around SAS

When Jan Carlzon took on the role of President at Scandinavian Air Services (SAS) in 1980, the business was in trouble. After nearly 30 years of growth and profitability the business had stalled and was facing a huge loss of almost $20 million. SAS was not alone. All of the world's airlines were struggling with excess capacity in a stagnant market, following the oil crises in the 1970s.

Most airlines were responding by cutting costs in order to reduce their revenue deficits, but Carlzon did not see the logic in this. He argued that cost-cutting ultimately ended up hurting customers and demoralizing employees. Instead, he proposed that spending be *increased* with an investment of $45 million in customer service initiatives. His strategy was simple—in a stagnant market he set out to increase revenue by becoming 'the best airline in the world for the frequent business traveller'.

Such epithets sound common now, but in those days what he was proposing represented a shift in thinking from product orientation (where the business focused inwardly onto its own costs and processes) to customer orientation (where the business looked outward first to determine what customers wanted and then geared all of its operations around meeting customer needs).

Carlzon chose to focus on business travellers because they were a more stable part of the market than holidaymakers. They also had special requirements which SAS could develop services to meet. Thus Carlzon's $45 million investment went into all the things that were important to business travelers: including improving the traffic hub at Copenhagen; launching a comprehensive punctuality campaign; offering service courses for up to 12,000 employees, and even restoring the olive in customers' martinis!

First-class tickets were scrapped. Instead, 'EuroClass' was created, which was cheaper than first class, but sold at full fare, not the discounted prices where many airlines lost money. EuroClass offered business travellers quicker check-in and boarding, better food, and comfortable lounges at airports. This increased the number of full-fare-paying passengers by nearly 25% in three years and led to SAS receiving the accolade 'best airline for business travellers in the world' by *Fortune* magazine in August 1983.

At the same time Carlzon brought about another revolution. He recognized that customers don't care about the constituent parts of a company, as long as they are treated as individuals and have a good experience. Carlzon calculated that each SAS customer came into contact with approximately five SAS employees, from check-in staff to cabin crew. The quality of these contacts—or how well the customer was treated—defined the customer's perception of the company. He called these contacts 'moments of truth' and calculated that each year SAS created 50 million moments of truth.

He thus realized the importance of motivated and empowered employees and went about changing the structures and cultures of his company to accommodate this. Each member of staff received a little red book entitled *Let's Get In There and Fight* and internal communication was improved, so that everyone understood the business objectives. Information and responsibility was diffused amongst the staff, helping employees to feel involved and valued. The result was a huge turnaround in employee attitudes, a surge of energy, and 20,000 employees all striving towards a single goal—customer satisfaction.

Neither did Carlzon stop at making his customer-focused changes at SAS—he also took them to his suppliers. Carlzon realized that though modern airliners had been increasing in technical sophistication, the bit that really mattered to passengers—the cabin interior—had not improved. In one famous instance, he refused to follow his rivals in buying the new technically advanced Boeing 737 aircraft, preferring to stick with the old DC9s his company had been flying for some time. When asked why, he pointed out that the DC9 had rows with three seats on one side of the aisle and two seats on the other. The more advanced Boeing 737 had three seats on each side. In other words there were more middle seats—the seats that no passenger wants by choice. He could offer a better service to his customers (and thus continue to boost his competitiveness and profitability) by continuing with the DC9.

Carlzon and his team thus pioneered the quest for the 'Passenger Pleasing Plane' (or 3P) and set off to Boeing to convince them to build one. At first they were greeted with incredulity by the worlds' biggest aeroplane manufacturer. But gradually Boeing came around to their way of thinking. After all, it is the passenger who ultimately pays for the plane! Today all new aircraft are designed with Carlzon's 3P approach in mind and all airlines have come to recognize the importance of this.

Everything Carlzon did was aimed at improving the customer experience. He convinced the airport authorities in Copenhagen to position planes at departure gates that were most convenient for transferring passengers, rather than planes—'I've heard many a traveller swear up and down about having to rush around between the concourses at Copenhagen Airport—but I've never heard an airplane complain about being dragged a couple of hundred yards.' He also used his relationships with the Swedish government and Civil Aviation Authority to block Air France's attempts to force SAS to charge higher prices for EuroClass.

Carlzon's policies not only turned around SAS, they ushered in a whole new way of thinking about the way in which businesses developed their marketing.

Questions

1. Why was Carlzon's approach revolutionary at the time?

2. Was what he did to turn around SAS within the remit of an average company marketing department?

3. Try to apply the Six Markets Model to SAS. How many relationships can you identify?

4. What is a 'moment of truth' described by Carlzon? Consider your moments of truth with any organization of which you are a customer. What are the implications of these?

Source: Adapted from Carlzon (1987) *Moments of Truth*, Ballinger.

Discussion Questions

1. What is relationship marketing? How does it differ from other forms of marketing?

2. What are the main criticisms of traditional 4Ps marketing?

3. Do the criticisms of the 4Ps approach mean that it no longer has any value in marketing?

4. Why did the marketing of services and industrial marketing have such a big influence on the development of RM thinking?

5. Why should RM be concerned with anything other than customer relationships?

6. How do the values of RM differ from those of transactional marketing?

7. Take the nine areas identified by Gummesson as distinguishing RM and apply them to: (a) a university; (b) a restaurant; (c) a car manufacturer; and (d) a soft drinks manufacturer. Did they apply equally well in each case?

8. Explain with examples how *influence markets* can affect the organization's strategic marketing.

9. How might an organization make use of Gummesson's 30Rs?

10. Why has RM attracted criticism in some quarters?

11. Can the principles of RM be covered through a more traditional framework such as the 7Ps?

12. If the Six Markets Model is adopted, who in the organization should be responsible for its implementation?

Further Reading

Christopher, M., Payne, A., and Ballantyne, D. (1991) *Relationship Marketing: Bringing Quality, Customer Service and Marketing Together*, Butterworth Heinemann, Oxford.

Grönroos, C. (2007) *Service Management and Marketing: Customer Management in Service Competition* (3rd edn), John Wiley & Sons, Chichester.

Gummesson, E. (1987) 'The New Marketing—Developing Long Term Interactive Relationships', **Long Range Planning**, 20(4), 10–20.

Gummesson, E. (2002) *Total Relationship Marketing. Rethinking Marketing Management: From 4Ps to 30Rs* (2nd edn), Butterworth Heinemann, Oxford.

Palmer, A. (1996) 'Relationship Marketing: A universal paradigm or a management fad?', **The Learning Organisation**, 3(3), 18–25.

References

Baker, M. (2000) *Marketing Strategy and Management* (3rd edn), MacMillan Press, Basingstoke.

Baumgartner, J. (1991) 'Nonmarketing Professionals Need More than 4Ps', **Marketing News**, 22 (July), 28.

Berry, L. (1981) 'The Employee as Customer', **Journal of Retailing**, 3 (Mar.), 33–40.

Booms, B. and Bitner, M. (1981) 'Marketing Strategies and Organization Structures for Service Firms', in Donnelly, J. H. and George, W. R. (eds), *Marketing of Services*, American Marketing Association, Chicago, IL, 47–51.

Borden, N. (1964) 'The Concept of the Marketing Mix', **Journal of Advertising Research**, 4 (June), 2–7.

Brady, J. and Davis, I. (1993) 'Marketing's mid-life crisis', **The McKinsey Quarterly**, 2, 17–28.

Bund–Jackson, B. (1985) 'Build Customer Relationships That Last', **Harvard Business Review**, Nov.–Dec., 120–8.

Carlzon, J. (1987) *Moments of Truth*, Ballinger.

Christopher, M., Payne, A., and Ballantyne, D. (1991) *Relationship Marketing: Bringing quality, customer service and marketing together*, Butterworth Heinemann, Oxford.

Christopher, M. and Peck, H. (2003) *Marketing Logistics*, Butterworth–Heinemann, Oxford.

Denison, T. and McDonald, M. (1995) 'The Role of Marketing Past, Present and Future', **Journal of Marketing Practice: Applied Marketing Science**, 1(1), 54–76.

Doyle, P. (1995) 'Marketing in the New Millennium', **European Journal of Marketing**, 29, 23–41.

Egan, J. (2004) *Relationship Marketing: Exploring relational strategies in marketing* (2nd edn), FT/Pitman.

Ford, D. (ed.) (2002) *Understanding Business Marketing and Purchasing: An interaction approach*, Thomson Learning.

Gordon, I. (1998) *Relationship Marketing*, John Wiley & Sons, Canada.

Grönroos, C. (1997) 'Value-driven Relational Marketing: from products to resources and competencies', **Journal of Marketing Management**, 13(5) (July), 407–19.

Grönroos, C. (2007) *Service Management and Marketing: A Customer Relationship Management Approach* (3rd edn), John Wiley & Sons, Chichester.

Gummesson, E. (1987) 'The New Marketing—Developing Long Term Interactive Relationships', **Long Range Planning**, 20(4), 10–20.

Gummesson, E. (2002) *Total Relationship Marketing. Rethinking Marketing Management: From 4Ps to 30Rs*, Butterworth Heinemann, Oxford.

Jobber, D. (1998) *Principles and Practice of Marketing*, McGraw Hill, London.

Kashani, K. (1996) 'A New Future For Brands', **Financial Times**, Mastering Management, Part 3.

Kotler, P. (1967) *Marketing Management: Analysis, planning, implementation and control*, Prentice Hall, New Jersey.

Kotler, P. (1984) *Marketing Management: Analysis, planning, and control*, Prentice-Hall, New Jersey.

Lauterborn, B. (1990) 'New Marketing Litany: Four Ps passe: C-words take over', **Advertising Age**, 61(41), 26.

McCarthy, E. J. (1960) *Basic Marketing: A Managerial Approach*, Richard D. Irwin, Homewood, IL.

Meldrum, M. (1997) 'Overcoming the Barriers to TQM's Success', **Quality Progress**, (May), 53–5.

Morgan, R. and Hunt, S. (1994) 'The Commitment–Trust Theory of Relationship Marketing', **Journal of Marketing**, 58 (Oct.), 20–38.

Palmer, A. (1996) 'Relationship Marketing: A universal paradigm or a management fad?', **The Learning Organisation**, 3(3), 18–25.

Palmer, A. (2000) *Principles of Marketing*, Oxford University Press.

Parasuraman, A., Zeithaml, V., and Barry, L. (1988) 'SERVQUAL: Multi-item scale for measuring consumer perceptions of service quality', **Journal of Retailing**, 64(I), 2–40.

Peppers, D. and Rogers, M. (2004) *Managing Customer Relationships: A strategic framework*, John Wiley & Sons, New Jersey.

Peters, T. (1988) *Thriving on Chaos: Handbook for a management revolution*, Macmillan, Harper & Row.

Petrov, J. (1997) 'Relationship Marketing: The wheel reinvented?', **Business Horizons**, Nov.–Dec.

Reichheld, F. and Sasser, W. (1990) 'Zero Defections: Quality comes to services', **Harvard Business Review**, Sept.–Oct.

Veloutsou, C., Saren, M., and Tzokas, N. (2002) 'Relationship Marketing. What if . . . ?', **European Journal of Marketing**, 36(4), 433–49.

Webster F. Jr., and Wind, Y. (1972) *Organizational Buying Behaviour*, Prentice Hall, Englewood Cliffs, New Jersey.

Websites

http://www.bankofengland.co.uk/statistics/ms/2006.htm accessed 21/10/06

http://www.cim.co.uk/cim/ser/html/infQuiGlo.cfm?letter=M accessed 09/09/06

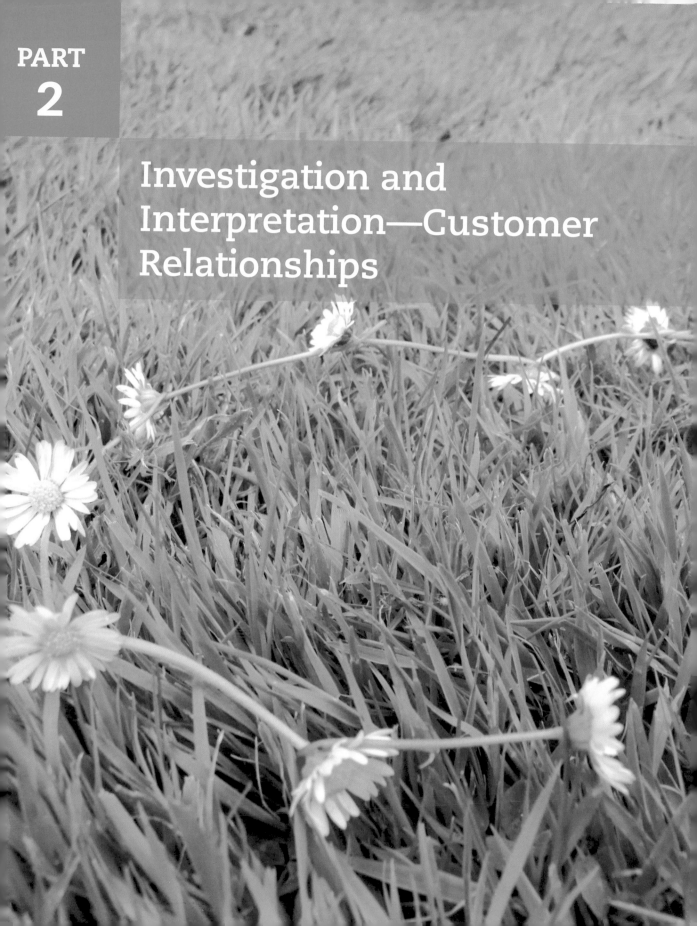

Investigation and Interpretation—Customer Relationships

The Nature of Relationships

Chapter Outline

Learning Outcomes

After reading this chapter you should be able to:

- appreciate the different possible bases for a customer relationship;
- understand how a relationship can add value;
- explore the ways in which businesses can meet the individual needs of their customers;
- understand the role of personal and social networks in marketing;
- recognize the extent of networks in B2B marketing;
- accept the significance of the human element of services marketing;
- debate the extent to which all customers want a relationship.

Introduction

This chapter starts to explore the first and potentially most important relationship—the one that Gummesson calls the classic dyad—the relationship with customers. Before we can do this, however, we need to be clear about what we actually mean by relationships with customers. Despite all the books and papers that have been written about relationship marketing, there is no clear consensus of opinion as to what constitutes a customer relationship. This has led to something of a free-for-all, with researchers and businesses claiming definitions which suit their own ends (Egan, 2001). The result is a range of initiatives from simple database marketing to complex networking involving all aspects of the business.

Even if we accept a broad definition of customer relationship marketing and that a true relationship should be a two-way affair, we need to ask: what's in it for the customer? This chapter therefore explores the ways in which businesses can develop relationships which add value for the customer, either by listening more closely to their needs, generating trust, or bringing a personal touch to doing business.

However, this is only looking at one side of the coin because it is assuming that the whole process of developing customer relationships is controlled and driven by businesses and that it is companies who determine how, where, and when the relationship takes place. In actual fact many businesses have to work within relationships that already exist in the market. For some this is an opportunity which smoothes the path of doing business. For others it is a formidable barrier which effectively locks them out of the market. We are talking here about personal and social networks, overlooked by traditional marketing but which can nevertheless drive customer relationships.

Given that relationships, for the most part, involve a human element, we shall take a look at the extent to which the 'human touch' can differentiate a business and add value for its customers. This is particularly apparent in service industries where face-to-face encounters play an important role in developing customer relationships. However, we shall also see that the human touch can help develop good customer relations even in manufacturing or product-based industries. Some of these issues are introduced in the Opening Case, The Beauty of Neighbourhood Networks.

Finally, however, even accepting all of the above, it is apparent that the concept of relationship marketing works better in some market situations than others; it is, in the words of Veloutsou *et al.* (2002), 'context specific'. We therefore finish off this chapter by asking what types of market are more suited to customer relationships and just how far a business can take those relationships.

Opening Case Study with Questions

The Beauty of Neighbourhood Networks

In today's age of digital technology and the World Wide Web it would be easy to dismiss door-to-door direct sales companies as something of an anachronism. Borne out of nineteenth-century America, where door-to-door salesmen peddled everything from health tonics to encyclopedias, direct selling was as much a means of self-employment as it was for companies trying to reach outlying communities. However, the success of the direct-selling model has led to its adoption in virtually every country in the world and its growth into the global, multi-billion dollar industry we see today.

According to the Direct Selling Association (DSA), direct sales account for over £2 billion a year in the UK and the industry is the country's 'largest provider of part time, independent earning opportunities'. The DSA represents a wide range of companies covering a variety of products, who between them make up nearly 80% of the UK direct sales market. Big names include Kleeneze (household products), Avon (cosmetics), Betterware (household products), and Herbalife (health supplements).

Of these, Avon is perhaps the oldest. The company was founded in 1886 by door-to-door bookseller David McConnell. As a sales incentive, he gave customers a bottle of perfume with each book purchase. He soon realized that the perfume was more popular than the books and so began selling this instead. McConnell now found himself very much in a woman's world and thus came up with the idea of using women to sell to women. The first 'Avon Lady', Mrs P. Albee of Winchester, New Hampshire, was therefore hired. She quickly established the role of 'general agent' and used her networks to recruit other women as 'depot agents', thus establishing the Avon business model we recognize today. The actual name 'Avon' was adopted by McConnell after visiting Stratford-on-Avon in England and being struck by its beauty.

The Avon company itself did not arrive in the UK until 1959 where its fashionable products and quirky 'Avon Calling' catchphrase quickly established it as a top beauty products brand. Avon Ladies (or sales representatives, as they are now known) began by selling to their friends or colleagues through a catalogue containing all of the products. They could work either independently or build up a network of their own agents in order to boost their income. The company gives numerous examples:

- Kay: 'started working for Avon when she was just 18—selling beauty products to college friends'

- Sarah: 'I can sell to mothers at the toddler group, neighbours and people in the area'

- Charlie: 'started selling Avon when an expectant friend from her daughter's playgroup asked her to lend a hand on her rounds'

- Lucinda: 'likes the networking opportunities offered by her Avon life and feels Avon has brought everyone together in the community'

Indeed, one of Avon's greatest strengths is its ability to attract sales representatives who can build up business through their own networks. The company now employs over 160,000 representatives in the UK, selling to around six and a half million women. Avon's successful formula has attracted newer rivals to the direct selling market including Oriflame and Virgin Cosmetics, but it still remains first choice for most women who buy their cosmetics direct from an agent.

But has the source of Avon's success—its direct selling model—now become its strait-jacket? Growth in the UK has stagnated and share prices have dropped. The younger market in particular has struggled to identify with Avon's brand and image and with no High Street or media presence this presents a problem. In the overall global beauty market Avon has slipped behind rivals who use a multitude of channels to reach the market:

World's Top Beauty Companies (ranked by 2005 revenues from beauty products only)

- L'Oréal ($18.1 billion)
- Proctor & Gamble ($17.9 billion)
- Unilever ($12.1 billion)
- Estee Lauder ($6.3 billion)
- Shiseido ($6.1 billion)
- Avon Products ($5.8 billion)
- Beiersdorf ($4.6 billion)
- Johnson & Johnson (($3.3 billion)   (*adbrands.net, 2005*)

In the UK, Avon is fighting back with a raft of new products (including male cosmetics—along with male sales agents!) and brand-building repositioning initiatives (such as TV sponsorship deals with hit drama show *Footballers Wives*, or product endorsements from girl band Atomic Kitten). Interestingly, the company has also embraced the Internet. Around half of the company's UK representatives now manage their accounts online, but perhaps more significantly, customers can now buy direct online too.

Questions

1. When David McConnell started the Avon business, why didn't he just open a shop?

2. How does direct selling add value for: (a) the customer; and (b) the company?

3. What role do relationships play in the Avon business model?

Sources:
Avon Cosmetics Ltd http://www.avon.uk.com accessed 12/01/07
Direct Selling Association http://www.dsa.org.uk accessed 12/01/07
BBC/Open University http://www.open2.net/blogs/money accessed 12/11/06
adbrands.net http://www.mind-advertising.com accessed 12/01/07

Defining Customer Relationships

The word 'relationship' is an emotive one. Ask any class of students what comes to mind when the word 'relationship' is mentioned and most will think of boyfriends, girlfriends, partners, affairs, commitment, etc. The word suggests closeness, friendship, liking, warmth, even intimacy. Thus, a definition of relationships might be about people being linked together in some way, where the behaviour of one (or both) of the parties, will have some impact on the actions, behaviours, or feelings of the other. A colder, more precise definition might just describe relationships in terms of two or more parties interacting with each other.

Defining relationships with customers therefore becomes tricky. Do we mean close, human-based relationships incorporating things such as liking, friendship, or even passion? Certainly, many businesses like to use the terminology of human relationships when describing customers. Thus we have 'monogamous' customers, who remain loyal to a single brand or product over a number of years. Customers who generally remain loyal but occasionally show interest in other brands are described as 'flirting', whilst those who spread their business around, showing no commitment to any single supplier have been called 'promiscuous'!

As simple metaphors to describe different consumer behaviour types, these descriptions are harmless. We all know that a customer can't really flirt with a brand of fish fingers any more than he can be promiscuous with his car insurance policy, but when firms start believing that customers attach similar levels of emotion to the things they buy as they do to their personal relationships, the business can delude itself. In reality there is no human aspect to the producer–customer relationship for many products. As customers, we will never get to meet anyone from Kellogg's, whose cornflakes we eat, or Ford, whose cars we drive. It is the suppliers of these products with whom we will interact (the supermarket or the car dealership) and these represent service industries, as opposed to product manufacturers. This is not to say that product manufacturers don't have relationships with customers; it just means that they have to be realistic in defining the emotional intensity of those relationships.

An alternative way of looking at relationships is by simply considering them as interactions which take place between the supplier and the customer. Again, product manufacturers are going to find it more difficult to interact with customers than service providers, though this is not an insurmountable barrier. Kellogg's, for instance, has a large interactive website providing information on diet and nutrition, and recipes, and a community site promoting physical activity for all through partnerships with schools, local authorities, sporting bodies, and charities.

The problem, of course, is getting the customers to interact and reciprocate in the relationship. Too many companies believe that they are practising relationship marketing when in fact, following the initial transaction there is no customer interaction at all. For instance, would a customer consider herself to be in a relationship with an airline with whom she had once flown, but who continue to send her e-mails with special offers and new destinations? Or the insurance company from whom she once requested a quote but who sends a new quote each year? Although this is called customer relationship management (CRM), it can end up as one-way database marketing, and is not interactive.

The issue of how close a company can get to its customers is looked at in Chapter 4, whilst CRM and database marketing is discussed in more depth in Chapter 5. However, it is important to understand here that when deciding what constitutes a supplier–customer relationship, we need to be careful in ascribing human emotions and high levels of interaction.

How Relationships Add Value

Value added
the difference between the perceived benefits and the perceived costs of a relationship

It is impossible to force someone into a relationship against their will—they will only enter if they perceive something attractive or positive within the relationship. Perhaps the best way to consider the supplier–customer relationship, therefore, is to consider it in terms of the value that is added by the relationship. Remember in the last chapter that we talked about relationship marketing being a 'win–win' concept? This means that the relationship must be worthwhile from the point of view of both the supplier and the customer. The benefits for the supplier derive from customer loyalty and retention, but what value can customers get out of a relationship? Exchange theory would have it that customer value is the ratio of perceived benefits to the perceived costs and sacrifices that are involved in the purchase and consumption of a product or service (Christopher *et al.*, 2002). In other words, for customer value to exist, the customer must perceive that they are getting more out of the purchase than they are putting in.

The cost to the customer of doing business with a supplier is not just the price which is paid for the product or service; it also includes other costs. Some of these relate to the transaction itself (e.g. travel and parking outside the shop where the purchase takes place, or delivery and installation charges). Others relate to the ongoing costs of ownership (e.g. after-sales service, product and service guarantees, or even the disposal of the product at the end of its life).

However, there are other sacrifices which a customer makes when purchasing and consuming a product or service, and these are predominantly associated with risk. Risk manifests itself in a variety of ways, from the highly objective . . .

'Will this computer I've just bought be as reliable as the last one?'

'Have I got the best deal on the broadband and digital TV package I have just signed up for?'

to the highly subjective . . .

'Have I chosen the right university?'

'Does my bum look big in this?'

If the customer is confident that the perceived benefits exceed the perceived cost and sacrifice, then customer value will result. Relationships can add value in three main ways:

- First, by getting close to the customer and encouraging interaction, the supplier can ensure that the product or service meets the customer's requirements and expectations exactly. Where these expectations (or perceived sacrifices) are of a subjective nature, this might entail one-to-one marketing as each customer will have an individual opinion about what is of value and the organization can meet each customer's requirements more precisely.

- Second, by engendering a close relationship with the customer, the supplier is creating a bond based on trust, commitment, and belonging, enabling both parties to do business confidently together. This will defuse any worries that the customer might have in terms of whether or not they have made the right decision.

- Finally, as human beings we like to be treated as such, and not just as another number or statistic on a business's balance sheet. As products and services grow more standardized and less distinguishable from each other, it is the business

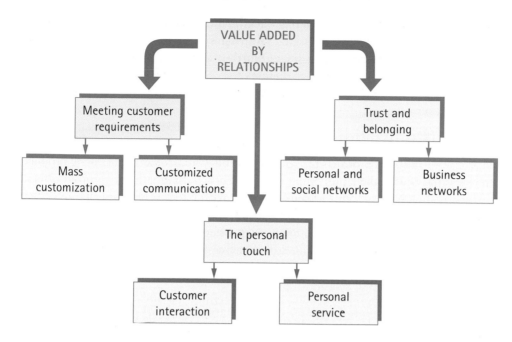

Figure 2.1 The value added by relationships

that can bring a 'human touch' to its dealings with customers that will often gain the advantage. The third way in which relationships can add value for the customer therefore is by enhancing the quality of the interactions he or she has with the business.

Each of these aspects can be divided into further areas as illustrated in Figure 2.1. Let us examine these important aspects of supplier–customer relationships in more detail.

Meeting Customer Requirements More Closely

Traditional marketing has been criticized because of its preoccupation with mass marketing, whereby groups of customers are aggregated together into large homogenous groups and targeted with the same products through the same messages. Where different needs are recognized, the markets are segmented according to demographic, psychographic, or product usage variables; but even here the principle is that segments must be large enough to be profitable and easy to reach. Critics argue that this is a supplier-centric approach—it is done because it makes things easier for the supplier rather than taking into account the needs of the individual customer.

Whilst this might be a valid response to markets which are characterized by mass production and mass consumerism (e.g. fast-moving consumer goods (FMCGs)), proponents of relationship marketing believe in a much more customer-centric approach in place of 'one size fits all'. This requires the tailoring of products and marketing communications for each separate customer. Whilst this has always been the case to a certain extent in the marketing of services and B2B marketing, it raises the prospect of what has become known as 'mass customization' in B2C markets.

Mass Customization

Mass customization

taking an individual approach to large numbers of customers

Mass customization of products recognizes that today's customers are seeking product offerings that match their individual requirements. Individually customized offers, represent a high level of value added for the customer and in markets characterized by stiff competition, companies that are able to do this will have an advantage. There are various ways in which a company can offer customized products to mass markets, four of which have been identified below. (See Figure 2.2.) The challenge is to be able to do this profitably and this often requires the careful management of supply chain and internal relationships.

Combination of Options. Compare the car market of today with that of Henry Ford's black Model T. Most car manufacturers today will offer the chance to 'build your own car' by logging on to their websites and selecting the desired options in terms of colour, engine specification, interior trim, wheels, etc. As the different choices are clicked, the car appears on the screen—the customer is therefore interacting with the company (see Minicase 1, Car Manufacturers 'Pimp Their Rides'). What the company is doing is enabling the customer to create a 'unique' vehicle. How unique the vehicle actually is will depend on the number of option combinations that are permissible and this in turn will reflect how flexible the factory can be.

Figure 2.2 Providing a customized product

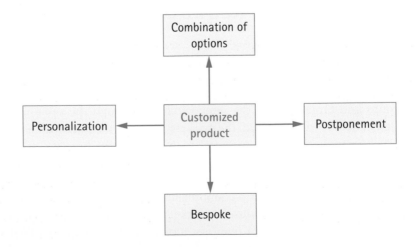

Minicase 1

Car Manufacturers 'Pimp Their Rides'

As car markets become more and more competitive and the cars themselves become less distinguishable from each other, many manufacturers have opted to allow the customer to 'build their own cars'. One only has to look at the websites for Jaguar, Honda, Smart Car, and MINI to see this phenomenon in action. All of them ask you to select a model, then an engine size, a body style, a colour, an interior trim level, a wheel type, and other accessories to personalize your car. As you select each option, the model appears on the screen in front of your eyes, along with the final price that your choices add up to.

Offering accessories for cars is nothing new but, traditionally, the list of options has been limited to items of equipment such as air conditioning, cruise control, CD changers, automatic gear boxes—even car mats. Visually, car buyers have been able to personalize their cars through a few different colours, including solid and metallic shades and two or three different interior trim options. Although these options enabled some personalization, many of them were limited to only certain models within the range, e.g. leather seats available only on the top-of-the-range models. Customers really wishing to drive something different had to customize the car themselves and places such as Halfords sold all the kit they needed from snazzy racing alloys to furry dice and go-faster stripes. However, most people only did this with old cars—and budding boy-racers queued up to 'pimp their rides'. New cars remained in their factory-finished blandness until their value dropped to a level that justified the risk of chopping and changing them around.

The BMW MINI has changed all this. Although their range consists of just five basic models, they offer a bewildering array of extra features which allow customers to personalise their new car. Externally these include the addition of aerodynamic features, bonnet stripes, chrome air intakes, exhaust modifications, light surrounds, mirror caps, mud flaps, nine alternative alloy wheel designs and no less than 19 different roof graphics, all of which are applied at the factory. Inside the car the customer is faced with a choice of chrome accessories, special instruments, interior trims, sun blinds, and floor mats, as well as all the usual technical specification options under the bonnet. As each car is built to order, MINI claim that it is very rare to find an identical car—not surprising when the company's Communications Director claims that there are theoretically 150 billion combinations of options!

The new MINI has become a cult car all over the world, not least in the USA where it has already outsold the original Mini by five times. However, another manufacturer in the States is taking the 'brand new custom car' to even greater heights. Usually associated with mass production, Toyota has launched a separate brand called Scion in the USA to target younger customers. Unlike standard Toyotas, such as the Camry which offers several different trim levels at different price points, all Scions have one basic trim. Known as 'monospec' this allows each driver uniquely to customize the car to his or her own requirements. Although Scion offers some accessories, it is left to other companies to offer the huge range of options that enables each Scion to be unique to its owner. These range from superchargers to sub-woofers and body decals to canvas roofs. What Scion is doing is no different from a house-builder who sells you a brand new empty shell—how you furnish and decorate it is up to you.

> **Questions**
>
> 1. How does Scion's approach to mass customization differ from MINI's?
> 2. What are the implications of this for each manufacturer?
> 3. Are all MINI's unique to their owners? If not, why not?
> 4. Why haven't all car manufacturers followed an approach like MINI's or Scion's?
>
> Sources:
> http://www.mini.co.uk accessed 10/01/07
> http://Auto Express News accessed 20/11/06
> http://www.scion.com accessed 09/01/07

However, the important thing to note is how relationships are being created with the customer. By interacting with the website and 'creating' their own car, customers feel as if they have some control over the relationship. They are being treated as individuals, just as they would be in a normal, human relationship, and the fact that they end up with a product which they perceive to be unique to them helps engender this feeling.

Postponement

delaying the final configuration of a product for as long as possible down the supply chain

Postponement. Whereas a combination of options enables a single manufacturer to practise mass customization, postponement involves the whole supply chain. The principal of postponement is that all of the components of a product are manufactured and moved along the supply chain, but they are not brought together into the final product until the last possible moment. This allows the last supplier in the chain to tailor the product to the customer's exact requirements.

A typical example of postponement is computers, where specialist retailers will build a product to a customer's exact specifications using components sourced from a number of different suppliers. A more humble example is the sandwich shop which makes the sandwich exactly as the customer likes it. Although computers and sandwiches can be bought off the shelf as standard items, the fact that they can also be created in exactly the way the customer wants, adds value to the relationship and gives the customer an element of control.

Postponement requires careful management of supply-chain relationships in order to add value for the customer and clearly reflects the win–win philosophy of relationship marketing.

Personalization

taking a standard product and personalizing it in some way for the customer

Personalization. Mass customization can also be achieved by enabling the customer to personalize his or her product at purchase. Shops such as Personally Yours and Things Engraved have long enabled customers in North America to have their name stitched, engraved, printed, or stamped onto a range of products such as tankards, clocks, pens, towels, and bedding. Gilmore and Pine (1997) have termed this 'cosmetic customization', as the products that are customized are mass-produced standard items.

Advances in digital technology have enabled this type of customization to reach new heights. In the UK, for example, Asda can print customers' photographs onto a birthday cake, whilst Storybook Stars offer a range of books and CDs which incorporate the name of the customer's child along with her age, home town, and the names of three of her friends into a fully fledged story!

Bespoke Products. Products which are created from scratch (i.e. not from a bank of standard components) to the customer's exact requirements are known as bespoke. The bespoke tailor was once the mainstay of the men's-suit market, but has now largely been replaced by off-the-peg retailers. However, examples of bespoke products still exist and these would include things such as wedding dresses, garden conservatories, or even holidays if the travel agent is able to create a specific itinerary. Strictly speaking, these might not be classed as mass customization, but they are included here in order to illustrate the high level of collaboration necessary between the supplier and the customer in their production.

Bespoke products are necessarily very expensive, but they represent the ultimate in added value, as the customer is benefiting from a one-to-one, interactive relationship and getting a product and service which is totally unique to them.

> **Bespoke**
> products and services which are created individually to meet the customer's exact requirements

Customized Communications

Mass customization does not just stop at products. The major enabling factor for closer customer relations in all markets is how companies communicate with their customers. Traditionally, mass marketing has entailed the use of mass-promotional media such as television, newspapers and billboards. This form of marketing communication can be described as 'broadcasting' (Gordon, 1998), because it is one-way and targeted at a wide audience. There is no attempt at relationship-building here and little or no added value for the customer. As companies have tried to get closer to their customers, however, they have personalized their communications in the form of direct mail, facilitated by databases.

Unfortunately, a lot of direct mail is neither welcomed by the customer nor conducive to any sort of relationship. Any form of marketing communication that attracts names such as 'junk-mail' or 'spam' is unlikely to add any value for the customer.

Figure 2.3 From broadcasting to individual, two-way communication

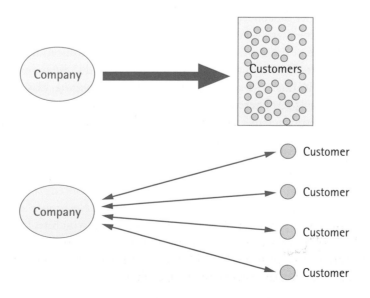

However, when the company starts using its knowledge of previous purchases to come up with individually tailored offers for specific customers, it is possible to add value. For instance, if a customer's local theatre knows that she likes thrillers, they can send details of forthcoming performances that she might like, perhaps with advance booking options for the best seats. This sort of thing is classic CRM and will be covered in depth in Chapter 5. What is important to note here is that it is a form of mass customization which adds value for the customer and can form the basis of a good relationship.

Trust and Belonging

So far we have considered how value can be added for the customer through the customization of products, thereby creating elements of an individual relationship. However, a further means by which value is added is through trust and belonging, particularly where the customer perceives an element of **risk** in the purchase. Reduction of risk is one of the most valuable things that a relationship can bring for the customer and is possibly one of the oldest forms of marketing. Before the days of mass production and mass marketing, goods were made and traded in local areas. **Trust** was a key element in doing business, buyers and sellers had to know each other, and dealing with a stranger was a risk. Doing business was a very personal thing—one generally knew the person who had produced the crops, vegetables, clothes, jewellery, or furniture that one bought. There were few distribution networks. Customers relied on relationships with people they knew, often in the same village, in order to exchange their goods and services for the things that they needed.

The benefits of small groups of people trading together were that they knew each other and where they stood in the exchange relationship. There was no need to go out and find a market as they automatically belonged to one. The need for overt marketing in the traditional sense was therefore less. This reinforced the close relationship between producer and buyer as both parties knew that they could trust one another. This relationship was fostered by direct and interactive communication—two parties talking with each other! For an outsider, trying to do business in these close-knit communities was very difficult, as they had to build up trust. Conversely, anyone within these communities who lost this trust, or acquired a reputation for dishonesty was treated as an outcast. Word spread fast and these people would find it very difficult to do business at all. In other words, *belonging* was an important benefit of relationships. (There are some striking similarities here with modern Internet shopping sites such as eBay where a supplier who gets a bad rating by other users can find it difficult to do business.)

But then everything changed. As the industrial revolution which began in Britain in the eighteenth century spread across the world, the close relationship between producer and buyer was broken. Armies of people were uprooted from the countryside and taken to burgeoning industrial towns and cities. No longer able to supply their own needs directly, they now relied on a wage with which to buy everything they needed. These products were now mass-produced in factories. The consumers' personal contacts were now with retailers who sold the products, not with the companies that made them. A single retailer could now serve hundreds of different

Risk
the potential for loss or other bad consequences arising from a business transaction

Trust
a firm belief in the integrity of a person or thing

customers, making a personal relationship with each less likely. What customer relationships there were had now shifted from manufacturer to middleman—a situation which remains unchanged today. If a customer's new car goes wrong, he returns it to the dealer, not the manufacturer.

Manufacturers who do not have a direct link to their final customers have resorted to other methods of building up trust and belonging, most notably through heavy promotion and strong branding. Some have argued that trust is no longer of overriding concern to today's customers (Palmer, 1996) as their increased confidence has reduced their need for risk reduction. Nevertheless, there are still numerous examples in B2C, B2B, and services marketing where social networks and personal contact play a big role in creating feelings of trust and belonging in the supplier–customer relationship.

Social Networks

Personal and social relationships are pivotal in many supplier customer relationships, because as human beings, we still prefer to conduct business with people we know and like. Networks are simply an extension of our relationships, allowing us to interact confidently with large numbers of people, whom we might otherwise not have known. Although we might not know all of these people personally, we know that we can trust them, because they are already known and trusted by someone close to us. It is exemplified in the oft-heard statement 'sorry I can't help … but I know a man who can!' Networks such as these can help in all areas of business, from raising capital to sourcing suppliers and finding customers.

In marketing terms these networks are very important as they can often dictate whether or not you can do business. For instance, imagine a firm is trying to sell fresh vegetables to a local restaurant. Its products are of a very high quality and keenly priced. However, the proprietor says that he buys all of his vegetables from his brother-in-law. The firm might be forgiven for thinking that you could never win this business, no matter how fresh their products, or keenly priced, because the customer is unlikely to break a close family relationship.

Social and personal networks can be loosely classed as formal, informal, or cultural. Some examples of these are given in Figure 2.4 below.

Figure 2.4 Examples of social and personal networks

Formal networks	Informal networks	Cultural networks
– Sports clubs	– Friends	– Ethnic background
– Church groups	– Family	– Religion
– Working men's clubs	– Neighbours	– Nationality
– Professional associations	– Colleagues	– Language
– Social clubs and societies	– Acquaintances	– Social class
– Alumni groups		
– Rotarians		
– Freemasonry		

Personal and social networks
an extended set of relationships based upon an individual's immediate circle of contacts

Formal networks, such as clubs, groups, and societies to which individuals belong can add much value to supplier–customer relationships. Customers do not have to hunt around for a supplier. Suppliers don't have to promote themselves to find customers, and both parties know that they can trust each other. Some societies, such as the Rotary Club, the Oddfellows, the Foresters, or the Freemasons have long histories and have built up memberships of people from all walks of life. Usually, membership of these organizations is by invitation only, which helps to maintain the bonds of trust and perpetuates the feeling amongst members that they are doing business with like-minded individuals. Whilst clubs such as the Oddfellows and the Foresters are friendly societies, whose original objective was to provide aid to members suffering hardship, the Rotary Club and the Freemasonry were developed specifically as business networking organizations.

Informal networks, such as friends or family do not require membership; they form naturally within groups of people with whom we are in close contact. In many ways they are even harder to access for outsiders than are formal clubs and societies. In the UK such relationships tend to be more apparent within smaller businesses, which may often be family run. However, even transactions between larger organizations can be influenced by personal or social relationships between the buyer and the seller. 'The Old School Tie', for instance, refers to an informal network made up of people who have attended the same public school, or more loosely, those who belong to the same social class. Doing business within these networks effectively debars outsiders and has been frowned upon in some circles as 'cronyism'. As a result, many organizations have introduced strict tendering processes, to ensure that contracts with suppliers are awarded on basis of price and quality rather than existing relationships. Nevertheless, a great deal of business is still conducted over a game of golf or a drink in the club-house.

Cultural networks have clearly delineated boundaries, usually defined by place of birth or religion. As such they can be very powerful and form formidable obstacles to outsiders. Any company wishing to do business overseas must understand the depth and significance of the personal and social networks that are part of that country's culture. In Japan, for instance, relationships are expected to last a lifetime. Furthermore, whereas western countries tend to have sets of relationships (e.g. relationships with family, relationships with friends, relationships with business partners, etc.) in Japan all these sets of relationships are rolled into one. These cover individuals across different industries, the government, civil service, police, universities, hospitals, etc. This leads to far-reaching networks of both individuals and the companies for which they work.

Japanese company networks (known to outsiders as *Keiretsus*) present big obstacles to western companies trying to do business in Japan. Indeed, many have complained that this represents an unfair form of competition as Japanese companies do not have to contend with the same sort of thing when they export to the West. Such complaints miss the fact that Keiretsus are not deliberate barriers to trade; they are an indigenous form of Japanese culture and although it can be difficult to get accepted as an outsider, once achieved, relationships do last. Those foreign companies who can recognize this and work with it have succeeded (see End of Chapter Case).

A similar situation exists in China, where it is impossible to do business unless one is already known and close business relationships, known as guanxi, are critical for success. The Chinese word **guanxi** literally translates as 'relations' although there is no equivalent English word to sum up everything for which guanxi stands. Put simply, guanxi is a deep-seated relationship between two or more individuals that has developed over a long period of time. Although guanxi involves the frequent exchange of favours and gifts, the crucial elements are the states of mutual obligation, respect, and trustworthiness which exist between individuals. Guanxi is more than just a friendship, it is an accepted code of business practice in China. As such, whole networks of guanxi exist, often representing a bewildering obstacle to western companies used to doing business along traditional marketing lines.

> **Guanxi**
>
> a deep-seated network of personal, social, and cultural relationships through which business in China takes place

However, it is not just when doing business in foreign countries that cultural networks may be encountered. All over the world people with the same ethnic or religious backgrounds have historically traded together, particularly when these groups are new to a country. Research by Fadahunsi *et al.* (2000) found that ethnic minorities in north London, for instance, were far more likely to use their own personal networks when developing their businesses than they were to use the mainstream business support agencies such as the banks or government-funded 'Business Links' or 'Enterprise Councils'.

With the world's population in flux, there is a higher incidence of immigrant communities in many countries, so this social and personal aspect of doing business is as strong as ever. The task for the marketer, therefore, is not just to get the marketing mix right, but to ensure that the key people in his or her organization move in the right circles and belong to the right clubs. In marketing terms this entails finding some way of belonging in order to do business and this may involve buying into companies already accepted within a particular group or of employing people who already belong. Many UK universities, for example, have employed Chinese nationals and even opened offices in China in order to attract Chinese students to the UK. Others have gone into partnership with Chinese colleges and universities for the same reason. In practice, things like this are over and above the remit of an average Marketing Manager and comes down to the Managing Director or Chairman.

Advantages of Close Personal or Cultural Relationships in Business

These examples of social and cultural networks illustrate one of Gummesson's key principles of Relationship Marketing—that 'market mechanisms are controlled externally' (Gummesson, 1987). What this means is that often in business, it is not *what you know*, but *who you know* which makes the difference. In other words, normal market mechanisms can be distorted or overruled by existing webs of relationships such as friendships, nepotism, club memberships, etc. Apart from the obvious benefit of trust, Gummesson (2002) points out that there are two other big advantages of doing business within personal or social networks.

First, such relationships tend to be enduring and last for long periods of time. Family ties and friendships are not easily broken. Business relationships formed within like-minded cultures are also often expected to last the course of time. Japanese business relationships can last whole lifetimes and this often leads to culture clashes when relationships are formed with western companies. Honda, for instance, was stunned when its UK partner, Rover, pulled out of a joint manufacturing and product development deal after just six years. The benefit of long-lasting business relationships is that they allow companies to plan ahead with more confidence. From the supplying company's point of view, if they know that through their relationships, they have a supply contract secured on an ongoing basis, they can divert their resources away from selling and put them into other areas. Conversely, the buying organization does not have to go through a potentially lengthy search for suppliers each year, thus enabling it to concentrate on more productive areas.

The second reason why personal, social, or cultural relationships are good for business is that they can weather bad times. In times of recession when companies are making cutbacks, they are less likely to cut suppliers or contractors with whom they have a close, personal relationship, than they are those with whom they have no relationship. Similarly, if a supplier makes an error, e.g. misses a delivery or experiences a lapse in quality, the buyer with whom they have a close personal relationship is likely to be more forgiving. Even if a cheaper rival comes along with a better product, suppliers who are close to their buyers will be told about it and given the chance to improve their own offers. This would not necessarily happen if the supplier did not have the personal relationship—they would just find themselves out in the cold and wondering why.

Disadvantages of Close Personal or Cultural Relationships in Business

It should be noted, however, that close relationships can also bring problems in business. The main reason is economic. Close relationships lead to closed markets because outsiders are excluded. This is why the ruling Communist party in China has opened up the market to western investors. Despite the existence of guanxi, they need the investment, technology, and know-how that the West can bring in order to develop the Chinese economy. As many of the old state-owned enterprises in China have stagnated and struggled to compete, a burgeoning private sector has developed, largely based around western investment. Of course, guanxi still plays a big part in determining which western companies get the chance to invest, but the Chinese market is nowhere near as closed as it used to be.

Gummesson (2002) also mentions another potentially negative outcome of close personal business relationships, which he terms 'the friendly thief'. He uses the example of home-selling parties, such as Tupperware, where people feel obliged to buy something because they have been invited there by a friend, even if they don't really want the product. In other words, business relationships which are built around friendship or social ties may lack the objectivity of rational commercial decisions. Nobody likes to refuse a friend, but just how far can one mix business with pleasure?

Business Networks

Interactive Business Networks

It has long been recognized that relationships in industrial (B2B) marketing add value by enabling organizations to network amongst each other. Indeed, studies of interactive business networks and their impact on overall competitiveness were underway long before research into relationship marketing took off. These studies were led by the Industrial Marketing and Purchasing (IMP) Group. Formed in 1976 by a group of European researchers from the Universities of Uppsala, Bath, UMIST, ESC Lyon, and the Ludwig Maximilians University in Munich, IMP set out to explain the effects of relationships between buyers and sellers in industrial markets through a concept which they termed the **Interaction Approach**.

The basic gist of the Interaction Approach is that business markets consist of myriads of relationships both within and between organizations. As Hakansson (1995) puts it, the 'market' is often described as some sort of impersonal mechanism which simply exists 'out there', whereas in reality it is made up of individual buyers and sellers, each with their own personalities. Some are easy to get along with, others less so, some familiar, others unknown. Over time, the interactions between these individuals develop into networks and can become extremely strong, depending on the characteristics of the participants and the environment in which the interactions take place. In other words, relationships are formed through personalities and individual experiences. Because these relationships form part of a complex network, they are interdependent on each other and what happens in one relationship will have a knock-on effect in others (Hakansson and Snehota, 1995; Ford *et al.*, 1998). As a simple analogy, imagine a couple splitting up. This might well mean that the couple's friends have to break off their own friendships with each other, as, inevitably, some will side with one party and some the other.

On the positive side, this network of relationships can help companies to become more successful by giving them the opportunity to develop their business. The existence of these networks is critical for both small companies and larger ones, although it has been argued that smaller companies can gain more from networks because they represent an extra resource (Chaston, 1998). For example, haulage firm Eddie Stobart rose from small beginnings to become one of the UK's top ten hauliers—and certainly the most well known—by offering a faultless service and also by networking. Links made in the early days with potential clients such as Metal Box and even competitors such as Robson's of Carlisle were to pay off in later years and enable Stobart to achieve phenomenal growth in what is a hugely competitive market (Davies, 2001).

> **Interaction Approach**
> the acceptance that business markets consist of multiple interactive relationships both within and between organizations

Business Networks in Practice

It should be noted that companies do not simply select their networks; neither are they imposed upon them. Business networks are not formal affiliations like joint ventures between companies; nor are they fixed and rigid with clearly defined boundaries. As some opportunities open up, others will close. In this sense they are similar to the networks to which we all belong as individuals. As you read this, your network will consist of friends and family, who are likely to be long term, but also perhaps, class-mates, neighbours, the barmaid in your local pub, the mechanic who services your car. Twelve months from now these may no longer be part of your network. Furthermore, each person in your immediate network will have their own network, which you may tap into, but this will also be constantly shifting.

So it is in business. No one company manages or controls the network—if they did, it would be a hierarchy, not a network. Rather, the task of companies is to manage their own relationships within the network (Hakansson and Ford, 2002) and their overall performance will depend on how well they are able to do this. It would seem, then, that relationships within business networks can add value, but that the networks themselves are outside the control of individual companies. Furthermore, Hakansson and Ford (2002) point out that business networks present a number of paradoxes for companies trying to take advantage of them.

First, although strong relationships within the network can lead to success, the network itself can form a prison as companies within the network become locked into a way of dealing with each other. This is particularly true of networks that have been built up over time, where each company has invested economic, technical, and social resources into the relationships. This limits their freedom to react to changing market conditions or new entrants. For instance, in the PC industry, existing competitors were unable effectively to compete when Dell came along with its direct business model. Instead of manufacturing PCs as stock items and then selling them through distributors, Dell sourced components from a number of different suppliers that could be mixed and matched to meet a customer's individual requirements, before being shipped directly to the customer by courier. Companies such as HP, IBM, and Compaq were tied into existing networks of suppliers (with whom they undertook design and development) and distribution chains whereby they sold their products in the market. As a result they could not easily emulate Dell's business model.

The second paradox of business network relationships relates to how much control a company actually has. Put simply, are a company's relationships affected by its own strategies and actions, or are the strategies themselves influenced by the relationships? It's a 'chicken and egg' situation—which comes first? The answer, according to Hakansson and Ford, is that both come about and exist at the same time. In other words, the network is both a way to influence and to be influenced. The implications for businesses is that the management of relationships within networks becomes a balancing act between being proactive and reactive and requires a much greater skill to get the most out of the relationship. It's about listening as much as it is talking and also about giving as well as taking.

The third paradox described by Hakansson and Ford recognizes that companies will want to make the most out of business networks and will therefore seek to control them. However, if one company is able to dominate a network with its own policies and ways of doing things, the network loses its effectiveness. The value of the network is that it brings along new ideas and fresh thinking and in order to do this it needs the ability to develop organically (i.e. in a natural or controlled way, without deliberate interference). Networks that are free to develop without control tend to do so more quickly and more effectively. Companies exercising tight control over a network run the risk of strait-jacketing themselves and being overtaken by their competitors.

The Role of Individuals in Business Networks

So far, we have discussed business networks in the sense that they exist between organizations, but any relationship within a network ultimately comes down to individuals. The simple business relationship is that between the supplier and the customer—what Gummesson (2002) calls the 'classic dyad'. Most businesses have more than one relationship, however, which is why Gummesson talks of networks.

In B2B marketing, a number of individuals are often involved in the buying process: the initiator, the user, the influencer, the decider, the buyer, and the gatekeeper. The same is also true of the selling organization, where, for example, we might have:

- researchers, who pre-empt the needs of the market;
- designers, who ensure that the product fits the customer's needs;
- engineers, who build the product to the customer's requirements;
- marketing people, who amongst other things promote the product;
- salespeople who negotiate the contract;
- finance people who draw up payment terms and invoice the customer;
- installation and after sales staff, who ensure that the product is working correctly in the customer's premises.

All of these people in the selling company will interact with their counterparts in the buying company and thus create networks between the two companies. (See Figure 2.5.) Simply put, networks are sets of relationships through which interaction takes place. Business networks can be internal as well as external and we will see later in this book how managing internal relationships helps organizations to manage their external relationships better.

For some organizations, the networks to which their individual employees belong represent huge sources of value to the company. This was clearly recognized by

Figure 2.5 Networks between companies

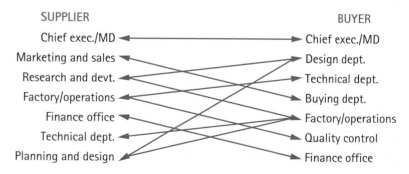

Gummesson when he reflected on his own experiences of working for a large international consulting company in Stockholm. He observed that despite ignoring everything that was being taught in traditional marketing textbooks, the company was highly profitable and expanding. He quickly realized that it was 'the network of relationships that the individual consultants belonged to through professional achievements, birth or membership' that drove the company's success (Gummesson, 2002). In other words customers perceived that their relationships were with the individual consultants and not necessarily with the company, and that consultants were using their personal networks to drive the business.

The implications of this for businesses are quite profound. If the consultant with whom the customer has the relationship leaves and joins another company, he or she will most probably take their customers with them. Companies are therefore prepared to pay handsomely for individuals who bring large or profitable networks of clients with them and will go to great lengths to ensure that they do not leave the business. Many companies will have a clause in their employees' contracts that prohibits the employee from setting up a rival company (using their networks of clients) within two or three years of leaving. Such situations are not just confined to business consultancies. Other areas where personal networks are important include marketing agencies, such as advertising, design, or PR; financial consultants; solicitors; journalists; and key account sales personnel. Even universities have realized that the industrial contacts which new staff can bring with them are potentially useful sources of revenue.

The Personal Touch

Interaction in Service Relationships

The final big area where relationships can add value for the customer is predominantly linked with the delivery of services—be they B2B or B2C. B2B services include things like agencies and consultancies, contract cleaners, security and shipping services, as well as financial and legal specialists. On the B2C side, large service sectors exist in retailing, catering, transport, banking, insurance, education, healthcare, fitness, leisure, and entertainment industries.

Unlike a product, the delivery and consumption of a service requires some form of interaction with the customer. Usually the service is delivered by the front-line personnel within a service organization (e.g. the waiter in a restaurant, the check-out staff in a supermarket, or the delivery driver of a courier company). The service company, its front-line personnel, and the customer can therefore be described as points on a triangle, who work together to develop, promote, and deliver services (Zeithaml and Bitner, 2000). This can be illustrated in the services marketing triangle. (See Figure 2.6.)

The services marketing triangle clearly shows the context of interaction in services alongside external and internal marketing. Zeithaml and Bitner assert that all three of these areas are essential in the successful provision of service. External marketing will include aspects of traditional marketing, such as price and promotion, as well as newer concepts such as customer relationship management. Internal marketing is

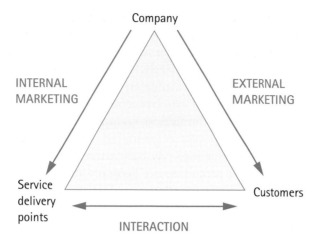

Figure 2.6 The services marketing triangle

critical in order to empower the front-line personnel who actually deliver the service to meet and exceed customer expectations. The interaction which then takes place between the customer and the service personnel then determines how satisfied the customer is and serves as a major opportunity for the service provider to add value.

Different types of Customer Interaction

It is clear that in the delivery of services the supplier can add value for the customer by the way in which interactions are managed. Gummesson (2002) describes four specific areas of interaction in the delivery of a service. (See Figure 2.7.)

Figure 2.7 Four areas of interaction in the delivery of a service

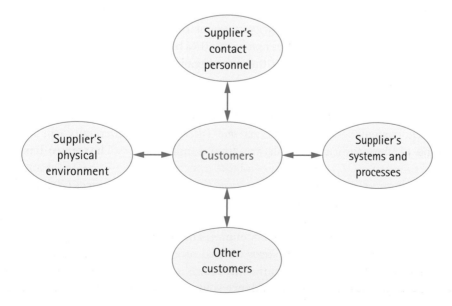

Interaction between the customer and seller's contact personnel are the 'moments of truth' described by Carlzon and discussed above. The implications for organizations employing customer contact personnel are far reaching. Not only does the service itself have to be performed efficiently, but the person performing the service has to live up to very high standards if they are to 'delight' the customer. Furthermore, it is not always front-line staff who have contact with the customer. Personnel in support functions such as IT, shipping, or invoicing can also affect the customer experience.

For instance, many UK universities regularly attract high numbers of overseas students on to their Masters programmes. Typically, from the first enquiry, the student encounters many contacts with various personnel within the university, including the academic who advises them about the course options and makes an offer, the student support officers who help with visas, the accommodation office who find them somewhere to live, right through to the administration staff who enrol them. All of these people are trained in dealing with international students and make customer care one of their top priorities. However, all of this relationship-building can be undone by an over-zealous Finance Office who turn students away if they cannot pay half of their fees immediately—even if the money is simply delayed as the students arrange their finances in the UK.

Clearly the finance personnel are not employed in a sales or marketing role, but Gummesson (1987) describes them as 'part-time marketers', reflecting the fact that their actions and attitudes will impact on the customer. It is for this reason that internal marketing becomes so important, so that all employees become customer-focused.

The second interaction Gummesson describes is that between the *customer and the seller's systems or processes*. These include things like the automated telephone help-lines or online banking. The successful management of customer relations via the telephone can prove to be especially challenging for suppliers and many have found themselves under fire for installing long-winded automated call centres which direct customers through numerous sets of instructions before they can speak to a real person. Overseas call centres can be another bone of contention for customers, who, rightly or wrongly, fear that their needs cannot be fully understood or acted upon by call-centre staff based in another country. Although the use of overseas call centres is growing in the UK, some companies, including the NatWest Bank and Powergen, have specifically advertised that their call centres are all UK-based. Managing customer relationships via the Internet can be equally challenging, but such is the magnitude of this area that a full chapter (Chapter 6) has been devoted to it.

Third, Gummesson describes *interaction between the customer and the seller's physical environment* such as the furnishing in a hairdressing salon or the appearance of a theme park. Customers will quickly form impressions about an organization based on the psychical aspects they encounter. For instance, if you go to a restaurant and find that the cutlery has not been washed properly, you start to wonder what other 'nasties' might be lurking in the kitchen. No matter how good the food is or how friendly the staff are, your experience is likely to be tainted.

Peters and Austin (1985) coined the term **coffee stain management**. This was based on the observation that a passenger on an airliner who flips down the tray in the seat back and finds a coffee stain, might wonder if the airline is as careless in its engine maintenance as it is in its cabin cleaning. 'Managing the coffee stains' became a euphemism for ensuring that all the physical aspects of the business with which the customer comes into contact leave the right impression (Ford *et al.*, 1998). Haulage entrepreneur Edward Stobart used this effectively to help build his business. See Minicase 2, Ready, Steady, Eddie.

Coffee stain management
managing the smallest details of each customer interaction to ensure that a consistently high message of quality is projected across the organization

---

Minicase 2

Ready, Steady, Eddie

No one understands the importance of image better than Edward Stobart, the man behind Britain's best-known haulage firm. Such is the iconic status of his business that even the company's fan club and merchandising division has an annual turnover of £1.5 million—more than many small haulage firms in themselves. The total business turnover is in excess of £135 million, employing 2,500 staff and a fleet of 800 trucks with 1,700 trailers, making it the tenth largest haulier in the UK.

But it wasn't always so. Contrary to popular opinion, Eddie Stobart Ltd is not named after Edward Stobart, the man who built the current business and still runs it today. Rather, it is named after his father Eddie who in 1957 founded a small agricultural contracting business based in Hesket Newmarket in the Lake District. Eddie's business consisted primarily of fertilizer spreading—mainly phosphate slag and lime—and he soon branched out into the buying and selling of fertilizers and other agricultural products. Eddie had a small fleet of lorries to transport the fertilizers, and occasionally he used these trucks to do other haulage jobs. Ironically, however, Eddie Stobart himself was never much interested in the lorries, preferring the agricultural side of the business.

It was his son Edward who saw a future in the lorries. He had been working in the family business since leaving school at 15, first spreading lime on the fields and then driving the lorries. When his father Eddie broke up the business in 1976, he took the farm shop and agricultural side of the business under a separate name, leaving young Edward in sole charge of the lorry haulage side of things, which continued under the name of Eddie Stobart Ltd. At this time the business was relatively small; existing mainly on subcontracted work from the big haulage firms. These tended to be last-minute rush jobs, or unpopular night-work. Additionally, they still relied heavily on transporting low-cost, dirty loads such as phosphate slag.

Edward was determined to change all of this. He wanted the clean, high-value loads, such as food products for supermarkets. But in 1976 there were nearly a million lorries in the UK, many of them run by small haulage firms such as Eddie Stobart's, all competing for the best work. Edward's approach was to make his lorries stand out from everybody else's by making sure they were always clean. Every weekend they were hand-washed with hosepipes and brushes and parked up ready for the next week's work. Often Edward did this job himself, even though he was the boss of the company. The lorries themselves were painted in an attractive post-office red and Brunswick green colour scheme and each one was given a girl's name, painted prominently on the panel below the windscreen.

Customers soon began to notice Edward's lorries and reasoned that clean, well-kept lorries must mean an efficient well-run service. As business increased, Edward was able to invest in state-of-the-art curtain-sided trailers, which not only kept the goods inside clean and dry, but also gave him the chance to emblazon the company's name down the side in huge orange lettering. No one could miss an Eddie Stobart lorry now. He also finally invested in a £22,000 Karcher washing machine but still continued to finish off the cleaning process by hand! As the lorry fleet grew, Edward maintained his strict control of the company's image. In 1987 he introduced a simple uniform of green work jacket and trousers for all the drivers. This was at a time when the average lorry driver was seen as a scruff. The move went down well with customers, so much so that three years later Edward insisted that all of his drivers wear a shirt and tie!

This was unheard of at the time, but out of 200 drivers only two refused to comply and left the company. The rest of them adopted the uniform, enduring the laughter and derision which often met them when they entered a transport café. The laughter was short-lived as, within a year, many of the big haulage firms had adopted the same policy. The shirt and tie smacked of professionalism and the days of the scruffy 'urban cowboy' lorry driver were numbered.

In the end it was not just customers who noticed Eddie Stobart. Hordes of other road-users began to show an interest, captivated by the bright, colourful lorries with the quirky title and the girls' names on the front—look out for this on the next Stobart lorry you see. And so the company became the first and only haulage firm in Britain to have an official fan club.

Questions

1. How did Edward's policy affect the interaction between the company and its customers?

2. Does it make sense for a company such as Eddie Stobart Ltd (a B2B enterprise) to maintain a fan club among the general public?

3. Can you think of any other companies where the way in which the customer relates to the physical aspect of the business has led to success?

Sources:
Davies, H. (2001) *The Eddie Stobart Story*, Harper Collins, London.
http://www.eddiestobart.co.uk accessed 24/01/07

So far, the interactions we have considered can be summed up as People, Process, and Physical Evidence—the three areas added to the original 4Ps to make the 7Ps, in an attempt to make traditional marketing theory more relevant to the marketing of services.

The final area described by Gummesson, however, relates to the *interaction between the customer and other customers*. Although this does not apply to all service sectors, it clearly has a big impact in some areas such as the camaraderie of club supporters at a football match or the willingness of other customers to get up and dance at a disco. We all know that the behaviour of other customers in a pub or a restaurant can adversely affect our own enjoyment, so it is important that businesses, who are delivering a service where customers interact with each other, ensure that these interactions are positive. This explains why some restaurants or nightclubs have a dress code, or why on occasions a disco might allow free entry for women, to ensure an even balance of the sexes. Holiday company Warner offers short breaks in the UK to adults only, in the recognition that many people do not want to be disturbed by the children of other customers when they go on holiday.

Personal Service

From a marketing point of view this underlines the significance of a two-way relationship, or interaction with the customer and how well this interaction is managed. In some service industries a long-term perspective is crucial. For instance, most banks can equal each other in terms of the transaction-based marketing mix. If one bank lowers its rates, or improves its product offering, the others quickly follow. What is critical to banks is that they keep their customers once they've got them and this is where the relationship approach clearly outdoes a marketing mix approach.

Grönroos (2000) draws a distinction between 'billable' and 'non-billable' services. Billable services represent the core elements of the service offering, such as the delivery and installation of a computer system. They are costed into the total price, charged to the customer, and calculated as part of the overall organizational turnover. Non-billable services on the other hand, represent the way in which customer relations are handled. These might include things like the friendliness of staff, the speed in which a telephone is answered, or the manner in which a complaint is dealt with—in other words the human face of the organization. Although the organization does not overtly charge for these, they represent added value for the customer and thus a crucial source of competitive advantage. The problem is that because these elements do not form part of the core service, many organizations fail to recognize their strategic potential. At best they are managed as administrative routines governed by cost constraints. At worst they are left to chance.

Service Elements Apply to Products Too

So far we have looked at how the interaction that takes place in the delivery and consumption of a *service* creates relationships which can add value for the customer. This implies a difference between services and products, but does it mean that the suppliers of products can't use interaction with customers to add value? In actual fact the line separating products from services is not always clear. We have seen that many *services* have a tangible product involved (e.g. the food in a restaurant) and many *products* have a service element involved (e.g. the delivery of a new television). It is thus useful to consider the difference between products and services not as a clear-cut distinction, but more as a spectrum ranging from pure product at one end to pure service at the other, with many cross-over permutations in between. (See Figure 2.8.)

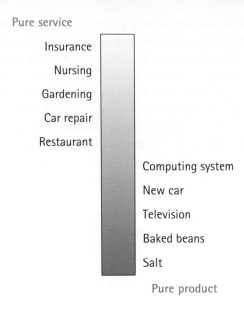

Figure 2.8 The service–product spectrum

It follows, therefore, that the manufacturers of products can also use service elements to differentiate themselves and build relationships. Grönroos (2000) identifies five categories of service function that might apply to a manufacturer of products. These are:

- before production (e.g. research and development on behalf of a customer or the drawing up of specifications to match the customer's requirements);
- during production (e.g. implementing quality control systems to meet the customer's standards);
- point of sale (e.g. delivery to the customer's premises, installation, raising the invoice paperwork, etc.);
- during consumption or use of the product (e.g. training the customer's staff, maintenance, and after-sales service);
- after consumption (e.g. dismantling, removing, and recycling the product at the end of its life).

Although these manufacturer service functions appear to apply to industrial marketing situations (such as the supply of plant, machinery, or computers) there are also examples in consumer marketing, particularly in terms of warranty claims or complaints handling. Just as in a pure service, the way in which these service functions are handled by manufacturers will determine to a large extent the customer's overall satisfaction with the product. For instance, Peperami's quick action in withdrawing all of its products from sale following a contamination scare in the 1990s showed that it had a duty over and above simply selling products. In fact the company went further and contacted all of its customers through broadcast adverts, asking them to return to the company any Peperami products they had bought, in return for generous money-off vouchers against future purchases. The problem was resolved and sales quickly returned to their former levels.

Peperami's actions illustrate a service element—public reassurance—which can be more important than the product itself in developing relationships with customers. Some have argued that the whole distinction between products and services is an outmoded concept. For example, Vargo and Lusch (2004) talk in terms of an overall 'value proposition' into which the customer buys, incorporating the 'co-creation of value' in the way that a customer consumes a product or service. This supports the philosophy of an individual, interactive approach between organizations and customers.

Is Relationship Marketing Suitable for All?

It is clear what a company can gain from having a relationship with its customers—loyalty and commitment and all the benefits that come with this. However, what happens if the relationship adds little or no value from the customer's point of view? Is pursuing a relationship marketing strategy still a realistic course of action for the company? Palmer (1996) highlights a number of reasons why customers might not be interested in a relationship:

- With one-off or infrequent purchases, the customer does not expect to need the supplier or its products again. For instance, when forced to use an airport hotel for a night because his flight had been grounded through bad weather, a traveller was surprised to be invited to join the hotel's loyalty scheme. This surprise turned to irritation when he realized that he was expected to fill in a lengthy application form with lots of personal details. From his point of view, he was never likely to need this hotel again. Likewise, is there any point in a baby buggy manufacturer trying to maintain a long-term relationship with its customers?

- Customers might wish to avoid tying themselves in too closely with a supplier for fear of restricting their choice. For instance, many power companies offer better rates if you buy both your gas and electricity from them. Car dealerships would like not only to sell you the car but also arrange the finance, the motor insurance policy, and on-going service arrangement—all, of course, wrapped up in an attractive deal. Similarly, many banks can offer a great deal if you undertake your insurance, mortgage, savings, and personal pension with them. All of them are trying to build in switching barriers by making it awkward or difficult to place part of your business with another supplier. However, if the customer feels that they are being pressured or restricted in some way, they will pull back from the relationship.

- Customers' confidence has increased which means that buying from an unknown source is now less of a risk. In some cases the need for trust has been replaced by protection through legislation or industry bodies. Consumer protection laws have put the onus on the supplier to ensure that goods and services are fit for purpose, so the customer can buy in confidence. Some market sectors, such as financial products, are heavily regulated to ensure that the customer is not misled or given poor advice. Industry watchdogs such as OFTEL in the telecoms market or ABTA in the travel industry exist to protect the interests of the customer. The result is that customers are more confident to shop around and try new suppliers and are less interested in developing a long-term relationship with one supplier.

All of this is not to say that relationship marketing has no value at all in many market sectors. It simply suggests that companies should look hard at their own markets and understand what is of value to their customers before trying to foist a relationship upon them. At the end of the day there will always be some sectors where transaction marketing is more appropriate than relationship marketing.

Chapter Summary

'Relationships' is an emotive word which when applied to marketing leads to some debate over the extent and relevance of pursuing customer relationships. Customers will only be interested in a relationship with a supplier if they perceive that they are getting some added value from the arrangement and organizations pursuing relationship marketing must be clear what this added value is and ensure that it is delivered.

It is suggested that relationships can add value for the customer in three ways: by more closely meeting their requirements; by engendering a feeling of trust or belonging; by enhancing service quality. The idea of 'mass customization' fits in with the notion that today's customer is more demanding and more empowered than previous generations and the successful organization will be that which most closely matches this new breed of customer's needs.

It is recognized that personal and social networks can play a big part in terms of trust and belonging, particularly B2B marketing and in many international markets. The challenge for organizations is not to try and control the networks, but to understand them so that they can manage them to best effect. This role cannot be easily undertaken by a functional department such as marketing, as the networks involve individuals from all over the organization.

Finally, as organizations struggle to differentiate their products and services, the importance of managing customer interaction becomes apparent. Whilst this has long been understood in the marketing of services, it is increasingly being applied to the marketing of products too.

Most arguments against relationship marketing revolve around areas where the relationship cannot add anything to the overall customer experience and this tends to occur in the marketing of low-risk, low-involvement products and services. Organizations trying to force a relationship onto customers in these circumstances are likely to be disappointed.

End of Chapter Case with Questions

Metro in Japan

Founded in 1964 by Otto Beisheim, Metro AG has developed from its base in Germany into a multi-national retail group, currently worth over €54 billion. The group is divided roughly equally between retail operations, where it has grown rapidly by acquiring smaller retail chains throughout Europe, and a wholesale/cash-and-carry division. The retail side of the business is the market leader in Germany and third only to France's Carrefour and the UK's Tesco in the whole of Europe. The group's retail brands include Real (large hypermarkets), Extra (smaller supermarkets), Galeria Kaufhof (department stores), Media Markt (consumer electronics stores), Saturn (DVDs, multi-media stores), and Praktiker (DIY stores).

However, it is the wholesale/cash-and-carry side of the business that has become truly global. Whereas the retail parts of the group sell to the general public, the wholesale/cash-and-carry operation sells to other businesses, predominantly smaller retailers and catering organizations such as restaurants and hotels. Known simply as Metro (or Makro in the UK) this division has seen most of its growth over the last few years coming from burgeoning Asian markets such as China, Vietnam, and Japan. However, Metro has had to work hard to get accepted in these markets where cultural differences and business norms are quite different than in Europe.

Metro Cash and Carry entered the Japanese market in December 2002, establishing its first store in Chiba. Almost immediately it was apparent to observers that this was a different venture than Metro's European cash-and-carry operations. For a start, the stores were much smaller than they were in Europe. Whereas a typical German Metro occupied a floor space of between 10,000 and 16,000 square metres, in Japan they opted to introduce 'Eco' class stores of between 2,500 and 5,000 square metres. This was partly a reflection of high land prices in Japan and partly to fit in with the expectations of the market which was not accustomed to large-scale cash-and-carry stores.

Indeed the whole concept of one-stop cash-and-carry wholesaling was alien to the Japanese market. Small retailers and restaurateurs traditionally bought their stock from a myriad of small suppliers based throughout Tokyo's dense street networks. If Metro were to succeed, it would need to win over these customers and change their buying habits. Two things were critical if this was to be achieved. First, Metro would need a wide product range with a high proportion of fresh food. This was what the customers were getting from the small, specialist street traders. Second, Metro would have to charge lower prices—its aim was to undercut its competitors by 20%. In order to do this Metro needed direct access to the suppliers and manufacturers. It could not afford to go through the numerous and complex stages of middlemen which characterized the Japanese market.

This, however, presented the company with a problem as long-established trading relationships within the market effectively meant that newcomers had to join the back of the queue. To circumvent this problem, Metro's Chairman, Dr Hans-Joachim Korber, entered into a partnership with the Japanese Marubeni Corporation. Marubeni is a giant trading company whose activities encompass agricultural, marine and forestry products, metals and minerals, textiles, chemicals, energy products, transport, and industrial machinery, with an annual turnover of $70 billion. Marubeni's President and Chairman, Tohru Tsuji, quickly saw the potential of the Metro concept in Japan and as part of the partnership deal the corporation took a 20% stake in Metro Japan.

That Metro was able to win over Marubeni was very much down to the efforts of its senior managers. Thomas Hubner, head of the group's cash-and-carry division, approached his Japanese counterparts with confidence and respect. German retail magazine *Lebensmittel Zeitung* reported that 'there is not a trace of arrogance about him and he does not consider it below his dignity to pour coffee out for a group of visitors'. Metro's manager in Japan, Anton Knijf, went even further when he delivered his speech in Japanese at the store's opening ceremony, instantly winning the respect of the Marubeni managers.

In consequence the Marubeni partnership has been good for Metro. Through their connections they were able to source the most suitable land sites for Metro's stores at competitive prices—no mean feat in a country where land is at a premium. They also used their experience and knowledge of Japanese business culture to steer through Japan's complex supply chains and enable Metro to buy direct from suppliers. For example, Marubeni licences with the fishing fleets allowed Metro to buy direct from the trawlers, thus avoiding the five wholesale stages operated through Tokyo's fish market and ensuring the freshness of Metro's products.

Questions

1. What new concept has Metro brought to the Japanese market? Has it adapted its strategy to fit the market?

2. What has been Metro's entry strategy for the Japanese market?

3. What benefits has Metro got through its partnership with Marubeni? What's in it for Marubeni?

4. Give examples of what Metro has done to acknowledge Japanese business culture.

Sources:
Lebensmittel Zeitung, 'What Metro stands for in Japan', December 2002.
http://www.metrogroup.de accessed 18/01/07
http://www.marubeni.com accessed 18/01/07

Discussion Questions

1. How useful is it to use metaphors from human relationships when describing an organization's relationships with its customers?

2. Describe the role of interaction in a relationship. Is it possible to have a relationship without interaction?

3. How can a relationship add value: (a) for the customer; and (b) for the company? Is it mutually compatible for both parties to take value from the relationship?

4. What is meant by mass customization? Give examples of products offering this.

5. What role do service elements play in the mass customization of products?

6. Is trust still a big concern of customers?

7. Discuss examples of where your own personal or social networks influenced your choice of supplier. How could a supplier outside the network have attracted your business?

8. Is it possible for a western company to achieve guanxi in China?

9. Are interactive business relationships a good thing? Explain your answer.

10. How can managing relationships address the four distinguishing factors of a service (tangibility, perishability, inseparability, variability)?

11. What is the difference between 'billable' and 'non-billable' services? Give examples.

12. Suggest whether relationship marketing might be more or less suitable in the following product/service sectors: industrial stationery (B2B); contract cleaning (B2B); security services (B2B); confectionery (B2C); tourist hotels (B2C); car insurance (B2C).

Further Reading

Gummesson, E. (1999) *Total Relationship Marketing. Rethinking Marketing Management: From 4Ps to 30Rs*, Butterworth Heinemann, Oxford.

Hakansson, H. and Ford, D. (2002) 'How Should Companies Interact in Business Networks?', *Journal of Business Research*, 55(2), 133.

Zeithaml, V. and Bitner, J. (2000) *Services Marketing: Integrating Customer Focus Across The Firm* (2nd edn), McGraw Hill.

References

Carlzon, J. (1987) *Moments of Truth*, Ballinger.

Chaston, I. (1998) 'Evolving "New Marketing" Philosophies by Merging Exiting Concepts: Applications of process within small high-technology firms', *Journal of Marketing Management*, 14, 273–91.

Christopher, M., Payne, A., and Ballantyne, D. (2002) *Relationship Marketing: Creating Stakeholder Value*, Butterworth Heinemann, Oxford.

Davies, H. (2001) *The Eddie Stobart Story*, Harper Collins, London.

Egan, J. (2001) *Relationship Marketing: Exploring relational strategies in marketing*, Pearson Education, Harlow.

Fadahunsi, A., Smallbone, D., and Supri, S. (2000) 'Networking and ethnic minority enterprise development: Insights from a North London study', *Journal of Small Business and Enterprise Development*, 7(3).

Ford, D. (ed.) (1998) *Managing Business Relationships*, John Wiley & Sons, Chichester.

Gilmore, J. and Pine, B. (1997) 'The four faces of mass customization', *Harvard Business Review*, 1, 101–10.

Gordon, I. (1998) *Relationship Marketing*, John Wiley & Sons, Canada.

Grönroos, C. (2000) *Service Management and Marketing: A Customer Relationship Management Approach*, John Wiley & Sons, Chichester.

Gummesson, E. (1987) 'The New Marketing—Developing Long Term Interactive Relationships', *Long Range Planning*, 20(4), 10–20.

Gummesson, E. (2002) *Total Relationship Marketing. Rethinking Marketing Management: From 4Ps to 30Rs*, Butterworth Heinemann, Oxford.

Hakansson, H. and Ford, D. (2002) 'How Should Companies Interact in Business Networks?', *Journal of Business Research*, 55(2), 133.

Hakansson, H. and Snehota, I. (1995) *Developing Relationships in Business Networks*, Routledge, London.

Palmer, A. (1996) 'Relationship Marketing: A universal paradigm or a management fad?', *The Learning Organisation*, 3(3), 18–25.

Peters, T. and Austin, N. (1985) *A Passion for Excellence*, Warner Books.

Vargo, S. and Lusch, R. (2004) 'Evolving to a New Dominant Logic for Marketing', *Journal of Marketing*, 68(1), 1–7.

Veloutsou, C., Saren, M., and Tzokas, N. (2002) 'Relationship Marketing. What if . . . ?', *European Journal of Marketing*, 36(4), 433–49.

Zeithaml, V. and Bitner, J. (2000) *Services Marketing: Integrating Customer Focus Across The Firm* (2nd edn), McGraw Hill.

The Significance of Customer Retention

Chapter Outline

Learning Outcomes

After reading this chapter you should be able to:

- understand the profit implications of retained customers;
- recognize the need for a balance between customer acquisition and customer retention;
- critically evaluate the relationship between customer satisfaction and customer retention;
- appreciate the role of customer care in retaining customers;
- identify the nature of customer defection in any given situation and suggest a means of managing defection;
- develop a customer retention plan.

Introduction

We noted in the first chapter that one of the bedrocks of relationship marketing (RM) theory is the importance of keeping customers over a long period of time rather than constantly going out and finding new ones—in other words valuing customer retention more than customer acquisition. It could be said that this distinction symbolizes the difference between traditional 'transaction'-based marketing (where marketing efforts are concentrated on making a single sale) and 'relationship'-based marketing (where the emphasis is on developing a long-term relationship with the customer with a view to encouraging ongoing repeat purchases).

This chapter therefore concentrates on issues around *customer retention*. We begin by looking at the value of customer retention and exploring the ways in which retention can add to overall long-term profitability. If Tom Peters was right when he said that it costs five times more to win a new customer than it does to retain existing ones, then why do many companies still gear their sales and marketing around customer acquisition instead of customer retention? We shall see that the choice between retention and acquisition is not always black and white and that for most businesses a balance must be struck.

Accepting that customer retention is desirable, the chapter goes on to consider customer satisfaction as a driver of retention. It seems logical to assume that customers must be satisfied, or they will not stay with a business. But is this enough? Just because a customer is satisfied with a product or service, does that mean that they will keep on buying it? What happens if a competitor can also satisfy the customer? Furthermore, customer satisfaction can be subjective in that what satisfies one person might not satisfy another.

If customer satisfaction is to lead to retention a business not only has to understand what its customers expect, it must ensure that it can satisfy customers more than its competitors can. This takes us into the realms of customer care and service quality and the chapter considers how these concepts can be managed to aid customer retention. Finally, the chapter looks at the practicalities of managing retention and defection and how a business might develop a customer retention strategy.

Opening Case Study with Questions

Rate Tarts Give Credit Card Companies the Run-Around

When Barclays launched their Barclaycard in 1966 they laid the foundations for what was to become a multi-billion pound industry. Back then the average credit limit was £100 and potential card applicants had to be recommended by their local bank manager. Today in the UK there are over 70 million credit cards in circulation, generating a spend of around £120 billion each year. It is estimated that two-thirds of the adult population have a credit card with an average of 2.4 cards per person. According to APACS (the UK trade association for payment service providers), there are approximately two billion credit card transactions a year, equating to 64 transactions per second. The average value of these transactions is around £60.

As in any industry that experiences rapid growth, the credit card sector has attracted hundreds of new players. As well as banks, today's credit card issuers include building societies, finance companies, insurance companies, retailers, and even the AA. Big suppliers such as Barclaycard have become multi-branded, offering Flexi-Rate, Platinum, Simplicity, Initial, Premiership, Charity, Student, and Graduate credit cards. Not surprisingly, competition between the various suppliers has become intense and card issuers have fallen over each other to give the customer the best deal.

One of the most common promotions over recent years has been the six-month 0% interest offer for customers opening a new account and transferring their balance over from another card provider. So popular has this promotion become that card-savvy customers have been able to switch their debts around, moving from one interest-free deal to another, just before the six months is up, thus avoiding paying any interest on their balances indefinitely. Such disloyalty has earned these customers the nickname 'rate tarts' and it is estimated that they have cost the UK credit card industry around £600 million a year in lost revenue.

Consumer organizations such as CardGuide and uSwitch have helped the rate tart by highlighting the best deals at any one time and how to get the best value from a card. As CardGuide reports, the intelligent rate tart knows that they should never use the same card for balance transfers as they use to make new purchases, as the existing debt will be paid off first, leaving any new debt to sit in the account at full interest rates. As a result, rate tarts have juggled numerous cards, in effect playing each of them off against each other.

There are signs now, however, that the party may be over for the rate tarts. Alarmed at the haemorrhaging profits, the credit card companies have finally woken up and have started charging fees for customers transferring balances across to take advantage of the 0% interest offers. Others are offering low interest rates (e.g. 3.9%) for the life of the transferred balance, not just an introductory six months. The companies are hoping that such initiatives will discourage the rate tart.

But will they? Most card providers are levying a charge of around 2.5% of the outstanding amount on transferred balances. Thus a £2,000 balance transfer would result in a one-off fee of £50. But when compared with the interest the customer would have paid at normal rates, £50 starts to look like a very good deal. Although the days of totally free debt look like they are numbered for the rate tart, there is still plenty of scope for promiscuous customers to cost the industry dear.

Questions

1. What are the objectives of the credit card companies in offering 0% interest deals?

2. Given the problems outlined in the case, why don't these companies simply stop offering these types of promotion?

3. Suggest any alternative marketing policies which the credit companies might use to maximize customer profitability.

Sources:
http://www.apacs.org.uk/resources_publications/card_facts_and_figures.html accessed 19/05/07
http://www.cardguide.co.uk/articles/rate_tart.html accessed 19/05/07
http://www.barclaycard.co.uk accessed 19/05/07
http://www.uswitch.com/CreditCards/Credit-Card-Companies-UK.html accessed 19/05/07

The Value of Customer Retention

It was back in 1988 when Tom Peters made his now often quoted claim that: 'it takes on average 5 times as much time, money and effort to gain a new customer as it does to retain an existing one' (Peters, 1988). This general principle has since become one of the cornerstones of RM, reflecting a focus on **customer retention** as opposed to customer acquisition.

Customer retention
keeping all or most of the customer's business over a continuous number of purchase cycles

Customer Retention and Profitability

Research into the link between retaining customers and profitability has been spearheaded by Frederick Reichheld. Reichheld leads the Loyalty/Retention practice at Bain & Company, a prominent Boston consultancy firm, and has long argued that 'the real enemy of profits is *churn*' (Reichheld, 1994). 'Churn' is the frequent turnover of customers requiring organizations to constantly seek new customers to replace those that they have lost. For many organizations churn is the driving force behind their customer acquisition-based marketing strategies. However, from studying hundreds of companies in all sectors, Reichheld found that the most successful were those that reduced churn by caring about and cultivating customer loyalty. Furthermore, this loyalty did not just apply to customers—Reichheld also found that loyalty amongst company employees and investors was just as important in successful organizations.

To prove his point, he teamed up with Harvard Business School academic Earl Sasser to find out just how much customer retention, as opposed to customer acquisition, might affect the bottom-line profitability of an organization. The results of their research, published in 1990, took many by surprise. They showed that just a 5% increase in customer retention could generate a massive net present value profit increase. The profit impact varied across different industry sectors, ranging from a 95% increase in an advertising agency to 35% in a software house, but in each case the profit increase was significantly higher than the increase in customer retention rate needed to achieve it. These figures are based on the 'net present value of the profit streams for the average customer life' (Reichheld, 1994). In other words they assume retention for as long as the customer is in the market. This is important because in many industries the initial cost of acquiring the customer means that the company will not make any profit until the second or third year. If the customer leaves after the first year, the company will make a loss.

Reichheld and Sasser demonstrate this by describing the profit flows generated by a customer of a typical credit card company. They suggest that it costs $51 to attract the customer in the first place. These **acquisition costs** are associated with the initial advertising and promotion and the administrative costs of opening a new account, performing credit checks, etc. The profits generated by that customer in the first year are only $30, rising to $42 in year two. It thus takes well over 12 months before the company breaks even and starts to make any profit. However, if they can hang on to the customer over an extended period of time the annual profits will start to climb (see Figure 3.1).

Acquisition costs
costs associated with attracting a customer and persuading him/her to do business with the organization

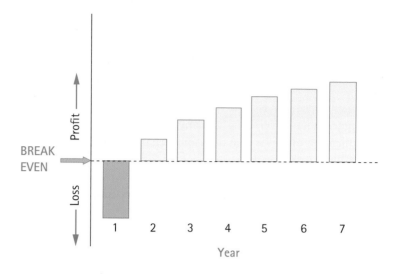

Figure 3.1 The importance of keeping customers over time

Source: Reprinted by permission of Harvard Business School Press, from Frederick Reichheld, *The Loyalty Effect* (1996), Boston, MA, p. 51

The Cost of Acquiring New Customers

Perhaps the most obvious reason why profits are higher with existing customers is that if all customers are retained, the business avoids the cost of acquiring new customers. This would include many marketing costs such as advertising and promotion, sales costs, and initial set-up costs.

Each year, UK companies spend over £19 billion (Advertising Association, 2005) on advertising their goods and services. Response hierarchy models, such as 'AIDA' or the 'Hierarchy of Effects' model are used to develop advertising messages and elicit a desired customer response (see Figure 3.2).

Typically, these messages will be built around a number of buyer-readiness states as follows (Kotler, 1997):

- awareness—letting customers know that the product exists;
- understanding—telling customers what the product does;

Figure 3.2 Advertising response stages

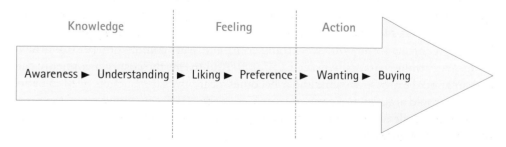

- liking—creating a positive feeling amongst customers towards the product;
- preference—persuading customers that this product is better than competitors;
- wanting—convincing customers that they need this product;
- buying—motivating customers to actually go out and buy the product.

All of these stages appear to assume that the customer is a new customer; in other words, they suggest that advertising is firmly rooted in the transaction marketing stable. The implication of this is that a business that retains all of its customers over a long period will not need to advertise. There is some merit in this argument. Many service industries such as restaurants, hairdressers, builders, plumbers, and car repairers never advertise as they simply rely on their existing customers to bring them business.

However, it should be noted that not all advertising is aimed at new customers. Sometimes, existing customers need to be reminded of how good the product or service is in order to assure them that they have made the right decision and ensure that they will continue to buy into the future (Barnard and Ehrenberg, 1997). Many car adverts for respected brands such as Audi or BMW are as much aimed at existing customers to remind them of why they bought the brand in the first place as they are at new customers. Nevertheless, it is clear that a business enjoying high rates of customer retention can save costs by not having to advertise to new customers.

But advertising is not the only cost of winning new customers. Many businesses employ promotions to acquire customers in the first place. For instance, each year the UK's banks try to attract the business of new students, offering a range of incentives from cash to free overdraft facilities. They are hoping that the students they sign up today will become the high earners of tomorrow and that they will remain with the bank they originally signed up with. Other businesses use similar tactics. For instance, many mortgage lenders offer to pay the customer's switching costs if they move their mortgage to them. Insurance companies offer free gifts or Marks & Spencer shopping vouchers just for a quote; mobile phone networks will give you the phone free if you sign up to their network and *Which?* magazine offered new subscribers a digital camera. Some of these businesses will tie the customer into a contract and make their money back that way, but many of them rely on new customers turning into long-term repeat customers in order to recoup their initial promotion costs. If the customer leaves after a short period of time, then the company might well make an overall loss on the transaction.

Advertising and promotion tend to be more geared toward first-time buyers in consumer markets (Kotler, 1997), whereas in business-to-business (B2B) marketing, much of the cost of winning new customers is based around the sales force. Employing a sales force is not cheap. In the UK the average annual salary of a sales manager is around £36,000 (workthing.com) and with commission and bonuses, on-target earnings can easily exceed £50,000. Add to this the cost of a company car and an annual expense account and it becomes clear why sales budgets need to be so big. One could argue that if companies maintained a 100% customer retention rate, the need for a sales department and all of its associated expenses would be far less. Of course, not all sales efforts are directed at finding new customers. Many businesses employ Key Account Managers whose job it is to look after big existing customers to ensure that they retain their business. However, in competitive markets a sizeable chunk of sales cost and effort is still directed at finding new customers.

Sales costs are not the only expense encountered in winning new customers in B2B markets. There are also set-up costs associated with doing business with a customer for the first time. These will vary depending on the industry, but will typically include things like design, installation, and the training of the customer's staff. This is because many products and services (such as industrial machines, security systems, IT systems, etc.) have to be tailored to fit each customer's individual specifications. Even tendering for a job can be a high-cost affair in some businesses where lengthy reports have to be meticulously researched and presented. Once a customer has been won, many of these heavy up-front expenses will not be incurred on second and subsequent sales, making customer retention a far more attractive proposition than customer acquisition.

Therefore, in service sectors and B2B markets, up-front marketing, sales, and set-up costs can be reduced or avoided by retaining customers. When it comes to fast-moving consumer goods (FMCGs), the situation is not so clear-cut. Supermarket shoppers are bombarded with promotions, from free plastic Shrek models in cereal packets to holiday competitions on shampoo bottles, as well as all of the money-off offers. In the evening, television adverts exhort consumers to buy this brand of chocolate or that brand of lager. Surely if customers remained loyal to one brand throughout their life, none of this would be necessary?

The problem is that these products tend to be 'low involvement' from the customer's point of view, in that their purchase carries little risk, either financially or emotionally. Furthermore, the customer has a huge choice of products all of which fulfil similar needs. This leads to the customer exhibiting 'variety seeking' behaviour. In effect every sale is a new sale as the customer has to be persuaded all over again to buy that product instead of a rival one. There is thus no escaping the high cost of advertising and promotion. Even when a customer exhibits brand loyalty, the message of what the brand stands for has to be reinforced over and over with constant advertising and promotion. It would appear that when it comes to up-front customer acquisition costs, the potential savings from retained customers are far lower for companies operating in business-to-consumer (B2C) FMCG markets than they are for B2B or service markets.

The Added Value of Existing Customers

Once the initial attraction costs have been absorbed, there are a number of reasons why existing customers are likely to be of higher value to the organization than first-time buyers:

Long-term Customers are More Likely to Enter into Collaborations

In many hi-tech industries such as consumer electronics, automotive, or aerospace, the supplier and customer will enter into joint product design initiatives, sharing each other's knowledge and resources in order to reduce costs. Similarly an integration of the supplier's and the customer's IT systems might enable the implementation of a just-in-time (JIT) delivery system in order to reduce inventory in the supply chain and reduce overall costs. Such collaborations require investment from both the supplier and the customer and usually tie both of them into a long relationship. With so much at stake, both sides will only be willing to risk this if they trust and are fully familiar with the other party. It is more likely that this will occur between long-term retained customers and their suppliers.

Existing Satisfied Customers are Likely to be Less Price-Sensitive

There is an old saying in business that no matter how good your prices are, someone somewhere will be charging less. Such a sentiment echoes the frustration of operating in a competitive industry where price competition is the norm. This happens in B2C markets such as supermarket groceries or petrol, as well as in B2B markets such as steel rod or stationery supply. It is also common in service industries such as insurance, banking, airlines, and utility supply (gas, electricity, etc.). Price-based competition tends to be transaction-based in that its goal is to win new customers by taking them from the competition. The problem with price-based competition is that it reduces overall profitability and can lead to price wars. An alternative to price competition is service-based competition, where the goal is to ensure that the customer experience is so good that they will be happy to pay the price, even if it is not the lowest price available. This tends to be a relationship-based approach.

However, it is not always easy using service features to differentiate a business. For petrol retailers, price and convenience are the determining factors. Banks and building societies have also found it difficult to differentiate themselves and end up competing on price. In these situations long-standing customers become very valuable as they are less likely to jump ship if a better offer comes along somewhere else, which invariably it will sooner or later. Ideally, a business should try to attract new customers with special offers and price promotions and maintain existing customers through exemplary service. However, this can lead to problems if existing customers feel that they are being disadvantaged. Some years ago the author of this book complained bitterly to Barclaycard that although he had been a loyal customer for 20 years, he was now being asked to pay a £12 annual card fee, when new customers, who had not yet shown any loyalty, were having this fee waived. The company quickly responded with an apology and refunded the £12. Shortly afterwards the annual fee was dropped altogether. This illustrates a problem for companies in the way in which they deal with different types of customer. Retained customers (whether loyal through genuine affection, or simply through inertia) will be less price-sensitive because they believe that they are getting good overall value from the company (Reichheld, 2006), but the company should be careful to maintain this overall added value and not be seen to be taking advantage of loyal customers.

In B2B marketing, frequent price-switching customers are less common because price is often not the only factor in determining a supplier. Other considerations such as continuity of supply, reliability of delivery, and quality standards will also play a part. However, if a customer knows that more than one supplier can meet its needs, then it might play the different companies off against each other in an effort to lever a better deal. In a long-standing relationship customers are less likely to leave without warning.

Regular Customers make for Easier Business Planning

Regular customers place frequent, consistent orders and are therefore usually less costly to serve. Knowing that a particular order will come in at the end of the month helps to take the heat out of production and financial planning. Factories can be geared to producing what is needed when it is needed. With no surprise rush jobs, output can be managed for maximum cost efficiency. At the same time, ongoing cash flows are predictable, which enables investment and expenditure decisions to be taken with confidence. The logistics are also easier to manage as transportation and warehousing can all be arranged in advance. As the years go by, retained customers' buying behaviour falls into patterns, thus helping the supplier's strategic planning process.

Existing Satisfied Customers are More Likely to Give Referrals

Word-of-mouth referrals from existing customers are a powerful marketing tool because the message is likely to be taken more seriously than an advertising message sent out by the company itself. Indeed, such is their significance that Christopher *et al.* (1991) include 'referrals' as one of the relationship markets in their Six Markets Model (see Chapter 1). Within this, they distinguish between customer referrals that are initiated by the customer themselves and those that are prompted by the company.

Customer-initiated referrals (or 'advocacy referrals') are common in many service sectors, where the customer feels that they have received exemplary service. Thus, many restaurants do little advertising but rely on referrals and repeat customers for much of their business. The same can be true of other services, such as solicitors, builders, or car mechanics. The development of the Internet has given the power of customer referral a huge boost as satisfied customers can now tell thousands of others about their experience. An example of this is the web log sites which have sprung up amongst Taiwanese students wanting to study in the UK. Students already studying in the UK use the sites to tell others about the different UK universities and are able to answer questions and enter discussions with their peers who are considering studying in the UK. Customer-initiated referrals also occur in B2B marketing situations, particularly where networking occurs (e.g. at conferences, exhibitions).

The other type of customer referral described by Christopher *et al.* is company-oriented. This too is common both in B2C and B2B marketing. Here, the company asks customers if they will provide a referral. Thus, book and music club members are encouraged to recommend them to a friend in return for free gifts, fitness clubs offer a month's free membership if you can 'sign up a new member', and mobile phone companies offer similar incentives. Many universities publish pictures of satisfied students in their brochures and prospectuses, alongside some form of 'testimony' where the student relates how much they have enjoyed the course or what studying at that particular university has meant to them.

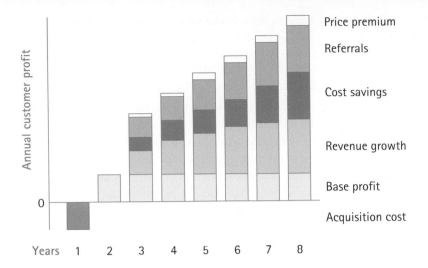

Figure 3.3 Incremental profit increases from retained customers

Source: Reprinted by permission of Harvard Business School Press, from Frederick Reichheld, *The Loyalty Effect* (1996), Boston, MA, p. 39

Long-Standing Customers are More Forgiving

Finally, existing satisfied customers are likely to be more forgiving if something goes wrong. If someone has been buying Ford motor cars all of their life, they are not as likely to ditch the brand after one fault as they are if this is their first Ford. The same is true of restaurants, banks, etc. However, it is important to remember that one of the principal tenets of RM is that complaints and problems should be handled speedily and effectively—this in itself can instil loyalty whereas badly managed complaints can make the situation worse.

Taking all of these factors into account, profits from retained customers start to climb. (See Figure 3.3).

The Lifetime Value of a Customer

Attracting the right type of customer—one who will remain loyal over many years—can pay dividends. Heskett *et al.* (1994) have calculated that a loyal pizza customer can easily spend $8,000 with the company in his or her lifetime, while a Cadillac customer can bring in excess of $332,000. If these figures are calculated as a net present value in today's terms it can be seen why retaining the right customers makes sense. The overall **lifetime value** of a customer is therefore something of which every business should be aware.

Lifetime value

the net worth of a customer's purchases of a particular product or service over his/her lifetime

Furthermore, as Reichheld points out, customer retention is a virtuous circle. The extra profits generated through customer retention cannot only be used to improve customer service even further (which will help to attract and retain even more customers); it can also be used to pay staff higher wages. According to Reichheld, staff retention is just as important as customer retention. Better wages will attract better staff, who will in turn give customers a better service and so the cycle is repeated. Companies with poor customer retention rates by comparison will end up spending more on customer acquisition. With lower profits they will not be able to invest in the same service levels and will attract less qualified staff. As customer retention slips even further, the vicious circle is intensified.

The Importance of Winning New Customers

The discussion so far suggests that customer retention should be given priority over customer acquisition and that organizations should rebalance their marketing efforts towards looking after existing customers. However, this would be a dangerous view to take and as Maister (1989) points out, there are several good reasons why organizations should not forget the importance of winning new customers.

First, new customers are needed to 'reseed the gene pool'. Put literally, existing customers will not be there for ever. They will eventually die or move away. If these organizations do not attract new customers, in time their existing customer base will have died away. There are hundreds of examples of organizations that have legions of satisfied existing customers, all gradually ageing away. In the late 1990s Marks & Spencer found itself in trouble because it was not attracting enough new customers. Although existing customers were perfectly happy, high-spending younger buyers were put off by the staid image and ageing customer profile. The company had to take drastic action and ended up ditching its long-standing St Michael brand in favour of new brands such as Per Una, along with completely revised management, purchasing, and merchandising structures.

However, it is not always easy for an organization used to serving a strong base of established customers to move to a strategy of new customer acquisition. Sometimes it means alienating the existing customers in order to attract new ones. (See Minicase 1, A Drop of the 'Red Stuff'?)

Minicase 1

A Drop of the 'Red Stuff'?

From humble beginnings in eighteenth-century Dublin, Guinness has grown into one of the world's iconic drinks brands. Enjoyed in over 150 countries around the world, Guinness's latest conquests include Russia and Nepal. It has already taken Africa by storm, where it is brewed under licence, and is performing strongly in Latin America and Asia. In North America, the drink's Irish heritage has helped sales, where quantities drunk on St Patrick's day can exceed those in Ireland. To reflect its global celebrity status, the Guinness Visitor Centre in Dublin, known as the Storehouse, has been promoted as Ireland's number one tourist destination, attracting over one million visitors within two years of its opening.

But Guinness's glittering worldwide performance disguises a worrying trend closer to home. Sales in its native Ireland have been falling steadily for a number of years now. Although it remains the number one alcoholic beverage in Ireland, this decline is accelerating and is threatening to undermine the international brand strategy—that Guinness represents Ireland and all things Irish. Some have even speculated that Guinness's owners, Diageo, may be forced to sell the brand in order to concentrate on its more profitable spirit and wine brands—a claim hotly refuted by the company.

There are a number of possible reasons for Guinness's decline in its home market, most of which come down to changing lifestyles. In common with the UK, Ireland has seen a shift in drinking habits, with more consumers choosing to consume alcohol at home rather than in the pub. The introduction of a smoking ban in pubs has exacerbated this trend. At the same time, cosmopolitan lifestyles have seen a shift away from traditional beers towards wine and continental lagers. Global mega-brands such as Budweiser and glitzy new cider brand Magners have ensured that the modern drinker has a choice of fashionable drinks to suit his or her lifestyle.

All of which makes Guinness look a bit dated. Guinness is a draught beer designed to be served in pubs and drunk from a glass, and, as we were famously told, it takes 1 minute and 59 seconds to pour the perfect pint. *Guardian* journalists Owen Bowcott and Simons Bowers sum it up. Many younger consumers associate Guinness with an older generation, more used to sitting long hours in pubs playing dominoes, discussing politics, and listening to folk music. Its warm, heavy texture and lengthy pour time do not fit with a 'clubbing' culture and fast-moving city bars where the next drink is never more than the flip of a bottle cap away.

Recognizing that they need to attract the younger drinker, Guinness has embarked on a number of new product launches and marketing initiatives. In 1999 came Guinness 'Extra Cold', chilled to just 3°C—an ideal temperature for young lager drinkers. Next came 'Bottled Guinness Draught', featuring a patented 'widget' designed to simulate the smooth texture of the draught version while allowing the user to drink straight from the bottle—ideal for clubbing. A device to enable fast pour in pubs followed in 2002. More recently the company trialled Guinness 'Toucan' (2006) which some described as being sweeter and less bitter than the traditional drink, and Guinness 'Mid-Strength' (2007) with a reduced alcohol content. Perhaps the wackiest new product variant is 'Guinness Red', similar to traditional Guinness, but using lightly roasted barely to give it a rich red colour.

So far, none of these variants has arrested the slide in sales of Guinness in Ireland and the more the company tinkers around with the core concept, the more it runs the risk of alienating the loyal drinkers it already has. The Extra Cold version in particular was heavily criticized by traditionalists, who claimed that the chilling process made the drink totally flavourless. Many of the Extra Cold pumps have now been removed from bars in Ireland. Similarly, the fast-pour concept flew directly in the face of Guinness's long-standing positioning message that 'good things come to those who wait'. Above all, how can a drink colloquially known throughout the land as 'a drop of the black stuff' suddenly become 'a drop of the red stuff'?

Questions

1. Suggest how Guinness might divide its marketing policy between existing customer retention and new customer acquisition. What are the pros and cons of each extreme?

2. Is it possible for long-established brands and products to re-establish themselves for younger markets? Give examples.

3. Does it matter that Guinness sales in Ireland are declining, if the product is still doing well in the rest of the world?

4. Can it be argued that Guinness is nearing the end of its product life cycle?

Sources:
'Guinness sees red over new coloured brew', *Daily Mail*, 26 January 2006
'Dark days for Guinness', *Guardian*, 29 August 2006
http://www.guinness.com/gb_en/ accessed 27/05/07

A further reason why organizations can't always afford to rely on existing customers is that they can become saturated. There is only so much that any one customer can buy from an organization and once this point is reached, no further growth can occur. Maister (1989) likens some organizations to 'leeches' in their relentless pursuit of ever more business from existing customers. Once this happens, there is a risk that the customer will back away. Many banks, for instance, try to encourage current account customers to move his or her savings accounts to the same bank too. They will then go on to encourage the customer to move her mortgage to them and with the mortgage all of the insurance for buildings, contents, payment protection, etc. If they can, they'll get the customer's pension business too. This is fine to an extent, but many customers do not wish to have all of their eggs in one basket. Frenzied overselling to the same customers could end up pushing them away.

Finally, Maister points out that the better the firm is at retaining customers, the more profitable will be its new client-marketing activities, because new clients will turn into long-term profitable existing clients. Thus, the Corgi model company is banking that the young collectors it attracts today with its Superhauler range will turn into lifelong collectors of the much more expensive adult-targeted Road Transport models. The banks giving away free gifts and promotions for students today have a clear eye on the potential profits of a loyal customer of the future.

So, although it makes sense to target a sizeable amount of the marketing effort at existing customers, there is also a strong case for attracting new customers. In practice, therefore, the question should not be whether to pursue new or existing clients, but rather, what the balance between the two should be and the marketing budgets allocated accordingly. We will consider how an organization might decide on this split later in the chapter when we look at designing customer retention strategies.

The Link Between Customer Satisfaction and Customer Retention

Logic suggests that the first step towards making sure that customers stay with a business is to ensure that those customers are satisfied. After all, a customer is hardly likely to return for more if he or she is not satisfied. Until the 1990s most measures of a business's performance concentrated on financial (e.g. sales, profitability, and cash flow) and operational (e.g. production output, costs, and stock control) perspectives. The problem with these measures, however, is that they are descriptive, not diagnostic. In other words they are good at telling an organization what *has* happened but less useful when it comes to predicting what *will* happen, or telling the organization what it must do to make things improve. Such performance measures often lead to cost cutting when the business runs into trouble and customer service often suffers, leading to customer dissatisfaction and high churn rates.

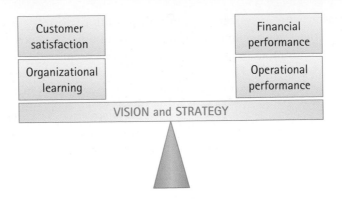

Figure 3.4 The Balanced Scorecard

Source: Reprinted by permission of *Harvard Business Review*, from R. Kaplan and D. Norton, *The Balanced Scorecard Approach—Measures that drive Performance*, Jan./Feb., 1992, pp. 71–9

Measuring Customer Satisfaction

The Balanced Scorecard

balances hard, quantitative measures of organizational performance against softer, more qualitative measures

An alternative approach called 'The Balanced Scorecard' was developed by Kaplan and Norton in 1992 to address these criticisms. **The Balanced Scorecard** (Figure 3.4) approach is based around four performance measurement perspectives including the two traditional measures—Financial and Operational—and two new measures—Customer Satisfaction, and Organizational Innovation and Improvement. The first two measures show an organization where it is and the second two show it how it can move forward.

The Balanced Scorecard Approach helped establish customer satisfaction as a strategic tool and as a result the pursuit of customer satisfaction became something of a 'holy grail' amongst many organizations. This can be seen in a proliferation of customer satisfaction surveys, whether it be when checking out of a hotel or getting a call from the garage to ask if a service has been carried out satisfactorily. Indeed, some organizations, such as J. D. Powers, have made their business out of measuring customer satisfaction (see Minicase 2, What Power Customer Satisfaction Surveys?).

Minicase 2

What Power Customer Satisfaction Surveys?

Regular viewers of the BBC's television programme, *Top Gear*, will be familiar with the show's annual customer satisfaction survey. Thousands of drivers are invited to take part in the survey by rating the model of car they drive across a number of pre-determined quality and overall satisfaction benchmarks. The results are often surprising and each year a big fanfare is made of the winning car makes, who quite naturally go on to use the accolades in their advertising and promotion. Likewise, attention is drawn to the losers, who are publicly admonished—on one memorable occasion by having a large amount of farmyard manure ceremoniously dumped over the car.

Top Gear's customer satisfaction surveys are run by American-based research company J. D. Power and Associates. Formed in 1968, J. D. Power and Associates is best known for its customer satisfaction surveys in the automotive industry. However, the company works with a number of industries including travel and hotels, healthcare, telecommunications, marine, utilities, consumer electronics, and financial services. The bulk of its customer satisfaction work is delivered through syndicated research, whereby companies within various industries subscribe to receive the data on an ongoing basis. However, the company also carries out customized, one-off research studies as well as business consultancy and training.

However, measuring customer satisfaction is not easy—to quote the company's founder, J. D. Power III: 'quality and customer satisfaction mean different things to different people'. To get around this problem, J. D. Power and Associates have developed a series of standard industry benchmarks against which customers can score their suppliers. In the UK car market this covers 77 attributes, grouped into four basic factors of satisfaction: vehicle quality and reliability; vehicle appeal (including performance, design, comfort, etc.); dealer service, and ownership costs. The resulting data is broken down and computed into a customer satisfaction index score for each make and model. Strict sampling control ensures that customers can only score models which they have owned and run over an average period of two years. In 2006 over 56,000 UK drivers took part in the survey.

Each year the industry awaits the results with almost an air of inevitability as the top ten places are usually dominated by Japanese brands such as Honda, Lexus, Subaru, Toyota, and Mazda. However, one marque has consistently defied its critics and surprised industry pundits by coming near the top of the rankings. Skoda, once the butt of motoring jokes, has appeared in the top five every year since 1995 and was voted the overall number one car manufacturer of 2006, taking the coveted spot from Lexus.

Skoda has rightly taken advantage of its high industry rankings and over the years has gradually increased its market share. In 2006, it set a new annual sales record in the UK, selling nearly 40,000 cars and taking a 1.7% share of the market. However, good news as this is for Skoda, it does raise the question that if this manufacturer is so good, why has it only got a 1.7% share of the market? Indeed, if one looks at any of the top-rated cars in the J. D. Power's survey, hardly any of them appear in the top ten best-seller lists according to the Society of Motor Manufacturers and Traders (SMMT). In fact the market sectors of 'Mini', 'Supermini', 'Lower Medium', 'Upper Medium', 'Executive', 'Utility', and 'MPV' are dominated by cars that don't do so well in the customer satisfaction rankings—some even appearing in the bottom ten.

Why the anomaly? Well as J. D. Power themselves acknowledge, customers buy different cars for different reasons. Brands such as Daihatsu and Kia are bought for their practicality and economy, Alfa Romeo and Jaguar for their image, and Volkswagen and Mercedes-Benz for their solid reputations. But as the editor of *Top Gear* points out, 'Companies that find themselves at the bottom [of the J. D. Power satisfaction rankings] each year need to get their act together before it's too late.' The thing is, he said this back in 2000 and the same companies still appear at the bottom of the rankings. Many of these same companies continue to dominate the UK sales charts. It would seem that customer satisfaction is not the be all and end all of selling cars in the UK.

Questions

1. Does the J. D. Power and Associates customer satisfaction survey have any value? If so, who can benefit most from it?

2. Suggest why companies such as Skoda and Honda do not have a higher share of the UK car market, despite their customer satisfaction rankings.

3. What are the factors which might contribute to customer retention in the UK car market?

Sources:
http://www.jdpower.com/corporateaccessed 20/05/07
http://www.jdpower.com/jdpcc/global/uk/content/faq_auto.jsp accessed 21/05/07
http://www.easier.com/views/News/Motoring/Skoda/article-1000 accessed 21/05/07
SMMT—Motor Industry Facts, 2006

Szwarc (2005) defines customer satisfaction as 'how customers view an organization's products or services in light of their own experiences with that organisation'. Thus, a member of a health club may find that all of the aspects of that club, such as the exercise equipment, the changing rooms, the showers, and spa area are adequate and theoretically should therefore be satisfied. However, Szwarc further states that in addition to their own experience with the organization, customers' satisfaction will also be based on comparisons with 'what they've heard about other companies or organisations'. Thus, the health club member might find the facilities in his present club are adequate but not be satisfied because he's heard that a gym down the road has a bigger pool or more modern equipment. Furthermore, customer satisfaction is essentially subjective and is therefore specific to each individual. A customer checking into a hotel might be dissatisfied that he is given a room at the back which has no view, while another customer might be perfectly happy with no view as long as he gets a good night's sleep.

As a result, we have to approach the subject of customer satisfaction with some caution. Donaldson (1995) is careful to make a distinction between the concepts of customer loyalty and customer satisfaction. Customer loyalty does not necessarily mean satisfaction—customers might remain simply due to inertia or because there are no alternative products or services available to meet their needs. Conversely, just because a customer is satisfied does not mean that they will necessarily be loyal to a business. She might be perfectly satisfied with the Mars Bar she has just eaten, but it does not mean that Mars Bars will be the only chocolate bar she will ever choose to eat in the future.

The Dangers of Concentrating on Customer Satisfaction

Reichheld (1996) is particularly critical of using customer satisfaction as a measure of success. Citing the automobile industry, he suggests that many manufacturers regularly achieve satisfaction scores of 80 and 90% but only manage to retain 40–50% of their customers; yet many car companies still regard high customer satisfaction rates as their ultimate goal, leading them into what Reichheld describes as the **Satisfaction Trap**.

The problem is twofold. First, raising customer satisfaction over and above the basic expected levels can be very expensive. Most organizations will initially go for the relatively easy things that will please the customer (what Reichheld describes as the 'low hanging fruit'). Thus a hotel might put out fresh flowers in the guests rooms each day or leave a complimentary chocolate on their pillow. However, it is unlikely that these in themselves will generate loyalty and they are easily copied by others. To truly delight the customer the hotel might have to totally soundproof the walls or have the bar and kitchen open for 24 hours. Such initiatives would require major investment and would need to be done with a full understanding of the type of customer the hotel was trying to attract and retain.

Second, concentrating too hard on satisfaction scores can lead to bad habits. Reichheld describes instances of salespeople pleading with customers to give them a high score as their monthly bonus, or even their job, relies on their achieving high customer satisfaction scores. As a result many satisfaction measures are meaningless and are not a good predictor of customer retention.

Thus, although customer satisfaction is a good first step in retaining customers, its subjective and emotional nature does not necessarily make it a good measure of long-term success. As Reichheld is at pains to point out, it is poor substitute for loyalty. As luxury car company Lexus openly acknowledges, the only true measure of satisfaction is repurchase.

> **The Satisfaction Trap**
> being led by customer satisfaction goals instead of customer retention ones

The Role of Customer Care and Service Quality

Achieving extremely high levels of customer satisfaction can itself be problematic as the things that evoke delight and excitement today quickly become the expected norms of tomorrow. Twenty years ago, features such as electric windows, air conditioning, and anti-lock braking systems could only be found on the most expensive cars. Today they are standard on even the most basic models. They do not create delight any more. Rather, if the vehicle doesn't have them, it does not even make it into the customer's initial choice set.

Generally speaking, as competing products such as cars or banks develop ever more advanced features, they remain indistinguishable from each other in the eyes of the customers and, assuming switching from one brand to another is relatively straightforward, customers have no reason to exhibit any sort of loyalty. As a result many businesses have turned to more intangible features, including the services associated with the purchase and consumption of the product. Such features generally come under the heading of **customer care** and while the value placed on these varies between different customers, customer care features are not always easy to copy and can therefore be used to differentiate the company. For example, Singapore International Airlines has become known for its focus on the customer, by including

> **Customer care**
> service elements associated with the purchase and consumption of a product/service

tangible innovations such as phones and TV screens in every seat and the less tangible features of staff courtesy and individual customer attention.

Customer care has become an important differentiator in both consumer and industrial markets, although the areas that generate satisfaction will differ. Consumers may value more subjective things such as friendliness of staff whereas business customers might be more objective in their service requirements such as consistency of delivery.

Features of Customer Care

Carson and Gilmore (1990) see customer care as a concept which encompasses at least four distinct kinds of activity:

- **Customer service**—ensures that all of the processes associated with buying and using a product or service go smoothly. This would include all advice and information sources provided by the organization to help the customer make the right decision. It would also include things such as order procedures, delivery, installation, etc. In other words this encompasses all of the activities which support the purchase and use of the core product or service. Examples would be making sure the organization's website is easy to navigate and secure, so that customers can place orders online. Another example might be the use of central call centres to handle enquiries. Many companies have been criticized for outsourcing activities like these to overseas call centres which inhibit the ability of the company to offer an efficient and knowledgeable service. In many respects, customer service boils down to how well the organizational structure enables the service to be delivered efficiently.

- **Product quality standards and measures**—set out to ensure that the product conforms to specifications and is fit for purpose. These relate to the core product or service and are pretty self-explanatory. No customer is going to be satisfied if the product itself does not do what it is supposed to do.

- **Service quality**—relates to the way in which the organization deals with its customers, focusing on the customer's experience during the process of the transaction. Service quality is one of the bedrocks of RM as it explores the interface between the organization and its customers (as highlighted by Carlzon (1987) when he talks about 'moments of truth'). Service quality will involve the interpersonal skills of employees who interact with customers as well as the customer's own perceptions of how the organization fulfils their expectations of quality.

- **After-sales service**—is the final area identified by Carson and Gilmore as being a distinct part of customer care. This would include enquiries and complaints handling, repair and ongoing maintenance. It could be argued that after-sales service falls under the general umbrella of customer service.

Clearly, the scope of customer care is extremely broad. In its widest sense it embraces everything that an organization does in order to establish and maintain a relationship

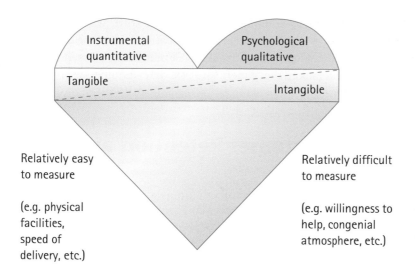

Figure 3.5 Dimensions of customer care

Source: Carson and Gilmore (1990). Reproduced with the kind permission of the *Irish Marketing Review*

with its customers. Donaldson (1995) defines customer care as: 'All those activities provided by the seller which have value for the buyer, thus increasing satisfaction and encouraging patronage and loyalty between the parties.' We have laboured the point about what customer care actually is because each organization has to identify what they can do to enhance it (and they can't enhance it unless they know what it is). It can be seen from the above discussions that customer care activities fall into two broad areas; the tangible and the intangible. This is illustrated by Carson and Gilmore in their 'Dimensions of Customer Care' (see Figure 3.5).

The tangible elements include the hard, objective elements that will deliver customer satisfaction. These can generally be measured fairly easily and often become part of an organization's quality control processes. Tangible customer care initiatives might include things like how fast the telephone is answered, how clean a restaurant is, or how easy it is for a customer to navigate a website. Because they can be measured relatively easily, tangible customer care initiatives are easier to adopt and to control. However, they are also more likely to be copied by competitors, thus cancelling out any advantage the organization might have accrued.

The intangible elements are often the most difficult to measure because they are subjective, but they are often the most likely to influence the buyer's ultimate experience. It is clear that the less tangible elements are largely services performed by front-line staff. It is possible to automate some of these services, such as replacing telephone operators with automated call centres but these can cause friction with customers, particularly when the nature of the customer's enquiry is not straightforward. The challenge of building relationships under such circumstances will be explored in more depth in Chapter 6.

It is possible to train people to achieve and sustain a high level of service delivery, underlining the importance of internal marketing (which will be looked at in

Chapter 9). In addition to training and motivating staff, a company should pay attention to other trappings, e.g. appearances, locations, etc. One of the reasons that Euro Disney struggled when it first opened was that being located in Paris, France made it too French! It lacked the 'American-ness' that customers associated with and valued about the Disney experience.

Managing Customer Retention and Defection

Plenty of organizations concentrate their management efforts on achieving customer satisfaction and high levels of customer care, but fewer of them seem actively to manage customer retention. If, as Reichheld suggests, customer retention is the only objective that matters, how then can organizations go about managing it?

Measuring Customer Retention Rates

If you don't measure something, you can't manage it. Every organization will measure elements of their business performance, usually in the form of sales turnover and profitability; but fewer of them bother to measure their customer retention rates. One reason for this might be because measuring retention is by no means easy or straightforward. For example, imagine a company making ball-bearings. It is easy for them to measure their sales (the amount of orders placed per month, or the amounts of monies invoiced over a period). It is also relatively easy for them to measure profitability (total net revenue minus costs over a period). How do they measure customer retention, though?

Presumably they would try to calculate some sort of index to measure how many existing customers are repurchasing; but how long a period of time should they consider? Some customers will use ball-bearings much faster than others and have to reorder them more frequently. The company will therefore need to find out what the repurchase cycle is for its customers before it can class them as retained or not. Even then, they will have to decide how many times the customer has to repurchase the ball-bearings before they can be classed as retained. Should a customer placing two orders over a 12-month period be classed as retained if other customers have placed three or four orders over the same time frame? Further questions might also be asked—for instance, is a retained customer classed as someone who buys all of their ball-bearings from the company? What about another customer who places regular orders but also gives orders to competitors?

There is no simple answer to this—each company must work out a retention index which is meaningful for them. A simple retention rate would measure the percentage of customers that are retained over a period (e.g. six months or one year, depending on the repurchase cycle for that particular market sector). However, a more meaningful measure would be one that is weighted so that customers who bought more were valued more highly than low users. If customers buy from a number of different sellers, then some sort of weighting should also be given, depending on the size of the share of their business (Payne, 2000).

Shajahan (2004) reminds us that customers will exhibit different levels of 'stickiness' depending on the stage of their relationship with the firm. Thus, first-time buyers are relatively less likely to buy again than those who have already bought several times. Any measure of retention, therefore, should perhaps be weighted according to the likelihood that a customer will buy again, so that alarm bells can be triggered if a long-standing customer defects.

Analysing Customer Defection

Defection is the opposite of retention. Thus, customers who defect do not make any repeat purchases from the company and are often assumed to have switched to a competitor. Reichheld and Sasser (1990) liken customer defection management to Total Quality Management (TQM) principles. Whereas TQM strives for zero defects, the goal of defection management is zero customer defections. Just as quality defects in a factory will result in lots of scrap material, customers who defect from a company can also be regarded as scrap as all of the investment that the company has put into them will be wasted. By measuring customer retention amongst different segment profitability groups, it will become clear to the company where the highest levels of customer defection are. We will see that it is not possible to retain every customer, but by analysing where and why defections are occurring, the company can better understand where it needs to concentrate its retention efforts. Payne (2000) suggests four approaches to determine the cause of defection:

> **Defectors**
> customers who cease to make ongoing purchases from the organization

- root cause analysis;
- trade-off analysis;
- competitive benchmarking;
- customer complaint analysis.

Root Cause Analysis

The aim of root cause analysis is to find out what really happened. Too often a company will just accept that it has lost a customer without trying to find out why. Every day, customers cancel insurance policies, switch their mortgage providers, or trade in their old cars for a different make. Unless organizations try to find out why these customers have defected, they stand little chance of improving their retention rates. Even when organizations do ask customers why they are leaving, the questioning is simple and often presumptuous. Thus an insurance company might accept a reason for defection as 'cover no longer required' or 'cheaper price elsewhere'. These are easy get-outs for the customer but end up telling the company very little (Payne, 2000). The real reason might have been that the customer does not like the overseas call centre the insurance company operates or that they were unhappy with the length of time it took to settle a claim.

Unless companies ask the right questions they will not always be able to find out why they lost a customer. Payne argues that root cause analysis should be undertaken by skilled researchers who can discover the real reason for defection. Properly done it will determine whether the defector was a customer who the organization wanted to keep in the first place. De Souza (1992) identifies six different types of defector:

Price Defectors are those customers who switch to a competitor who is offering a better price. The good thing about price defectors is that they can be bought back if you cut your prices. The bad thing is that they'll probably defect again as soon as a cheaper price comes along elsewhere and you'll run the risk of ending up in a price war. For this reason price defectors are often referred to in disparaging terms such as 'promiscuous' or 'rate tarts'. Recognizing that these customers are never likely to be profitable long-term prospects, some companies try to avoid them. For instance, GM's Saturn division has established a non-negotiable price list at dealer level, to discourage discount seekers, as this group makes up one of the least loyal segments (Reichheld, 1994). Businesses that don't have to worry about price defectors are those who have been able to add value in other ways, such as brand image (e.g. BMW), product quality (e.g. Marks & Spencer), or superior service delivery (e.g. Singapore International Airlines).

Nevertheless many market sectors can do little to avoid price defectors, particularly in things like commodities (e.g. petrol), non-core business services (e.g. office cleaning or stationery supply), and products and services which are difficult to differentiate (e.g. motor insurance). Trying to retain customers in markets such as this is notoriously difficult and explains why they are perhaps better suited to transactional marketing as opposed to RM strategies.

Product Defectors are much more difficult to win back. They have left the business because either they are dissatisfied with the product, or a competitor has come along offering a much better product. This is what happened to the British and American motorcycle industries. In the 1960s the British motorcycle industry was suffering from years of underinvestment and lack of development. Their products were technically archaic and they were unreliable. When Japanese bikes such as Honda arrived, they presented a revolution as they were clean, stylish, technically advanced and, above all, reliable. Furthermore they did not cost any more than their British counterparts. Customers flocked to them in droves and the writing was on the wall for British bikes. This was a blow from which they have never been able to recover because, although the design and quality of British bikes improved enormously, they could never shake off the poor reputation they had gained.

Price is not usually a factor for product defectors so they cannot simply be bought back. Hoover and Electrolux found this out to their cost when the technically advanced Dyson dual cyclone vacuum cleaner came along and took away a huge share of their market. Despite costing nearly twice as much as a typical Hoover, Dyson became the best-selling vacuum cleaner in the UK within two years of its launch. Unable to break Dyson's patents, Hoover resorted to high-profile promotions, culminating in the disastrous 'free holiday flights to America' offer which ended up costing them over £40 million and turned into a public relations nightmare. Hoover has since struggled to retrieve their once dominant market position, even though they now have similar technology to Dyson.

Service Defectors are similar to product defectors except that here it is poor service which drives them away from a company. Here too it is extremely difficult to win a customer back once the business has a reputation for poor service, particularly if there are plenty of alternative suppliers for customers to choose from. Having enjoyed years of monopoly status protection, the big utility companies such as British Telecom and British Gas could not count customer service amongst their strong points. As a result, when the markets were de-regularized and opened up to competition, millions of customers defected to competitors. Although they are now winning back some of these customers, this is probably as much to do with the poor service that customers have received from competitors as it is to do with anything that BT or British Gas have done.

Like product quality, once an organization has a reputation for poor service, it is difficult to shake off. Many bus users have defected to other means of transport, particularly cars, over the last ten to fifteen years. Despite the high running costs of cars, the congested roads, and the difficulty of parking them in cities, customers were fed up with waiting at bus-stops for buses that never arrived, or arrived so overdue that two came together. They were tired of sitting on grubby seats and having to wipe a hole in the condensation to see out of the window. They were unimpressed by the surly drivers and the noise, smells, and vibration from vehicles which were long past their sell-by dates. Huge numbers of ex-bus-users still believe it to be like this despite the investment bus companies have made in new vehicles which are cleaner, faster, quieter, and more comfortable. Old opinions die hard and it will take a major shift in opinion (or legislation) to get people back on buses.

Market Defectors are customers who have left the market altogether because they simply don't need the product or service any more. This can be due to any number of reasons, but most commonly it is because of a change in personal circumstances. The mother whose children are growing up will no longer need the nursery she has been using for the last few years. The couple who get married are likely to forget about 18–30 holidays and will look for a different type of holiday, while the businessman who secures a job in Scotland is no longer going to need to catch a train to London every day. In B2B markets loyal customers can disappear overnight if they go into liquidation or relocate abroad.

There is nothing a company can do to prevent the loss of customers in this way. Some will be more exposed to market defectors than others, especially if they are targeting customers of a particular age or life-stage (e.g. fashion shops, night clubs, or universities). For businesses who can potentially keep customers over a lifetime, however, they need to look very closely at environmental trends and their own customer profiles to ensure that they are not over exposed to the risk of market defection.

Technological Defectors are customers who switch their business to an altogether different company outside the industry, usually because this company has been able to use their technological skills to offer a better product or service solution. For example, Kodak has seen millions of customers defect to companies such as Sony and Panasonic. These were never traditional competitors of Kodak but because they had a lead in digital electronics technology, they were able to develop the digital photography market and attract Kodak's customers (see End of Chapter Case).

The same thing has happened in other industries (e.g. computers, musical instruments, watches, and newspapers).

Once again the company should be scanning the environment to keep on top of technological developments. This might mean forming alliances with companies in other industries in order to be able to offer customers the same technologies as competitors. However, careful analysis of customer defections can sometimes highlight technology defections which the company might not have seen coming. For example, sales of watches have been falling in recent years, largely because young people simply tell the time from the digital display on their mobile phone.

Organizational Defectors are those customers who are prevented from buying the product again because of 'political' reasons, and not because there is anything wrong with the product or service. For instance, several years ago students were asked to boycott KitKat chocolate bars and the products were withdrawn from many Student Union shops. The reason for this was that KitKat's parent company, Nestlé, was promoting powdered baby milk to poorer African states, thus discouraging natural breastfeeding. The Students Union opposed this policy, believing that it was disadvantaging poorer communities and undermining their health, hence the edict to stop buying any Nestlé products.

If a company finds that it has many organizational defectors, there is little it can do other than try to build relationships with whoever is pulling the strings. These examples fall under what Gummesson (1999) terms 'Mega Relationships'. We will be looking at these in more detail in Chapter 8.

Trade-off Analysis

Once the organization has an understanding of which customers are defecting and why, it can start to concentrate its resources in retaining those customers whom it needs to keep. The next step is to identify those areas of customer service which the customer really values and which if performed well will help to promote retention. Different types of customer will have different service priorities and it is more than likely that some sort of trade-off will have to take place so that the service priorities of the highest value customers take precedence.

In recent years many pubs have found themselves making tough decisions about the type of service they want to offer in order to appeal to the most valuable customers. Some pubs have gone up-market, getting rid of dartboards, pool tables, juke boxes, and beer mats in favour of designer furniture, staff uniforms, and an emphasis on food and wine rather than beer. In doing so they have alienated many long-standing traditional customers but they think it is worth it because they will attract and hopefully retain higher spending customers. Other pubs believe that the traditional pub drinker is the best long-term bet and have catered for their needs with satellite TV, fruit machines, and an emphasis on drinks rather than food. At the same time some pubs are 'family friendly' while others have a policy of no children at all. No pub can be all things to all people, hence the trade-off, but a pub does have to know which customers represent its best long-term potential and make sure that it knows what the service priorities of this group are.

Competitive Benchmarking

The third area suggested by Payne in analysing customer defection is for the organization to compare its performance on those service features which have been identified as customer priorities with the performance of its competitors in this area. Clearly, the objective should be to at least match, or if possible exceed the standards of its competitors. If it cannot do this it is likely to suffer customer defections.

Thus, a car repair shop might use **benchmarks** such as the average time taken to book a car in, the qualifications and experience of the staff, the cleanliness of the premises, the provision of a comfortable waiting area, and the explanation to customers of work that has been carried out. The organization should seek to exceed the performance of its competitors in those areas which have been identified as customer priorities. Low-cost airlines used this to great effect when developing their 'no frills' services.

Benchmarking comparing actual performance against pre-determined industry standards

Customer Complaints Analysis

Finally, the organization should look at the customer complaints it receives. When they receive a complaint, many organizations will concentrate on placating the customer there and then, perhaps with a quick refund, instead of really analysing what is going wrong. A deep analysis of complaints over time can identify trends and act as an early warning system of possible problems ahead. For every customer who complains, there will probably be many more who don't complain, but simply walk away never to return. Any complaints that are received should therefore be taken seriously as they could well indicate a serious underlying problem which is causing customer defection. Sometimes these can be in areas which the organization had not considered to be a problem, such as the attitude of a staff member, and they can often reveal what the customer's true service priorities are.

Therefore, it makes sense for an organization to analyse complaints data at a strategic level. This will not only tell the organization what is important to the customer and where it is getting things wrong, it will also enable them to fix problems that are causing defection. Furthermore, swift action at an operational level will prevent disgruntled customers from telling others about their experience and may even help to strengthen the relationship.

Corrective Action to Improve Customer Retention

Once an organization has identified its rates of customer defection, the types of customers who are defecting, and the possible reasons for their defection, it can start to take action to improve retention of the most valuable customers. Each organization will be different and plans to improve retention will therefore be highly specific to the organization concerned However, De Souza (1992) suggests a number of broad strategies that any organization can take to improve its customer retention rates.

Identify Switching Barriers and Build them into the Product or Service

We have to be careful with the use of the word 'barrier' as it can have negative connotations. A barrier is usually there to keep us in or to stop us from getting

Switching barrier

something which makes it difficult, risky, or not worthwhile for a customer to take his/her business elsewhere

somewhere. **Switching barriers** in business makes it difficult, onerous, or risky for the customer to defect to a competitor. For instance, switching bank accounts involves some effort on the part of the customer as they have to re-arrange all of their direct debit and credit arrangements. Switching a mortgage is even more complicated as it can involve having property surveys carried out and will usually also require the customer to pay a hefty fee. Such barriers will certainly result in customer retention but will probably also result in an unhappy and ultimately unprofitable long-term customer.

As a result switching barriers should only be created if they are of benefit to both the customer and the supplier. Product-bundling, for example, usually entails the customer receiving an overall discount if they take more than one product from the supplier (e.g. customers buying both gas and electricity from nPower get both at a cheaper rate). In B2B situations a supplier may help the customer with their own sales and marketing (e.g. joinery manufacturer John Carr overprinted their trade catalogues with the name of their customer, Jewson. This gave Jewson a ready-made sales catalogue which they could promote to builders. Both John Carr and Jewson benefited from this arrangement). Sometimes the working relationship becomes even closer (e.g. through joint product development or electronic data interchange (EDI) to facilitate JIT operations). In such cases there is a clear disincentive, or switching barrier, for the customer to defect.

Visible Top-Management Endorsement

We saw earlier in this chapter that retaining customers is not always seen as exciting or valuable as winning new customers. For this attitude to change, the top management in the organization needs to show that they are fully behind a strategy of customer retention. What is important however is that this is not seen simply as a 'management fad'. Rosenberg and Czepiel (1984) suggest going further and reconfiguring the organization to aid customer retention, e.g. by assigning executive accountability for customer retention and retained turnover. Key account management is an example of this.

Concentrate on an Internal Customer Service Climate

Many studies have shown that organizations with a strong internal customer service ethos generally enjoy greater levels of employee satisfaction and greater levels of customer retention (e.g. Ogbonna and Wilkinson, 1990). Developing the interpersonal skills of front-line staff should therefore become an organizational priority. Lynn Shostack (1985) proposes that the service encounter should be carefully planned, while Carlzon (1987) emphasizes the importance of organizational customer interface. The whole area of staff relationships and their impact on customers will be looked at in depth under 'Internal Marketing' in Chapter 9.

Chapter Summary

There is strong evidence to suggest a positive link between an organization's profitability and its ability to retain customers over a period of time. While the strength of this link varies across different industry and market sectors, many companies overlook the importance of retaining customers and concentrate the bulk of their marketing efforts on customer acquisition. Getting the balance right requires a clear understanding of the costs of acquisition and the lifetime value of a retained customer.

It is easy to assume a link between customer satisfaction and customer retention, but this can be dangerous as customer satisfaction becomes a basic expectation rather than any guarantor of loyalty. To truly delight the customer, the organization must increasingly look to the less tangible features of customer care and service quality as it is in these areas where it can begin to differentiate itself from the competition and give customers a reason for coming back.

Ultimately an organization must take a strategic approach to managing customer retention. This entails identifying the types of customer it needs to retain and ensuring that defection amongst these groups is kept to a minimum. Reducing customer defections will require a proactive approach from a high level within the organization.

End of Chapter Case with Questions

Brands Fight to Stay Ahead in a Shifting Market

For over a century Kodak was a dominant name in the world of photography. Having pioneered the development of mass-produced, easy-to-use cameras, Kodak's founder George Eastman led the way in developing new products and processes, in both cameras and the film that they used. Today, Kodak still leads the world market in celluloid film, but the market is in steep decline. The company has already ceased making traditional reloadable cameras and is fighting hard to embrace the new technology which it needs to keep the Kodak brand name at the forefront of a rapidly changing photography market.

The onset of digital technology shifted the nature of photography from a chemical process base to an electronic process. This brought a raft of new entrants to the camera market, in the form of established electronics companies such as Sony, Canon, and Samsung. Kodak and other traditional camera producers were forced to react to protect their market and move into the new technology. However, despite investing $3 billion to keep up, Kodak saw Sony grab 20% of the worldwide market in digital cameras by 2004. Some argued that Kodak had reacted too late as the company's profits and share prices slid. Nevertheless, Kodak was successful in developing its own range of digital cameras which in the US market overtook those of Canon and Sony. It seemed that consumers' association with Kodak and cameras had been maintained.

But now it is predicted that the growth in the digital camera market has peaked as more consumers turn to mobile phones with cameras built in. In 2006 Konica Minolta pulled out of the digital camera market altogether and companies such as Canon and Sony are banking on the top-end digital SLR market for big future growth. Not to be outdone, Kodak's chief executive Antonio Perez wants the company to be 'the indisputable leader for digital capture for consumer applications' by 2010. To this end he has signed a deal with Motorola to provide silicon camera sensors in mobile phones. 'We are going to collaborate and co-design cellphones so they become real cameras', says Perez, 'we're talking about information and imaging becoming one'.

It's all come a long way from the original Box Brownie!

Questions

1. What are the challenges facing Kodak as it tries to maintain its brand identity?

2. Is it possible for a company synonymous with a particular type of product or technology to successfully reinvent themselves? Use examples to support your answer.

Sources:
'Digital-camera growth has peaked, study says' http://www.news.cnet.co.uk/digitalcameras accessed 05/08/05
'Kodak to finish camera making', *Times*, 2 August 2006
'Kodak's moment: once-great brand hopes to become global name again', *Guardian*, 28 September 2006

Discussion Questions

1. Do all product and service sectors experience high initial costs when winning new customers? Explain your answer with examples.

2. Can a clear distinction be made between advertising and promotion designed to attract customers as opposed to those designed to retain customers?

3. What are the potential risks of targeting new customers with generous promotional offers? How might an organization mitigate these risks?

4. Why is customer retention a less realistic proposition in fast-moving consumer markets than it is in B2B or service markets?

5. What are the benefits to a customer in remaining loyal to an organization or brand over time?

6. Should customer retention be the responsibility of the sales department? If not, which other functions within the organization might have a part to play?

7. Should a company with lots of loyal, satisfied customers worry about getting new customers?

8. What are the problems associated with measuring customer satisfaction?

9. When Reichheld talks about the 'satisfaction trap', is he implying that the pursuit of customer satisfaction is not worthwhile?

10. What challenges might an organization face when trying to differentiate itself through customer care initiatives?

11. Why is measuring customer retention not as straightforward as it sounds?

12. Why is it important for an organization to allow dissatisfied customers to complain?

Further Reading

Reichheld, F. (2006) *The Ultimate Question: Driving Good Profits and Good Growth*, Harvard Business School Publishing Corporation.

Jones, T. and Sasser, E. (1995) 'Why satisfied customers defect', **Harvard Business Review**, Nov./Dec., 88–101.

Szwarc, P. (2005) *Researching Customer Satisfaction and Loyalty*, Kogan Page.

References

Barnard, N. and Ehrenberg, A. (1997) 'Advertising: Strongly Persuasive or Nudging?', **Journal of Advertising Research**, Jan./Feb., 21–31.

Carlzon, J. (1987) *Moments of Truth*, Ballinger.

Carson, D. and Gilmore, A. (1989/90) 'Customer Care: The neglected domain', **Irish Marketing Review**, 4(3), 49–61.

Caruabna, A. (2002) 'Service Loyalty. The Effects of Service Quality and the Mediating Role of Customer Satisfaction', **European Journal of Marketing**, 36(7/8), 811–28.

Christopher, M., Payne, A., and Ballantyne, D. (1991) *Relationship Marketing: Bringing quality, customer service and marketing together*, Butterworth Heinemann.

De Souza, G. (1992) 'Designing a Customer Retention Plan', **Journal of Business Strategy**, Mar.–Apr., 24–8.

Donaldson, B. (1995) 'Customer Care' in Baker, M. (ed.), *Marketing: Theory & Practice* (3rd edn), Macmillan, London.

Gummesson, E. (1999) *Total Relationship Marketing. Rethinking Marketing Management: From 4Ps to 30Rs*, Butterworth Heinemann, Oxford.

Heskett, J., Jones, T., Loveman, G., Sasser, G., and Schlesinger, L. (1994) 'Putting the Service Profit Chain to Work', **Harvard Business Review**, Mar.–Apr., 164–74.

Kaplan, R. and Norton, D. (1992) 'The Balanced Scorecard Approach—Measures that Drive Performance', **Harvard Business Review**, Jan.–Feb., 71–9.

Kotler, P. (1997) *Marketing Mangement. Analysis, Planning, Implementation and Control* (9th edn), Prentice Hall International.

Maister, D. (1989) 'Marketing to Existing Clients', **Journal of Management Consultancy**, 5(2), 25–32.

Ogbonna, E. and Wilkinson, B. (1990) 'Corproate Strategy and Corporate Culture: The view from the checkout', **Personnel Review**, 19(4), 9–15.

Payne, A. (2000) *Marketing Management: A Relationship Marketing Perspective*, Cranfield School of Management, Macmillan Press Ltd.

Peters, T. (1988) *Thriving on Chaos: Handbook for a Management Revolution*, Macmillan, Harper & Row

Reichheld, F. (1994) 'Loyalty and the Renaissance of Marketing', **Journal of Marketing Management**, 2(4), 0–21.

Reichheld, F. (1996) *The Quest for Loyalty*, Harvard Business School Publishing Corporation.

Reichheld, F. (2006) *The Ultimate Question: Driving Good Profits and Good Growth*, Harvard Business School Publishing Corporation.

Reichheld, F. and Sasser, E. (1990) 'Zero Defections: Quality Comes to Services', *Harvard Business Review*, Sept.–Oct., 105–11.

Rosenberg, L. and Czepiel, J. (1984) 'A Marketing approach for Customer Retention', *Journal of Consumer Marketing*, 1, 45–55.

Shajahan, S. (2004) *Relationship Marketing: Texts and Cases*, Tata McGraw Hill, New Delhi.

Shostack, L. (1985) 'Planning the Service Encounter', in Czepiel, J., Solomon, M., and Surprenant, C. (eds), *The Service Encounter*, Lexington Books, pp. 243–53.

Szwarc, P. (2005) *Researching Customer Satisfaction and Loyalty*, Kogan Page.

Websites

The Advertising Association http://www.adassoc.org.uk accessed 29/03/07

Workthing.com http://www.workthing.com/career-advice/industry-qualifications/sales/training_payanddisplay.html accessed 15/05/07

Customer Loyalty and Involvement

Chapter Outline

Learning Outcomes

After reading this chapter you should be able to:

- describe the different levels of customer involvement;
- understand the concept of loyalty and recognize the difference between retention and loyalty;
- suggest policies to move customers up each stage of the loyalty ladder;
- evaluate the effectiveness of loyalty schemes;
- appreciate the limitations of involving *all* customers in *all* markets;
- know-how to build customer involvement into the strategic marketing plan.

Introduction

Chapter 3 highlighted the significance of long-term customer relationships and the value of retaining customers. Relationships, however, are about involvement and interaction by both parties. To illustrate this, consider a human relationship which is only one-sided. The words 'infatuation' or 'stalking' come to mind, whereby one party believes they are in a relationship, but the other definitely does not!

This chapter therefore considers the ways and means that customers can be involved with a business and how this translates into loyalty. Whereas loyalties within human relationships (e.g. between friends) are fairly easy to recognize and understand, loyalties between customers and businesses are more difficult to quantify, particularly when the organization has many thousands of customers (this explains why this chapter concentrates more on business-to-consumer (B2C) marketing situations than business-to-business (B2B), where networking and personal relationships are more common). Many businesses believe that they have loyal customers when in fact all that their customers are doing is exhibiting repeat purchasing behaviour for some other reason.

It is important therefore for organizations to have an understanding of the drivers of loyalty and how much customer loyalty and involvement they can reasonably expect. The Ladder of Loyalty (Christopher *et al.*, 2002) is used here as a frame on which to base these questions, as it suggests that customers can progress from being mere prospects with whom the organization might do business, right through to being partners of the organization. Along the way, the shift from transactional marketing to relationship marketing can be seen and the difference between spurious loyalty and sustainable loyalty becomes apparent.

Against this background, organizations pursue a number of strategies to try and encourage and maintain customer loyalty and involvement. We are all familiar with the 'loyalty scheme' and these are discussed in some depth here, including the question on every marketer's lips, 'do they work?' The answer appears to be a heavily qualified yes . . . but only at relatively low levels of the loyalty ladder. Other means of involving customers in closer relationships are therefore investigated, including permission marketing, customer membership schemes, and branding.

The Opening Case illustrates how Microsoft has attempted to build loyalty by involving the customer.

Opening Case Study with Questions

Microsoft Turns Customers into Partners

When Bill Gates founded Microsoft 30 years ago, he had a vision that in the future everyone would have access to a personal computer (PC). At a time when no one even knew what a PC was, his venture demonstrated extraordinary foresight and in business terms was a daring act of bravado. Today we find it hard to imagine a world without PCs and Bill Gates' vision has made Microsoft into a multi-billion dollar company and turned Gates himself into the world's richest man, with a personal worth of over $50 billion.

Although familiar to most of us through its B2C operations, the major part of Microsoft's business is based on its B2B sales, with millions of companies across the world relying on Microsoft products. The diversity in demand has led to many companies setting up to customize Microsoft products for individual business solutions. Whole industries have been built up around business support providers, system builders and integrators, training providers, consultants, applications, and e-commerce solution developers along with independent hardware and software vendors, many of whom use Microsoft products as their base.

In B2B markets, then, Microsoft finds itself in a supply chain, relying on businesses further down the chain to develop and use its products to provide solutions to end users. Recognizing the key role that these customers have in maintaining their market share, Microsoft has created a 'Partner Scheme'. Microsoft Partnerships come in three different levels: Registered Member, Certified Partner, and Gold Certified Partner. Customers qualify for partnership at the two higher levels through 'Partner Points' which are earned in a number of ways including:

- demonstrating competencies with Microsoft products;
- staff achieving Microsoft professional certifications;
- developing software solutions which meet Microsoft's quality requirements;
- end customer satisfaction;
- unit sales of Microsoft learning products;
- revenue generation through sales of Microsoft software licences.

In addition, customers wishing to become Certified or Gold Certified Partners, pay a fee to Microsoft.

In return for their partner status, customers are given help to develop technical competencies with Microsoft products and access to commercial support resources including use of logos, company newsletters, and assistance with sales and marketing planning. Additionally, Microsoft will refer business directly to its partners and they are encouraged to network between one another to develop business opportunities. Possessing Microsoft Partner status gives companies a powerful sales and marketing tool within their own markets, e.g. UK-based consulting firm Compusys proudly announces on its website that it is a Microsoft Gold Certified Partner.

Microsoft is not the only IT company using a partnership scheme to get close to its key customers—rivals HP and Cisco offer similar schemes, leading to competition between schemes in order to woo partners.

Questions

1. To what extent are Microsoft's Partners true partners in a business sense?

2. How effective do you think such partnership schemes are in securing loyalty?

3. Who benefits most from the Microsoft Partnership programme?

Sources:
http://partner.microsoft.com.global accessed 06/11/05
http://www.compusys.co.uk/compusys/consulting accessed 07/11/05

A Word About Loyalty

For many marketers, particularly those adhering to the principles of relationship marketing, customer loyalty has become something of a holy grail. The more loyal customers an organization can count amongst its market, the closer it comes to reaping the benefits of customer retention outlined in Chapter 3. For this reason, any study of relationship marketing would be incomplete without a consideration of the concept of loyalty. However, the actual meaning of loyalty when applied to customers' relationships with businesses can be problematic. What constitutes a loyal customer and what can businesses do to encourage loyalty?

Defining Loyalty

The first problem to overcome is to define what we mean by loyalty. Various quantitative suggestions have been put forward, such as the customer retention rate, purchase frequency, or customer's share of wallet. These are all easy to measure, but do not necessarily explain or predict a customer's true loyalty. Some definitions are therefore more qualitative. Uncles *et al.* (2003) suggest that loyalty is a positive feeling that consumers may exhibit towards brands, services, stores, product categories, and activities; but this is rather vague. More useful is Little and Marandi's (2003) definition: 'a commitment by a customer to a supplier which is based on choice'. For our purposes we will assume that consumer loyalty is: 'a consumer's firm and unchanging friendship, support and belief in an organization, or its products, brands and services and a propensity to act in support of these feelings'. Words such as 'friendship', 'support', and 'belief' carry a certain emotional resonance which is difficult to apply to many products and services. While we may shop at the same supermarket each week, buy our petrol from the same garage or stick with the same electricity supplier year in year out, how many of us can claim that this is through friendship, support, or belief?

Genuine Loyalty versus Repeat-buying Behaviour

Repeat buying
customers making subsequent purchases of the same product or service over time

Genuine loyalty
a customer's firm and unchanging friendship, support, and belief

The reason for making this distinction is to highlight the first contentious area in the study of customer loyalty—the difference between simple **repeat-buying behaviour** and **genuine loyalty**. Many businesses mistakenly believe that they have loyal customers, when in fact all that their customers are doing is demonstrating repeat-buying behaviour for other reasons. These reasons might be:

- Lack of choice. There are hundreds of bus companies in the UK, but the chances are that anyone using buses regularly will always use the same company—not through loyalty, but because that is the only bus company operating on the route the traveller uses.
- Convenience. A driver who fills her car up with petrol at the same garage every week is not necessarily demonstrating loyalty—it might simply be because the garage is on her route to work in the morning.

- Lack of information or ignorance. People sticking with the same utility suppliers (telephone, electricity, water, etc.) may do so not through loyalty, but because they simply do not know what alternatives there are.

Inertia. Many people stick with the same bank or building society over many years, not through loyalty, but because they can't be bothered to change. The prospect of looking around for the best deal and filling in lots of paperwork to open a new account somewhere else puts them off.

Many businesses have relied on customer inertia to make their profits. A recent study by Zurich Bank suggested that in the UK, inertia was costing consumers £4–£5 billion a year! While there is nothing wrong in businesses taking advantage of repeat custom for these reasons, it is important to recognize that this custom could be fragile in the sense that it does not constitute a close relationship with the customer. There are signs however that things are changing as competition increases and customers are actively encouraged to switch to better deals. (See Minicase 1, uSwitch Tackles Customer Inertia.) As management guru Gary Hamel (2002) puts it, inertia may no longer be a source of profit for many organizations.

> **Inertia**
> customers remaining with an organization, not through loyalty, even when better offers are available elsewhere

---

Minicase 1

uSwitch Tackles Customer Inertia

In September 2005 British Gas announced that it was increasing its prices by 14%—a move that was greeted with gasps of dismay from industry commentators and predictions of a mass exodus of customers to other gas suppliers. The company had already lost nearly 900,000 customers following its last price increase in 2004 and yet remains the clear market leader with over 12 million household customers and a 70% market share. Indeed, despite a number of price rises above the industry average, the company's market share has not eroded nearly as much as some market pundits predicted.

According to Alan Tattersall, Director of Home Services at uSwitch.com, the average British Gas customer could save over £100 a year by switching gas supplier. uSwitch is a business set up to help customers find a better deal in markets which are characterised by inertia. These include energy supply, telecom services, credit cards, banks, and mortgages. They are services which we consume continuously, yet purchase relatively infrequently as they are things that we 'sign up for' and are often sold on a contract basis.

It is ironic that customers now have a bigger choice than ever before in terms of banks, credit card providers, mortgage lenders, and energy suppliers, but still stick with their original provider. Even more surprising is that many of these 'loyal' customers are openly dissatisfied with their providers. Research by uSwitch suggests that 66% of British Gas customers thought that their loyalty was being abused, while in Australia 60% of customers claimed to be unhappy with their bank, but less than one-third of these had bothered to change (BankWest, 2005). Why then does this inertia persist?

Many reasons have been suggested, including laziness, disinterest, lack of access to impartial comparative figures, lack of time, fear of the unknown, and the difficulty of switching. One thing that all of these businesses have in common is the lack of fun in shopping for their products. No one enjoys hunting round for the best bank, or filling in forms to change credit card suppliers. As John Kay, writing in the *Financial Times* points out, 'making mortgages glamorous is beyond even the most inspired of marketeers'. So just as we put off doing those things we know we should, like going to the dentist, or going to the gym after work, so we put off reviewing purchases which are by their nature unattractive to us.

uSwitch hopes to take away some of the burden of switching, by doing the leg work for the customer. In return they receive commission from those businesses where they are able to sign up new customers. However, there are still many businesses out there that are hoping that customer inertia is going to be around for a while yet.

Questions

1. What is the difference between customer inertia and loyalty?

2. Is inertia a bad thing?

3. Who are uSwitch's customers?

4. How can companies such as British Gas engender true loyalty amongst their customers?

Sources:
BBC News: 'British Gas prices to rise 14%' http://news.bbc.co.uk accessed 09/09/05
'Inertia stopping Australians from getting a better deal' http://www.bankwest.com.au accessed 05/11/05
'Customer inertia and the active shopper', *Financial Times*, 17 December 2003
http://www.uswitch.com accessed 05/11/05

It is not just inertia that leads to repeat-buying behaviour. Products which are cheaper or offer superior value in some other area may also enjoy repeated custom. But is this loyalty? The acid test is to ask what would happen if another supplier came up with a similar or superior offer—would the customers switch to the new supplier?

The Changing Consumer

In many ways the above question highlights the difference between transaction marketing (which would include special offers and promotions to make customers switch) and relationship marketing which plays on stronger, more emotional bonds to generate true loyalty. In recent years there has been a shift in consumer attitudes and true loyalty is getting harder and harder to achieve. (See Figure 4.1.)

Being time-poor leads many consumers to value convenience over other brand attributes. Shoppers are thus less likely to go out of their way to be loyal. At the same time, today's consumers are more individualistic and are therefore less content to stick with the same products and services as their parents did. Levi's found this out to their cost when, despite having an excellent product and an enviable brand pedigree, youngsters shunned them as belonging to the older generation. This was irreverently dubbed at the time as the 'Clarkson Effect' after 40-something television presenter Jeremy Clarkson became known for wearing Levi's.

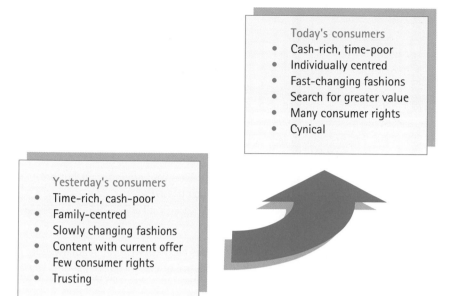

Today's consumers
- Cash-rich, time-poor
- Individually centred
- Fast-changing fashions
- Search for greater value
- Many consumer rights
- Cynical

Yesterday's consumers
- Time-rich, cash-poor
- Family-centred
- Slowly changing fashions
- Content with current offer
- Few consumer rights
- Trusting

Figure 4.1 Changes in the consumer

Today's consumers demand fashion or style changes much faster than the previous generation. Witness the rise and fall of the 'alcopop' market. The drink that started it all, Hooch, was quietly withdrawn in 2003, a bare eight years after it started the alcopop revolution in the drinks market. It seems these days that companies have no time to generate any loyalty before the market shifts again.

On top of all this, customers are now much more demanding, more discriminating, and more willing to complain if things go wrong. They know their rights and they expect to be rewarded for their custom and will seek out the best value. In the airline industry, for instance, a company is no longer seen as standing above its rivals by offering a good frequent flyer programme—rather, it is seen as standing below its rival if it doesn't—a subtle but important difference which is expanded on later in this chapter when we look at loyalty schemes.

Finally, consumers' attitudes towards companies' messages have become more cynical. We are surrounded by adverts and promotions every day, the vast majority of which we blank off. Many companies have abused the tools of customer relationship management (CRM) and bombarded us with junk mail, spam, and unwanted telephone calls to the extent where we employ other companies to block them. At the same time consumer programmes such as *Watchdog* have highlighted cases of the abuse of our trust and famous debacles such as the ill-fated Hoover 'free flights to America' offer have all taken the gloss off traditional marketing messages and made customers more wary of committing to a relationship. As such, organizations have to manage customer loyalty very carefully. One tool which has been suggested to help in this area is the Ladder of Loyalty.

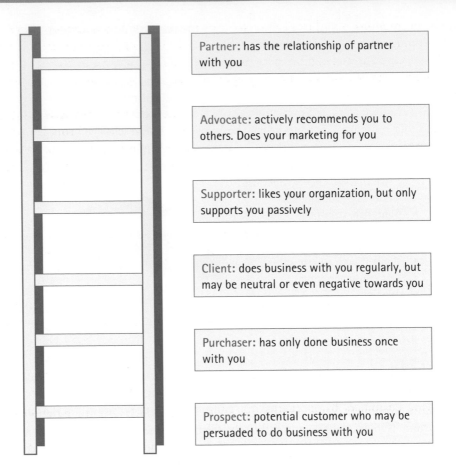

Partner: has the relationship of partner with you

Advocate: actively recommends you to others. Does your marketing for you

Supporter: likes your organization, but only supports you passively

Client: does business with you regularly, but may be neutral or even negative towards you

Purchaser: has only done business once with you

Prospect: potential customer who may be persuaded to do business with you

Figure 4.2 The Ladder of Loyalty

Source: Christopher *et al.* (1991): *Relationship Marketing: Bringing Quality, Customer Service and Marketing Together.* © Elsevier. Reproduced with kind permission.

The Ladder of Loyalty

The extent to which every product or service can aspire to a high level of relationship and 'genuine loyalty' with its customers is a matter of debate. Christopher *et al.* (2002) have suggested that customers can move towards a closer relationship with a supplier in a series of stages over time. They have termed these stages 'the Ladder of Loyalty' as each rung on the ladder takes the customer to a higher level of relationship. (See Figure 4.2.) In practice, supporters of the Ladder of Loyalty suggest that this can be used by businesses to identify customers at different stages of relationship and direct their marketing resources accordingly.

Rungs on the Ladder

Thus a business with lots of 'prospects' should concentrate on turning these into 'purchasers'. This is the bedrock of traditional transactional marketing, using special offers, promotions, and direct selling to attract customers. It was seen in Chapter 3 that although there might be more profitability in keeping existing customers, no business can completely ignore new customers. Loyal, long-term customers are not born—every single customer that a business has will have begun as a prospect at the bottom of the ladder.

However, once attracted onto the first rung of the ladder the objective should be to encourage repeat custom and turn the 'prospect' into a 'client'. From here on in the approach is more in line with traditional relationship marketing thinking where the emphasis is on customer retention. Thus, 'purchasers' are turned into 'clients' and 'clients' are turned into 'supporters'.

From Clients to Supporters

It is important to recognize the difference between 'clients' and 'supporters' because this is the jump where loyalty and involvement begin. On the Ladder of Loyalty, 'clients' are repeat purchasers but do not necessarily have any loyalty, or even liking for the business. Their repeat custom may simply be due to lack of alternatives, ignorance, inertia, etc. They may even be dissatisfied customers who have not switched, in which case they might become critics of the organization. It is only when the next rung of the ladder is reached that customers become 'supporters'—and have a positive attitude towards the business or its products. Although this support is only passive at this stage, it does give the business some degree of security as customers who are 'supporters' are less likely to defect than those who are merely 'clients'.

Moving customers from 'clients' to 'supporters' is therefore a very important objective for most businesses. Some argue that a favourable opinion of a product or service develops over a number of repeated purchases, assuming of course that the customer is satisfied. Oliver (1997) calls this 'affective loyalty'—a loyalty that comes about as the result of 'repeated confirmations of expectations'. For instance, a customer using a particular hotel over a number of occasions may find that the service is efficient, the room is clean and comfortable, and the tariff is reasonable. These are all things that would be expected from any hotel, but because his expectations have been met over a number of occasions, the customer comes to rely on this standard and the risk of trying a different hotel increases. He has reached the 'supporter' rung on the Ladder of Loyalty.

Businesses must therefore strive to offer the highest quality and maintain these standards in order to turn their repeat customers into supporters. For example, McDonald's see their key loyalty drives as quality, service, value, cleanliness, and convenience (Woolf, 2002). These are the factors that create satisfaction amongst McDonald's customers and will, all other things being equal, ensure a positive attitude and continued repeat custom. But meeting these satisfaction criteria and generating this positive attitude is not always enough in itself to produce genuine loyalty—particularly in a competitive marketplace. As long as competitors such as Burger King and Wendy's can match the standards which customers expect, McDonald's will still have to go back to transactional marketing tactics such as short-term promotions to hold on to their market share. Remember we are still only half-way up the Ladder of Loyalty and although relationship marketing starts to kick in at this level, genuine loyalty does not appear until higher up.

Supporters to Advocates

The next rung above 'supporter' is 'advocate', the stage where customers take their level of support for a business and actively promote it. The jump from 'supporter' to 'advocate' is relatively small, but hugely important. Christopher *et al.* (2002) lay especial emphasis here as a customer who is an 'advocate' will do a lot of marketing through word of mouth. Indeed, referrals from existing satisfied customers make up one of the components of the Six Markets model discussed in Chapter 1. Personal word of mouth is a particularly strong means of marketing communication, as it legitimizes a message far more than a commercial message, such as an advert. Of course, for a customer to become an 'advocate' for a product or service, they must be satisfied with it. However, we have already seen that satisfaction in itself does not necessarily generate loyalty. True loyalty requires an extremely high level of customer satisfaction—higher than what was simply expected so that the customer is not just satisfied, but is delighted (Jones and Sasser, 1995).

Another (and perhaps higher) level of customer advocacy is achievable to organizations that possess a strong aspirational brand name. Branding is an important means by which an organization can involve its customers and develop relationships and as such is discussed in more depth later in this chapter. However, it is worth recognizing here that a customer who is willing to walk about with a prominent brand name across their chest is perhaps the ultimate in product advocacy. Here, the advocacy comes not from delight about the product's performance but more from aspirational and emotional attractions. The product says something about the person advocating it.

Advocates to Partners

This brings us to the final rung of the Ladder of Loyalty whereby the customer assumes the role of 'partner'. The oft-quoted examples of this level of the ladder are of customers who are so delighted with a product that they go into business with the organization—literally becoming partners. In B2C marketing this is extremely rare. A more realistic view of customers as 'partners' is those who share a part of their life with the organization. These customers invest more than simply the purchase price of the product—they become involved! Examples would include customers proudly displaying designer labels, as the brand has become part of who they are and how they project themselves. A more mundane example would be pub customers who not only represent satisfied repeat purchasers, but whose loyalty extends to representing the pub in darts matches or playing on the pub's football team.

Partnership is more common in B2B marketing, as organizations will often link up with their suppliers further down the supply chain to share end-market information or collaborate in the development of new products. The relationship with partners and suppliers is dealt with more fully in Chapter 8.

The Move from Transactional to Relational Marketing

The Ladder of Loyalty is therefore a potentially useful tool for organizations to understand and manage customer loyalty and involvement. But is it practical or realistic to try and move all customers to the top of the ladder? Think about the burger chain again. While it is well within their capabilities to satisfy their customers, can they ever truly delight them to the extent that they rave about the experience to all of their friends? Can customers ever become 'partners' of McDonald's? With 14 million customers McDonald's has to know more about what actually constitutes loyalty and what is a realistic level of loyalty to which they can aspire.

The Customer's Perspective

So far we have looked at customer relationships from the organization's viewpoint. What about the customers—do they want relationships with their suppliers? Piercy (1999) accuses many organizations of 'relationship marketing myopia' by not recognizing that not every customer is interested in having a relationship with their supplier. He argues that there are four types of customer and that organizations would do well to recognize these types when deciding which customers to focus their relationship building efforts upon. The four types are:

- relationship seekers—customers who actively pursue a long and close-term relationship with their suppliers;
- relationship exploiters—customers who take all of the benefits offered to promote loyalty, but in practice demonstrate no loyalty at all;
- loyal buyers—customers who remain loyal but do not want a close relationship;
- transaction buyers—customers who have no interest in relationships with suppliers and exhibit no loyalty to any particular supplier.

The four different types would make a useful segmentation base from which to manage customers but organizations developing relationship strategies need to have a deep knowledge of the customers in their market. For instance, a customer might be a relationship seeker in one market (e.g. designer clothes) but a relationship exploiter in another (e.g. supermarket loyalty schemes). Money spent on 'relationship' exploiters is wasted, while relationship strategies aimed at loyal buyers might end up causing irritation.

Measuring Loyalty

To try to understand this, we need to think about what constitutes loyalty from the organization's viewpoint. We have already seen that definitions of loyalty can veer between those that are largely quantitative and those that are qualitative. This is mirrored in two schools of thought: the behavioural approach to measuring loyalty and the attitudinal approach.

The Behavioural Approach

Behavioural loyalty is clearly observable and is based on existing and past purchase patterns (Uncles *et al.*, 2003). Basically, customers who are seen to buy the

Behavioural loyalty
customers who demonstrate repeat-buying behaviour over a period of time

same product or service over a period of time are classed as loyal. Thus, loyalty can be gauged by market statistics such as repeat buying, frequency of purchase, market penetration, share of basket, etc. Naturally, the behavioural approach to loyalty is popular amongst marketing practitioners because it is easily measurable. It also provides organizations with a solid base to try and build customer loyalty as it assumes that the drivers of loyalty are 'hard' dimensions such as price, quality, value for money, convenience, ease of use, etc.

Critics of the behavioural approach to loyalty argue that it offers no indication of genuine loyalty or customer involvement. In effect it is a mercenary approach where loyalty can be bought by the organization offering the best incentives and customers feel little or no emotional bond to the product or service. To illustrate this, Jones (1994) draws the analogy between the 'cupboard' loyalty of a **cat** and the more unquestioning, faithful loyalty of a **dog**. The behavioural approach to loyalty is common particularly in sectors such as fast-moving consumer goods (FMCGs), where purchases are frequent, customer involvement is low, and competition is fierce. Some would question whether true customer loyalty is possible at all in these circumstances, so businesses adopt reinforcing incentives to encourage continuous repeat purchases.

Such policies are needed in markets where customers display what Uncles (1994) refers to as switching, promiscuous, or polygamous behaviours. Switching customers are loyal to either one brand or another, but not to both at the same time. Thus a shopper may use Tesco repeatedly over a number of weeks before growing tired of them and switching to Sainsbury's. After a while they may switch again, this time to Morrison's. Promiscuous customers are similar, except here the customer may ditch Tesco and spread his or her purchases over a number of alternative shops. Finally, polygamous customers tend to divide their purchases between one brand and a number of others. Thus a shopper may buy basic grocery products from Tesco, frozen products from Iceland, and more expensive 'luxury' products from Sainsbury's.

Each of these stores will try to retain the customer exclusively, or at least obtain the lion's share of their business—usually through the use of reinforcing promotions such as advertising and incentives such as loyalty schemes. (A full discussion of loyalty schemes appears later in this chapter.)

The Attitudinal Approach

The alternative way of considering customer loyalty is to take an attitudinal approach similar to the dog loyalty described above. Whereas behavioural loyalty is based on easily measurable factors such as market share or repeat purchase, **attitudinal loyalty** is based on more intangible dimensions such as positive feelings and emotions (Dick and Basu, 1994). Customers displaying attitudinal loyalty are much less likely to be swayed by price offers and other incentives. Their attachment and involvement with the product or service goes much deeper and they are far more likely to occupy the higher rungs of the loyalty ladder.

Organizations pursuing attitudinal loyalty among their customers face a much tougher task as this kind of loyalty cannot be simply bought. The emphasis here is on

Cat loyalty

spurious, open to switching if a better offer is received

Dog loyalty

genuine and unquestioning, based on an emotional attachment

Attitudinal loyalty

customers who hold positive feelings or emotions towards an organization or brand building long-term relationships based not only on repeated customer satisfaction but also by engendering a feeling of belonging within the customer. In some respects it is easier to do this in the service sector than it is with products. Services rely on human contact and relationships to develop trust and commitment and even friendship. Such relationships may also be more common in B2B transactions where the buyer and the seller are mutually acquainted (see Chapter 2).

Those organizations which do not have any human contact with their customers need to find another way of engendering attitudinal loyalty among their customers and this is where branding comes in. In some cases, customers' relationships with brands can reach similar levels to human relationships. Brand relationships are explored in more depth later in this chapter. What should be made clear, however, is that just as it is impossible to get all customers to the top of the Ladder of Loyalty, so it is impossible to generate attitudinal loyalty in all customers. Moore and Sekhon (2005) suggest that attitudinal measures of loyalty are of little value in consumer markets characterised by low risk, low involvement, frequent purchase, and multi-brand purchasing.

Categorizing Customer Loyalty

While the simple distinction between behavioural loyalty and attitudinal loyalty appears outwardly valid, neither approach on its own is sufficient to explain or classify customer loyalty. For instance, behavioural measures make no distinction between simple repeat purchases made through convenience or inertia and those resulting from more genuine loyalty. Likewise, attitudinal measures tend to fall back on customer satisfaction as an indicator of loyalty, even though numerous studies have shown that satisfaction does not necessarily lead to loyalty. Dick and Basu (1994) have therefore come up with a simple matrix which combines behavioural and attitudinal measures of loyalty to give different categories of loyalty each of which has implications for the organization (Figure 4.3).

The model combines two dimensions of loyalty: relative attitude towards a brand and purchase history of that brand. Relative attitude includes latent satisfaction with the brand compared with alternative brands, thus providing a measure of preference.

Figure 4.3 Categories of loyalty

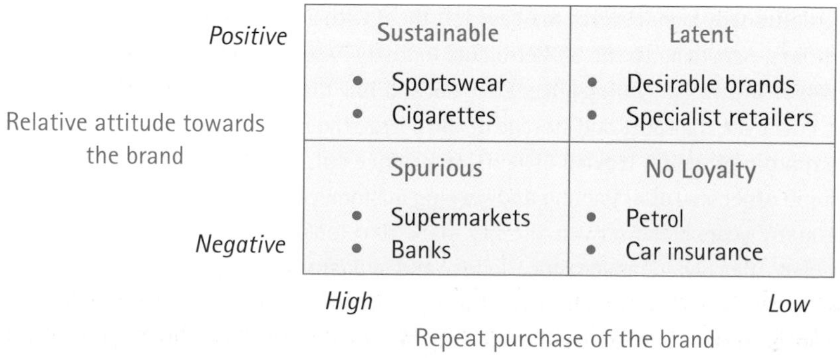

	High	Low
Positive	Sustainable • Sportswear • Cigarettes	Latent • Desirable brands • Specialist retailers
Negative	Spurious • Supermarkets • Banks	No Loyalty • Petrol • Car insurance

Relative attitude towards the brand

Repeat purchase of the brand

Purchase history includes traditional market measures such as frequency, relative value, and market share. This combination gives four broad categories of customer loyalty: no loyalty, spurious loyalty, latent loyalty, and sustainable loyalty.

No Loyalty

Brands with low repeat purchase and relatively negative customer attitudes can be classed as enjoying no loyalty. Products such as petrol or car insurance might fall into this category. Lack of differentiation between petrol brands has led petrol retailers to attempt to raise customers' switching costs through reward accrual schemes in the attempt to turn 'no loyalty' into at least 'spurious loyalty' (O'Malley, 1998). (See Minicase 2, Petrol Retailer Accrual Schemes.) Basically, any undifferentiated product which is bought purely on price tends to fall into the 'no loyalty' category. Other examples include car insurance (how many drivers switch their car insurance each year to get a slightly better premium?) or consumables such as office supplies in a business. Many insurance companies offer product bundling whereby customers buying car insurance through them can get discounts on home or travel insurance. Office supply companies may offer quantity discounts or super-quick delivery times to try to win the business. The objective of any business which finds itself with 'no loyalty' products is to create 'spurious loyalty' through special deals and promotions. While not perfect, this is better than no loyalty at all. In effect, companies operating in these conditions are limited to transaction marketing rather than relationship.

Minicase 2

Petrol Retailers Fight for Customer Loyalty

Nobody loves petrol. Few of us even give it a second thought, except to bemoan the high cost of filling our cars with it. We have no involvement with petrol. It is an invisible product and as long as it propels our cars effectively, we will buy it from wherever it is cheapest or most convenient. We take no pleasure in its purchase; in fact we deliberately try to consume as little as possible. For many of us it is a distress purchase as we will only fill up when absolutely necessary. And unlike clothes, cars, music, food, or even birthday cards, the type of petrol we buy says absolutely nothing about who we are as individuals.

All of this makes petrol the classic 'commodity'—an undifferentiated, low-involvement product which is predominantly bought on price. Unfortunately for UK petrol retailers, however, traditionally high levels of tax have left them with very little margin on which to make price offers. According to the UK Petroleum Industry Association the petrol retailer receives only 6% of the average pump price, after tax and raw material costs are taken off. This 6% has to cover the transport and storage of the petrol, the running costs of the filling station, plus a margin for profit, leaving little room for price cuts. Petrol retailers therefore have to find some other way of attracting and keeping customers.

For many years branding was the key marketing tool, with the big retailers promoting themselves heavily in advertising, logos, and slogans. Esso's campaign in the 1960s famously told us to 'Put a tiger in your tank'; while for many years Shell reassured us that 'You can be sure of Shell'. New market entrants such as Repsol and Q8 in the 1980s and the beginning of supermarket involvement led the established retailers to proclaim that their petrol was better for your engine, that you risked serious long-term damage by using inferior brands. The customers, however, were not convinced. The general consensus seemed to be that it all came from the same place anyway, so there was no difference.

Petrol retailer accrual schemes began in the 1960s with the onset of Green Shield Stamps, but really came into their own in the 1980s. Customers earned stickers or tokens for each gallon of petrol they bought from a particular retailer. These could be exchanged for gifts when a pre-specified amount had been accumulated. The core objective was to keep customers going back to the same petrol station each time they filled up, but they were also useful for high mileage business drivers who could accumulate the tokens all over the country, as long as they always filled up with the same brand.

The gifts themselves were pretty basic and often formed part of a set, such as four wine glasses or six soup mugs. Frustration often arose amongst customers when a particular offer was withdrawn before they had collected the full set and many a sales rep's drinks cupboard was filled with an odd assortment of cheap wine glasses and whisky tumblers from petrol promotions. The cheap glasses and crockery gifts gradually gave way to a better choice of quality products from a catalogue, though the frustration of a scheme being pulled when you were just short of enough points for the food blender you'd been saving for often remained.

During the 1990s, competition in the petrol retail industry took a new turn. Low margins, expensive health and safety requirements, and the onslaught of competition from supermarkets forced many petrol retailers out of business. Between 1992 and 2004 the number of petrol stations in the UK fell from 18,000 to just over 12,000, while the average sales of each site increased from 1.67 million litres to 2.45 million, reflecting the much bigger size of the new sites. Supermarkets now account for over 30% of the total petrol market in the UK.

The change in the market saw the end of the old accrual schemes, which were replaced by glitzy new loyalty cards where the supermarkets had an immediate advantage. Motorists could now gain points for petrol and groceries on the same card, giving them a much better opportunity to save for better rewards. Supermarkets also began to tie in their petrol customers by bundling product benefits together—at the moment if you spend £50 or over in the supermarket, Sainsbury's will give you 5 pence a litre off at the petrol pump. Most of the other petrol retailers have introduced loyalty cards—some have been in conjunction with other retailers (e.g. BP with Nectar) while others have concentrated on offering loyalty benefits to community groups and organizations (e.g. Texaco's Group Loyalty Scheme). The basic problem remains for retailers, however—nobody loves petrol.

Questions

1. Can petrol retailers ever get close to their customers?
2. Are the schemes described above promotions or relationship marketing? What is the difference?
3. What other products might be classed as 'commodities'? How do the producers of these products gain customer loyalty?

Sources:
DTI statistics http://www.og.dti.gov.uk accessed 09/11/05
UK Petroleum Industry Association http://www.ukpia.com accessed 09/11/05

Spurious Loyalty

Spurious customer loyalty is better than no loyalty at all because at least the business is getting repeat custom. The problem is that this repeat custom is not based on genuine loyalty but on some other factor such as price, convenience, ignorance, or even inertia. As a result it is relatively easy for competitors to induce switching behaviour by matching offers, undercutting prices, and generally appealing to what can be the promiscuous nature of the spuriously loyal customer. Examples of products affected by spurious loyalty are numerous and typically include FMCGs, supermarkets, banks and building societies, gas, electricity and telephone services, and some consumer durables such as televisions, DVD players, fridge freezers, and washing machines. In B2B markets this might include the services offered by staff agencies, energy suppliers, print houses, and transport companies, all of which tend to be undifferentiated and are usually purchased on the basis of price or convenience. The objective of businesses who are facing spurious loyalty from their customers is to maintain the loyalty, through traditional transactional marketing techniques (such as advertising, special promotions, etc.), or by tying the customer in (e.g. through contracts or clauses), although this will not endear the business to the customer and, like any prisoner, as soon as the customer can escape, they will and might never return! An alternative might be to move customers to a more sustainable loyalty. On the Ladder of Loyalty this would equate to customers climbing from client to supporter. This may involve building up relationships by offering a personalized service or involving the customer in some other way.

Latent Loyalty

Both 'no loyalty' and 'spurious loyalty' are based on the premise that customers have a relatively negative (or at best neutral) attitude towards the company or the brand. However, it is possible for customers to have a relatively high opinion or attitude towards the brand but not display repeat-buying behaviour. This is known as 'latent loyalty'. Common reasons for this are that the customer is unable to buy the product because it is not sold locally or that it is out of stock. We have all heard stories of ex-patriots living abroad who constantly implore their UK-based friends to send them stocks of Marmite, Stilton cheese, Branston pickle, Chivers marmalade, or other UK-based products that are not available overseas. Closer to home many beer drinkers are unable to enjoy their favourite pints on a regular basis because the pub companies deal with national beer distribution chains who only offer a limited repertoire of beer brands. Similarly, customers may love to shop at Selfridges, but if they live in the north of England, they are likely to be infrequent visitors to the store, which is based in London. Business travellers may prefer Singapore Airlines (SA), but if SA does not operate on their usual routes, their repeat business will be low. In all of these cases, the battle for the company is half won. Customers have a positive attitude and may already feel that they have a relationship with the brand. The objective of the company must therefore be to enable the relationship to be consummated by removing the barriers. The advent of the Internet has made it much easier to make products available by mail order and to develop strong, interactive relationships with the customers at the same time. Developing the product to make it more easy for customers to buy it is another way of removing barriers (e.g. small draught-beer producers may bottle their products for sale in supermarkets, or mail order, in order to bypass the pub distribution chain). SA might consider opening up new routes, going into partnership with other airlines, or even licensing their operations in order to tap into latently loyal markets.

Sustainable Loyalty

Sustainable customer loyalty encompasses high-repeat purchases with a high relative attitude towards the brand. This represents the 'Supporter', 'Advocate' and perhaps even 'Partner' rungs on the Ladder of Loyalty. According to Dick and Basu (1994), this category represents true loyalty. Typically, the sustainably loyal customer exhibits high involvement with the brand (e.g. BMW car drivers, Nike Sportswear users, or Marlboro cigarette smokers), or they have a very close relationship with the product over time (e.g. the locals in a pub, regular restaurant customers, or house-holders using the same plumber or electrician for years). In all of these examples, the customer will remain loyal to the brand or the company, even if competitors offer better prices or special deals. Businesses with sustainable loyalty need to recognize-what their customers value, and strive to maintain these values. This requires careful brand management and constant monitoring of customer service standards.

Loyalty Schemes

We have seen that achieving high levels of loyalty entails the development of close customer relationships and involvement. However, we have also seen that in many purchase situations, particularly where there is no strong positive attitude towards the brand, the customer will display promiscuity or switching behaviour, thus destroying any pretext of loyalty. The response of many companies, therefore, is to introduce a *loyalty programme* or *loyalty scheme*. For companies operating under conditions of no loyalty or spurious loyalty, the idea is that loyalty programmes will create more sustainable loyalty, while for companies already enjoying sustained loyalty the programmes will reinforce the relationship through rewards.

Uncles (1994) supports this view, believing that loyalty programmes create a sense of belonging amongst customers who are actively seeking an involving relationship with their brand. The idea is that loyalty schemes offer psychological reassurances to customers that the company is 'prepared to listen, willing to innovate on behalf of customers, and is caring, concerned and considerate'.

What is a Loyalty Scheme?

Basically a loyalty scheme exists to identify and reward loyal customers by offering discounts, or other benefits based upon the amount they spend. This is nothing new. In the 1960s and 70s many shops and petrol retailers offered pink or green stamps with each purchase, which could be saved up by the customer and eventually redeemed for rewards. One such scheme was Green Shield Stamps. Customers collected the stamps from participating retailers, including Woolworths, and could choose from a number of gifts from a catalogue, depending on how many stamps they had saved. The stamps could be exchanged at High Street redemption centres, typically for household goods such as food mixers or toasters. (These redemption centres eventually became Argos shops who, ironically, now have their own loyalty scheme—Argos Premier Points!)

By the 1980s, airlines had jumped on the bandwagon. The first airline reward scheme was set up by American Airlines in 1981 and called the 'Advantage Travel Programme'. The Air Miles programme we know today began in the UK in 1989 and is now franchised to third parties including British Airways. Air Miles are now given as rewards not just by airlines, but by credit card companies, hotels, car hire firms, and others. Such is the success of the scheme that a 2002 BBC news report suggested that the $500 billion worth of Air Miles in circulation made them the world's second biggest currency after the US dollar!

Today many retailers now have some sort of loyalty card. These schemes vary in the way in which they add value to the customer and include simple point accrual schemes, club cards, and even combined credit cards (see Table 4.1).

Objectives of Loyalty Schemes

If they are to design an effective loyalty programme, organizations must have a clear picture of whereabouts in Dick and Basu's box their customers sit and what kind of loyalty they are displaying (Moore and Sekhon, 2005). In the case of the airlines, for example, the role of the loyalty scheme is to reward and cement the relationship, while for supermarkets it is to reinforce repeat purchasing. (See Figure 4.4.)

Figure 4.4 Roles of loyalty schemes with different types of loyalty

Sustainable	Latent
Reward and cement the relationship, e.g. (for airlines) through added-value benefits such as quick check-ins, upgrades, air miles, discount car hire and hotels, etc.	*Loyalty schemes do not have a role here. Management must concentrate instead on removing barriers to doing business to pave the way for sustainable loyalty*
Spurious	No Loyalty
Reinforce and defend existing repeat purchase patterns through incentives such as money off or free gifts	*Differentiate the brand and attract customers through incentives such as money off or free gifts*

Table 4.1 All Retail Loyalty Schemes Are Not The Same

Scheme	Value	Points Earned	Points Redeemed	Comments
Tesco Clubcard	1 point = £0.010	£1 spent = 1 point at Tesco MFI Avis Powergen Marriot and others	In-store or online at Tesco or at four times face value in 'special deals' on travel and leisure	Widely see as one of the reasons for Tesco's success in the grocery business. Extra points used as a promotional tool to incentivise purchase of selected items in store.
Nectar	1 point = £0.005	£2 spent = 1 point at Sainsbury's Argos Debenhams Adams Kids Thresher Hertz BP Ford Cars and others	In-store or online at issuing shops or exchange for leisure and travel tickets or 'gifts and treats'	Launched in 2002, Nectar was the first big 'coalition loyalty card' in the UK. Like the Tesco Clubcard, the Nectar points can be used to manipulate buyer behaviour by offering extra points on certain purchases (e.g. online).
Boots Advantage Card	1 point = £0.010	£1 spent = 1 point at Boots	In-store or online at Boots	Widely seen as the most generous scheme with multi-point offers often available, but can only be used at Boots
WHSmith Clubcard	1 point = £0.010	£1 spent = 1 point at WHSmith	In-store or online at WHSmith	WHSmith have recently improved the offer to match Boots. Benefits can only be redeemed at WHSmith. Not available in all stores. Customers can check their balance online
Somerfield Saver Card	N/A	N/A	Rewards available in store	Somerfield does not offer points. Instead, card holders can take advantage of special in-store offers (e.g. buy one, get one free) and enter prize competitions (e.g. win a Mini draw)
Marks & Spencer &more card	1 point = £0.010	£1 spent = 1 point at M&S	In-store or online at M&S. Discounts on travel through the &more Travel Club	The &more card is also a MasterCard credit card, which can be used anywhere. Purchases made elsewhere from M&S earn 1 point for every £2 spent, but points can only be redeemed at M&S or its associated operations

Information based on individual retailer's websites, November 2005
Table based on consumerdeals.co.uk, November 2005

Do Loyalty Schemes Work?

To answer this question it is important to understand what the objectives of 'loyalty' schemes are. Basically these can be broken down into three main strands:

- to promote customer retention through reward;
- to gather information on customers and use this to manage profitable customer relationships;
- to defend against the actions of competitors.

Whether a scheme can be considered successful or not therefore requires further examination of these areas.

Promoting Retention by Rewarding Loyal Customers

This is how loyalty schemes originally began and seems most closely to fit our concept of loyalty. The premise is simple—the more you buy, the more you are rewarded. However, most commentators agree that many so-called 'loyalty schemes' do not produce genuine loyalty. To draw an analogy with human relationships, you would not dream of developing a scheme which rewarded your friends according to how loyal they were.

This has led to observations that most loyalty schemes are nothing to do with relationship marketing; some conclude that many of them are merely elaborate sales promotional activities (O'Malley, 1998) or at best, basic customer retention tools (Little and Marandi, 2003). This puts them firmly under the banner of transactional marketing, not relationship marketing. Is this a problem? We've already seen that many schemes operate in markets categorised by low customer involvement, high switching propensity and frequent purchase (e.g. supermarkets, petrol retailers, credit card companies). In other words, those that fit the behavioural notion of loyalty, as opposed to the attitudinal. In these markets, repeat purchase, even if it is just spurious loyalty, is the best for which a company can hope, so the schemes should not be seen as failing just because they do not create genuine relationships. Indeed it can be argued that relationship marketing itself is not appropriate in these areas.

Therefore, it might be concluded that the term 'loyalty scheme' is something of a misnomer. Far from promoting long-term customer involvement and loyalty, the best they can do is reduce switching behaviour and aid retention. However, some argue that they aren't even effective at this level. Stauss *et al.* (2005) point to general customer dissatisfaction with loyalty schemes and, given that satisfaction is one of the prerequisites for loyalty, they suggest that some loyalty schemes might even be creating disloyalty! They suggest that customer frustrations can be divided into two areas—those that are related to the operation of the scheme itself and, perhaps more worryingly, those that affect the customer's perception of the company behind the scheme. These are summarized below.

> ### Stauss *et al.*'s Loyalty Scheme Frustration Factors
>
> #### Scheme-related Frustrations
>
> Qualification barrier—the reward is tied to conditions that are difficult or impossible to fulfil. Example: '...for me as a private customer it is simply impossible to collect the necessary number of points in 12 months'.
>
> Inaccessibility—customers qualifying for rewards find it impossible to take them up. Example: '...the offer flights are only available at off peak times when the kids are in school and I can't get any time off work...'.
>
> Worthlessness—customers do not see the benefit they receive as being a reward because they find the additional value too low: Example: '...I've worked out that I have to spend over £2,500 just to get a free alarm clock...'.
>
> Redemption costs—customers can only access the reward by investing additional funds or mental costs. Example: '...the scheme only covers hotels on the outskirts or Paris, so we have to travel in each day...'.
>
> #### Organization-related Frustrations
>
> Discrimination—customers who do not qualify for a reward yet still demonstrate a strong commitment may perceive that the company does not value them. Example: '...how un-important must I be for the company that I do not even get this advantage...'
>
> Defocusing—customers believe that the company has directed too much resource towards the loyalty scheme instead of improving the core service. Example: '...I'd be happier if they'd spend more money on keeping prices down, instead of sending me all this junk mail...'
>
> Economization—loyalty schemes move the economic character of the relationship to the forefront, which might be a problem if the customer perceives that they have an emotional relationship with the company. Example: 'I've been coming here for 25 years. He's only been here five minutes and he gets the same offers as me...'

Stauss *et al.*'s research suggests that these frustration incidents lead to highly negative emotions. Scheme-related incidents may cause customer withdrawal from any attempts to build relationships, while organization related incidents can lead to defection—the exact opposite of what the schemes are designed to do. It is crucial, therefore, that organizations monitor their loyalty schemes very carefully to check that they are achieving their objectives.

What of loyalty schemes' broader role in CRM? If the reward aspect of these schemes is not sufficient to promote long-term loyalty, can the data they produce be used more effectively to develop and manage long-term relationships? This brings us to the second objective of loyalty schemes.

Gathering Data for CRM Purposes

CRM has become an important part of relationship marketing and it is in this area where loyalty schemes might be more successful in developing genuine loyalty through closer relationships. In the past, many so-called loyalty schemes were unable to gather much information about customers (collecting petrol vouchers for a set of wine glasses, for example), but most schemes are now similar to membership clubs, whereby the customer provides a large amount of information regarding their circumstances and buying behaviour. (Airline loyalty programmes clearly fall into this category, thus enabling tailor-made packages to be made available and targeted at specific groups of customers.) Supermarkets can combine the personal data they gather from their customers with the shopping behaviour they observe each time the customer uses their loyalty card.

The resulting information can be used to manipulate customer behaviour and develop closer personal relationships. Sainsbury's, for example, have combined personal details such as date of birth with observed shopping behaviour, such as infrequent store visits, and has sent birthday cards to customers, along with a voucher for a free bottle of celebratory wine, to customers who are not regular shoppers. Such a move works on two levels: first, as a basic promotion to attract customers into the store (most people would wish to redeem a voucher for a free bottle of wine, and hopefully go on to do the rest of their shop in Sainsbury's), and second, by generating a sense of gratitude and warmth, as one might feel if a friend gave you a birthday present that you did not necessarily expect. Even allowing for the fact that most customers can see that this is a form of company marketing, a psychological barrier has been crossed that is more likely to contribute to a longer term relationship.

However, there are criticisms that many schemes pay too much attention to data gathering and not enough to developing loyalty (O'Malley, 1998). For many businesses, the sheer scale of the data provided makes it difficult for the card providers to offer benefits that build up a personal relationship level. Instead, once again, there is a tendency for data to be used just in short-term promotions (e.g. a discount voucher for celebration cakes for someone buying a birthday card). Furthermore, there is evidence that customers are becoming more hardened to such tactics and will sign up for a number of schemes in order to obtain maximum benefits. As O'Brien and Jones (1995) have noted, many customers have 'become experts at getting something for nothing'.

In order to be part of a successful relationship marketing strategy, loyalty schemes must be managed as part of an overall CRM policy, whereby individuals or groups of customers are identified, targeted, and managed accordingly through close, interactive relationships (as many of the airlines have done). The average retailer loyalty scheme does not go this far, preferring instead to concentrate on offering incentives and short-term promotions. Once reduced to this level, many schemes merely end up as commodities, which the customer comes to expect. This leads us on to the third major potential objective of loyalty schemes—to enable companies to compete in a market.

Defending Against the Actions of Competitors

Organizations adopting loyalty schemes for competitive purposes tend to do so for two reasons. The first of these is for differentiation purposes. This is particularly true in markets where there is little perceived difference between competitors, such as credit cards or petrol. However, other retailers have embraced loyalty cards in an effort to give themselves more identity. High Street stalwarts Boots and WHSmith have witnessed a gradual erosion of their identities over recent years. Boots began life as a chemist (or drug store) and WHSmith as a stationer. However, both have expanded into additional areas and now find themselves in heavy competition across a number of retail sectors. In 1997 both companies launched their loyalty schemes—the Boots Advantage Card and the WHSmith Clubcard.

The key to achieving differentiation lies very much with the quality of the scheme. With its generous 4% return and the ability to earn bonus points, the Boots Advantage Card regularly comes out top in consumer surveys of loyalty schemes and has been successful in helping the company carve out a distinctive presence in the market. High-quality schemes will always include features that motivate customers, such as easy to understand, lots of ways to earn, no restrictions and easy/fast redemption (Kenley, 2005). There is also clear evidence of first mover advantage, as successful early schemes such as Boots and Tesco have remained at the forefront while late entrants have had to struggle to find a space in shoppers' wallets.

However, this brings us on to the second, less positive reason why organizations have introduced loyalty schemes—simply to keep up with the competition. In retailing, this has led to the surfeit of cards we see today. The problem is that once shoppers start to carry around more than one card, any possibility of the schemes generating loyalty, or even regular repeat purchase is seriously undermined. If a customer has a Sainsbury's loyalty card and a Tesco loyalty card, choice of which store to use will be based on some other criteria such as convenience, and use of the card will simply give away discount for no gain. When one takes into account the huge set-up and running costs associated with these schemes, this has serious implications for the organization's profitability.

Furthermore, as Denison (1994) surmises:

> As schemes proliferate, what began as a 'reward' turns into an 'incentive'—or bribe. As companies try to outbid each other's incentives they risk slipping into loyalty wars—price wars by another name. And as consumers learn to shop around for the best schemes, marketers risk fuelling the very promiscuity they set out to combat.

This has led some retailers to differentiate themselves by *not* having a loyalty scheme! Both Asda and Morrison's, for instance, make great play of their lack of loyalty cards, by claiming that all the costs saved are used in reducing prices in their stores. When combined with the 'hassle' factor of juggling a wallet full of cards and redeeming points, these companies believe that customers are not motivated by loyalty cards. By concentrating on 'every day low pricing' they are steering right away from notions of customer involvement and relationship marketing and are basing themselves instead firmly in the land of transaction marketing, where the 4Ps are the order of the day.

Multi-brand Schemes

In an effort to get around the problem of too many cards flooding the market some companies have merged their individual loyalty schemes to form one big one. These are known as 'coalition schemes'—perhaps the most well-known one in the UK being Nectar (see Minicase 4, Keeping Nectar Sweet). Coalition schemes aim to use their size and scope to re-motivate customers by enabling them to build up points quickly and redeem them in a variety of different ways, ranging from money off at the till to holidays, gifts, and other attractions. Additionally, the costs of running the scheme are lower as they are shared amongst a number of participants. However, such schemes are not without their critics. Research by Moore and Sekhon (2005) found that coalition schemes were no better in generating commitment, trust, or perceived relational benefits than single-brand loyalty schemes. Indeed, they concluded that many customers were unaware that their coalition loyalty card had a number of different sponsors and as such they tended to use the card for one brand only. This obviously devalues the scheme for both customers and companies.

Minicase 3

Keeping Nectar Sweet

At a time when customers' purses and wallets were already bulging with plastic loyalty cards, Nectar burst on the scene in September 2002, promising to cut through the clutter with just one card. The scheme was to be run by Loyalty Management UK Ltd, whose founder, Keith Mills, knew something about loyalty schemes, having been the originator of Air Miles 15 years earlier.

Nectar was the result of four of Britain's top consumer companies—Sainsbury's, Barclaycard, BP, and Debenham's—merging their existing loyalty schemes together under one brand. As such, Nectar became the UK's first 'coalition' loyalty card. Customers were able to earn points at each of the four participating companies and exchange these for a wide range of rewards including gifts, cinema tickets, days out, and holidays. According to Mills, the attraction of the scheme lay in the fact that 'customers will be able to earn substantially more points because they'll be pooling them from different retailers'.

Following a £50 million launch (shared between the four founders) the mood was upbeat. Nectar quickly signed up over 11 million customers and this had risen to 18 million by 2005. The scheme was also attracting an ever-increasing number of participating customers including Thresher, Magnet, Brewers Fayre, Adams kids, Ford, Dolland & Aitchison, and Vodafone. One of the principles of the scheme was that no competitors to existing sponsors would be allowed to join, although clearly some overlap existed in some areas.

However, to some observers the benefits of Nectar were not as sweet as might be. Consumer groups such as *Which?* pointed out a £5,000 spend on Barclaycard netted a measly £12.50 in points to spend, while Sainsbury's shoppers had to spend up to £1,000 to earn a couple of cinema tickets. The BBC reported that customers transferring points from the old Barclaycard scheme found that they were worth less under Nectar, meaning that they were further away than ever from the big rewards for which they had been saving. Analysis by Datamonitor estimated that within a year, only 56% of customers had redeemed their points. Many did not know who all of the participating companies were, or where they could use their card.

Furthermore, rumours persisted in that some of the big sponsors were less than happy with the scheme. One reason was the huge costs involved—promoting the scheme, issuing cards, maintaining databases, mailing customers, and redeeming rewards. Some industry analysts began questioning whether the value added to companies participating in the scheme was being off-set by the costs of being involved. Others claimed that the effectiveness of loyalty cards in general was doubtful. Research by KPMG Consulting suggested that only 2% of customers had been totally faithful to their cards.

In August 2005, two of the biggest backers—Barclaycard and Vodafone—announced that they were pulling out of the scheme. Barclaycard claimed that its customers valued more practical support from their credit card provider such as free travel insurance on trips booked through its Thompson-based travel company and paid for with a Barclaycard. Vodafone took a similar line, claming that they were going to focus instead on delivering customer value through price plans which allowed customers to save money when using their phones at evenings or weekends.

Loyalty Management UK, the company running the scheme, remained unabashed. One reason might be their 2005 signing of American Express. Their customers were allowed to earn Nectar points at a rate almost double that under the old Barclaycard. Furthermore, customers were able to 'double-dip', or earn points twice over, by paying with the Amex card and swiping their usual Nectar card at the same time.

Questions

1. What are the cost-benefit implications of a company signing up for Nectar?

2. Why would a company such as American Express join the scheme when rival Barclaycard had just pulled out?

3. What are the major problems that the Nectar scheme has faced?

Sources:
'Nectar hopes to keep customers sweet' http://news.bbc.co.uk accessed 05/06/02
'Nectar disap-points' http://news.bbc.co.uk accessed 27/02/03
'Nectar tastes less sweet as Barclaycard pulls out of scheme', *Sunday Herald*, 24 July 2005

Stored Value Cards

A relatively new tool in the development of customer loyalty schemes is the stored value card. In effect, a stored value card is a pre-paid debit card. The idea is simple—customers buy a card of a fixed value (say £20). Each time they make a purchase the card is swiped and debited for the amount they have bought until its value is used up.

This is nothing new—phone cards in the 1980s worked on exactly the same principle. However, these cards are now becoming more popular with retailers, particularly in the USA. One of the best-known stored value cards is the Starbucks scheme. This was originally developed to facilitate payment as an alternative to cash but its value as a relationship marketing tool is being increasingly recognized:

- By investing in a Starbucks stored value card, the customer is committing themselves to a number of future purchases, thus immediately meeting the important objective of repeat custom. Usage data from the cards in the USA suggest that the average customer uses the card on four separate purchase occasions (*Intele-Card News*, 2005).

- The Starbucks card can be topped up at any time, either in the shop or online. This ensures that the card remains in the customer's wallet over a long period of time. Ownership of the card and the interaction it stimulates between Starbucks and its customers enhances the level of involvement that customers have with the company and thus prepares the ground for long-term relationships.

- Ownership of the card also creates an effective switching barrier as customers are unlikely to try out a competing coffee shop as long as they have value on their Starbucks card.

- Finally, the stored value card can give exactly the same benefits to the company as a traditional loyalty card. Not only does Starbucks obtain demographic data for each card-holder for its database, it can also track each customer's spending patterns and purchase behaviour, thus enabling the implementation of a full CRM strategy. Furthermore, the company can, if it wishes, offer rewards through the card, for instance by offering special deals to card-holders.

The Need to Move Beyond Loyalty Schemes

It can be seen from the above discussion about loyalty schemes in general, that most of them appear at best to operate at a 'spurious' level of loyalty. They are thus fine in markets characterized by low customer involvement (e.g. supermarkets, dry cleaners) or lack of differentiation (e.g. petrol, credit cards), as good schemes can stimulate repeat purchase. When it comes to delivering genuine, long-term loyalty, however, most so-called 'loyalty schemes' fail to deliver, prompting the claim from many that they are nothing more than complex sales promotions.

It would appear that 'stored value loyalty cards' may get around some of the problems associated with traditional loyalty card schemes, as they involve a deeper level of customer commitment because the customer actually invests in the card. Clearly, the customer does not *have* to put money onto the card, as they can still buy coffees at Starbucks simply by using cash. The fact that they choose to invest in the card is an important step towards a reciprocative relationship with the company. Reciprocity, or interaction, between the customer and the organization is one of the key principles of customer involvement and is encapsulated in the thinking behind 'Permission Marketing'.

Permission Marketing

Permission marketing is a term coined by Seth Godin (1999), meaning that the customer has given his or her consent to receive marketing messages from an organization. As such they are more receptive to the organization because the messages are anticipated, personal, and relevant. The opposite of permission marketing is interruption marketing, which Godin claims, can lead to a 'lose–lose' situation. Interruption marketing occurs when the customer receives unsolicited direct marketing messages (see Figure 4.5). This can include direct mail, telephone calls, e-mails, and text messages. Godin argues that these things often end up wasting the customer's most precious commodity—time—and therefore lead to frustration. It is no coincidence that they are commonly referred to in the derogatory terms 'junk mail' and 'spam', because they are unwelcome. All too often the net result is a frustrated customer with no intention of buying and a marketer who has wasted his budget—lose–lose.

Godin acknowledges that **interruption marketing** will still be required for customer acquisition, but once the customer is on board, permission marketing takes over and the business of building a sturdy, long-term relationship through consent begins. Under permission marketing, customers will only be contacted with marketing information that they have said will be of interest to them and have given their consent to receive. In order to receive this consent, Godin acknowledges that some sort of incentive might need to be offered. This might be information, entertainment, competitions, prize draws, or just straight cash payment. Once permission has been given, the marketer has the customer's attention and can get down to focusing on the product's benefits and what it can do for the customer. As the relationship

Permission marketing
the customer gives consent to receive marketing messages from the organization

Interruption marketing
the customer receives unsolicited marketing messages from the organization

Figure 4.5 Interruption marketing versus permission marketing

INTERRUPTION MARKETING
- One-way sales push by the seller
- Intrusive information that is of little value
- A fixed offer with little insight into what the customer really wants
- No real relationship-building
- Danger of customer irritation

PERMISSION MARKETING
- Two-way dialogue that is permitted by the customer
- Contact which is focused, timely, tailored, specific, and relevant
- Flexible offers which can meet the customers' needs
- Building of relationships based on trust
- Satisfied customers

progresses, the marketer will seek to increase the level of permission given by the customer, thus gathering more information and being able to target products and services more personally.

Problems with Permission Marketing

Since Godin's book first came out, permission marketing has become something of a buzz-word with many companies trying to jump on the band wagon. The trouble is, many of these companies don't fully understand where permission begins and ends. To a certain extent, EU Directives have forced companies to seek permission to target them with further messages. The aim of the legislation is to prevent people's details being kept on a database or circulated to third parties without their consent. Organizations often use tick boxes at the bottom of an order form, a competition entry, or a questionnaire along the following lines: 'from time to time we may wish to mail you with details of other products or services which we feel might be of interest to you. Please tick here if you do not wish to receive these mailings.' Customers who do not tick the box are considered to have given their consent. The problem is that many companies then take this consent as a one-off, allowing innumerable further contacts stretching into the future. These further contacts are often devised around what suits the company, not the customer. Unless further contacts are welcomed by and are of value to the customer, the messages revert to junk mail or spam. Permission has to be earned at each step until a level of trust and mutual understanding is achieved and this is not always easy in the relationship between an organization and a customer.

Involving the Customer as a Member

One way of getting closer to the customer, involving them and gaining their permission all at the same time is to offer them some sort of membership status, whereby they gain benefits that are related to but stand apart from the core product or service. The customer as 'member' is one of Gummesson's (2002) 30Rs. However, Gummesson makes a distinction between 'pseudo membership' and 'genuine membership'.

Pseudo Membership

Pseudo membership tends to be characterized as follows:

- Price driven (the more the customer spends the more price reductions or other benefits they are entitled to). This would encompass many of the traditional loyalty schemes we looked at earlier in this chapter, e.g. Tesco ClubCard.
- Membership must be earned. This would include many airline loyalty programmes. For example, British Airways offers three levels of membership—Blue, Silver, and Gold—with ever-increasing benefits at each level. However, membership at each level can only be realized if the traveller flies more frequently and for longer distances.

Although very successful at generating repeat custom, often over long periods, pseudo membership schemes in themselves are not necessarily guaranteed to move customers to the higher levels of the Ladder of Loyalty.

Genuine Membership

According to Gummeson, genuine membership is not commercial, or at least only commercial in a cooperative sense. In practice, however, most organizations that involve their customers in membership schemes do so for commercial reasons; it's just that some are more overtly profit-oriented and some are more relationship-oriented. This can be seen if we look at the objectives of membership clubs.

- Membership for legal purposes. In the UK, businesses that want to sell products or services that are heavily regulated can only do so legally if customers are signed up as members. Casinos, late-night drinking establishments, or so-called 'gentlemen's clubs' might fall into this category. Membership is less to do with developing a long-term relationship than enabling customers to take up the service in the first place.

- To increase customer retention. Some organizations want to make sure that they retain business over a period of time by requiring customers to sign a contract, or an agreement to purchase a minimum amount during a given period (for example gyms, health clubs, book and CD clubs, etc). Whilst it is possible through exemplary service for a company to turn this sort of membership into a close relationship with the customer, the risk is that the customer simply becomes a prisoner. If this happens, the relationship has turned negative and will not generate any long-term loyalty.

- Affinity club tie-ins. Recognizing that traditional reward schemes have not always been successful, many credit card companies have attempted to go down the membership route by tying up with existing, strongly idealistic or associative groups such as charities, universities, sports clubs, or trade unions. The result is the affinity card. For instance MBNA and the charity World Wildlife Fund can now offer customers a credit card. Heavily branded with WWF imagery (the attractive side of the partnership) the card offers all the functions of a normal credit card (the practical side of the partnership), but MBNA guarantees to give a contribution to the WWF each time the card is used (the idealistic aspect). In effect MBNA is riding on the coat tails of customers' loyalty to the WWF, but everybody wins, including the customer.

- To increase share of wallet. Membership schemes which are not exclusive (i.e. those where the customer is not bound by any contractual obligation to use the product or service) can add value for a customer and encourage customers to switch more of their business in their direction. For example, UK-based toy and model manufacturer Corgi runs a Collectors Club which offers members advice and valuation on models, previews of new releases, a classified section for customers to buy and sell models, annual events such as 'swap meets', and price discounts. By building this affinity, Corgi is hoping that members will spend more of their budget on Corgi products than they will on those of competitors.

- Involving the customer. The final category of membership aims to take customers right up the Ladder of Loyalty by involving them both emotionally and physically with the brand or product. Common examples include football club supporters clubs and car and motorbike owners clubs. Here the customer puts as much into the relationship (if not more) than the company, by contributing their money, time, and emotional commitment, even changing their lifestyle to fit around the product. The customer at this level exhibits long-term, unshakeable loyalty (witness football fans). In these circumstances, the attraction of the product or service often exceeds its practicality or intrinsic value. Clearly, not every product can hope to achieve this level of commitment.

Customer membership schemes are not just limited to B2C markets; they can also work in B2B markets, e.g. Microsoft and its partners (see Opening Case). What is important however, when considering customer membership clubs, is to distinguish between those which encourage behavioural loyalty and those operating at more attitudinal level of loyalty. The second type is more likely to provide examples of good relationship marketing.

Involving the Customer at an Emotional Level

In a business sense, the strongest relationships are those which engage the customer in more than simply a commercial transaction. Here the relationship becomes something more personal—like a human relationship. If an organization is able to transcend to this level of relationship with its customers it is in a very strong position indeed.

The Power of Brands

For many years the brand has been seen by organizations as the handle around which they can build relationships. Originally developed for purposes of trust and differentiation, brands still work in these areas but have additionally taken on characteristics around which customers can build relationships. As Gummesson (2002) observes, brands have increasingly become the real output whilst manufacturing has become a network of partners and subcontractors (e.g. Virgin Mobile, which uses the network and supporting technology of T-Mobile; or Coca Cola, who licence production of the product to many different producers and bottlers around the world). The brand comes first, the product comes second.

This is further exemplified when one considers the difficulty in achieving lasting differentiation through core product features. Take cars, for example. Not so long ago, different makes and models varied enormously from one another—not just in the way they looked, but in the way they drove, the way they were engineered, the technology they employed, even in how reliable they were. Today, advances in production technology and design have ironed out these differences, so now all cars are well engineered, good to drive, reliable, etc. At the same time, consolidation of the industry has left just a handful of big corporations to compete with each other, each of whom can match one another in terms of product design, engineering, and price. As Gilligan and Wilson (2004) put it, the traditional sources of competitive advantage have been eroded. As a result, consumers have increasingly looked towards brand names when considering which product or service to buy.

Consumers' relationships with brands have therefore become all-important for organizations. One of the key aspects of any relationship is trust and Gilligan and Wilson highlight the development of 'trust brands', where the customer has a 'long-lasting and deep-seated faith' that the product will deliver what they want and that they will get a fair deal. Brands scoring high on trust can more easily be applied to a raft of different markets, as can be seen with Virgin, which has spread across airlines, mobile phones, retailing, financial products, soft drinks, etc., or Tesco, who have moved from grocery into financial products and clothing. Indeed, the principle of 'trust brands' explains the phenomena of the 'designer label' and explains why we can buy Jaguar watches, Marlboro leisure-wear, and Ralph Lauren fragrances.

Consumers' relationships with brands have been explored in further detail by Rapp and Collins (1995), who coined the term 'relationship brands'. Relationship brands go beyond simple trust; they encapsulate mutual respect and interaction. In their words, 'you no longer simply brand and promote what you sell. You brand and promote the relationship as well.' The Harley Davidson Owners Group discussed in Chapter 1 is an example of this. This is perhaps the ultimate in customer relationships. The brand has become part of customers' lives, a statement of who they are and what they believe in. Is this the top of the loyalty ladder? Perhaps—at least as long as the fashion lasts!

Chapter Summary

Relationships are all about getting closer to the customer, getting involved with them and thus securing their loyalty, and this chapter has considered the implications of this from a marketing point of view. We have seen that it is important to distinguish genuine loyalty from simple repeat-buying behaviour for other reasons and how changes in consumers' lifestyles and attitudes have eroded traditional loyalties.

The loyalty ladder is a model which can be used not only to assess the level of involvement a customer might have with an organization of its products and brands, but also a process by which the organization can move customers to ever-increasing levels of loyalty. The model can be used to illustrate the transition from transactional marketing, using promotions to attract customers and retain them on a week-by-week basis, to relationship marketing involving closer customer involvement. However, it becomes clear when considering Dick and Basu's categories of loyalty that some customers will never move beyond the bottom rungs of the ladder as they will exhibit either no loyalty or, at best, spurious loyalty. This is particularly true in markets categorized by lack of differentiation, low customer involvement, and ease of customer switching.

In recent years, many organizations have introduced customer loyalty schemes, but the effectiveness of these in generating long-term, sustainable loyalty is questionable. Indeed, many loyalty schemes seem to work better on a promotional level lower down the loyalty ladder, although the proliferation of schemes, customer dissatisfaction, and the high costs of running them can reduce their value for both the customer and the companies. Loyalty schemes are still evolving, through multi-brand cards such as Nectar, to stored value cards such as Starbucks, but still tend to be most effective in engendering behavioural rather than attitudinal loyalty.

As traditional bases of loyalty are eroded, organizations must find new ways of adding value and moving customers up the Ladder of Loyalty. The higher rungs of the ladder tend to involve reciprocative customer relationships, where interaction takes place. Permission marketing adds value for the customer because it allows them to have a say in the relationship, while membership schemes enable the customer to interact with the organization and with other customers, thus augmenting the core product and adding further value. Perhaps the closest of relationships are those that involve customers at an emotional level. Objects, symbols, and brands can do this, but have to capture the customers' imagination first, and with fickle customers this is no mean feat.

There are thus a number of approaches, working at different levels of the loyalty ladder and traversing the barrier between transactional and relationship marketing. This is summarized in Figure 4.6 below. In order to make any of these approaches work, the organization must carefully evaluate its market in order to identify what sort of customer loyalty it can realistically pursue.

Figure 4.6 Marketing approaches at different levels of loyalty

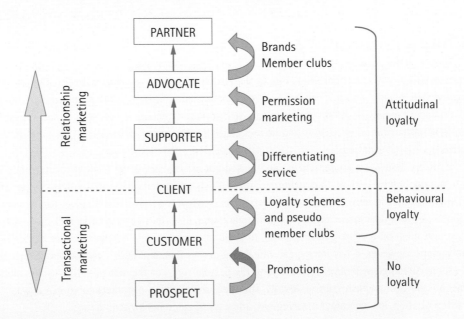

End of Chapter Case with Questions

Customer Loyalty at Heinz

Think of an archetypal FMCG brand and you might well think of Heinz. With its famous catchphrase '57 Varieties' and products such as tomato ketchup, soup, baked beans, spaghetti, and salad cream, Heinz has become a household name at mealtimes across the world. The company as we know it was founded in the USA in 1876 by German émigré Henry J. Heinz, producing bottled sauces and ketchup. Heinz products were of a high quality and sold well and the range rapidly expanded, the famous tinned baked beans being added in 1895. It was shortly after this that Heinz coined his famous slogan—'57 Varieties'—to get across to customers the depth and breadth of his company's product range. Ironically, by this time, Heinz already had many more than 57 varieties; he chose the number because it appealed to him. Today the company's product range numbers over 360. By the time he died in 1919, Henry J. Heinz's company was a market leader and has remained so ever since.

Heinz has always tried to keep close to its customers. Its first products appeared in clear glass jars (when its competitors were using coloured glass), so that the purity of the products could be clearly seen. Traditionally the company has always laid much emphasis on loyalty, and invested heavily in slogans, advertising, and branding. Henry J. Heinz himself once described true loyalty as a customer who, upon finding no Heinz products in a shop, abandons that shop altogether and goes in search of a shop which does sell Heinz. This is a powerful analogy—are there any brands that you like enough to walk out of a supermarket for?

As competition in the grocery sector has intensified, Heinz has fought hard to maintain its position. Initially, competition came from other brands such as Crosse and Blackwell and HP, but recently Heinz has had to contend with supermarkets' own-label products. Indeed, such is the power of the supermarkets that traditional brands have struggled to remain close to the final customer. With their size, range, and proximity to the final consumer, the big supermarkets have muscled in on customer relationships and can control to a great extent which products customers buy.

Heinz continues to promote its brand through advertising, point-of-sale promotions, and branded merchandise, but, in common with many other FMCG manufacturers has found it more difficult to pursue CRM strategies. At one time it was even suggested that if a customer spent less than £10 a year on Heinz products, CRM was not profitable (Treather, 1994).

These days, however, things have changed. Clicking on to the company's website (www.heinz.co.uk) customers can now obtain a host of information, from new product launches, recipes, tips about nutrition, and even classic adverts from the past. Heinz has also developed links to other sites, such as Tinytums (where customers can access advice on pregnancy and baby feeding) and Linda McCartney Promotions (for offers on products that are complementary to Heinz's own products). In addition, the site offers opportunities to enter competitions and a letters page, where customers can write in with questions or comments and read and reply to others.

Finally, the website offers customers the opportunity to sign up to 'Heinz Offers', by submitting their name, address, and contact details. In return, customers are entered into a prize draw, but also receive a regular e-mail newsletter, with details of news, promotional offers, and money-off coupons for Heinz products. Customers signing up for 'Heinz Offers' are covered by a privacy policy to protect the data they submit and must also agree to abide by the terms and conditions of the site.

To date, Heinz remains one of the UK's favourite and best-selling brands.

Questions

1. Taking Heinz's current strategies, at what point (if any) does the company move from transactional marketing to relationship marketing?

2. Why is it difficult for a traditional FMCG company such as Heinz to 'involve' the customer?

3. How does Heinz maintain customer loyalty?

4. Will customers signing up for 'Heinz Offers' be spammed with junk mail?

5. Having read this chapter, try to say whether Heinz is building customer relationships at each level of the loyalty ladder.

Sources:
http://www.heinz.co.uk accessed 02/08/06
Treather, D. (1994) 'Souped-up for direct attack', *Marketing*, 29 Sept., 18–19

Discussion Questions

1. How might the concept of customer loyalty differ between differentiated and undifferentiated products?

2. Can organizations continue to rely on customer inertia?

3. As a customer, apply the Ladder of Loyalty to yourself, identifying products and services where you play a different role (prospect, purchaser, client, supporter, etc.). What would the product/service provider that you have described at the different stages have to do to move you up to the next rung of the ladder?

4. How should an organization manage 'loyal buyers' who are not 'relationship seekers'?

5. Why might it be easier to engender attitudinal loyalty in a service or B2B market?

6. Discuss the pros and cons of a loyalty scheme of your choice.

7. Explain the difference between loyalty cards, multi-brand cards, and stored value cards. Do these represent short-term promotions or long-term marketing strategies?

8. Should marketers abandon 'interruption marketing'?

9. How might Piercy's four types of customer (relationship seekers, relationship exploiters, loyal buyers, transaction buyers) apply to customer membership schemes?

10. How can customers have a relationship with a symbol or object? Give some examples.

11. What added value does a strong brand bring to customer relationships? Can a newcomer to the market induce customer-switching in a market dominated by designer brands?

12. Suggest how the following companies might develop and maintain customer loyalty: Kellogg's, Virgin Mobile, HSBC, Dell, Marks & Spencer.

Further Reading

Christopher, M., Payne, A., and Ballantyne, D. (2002) *Relationship Marketing*, Butterworth Heinemann.

Dick, A. and Basu, K. (1994) 'Customer loyalty: towards an integrated framework', *Journal of the Academy of Marketing Science*, 22(2), 99–113.

Uncles, M., Dowling, G., and Hammond, K. (2003) 'Customer loyalty and customer loyalty programs', *Journal of Consumer Marketing*, 20(4).

References

Christopher, M., Payne, A., and Ballantyne, D. (2002) *Relationship Marketing*, Butterworth Heinemann, Oxford.

Denison, T. and Knox, S. (1994) *Pocketing the Change from Loyal Shoppers: The double indemnity effect*, Cranfield School of Management.

Dick, A. S. and Basu, K. (1994) 'Customer Loyalty: Towards an integrated framework', *Journal of the Academy of Marketing Science*, 22(2), 99–113.

Gilligan, C. and Wilson, R. (2004) *Strategic Marketing Planning*, Butterworth Heinemann, Oxford.

Godin, S. (1999) *Permission Marketing*, Simon & Schuster, London.

Gummesson, E. (2002) *Total Relationship Marketing*, Butterworth Heinemann, Oxford.

Jones, M. (1994) 'It's a Dog's Life Being at the Beck and Call of Marketers', *Marketing Business*, Feb.

Kenley, R. (2005) 'Loyalty is Pointless—or is it?', *The Wise Marketer*, 3 May.

Little, E. and Marandi, E. (2003) *Relationship Marketing Management*, Thomson, London.

Jones, T. and Sasser, E. (1995) 'Why Satisfied Customers Defect', *Harvard Business Review*, Nov./Dec., 88–101.

Moore, G. and Sekhon, H. (2005) 'Multi-brand Loyalty Cards: A good idea', *Journal of Marketing Management*, 21(5).

O'Brien, L. and Jones, C. (1995) 'Do Rewards Really Create Loyalty?', *Harvard Business Review*, 75–82.

O'Malley, L. (1998) 'Can Loyalty Schemes Really Build Loyalty?', *Marketing Intelligence and Planning*, 16(1).

Oliver, R. (1997) *Satisfaction: A Behavioural Perspective on the Consumer*, McGraw Hill, Maidenhead.

Piercy, N. (1999) 'Relationship Marketing Myopia', *Marketing Business*, Oct.

Prahalad, C. and Hamel, G. (2002) *Competing for the Future*, Harvard Business School Press.

Rapp, S. and Collins, T. (1995) *The New MaxiMarketing*, McGraw Hill, New York.

Stauss, B., Schmidt, M., and Schoeler, A. (2005) 'Customer Frustration in Loyalty Programmes', *International Journal of Service Industry Management*, 16.

Treather, D. (1994) 'Souped-up for Direct Attack', *Marketing*, 29(9), 18–19.

Uncles, M. (1994) 'Do You or Your Customers Need a Loyalty Programme?', *Journal of Targeting, Measurement and Analysis for Marketing*, 1, 45–51.

Uncles, M., Dowling, G., and Hammond, K. (2003) 'Customer Loyalty and Customer Loyalty Programs', *Journal of Consumer Marketing*, 20(4).

Woolf, B. (2002) 'What is Loyalty?', *The Wise Marketer*, 7 Feb.

Websites

BBC News: 'Air Miles "threaten dollar's"' http://news.bbc.co.uk accessed 03/05/02

Intele-Card News: 'Stored value cards as 21st century currency' http://intelecard.com accessed 08/01/03

Customer Relationship Management (CRM)

Chapter Outline

Learning Outcomes

After reading this chapter you should be able to:

- describe the parameters of CRM and its context within the overall study of relationship marketing;

- understand the difference between 'analytical' CRM and 'operational' CRM;

- appreciate the extent to which IT is an enabler of CRM;

- show how information about customers can be used by the organization to gain competitive advantage;

- determine the factors which will make the successful implementation of CRM initiatives more or less likely.

Introduction

At first glance it might seem odd to have a single chapter on 'customer relationship management' when the whole book is supposed to be about marketing relationships. However, it has been included here because customer relationship management, or CRM as it is usually abbreviated to, is often treated as a distinct set of activities that can be adopted by the organization to give it a customer-centric competitive stance.

Whereas the general field of relationship marketing (RM) can be viewed as a broad subject area that can be studied and researched, CRM is often treated as something more immediately practical—something which can be packaged, installed, and implemented in a fairly straightforward manner. For this reason, many of the books dealing with CRM (as opposed to relationship marketing per se) are written as management help books, rather than academic books. This is not to say that CRM is not a valid area for academic study. On the contrary, many writers have acknowledged the strategic significance of CRM and the value of effective customer information management. As such, CRM has become an important part of relationship marketing as it represents a tailored approach to an organization's dealings with customers.

This chapter therefore begins by exploring the background of CRM and putting the subject into context. Consideration is given to what some writers have termed 'Analytical CRM' whereby knowledge about the status of individual customers and their behaviours is used strategically and 'Operational CRM' which is more concerned with the day-to-day running of the business. Recognizing the role of IT as an enabler of CRM and customer knowledge as its resource, the chapter goes on to explore how customer data is collected, used, and managed by organizations to gain competitive advantage. This leads on to a discussion of privacy and the extent to which an organization can justifiably collect and use customer information. Finally, the chapter looks at the practicalities of CRM implementation through software packages and other initiatives have been used to target and develop relationships with individual customers. Possible reasons for CRM failure are also considered here. To begin with, however, it may be useful to consider the Opening Case which looks at how the UK's leading supermarket, Tesco, has used CRM to gain an advantage in the market. This is a useful introduction into the scope of CRM and its potential application.

Opening Case Study with Questions

Tesco's CRM Programme: The move from customer understanding to customer insight and then to customer/brand engagement
Source: © Professor Colin Gilligan (2007)

Synopsis

Tesco is currently one of the most successful retail organizations in the world. This case study explores how the organization has developed and how a key element of its strategy since 1995 has been its Clubcard-based loyalty scheme and its development of a strategic

CRM (Customer Relationship Management) programme that provides the basis for true customer insight and greater brand engagement.

Background

In 2003 *Management Today* voted Tesco the UK's Most Admired Company and its boss, Sir Terry Leahy, Most Admired Leader. In 2005, the company again picked up the two awards, a feat that had not been achieved since *Management Today*, in conjunction with Mercer Consulting, launched the Most Admired Companies scheme in 1989. In doing this, they also won outright two of the nine criteria used to judge companies: Capacity to Innovate and Use of Corporate Assets.

The Tesco story, particularly over the past 20 years, is one of sustained growth and financial success. With more than 2,100 stores in the UK (3,700+ stores worldwide) and group sales in 2007–8 of £52 billion, it is with more than 280,000 employees in the UK and 440,000+ worldwide, the UK's largest private-sector employer and the third largest grocery retailer in the world. In 2007–8, the company made in excess of £2.8 billion in profit (PBT) and accounted for more than £1 in every £7 of UK consumer spending. Its Internet shopping arm is the world's most successful online retail grocery operation.

The Strategy

Founded in 1924, the company for many years pursued a largely price-based strategy. However, at the beginning of the 1970s, with customers becoming wealthier and less concerned with price, the company began to rethink its pile it high, sell it cheap low cost/low price model. Throughout the 1970s and 80s, the management team restructured and began to focus upon superstores, new store layouts, store ambience, and a far wider product range. During the 1990s they launched a series of new store formats, including Tesco Express, Tesco Metro, and Tesco Extra. At the same time, they entered a series of overseas markets such as China, Japan, Thailand, Malaysia, France, Hungary, Poland, Slovakia, the Czech Republic, Ireland, and the USA. Speaking at the end of 2007, when overseas operations were generating £13 billion of sales, Leahy made the comment that the expectation was that by 2015 more than half of the company's turnover would be generated outside the UK.

The success of the company's strategy in the UK was reflected by it overtaking Sainsbury's in 1995 to become the UK grocery market leader. Since then the company has rapidly reinforced its dominance of the market by expanding both its product range and UK market share, which by the end of 2006 had reached 22%; this compared with Sainsbury's 16.3%. Its position in the UK has also been strengthened by its home grocery shopping service which in 2006 had sales of £1 billion, making the company the largest .com grocery business in the world. At the same time, the company was also the groceries market leader in five other countries.

However, at the beginning of the 1990s, the company's management team began to recognize that the key to future success would lie not just in pursuing a strategy of growth, but must be based on getting ever closer to the customer. It was this that led to the company's development of what has proven to be one of the world's largest and most successful CRM initiatives. Based on the company's statement of its core purpose of creating 'value for customers and *to earn their lifetime loyalty'* (author's emphasis), the CRM programme is seen by many to be a model of best practice.

The CRM Initiative

Tesco's move into CRM began in the early 1990s when the company started working with dunnhumby, a marketing services firm, and led in late 1994 to the preliminary test launch of a loyalty card scheme in six stores. The move was driven partly by an awareness of this sort of initiative in other parts of the world, but also by the results of some analysis which highlighted two significant facts:

- In many of their stores the top 100 customers were worth as much in terms of sales as the bottom 4,000.
- The top 5% of the company's customers accounted for 20% of sales, whilst the bottom 25% accounted for just 2%.

The scheme, which was underpinned with a major launch to the staff and the distribution of 140,000 educational videos, is based upon the Tesco Clubcard which rewards customers by giving them one loyalty point for every £1 spent with the company. These points can then be redeemed either for products in store or with a wide range of other organizations including leisure attractions, hotels, museums, zoos, holiday and travel companies, and restaurants.

However, the Clubcard scheme is far more than a simple customer reward programme. From the outset, the company has focused upon capturing, analyzing, and then, most importantly, *using* the data and information generated by the ten million+ transactions made each week. The starting point for this involves each of the transactions being linked to individual customer profiles. Data-mining techniques are then used to pinpoint when and where purchases are made, the amount that customers have spent, and the types of products that have been bought. These purchasing habits and behaviour patterns are then used as the basis for segmenting customers on the basis of 5,000 need segments.

How the Information is Used

Armed with this information, segments are targeted with tailor-made campaigns and advertisements, as well as invitations to join Tesco special interest clubs which include the wine club, the kids club, the food club, the baby and toddler club, and the healthy living club. Customers also receive regular mailings of a mass-customized magazine that has a tailored combination of articles, advertisements related to Tesco's offer, and third-party ads.

Internally, the information is used by the company's management teams as the basis for making a series of decisions about:

- management of the product range;
- new product development: Tesco's Finest, for example, was launched when analysis showed that some customers were defecting to Marks & Spencer for high(er) quality foodstuffs;
- pricing strategies that more precisely meet the needs and price sensitivities of different target groups;

- merchandising so that the product portfolio is based on *detailed* insights to customer profiles and purchasing patterns;

- inventory management;

- promotions, with greater rewards being offered to loyal customers;

- levels of customer service, with greater attention being paid to the stock levels and promotions on those products bought by loyal customers;

- measures of promotional and media effectiveness;

- customer acquisition by matching new products such as the entry to financial services and the launch of Tesco.com to specific customer types; and

- targeted communications (20% of Tesco's coupons are redeemed against an industry average of 0.5%).

The information is also used by the company as part of the process of identifying and evaluating product development opportunities, promotions, and when dealing with its suppliers.

Questions

1. The majority of CRM programmes fail to deliver what is promised or expected when they are introduced. Why has the Tesco scheme been so successful when so many others have failed?

2. What lessons emerge from the Tesco experience that might be applied within other organizations?

Sources:
Gwyther, M. and Saunders, A. (2005) 'Another Twin Win for Tesco', *Management Today*, Dec., pp. 35–43

Mukund, A. (2003) 'Tesco: the Customer Relationship Management Champion', ICFAI Centre for Management Research, Hyderabad, India

Newell, F. (2003) *Why CRM Doesn't Work: How to Win by Letting Customers Manage the Relationshi*, Kogan Page

What is CRM?

Although **CRM** today is based upon sophisticated technology and the manipulation of millions of pieces of customer data, the underlying principles are nothing new. Taking time to understand customers' needs and requirements has formed the basis of good business practice for hundreds of years. In this way businesses were able to identify the most lucrative customers and devise the best way of serving them in order to retain them. As we have already seen in previous chapters, however, the ability to pursue individual relationships with customers was lost in mass consumer markets where a business might well be serving thousands, even millions of customers across a vast geographical area.

Customer Relationship Management (CRM)

implementation of the principles of relationship marketing through the management of customer data and use of technology

Background of CRM

Over the years a number of labels have been applied to CRM-like activities, each one tending to reflect the writer's area of interest (Peppers and Rogers, 2004). Examples of closely related areas are integrated marketing communications and knowledge marketing.

Integrated Marketing Communications

Integrated Marketing Communications (IMC) was put forward by Shultz *et al.* (1993) as an American take on the Scandinavian-led CRM concept. Basically, IMC linked together all the separate communications that the organization had with the customer. Thus, at the touch of a button the organization could see all the different approaches that had been made to the customer and whether these had been in person, by mail, or telephone. In effect, it brought together what Peppers and Rogers described as 'the mishmash' of uncoordinated advertising, direct-mail campaigns, invoices, and other contacts with the customer into a consistent branding strategy. The idea was that the organization's message should remain consistent at all times. The customer's responses could also be tracked, including enquiries, orders, payments, complaints, etc. The term integrated was used in recognition that these customer touch points would most likely be across a number of different departments within the organization.

> **Integrated Marketing Communications**
> ensuring a consistent brand message across all of the organization's communications and customer touch points

Shultz has developed his original theories and argues that IMC has now become Integrated Brand Communications (IBC) in recognition that the organization's brand brings together all of what an organization is in the eyes of the customer. Shultz contends that traditional marketing communications has been focused on creating effects or changes in the customer's awareness, recall, comprehension attitudes, or intention to buy. In other words it is something which is done *to* the customer, rather than something which is done *for* the customer. IBC is more wide-ranging in that it attempts to create an overall relationship with customers. Its goal is to best serve customers profitably and it is thus an investment in customers, not an investment in tools or tactics. IBC thereby encompasses all brand touch points. An example of this in practice is Virgin Mobile. Here, the visual image of the brand logo, the colours and typefaces used, and the underlying brand values of simplicity, openness, and helpfulness are conveyed at every customer touch point including the phone itself, the telephone and website-based helplines, the top-up systems and procedures, and associated products and services.

In practice this is what CRM does too, but whereas IMC and IBC concentrate on marketing communications and branding, it is generally acknowledged that CRM takes this further, by, for instance, developing profiles of customers for use in strategic planning.

Knowledge Management

> **Knowledge Management**
> the treatment of knowledge as an economic resource which can be managed to generate competitive advantage

Knowledge Management (KM) is a more distinct discipline which has developed as a field of study in its own right. At the heart of KM is the acceptance that knowledge is an economic resource that can be managed like other resources to give the organization a competitive advantage (Drucker, 1996). Rowley (2004) recognizes that there are strong links and similarities between KM and CRM. However, she distinguishes the two by contrasting the range of knowledge covered by each of the two disciplines. Rowley contends that KM deals with a number of knowledge 'themes' that an organization might usefully be able to take advantage of including knowledge about markets, management, technical areas, and professional areas (e.g. medicine or law). Clearly, the idea of knowledge about markets or customers being a useful business tool sounds similar to the premise of CRM. However, the other themes do not appear to relate to CRM, although Rowley does acknowledge that they come close to the wider view of relationship marketing (e.g. as set out in the Six Markets Model). Interestingly, Gummesson (1999) includes the 'Knowledge Relationship' as one of his 30Rs of relationship marketing (see Chapter 1).

Thus, although certain aspects of KM are shared with CRM, we can conclude that the two are distinct from each other and can be viewed as separate disciplines.

Definitions of CRM

Most definitions of CRM are based around the collection and use of customer data for specific customer-focused activities (e.g. Xu and Walton, 2005). Peppers and Rogers (2004) broadly describe CRM as 'increasing the value of the company through specific customer strategies'. They suggest CRM is a set of business practices designed to bring an organization closer to its customers so that it can understand each customer better and thus deliver greater and greater value to each one. In this way each customer becomes more valuable to the firm. More precisely they describe CRM as 'an enterprise wide business strategy for achieving customer specific objectives by taking customer specific actions'. In other words, CRM is not just confined to the marketing department—it entails the whole organization being customer centric.

In a study of financial services companies, Rodrigues and Stone (2002) summarize a number of statements that have been put forward to define CRM. These break down into two basic areas:

- enhancing the customers' overall experience of the organization;
- getting closer to those customers who represent the greatest profit potential.

Rodrigues and Stone's own definition comes from one of the retail banks which formed part of their study: 'the business strategy and mode of operation deployed to maintain and develop relationships with profitable customers, and manage the cost of doing business with less profitable customers'.

The notion of an organization choosing which customers to get close to is one of the basic concepts of relationship marketing. It is based on the principle that relationships can apply leverage to the customer's long-term profit potential, but at the same time acknowledging that there are costs associated in developing and maintaining a relationship. This area will be explored in greater depth in Chapter 10 when the issues of implementing relationship and return on relationships are considered. It is worth noting here, however, that use of CRM in this way would constitute a strategic approach, which will be discussed in this chapter as *Analytical CRM* as opposed to *operational CRM* (see Figure 5.1).

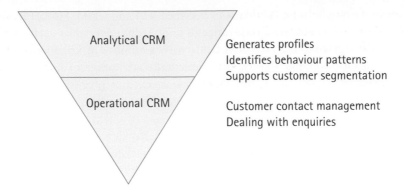

Figure 5.1 Levels of CRM

Levels of CRM

Analytical CRM

Analytical CRM

the strategic use of customer data in long-term relationship marketing decision-making

Analytical CRM involves the strategic use of customer data (sometimes known as 'knowledge management') to inform long-term planning and decision-making at the top of the organization. Questions such as which markets to serve and how to maximize customer profitability are addressed here. As such, analytical CRM will affect the shape and direction of the organization. *Reader's Digest* is a good example of an organization that has based its business on analytical CRM. By managing the data it gathers about customers through their previous purchases and responses to mailings, the company has been able to tailor its approach to individual customers, adding value for them and at the same time developing a competitive advantage. This is described in more detail in Minicase 1, *Reader's Digest*.

In business-to-consumer (B2C) markets, at a basic level this often entails capturing some individual demographic customer data such as name, address, date of birth, etc. which is then used to communicate directly with the customer with special offers, appeals, etc. Typical data capture tools include things such as competitions or prize draws. Guinness for example regularly runs competitions to win free beer, rugby tickets, or other prizes. In order to enter, the customer must provide contact details and date of birth (a declaration that they are old enough to drink). This data can be subsequently used to send personalized messages to the customer—a typical example being a birthday greeting and an invitation to go to the pub for a celebratory drink (of Guinness) with their friends.

More sophisticated CRM schemes not only capture the customer's demographic data, they also monitor the customer's behaviour in terms of what they buy, how frequently they buy, where they buy, etc. For example many banks use the information they have about their customers to target specific customer segments which they know will be most profitable in the long run. Some organizations gather this information through a loyalty or reward card—the Tesco Clubcard being a prime example. With this more detailed information the company can target individuals with specifically tailored offers. However, the pursuance of CRM in B2C markets can still be problematic, particularly if the customer does not see the need for a relationship or feels 'hounded' or 'spied upon'.

Minicase 1

Reader's Digest

The next time you find yourself in the waiting room of your doctor or your dentist, take a look at the pile of magazines that has been left there for you to read. Chances are one of them will be the *Reader's Digest*. Published in 21 languages, *Reader's Digest* has a global circulation of 18 million and an estimated 80 million readers, making it the world's best-selling magazine. *Reader's Digest* was founded in 1922 by American De Witt Wallace and his wife, Lila Bell. The original concept was to take topical news and journal articles of the day and 'condense' them into one magazine. As the business grew, books and music were added to its portfolio and today the company is able to meet a wide variety of interests from cookery to computers and country and western to classical.

The business's success has been attributed to its direct mail method of selling. Customers are targeted with mail shots and encouraged to reply through prize draws for large amounts of money and other prizes. By keeping a close record of the orders they receive, *Reader's Digest* can build up a picture of what sort of products are going to be of more interest to a particular customer. Even the replies from those who don't order anything and simply enter the prize draw are useful because they help keep the database up to date. By monitoring customer replies, some of which go back over many years, the company can tailor subsequent mailings more closely to individual customers and personalize the appeal.

Research undertaken by *Reader's Digest* in Germany found that mailings targeted at different types of customer with different products, depending on the customer's affinity, produced a response rate 62% higher than a 'benchmark' mailing where recipients received a standard offering which was not personalized. *Reader's Digest*'s German promotions manager Klaus Kicherer described the challenge in deciding how much personalization to include: 'deciding which elements to personalize was difficult . . . would they feel that we know too much about them and feel threatened by that?'

The value of the *Reader's Digest* database is not just in its ability to sell magazines, books, and music. Its prize draw responders list is also made available commercially to other organizations. Marketing company Howse Jackson described a *Reader's Digest* list as 'an outstanding file of responsive consumers with a wide range of interests' and offering 'a wealth of selections including geographic; gender; recency; age band; marital status; hotline 'latest' names; look-a-like profiling . . .'. A statement within *Reader's Digest*'s prize draw information alerts customers to the possibility of their information being passed on to 'other carefully selected companies whose offers may be of interest to you'. Customers are able to opt out of this if they wish.

In recent years *Reader's Digest*'s circulation has dropped as its customer base aged, and in 2006 the company was sold to investment group Ripplewood Holdings for $2.4 billion. Ripplewood already owns Direct Holdings Worldwide, which sells Time Life books, DVDs, and music around the world, so *Reader's Digest* looks like a good fit. Acknowledging that the way in which customers would want to read things might change in the digital age, Ripplewood's chief executive Tim Collins was confidant that '*Reader's Digest* is exceedingly well positioned be a leader in that transition'.

Questions

1. What are pros and cons of *Reader's Digest*'s business strategy?

2. How might *Reader's Digest* replicate its strategy in the digital age?

3. Identify other organizations that have used similar strategies. Have these enjoyed the same success as *Reader's Digest*?

Sources:
Reader's Digest http://www.rd.com accessed 12/06/08
'Easily digestible DM results for *Reader's Digest*' (2007) *Print Media Management*, May
'*Reader's Digest* sold to private equity frim for $2.4bn', *Times*, 17 November 2006
'*Reader's Digest* taken private for £1.3bn', *Guardian*, 16 November 2006

The principles of analytical CRM can also be seen in business-to-business (B2B) marketing. It is true that many businesses also serve large numbers of customers on a B2B basis (e.g. drugs suppliers, steel stockholders, commercial vehicle manufacturers, stationery suppliers, etc.) but in general the B2B customer is known to the supplier and is treated as an individual (Kotler, 2004). There are a number of reasons for this. For a start, there are more people involved in the typical B2B transaction (from buying, operations, finance, etc.) which means that each customer has to be treated in a different way. Furthermore, the business solution that is provided in a B2B transaction often has to be tailored to fit a specific client specification. Whether it is the design of the product or process, the packaging, delivery, installation, staff training, after-sales service, or invoicing arrangements—even the ordering process itself, it is unusual for two B2B transactions for different customers to be exactly the same.

As a result, instead of relying on advertising and other mass communications techniques, most businesses use a sales force whose job it is to deal with each customer separately. Larger, more important customers are often handled by Key Account Managers whose job is to stay close to the customer and ensure that their needs and requirements are fully met. Key account management reflects one of the basic principles of CRM—that the most profitable customers should be singled out for special treatment. Good key account management involves working closely with the customer on a one-to-one basis in order to develop solutions that will improve the profitability of both organizations (Christopher *et al.*, 2002).

Operational CRM

Operational CRM systems usually involve the processes and systems by which day-to-day customer-based activities such as customer enquiries, orders, shipment, and invoicing are managed. For example, the mail order firm MusicandFilm.co.uk uses customer information to manage its customer helpline. Customers enquiring about when a particular DVD they have ordered might be delivered, or querying their bill can be handled quickly and efficiently by the company's call centre. As these activities often involve different departments within the organization, operational CRM systems need to be functionally integrated, to enable all those who need to see a customer's history to do so at the touch of a button.

Operational CRM using data to enhance the customer's experience of the organization's day-to-day activities

This not only allows the organization to offer a smooth and seamless operation to the customer, it also presents the opportunity to cross sell different products and services. For example, an insurance company can not only see how many policies a customer holds and when they are due for renewal, it can also advise customers of new or additional products. Developments in IT have led to computer packages which can now track and record every point of contact that the customer has with the organization across every department across the whole company. As they can be bought off the shelf as software packages operational CRM systems are commonly adopted by businesses in the B2B and services markets where multiple transactions take place with known customers.

Siboni (2004) has thus described CRM as a highly leveraged business strategy whereby an organization can use knowledge about customers to anticipate their needs and meet their requirements more closely. This results not only in overall satisfaction and high customer loyalty levels, but also a greater propensity for that customer to give the organization a higher share of their business. Thus, from a given number of customers, a good CRM scheme can *leverage* a higher amount of profit from each by concentrating on *customer share* rather than simply going after *market share*.

That CRM is able to assert such leverage is down to the two dimensions of CRM identified earlier:

- advances in information technology (IT) which enable organizations to not only collect and process customer data, but also to integrate all of the functions within the organization in order to present a uniform face to the customer;
- the use of customer knowledge as a valuable resource to improve profitability.

Commentators have varied in their opinions of which of these dimensions plays the bigger part in CRM, but for now we shall accept that both areas play an equal and complementary role in effective CRM management. Let us now take the following sections to explore both of these concepts in greater depth.

Information Technology and CRM

It was noted earlier that businesses have long gathered information about their customers. With relatively few customers this could be stored in the head. For example, in olden days the village blacksmith would most probably know all of his customers by name. He would know what sort of horses they had, how often they rode their horses, and what kind of horseshoe they required. He would even know how good a payer they were and whether they were good for credit or not. However, whilst small businesses who are offering a personal service might still be able to do this, for most it has become impossible to know every customer without keeping some sort of record. For many years this entailed some sort of card index, whereby the customer's details were kept on file, together with rudimentary details about their recent purchases. The system worked well, but it was cumbersome and not particularly efficient. It also placed a heavy burden on the staff who had to use and maintain it.

The computerized database changed all of this. Like a card index, a database could be used for storing customer data. Unlike a card index, however, a database could be accessed from anywhere within the organization where there was a PC terminal. Furthermore, the advent of wireless technology meant that remotely located laptops could also tap into the database—ideal for the field sales representatives who were operating away from the office. For the first time, any number of staff could access customer data that was bang up to date. Furthermore, they were able to input data as and when necessary. Thus the sales department could record orders taken and the price that had been agreed, the factory could record when the order had been produced, the shipping department could record when the order was dispatched, and the accounts department could record when the order had been invoiced and payment received.

Managing the Data

Bradley (2007) describes how an organization relies on good quality information which it uses in three important ways. First, there is the data which tells it how well it's doing—things such as sales statistics, turnover, and profitability figures. This data is gathered on a continuous basis because it is used for ongoing evaluation. Second, the organization will need information about its markets and the wider environment so that it can plan for the future. This type of data can also be gathered continuously through things like environmental scanning, but is also gained through ad hoc marketing research exercises. Finally, each functional area within the organization will require its own information in order to carry out its operations effectively (e.g. purchasing departments will have lists of suppliers and prices, manufacturing divisions will have data on machine capacity, and throughput, etc.)

MIS or MkIS?

Marketing Information System

the ongoing channelling of all organizational data into a central location from which it can be used for marketing purposes

Sometimes all of this information is brought together and channelled into a 'Management Information System' or MIS. This is so that senior managers within the organization can have all the information at their fingertips before they make important decisions in areas like investment, expansion, or resource allocation. For *marketing* decision-making purposes, the information is channelled into a **Marketing Information System** or MkIS. (See Figure 5.2.) It is important to make the distinction between an MIS and an MkIS. The function of the MkIS is to assist in *marketing*-based strategic decisions involving things like new product development, market entry strategies, customer segmentation, targeting, and positioning decisions.

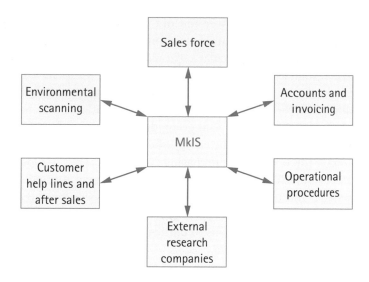

Figure 5.2 The Marketing Information System (MkIS)

Within the MkIS sits the database which drives CRM. The quality of the database is only as good as the information that it contains and it is important therefore that it is populated with data which can be accessed and used effectively. We noted above that most organizations will gather and use large quantities of data, or information, in the course of going about their daily activities. The problem is that this data is usually scattered across the organization in the hands of those functional areas which need it. The challenge for managing the CRM database is therefore to ensure that it is channelled through the MkIS into a format that can be used in marketing, as much of it is collected for non-marketing purposes

To illustrate the point, any airline has to gather large amounts of data about its customers just to enable it to generate a boarding pass. This information will include the customer's name and address, their flight destination, preferred seat location, flight class, amount and type of luggage, and any other requirements for the flight. From an operational point of view, once the customer has boarded and the plane has left, there is no further use for this data. However, from a marketing point of view, this data is hugely valuable as it can be used to identify different types of customers, such as frequent fliers, long-haul fliers, business fliers, etc. Coupled with the customer's address this knowledge can be used to make special personalized offers and start to create relationships with customers.

Data-mining

However, the function of a database is not just to store data; it also enables the user to manipulate and reorganize the data to provide meaningful information. As such, data across a number of data fields can be instantly retrieved and cross-tabulated to show trends, create profiles, etc. These data fields could include things like the customer's name, size, geographical location, date of last order, outstanding debt, etc.

This represents an improvement over the old card indices which could only be recorded in one dimension. For example, customers recorded in alphabetical order made it easy to pull out any particular customer's details, but if the user wanted something further, such as all customers in Scotland, they would have had to keep a separate data index based on geographical location. Trying to draw out something more meaningful, like the names of all customers in Scotland who had placed an order within the last three weeks, meant going through every index card.

CRM gets around this by using the power of databases to identify individual customers and keep a track on their purchasing behaviour. Thus a supermarket can look across its customer database, using information gained through its customer loyalty card scheme and using a simple search command, can quickly identify customers buying organic products and spending over £20 a week. This ability to cross-tabulate between different dimensions of data is called **data-mining** and is one of the reasons why CRM can now be so precise.

Data-mining
the reorganization and interrogation of data to provide meaningful information

Data-mining is used heavily throughout the market research industry to build up profiles of customers that can then be used to predict likely behaviour patterns and identify distinct segments. However, data-mining which results in customer profiling is only part of the story. With CRM the idea is to go beyond broad customer profiles and use the database to identify and target customers as individuals. With a good database, it doesn't matter how many customers the organization has because the purchasing behaviour of each one can be tracked and the customer contacted directly. This does not of course mean that someone at Tesco physically looks up every single customer to see what they've been doing. Rather, they use sophisticated data-mining programs to highlight opportunities to up-sell to a particular individual or ring alarm bells if it looks as if they are losing a customer. In other words, the data-mining programs are set up to be 'tripped' by certain observed customer behaviours, which then trigger an appropriate marketing response.

Using Information and Knowledge about Customers

Having considered IT as one of the defining characteristics of CRM, let us now turn our attention to the other—knowledge about customers. Whether the organization is using knowledge for analytical or operational CRM purposes, it is important to be clear about what information is needed. This generally breaks down into two areas: who the customer is (identifying the customer) and what the customer does (behavioural knowledge).

Identifying the Customer

The whole basis of CRM is that customers must be identified as distinct individuals so that they can be approached directly and a relationship established. This contrasts with much traditional marketing theory, which relies on aggregating customers together as markets or market segments (Peppers and Rogers, 2004). However, being able to identify each individual customer is easier for some organizations than it is for others. For instance, a university will know exactly who every one of its students is at any one time. Each student will have made an application, enrolled onto a course, and paid their fees. Their individual results will have been carefully recorded and gone through examination boards as they complete the different levels of their course. All of this data is held on a central database, or 'Shared Information' (SI) system, where it can be accessed by those who need it, such as course leaders and administrators.

Universities need this data in order to manage the delivery of their service to the student (in this case the provision of education and a learning experience). This is not uncommon—many organizations need to know their customers individually in order to provide their service. Banks, solicitors, accountants, insurance companies, travel agents, and utility suppliers (e.g. gas and water) are obvious examples. Additionally, companies offering direct delivery or mail order services (including Internet retailers such as Amazon) will also be able to identify individual customers. Indeed any company which knows your name, address, and perhaps other things about you is theoretically able to undertake CRM activities.

However, many organizations are not able to identify their customers separately. The manufacturers of products that are sold through a supply chain will not normally be able to know the identities of their final customers. This includes fast moving consumer goods such as baked beans and deodorants, newspapers and magazines (unless the customer has a subscription), clothes, CDs, DVDs, furniture, electrical appliances, and cars. One could be forgiven for assuming that only the providers of services can know their customers individually but this would not be true. Most shops, pubs, cafés, cinemas, theatres, bus and train companies would not be able to tell you the names of their customers, let alone where they live. If the organization does not have these basic details about its customers, it cannot theoretically practise CRM .

Peppers and Rogers suggest two steps that an organization can take to identify its customers in preparation for CRM activities. The first of these is to review what information the organization already has. The second is to get customers to identify themselves.

Reviewing Existing Information

We have already seen that many businesses gather information about their customers for operational purposes (e.g. the airline industry) and that this should be channelled into a central database or warehouse for it to be of value for CRM purposes. However, there can be risks and limitations involved in relying on existing data.

For instance, many organizations only have part of the data. Domino's Pizza for example knows the addresses of the customers to whom it delivers its pizzas. It also knows what sort of pizzas are preferred at that address (through its past delivery records). But it doesn't know the names of its customers. Although Domino's uses its database of addresses for direct marketing purposes, the best it can do is address its direct mail to 'Dear Pizza Lover'. Clearly this lacks the personal touch and may well limit the extent to which the company can form relationships with its customers.

Some organizations might think that they have all of the data but go on to misinterpret it. Some years ago a diehard football fan was keen to get tickets for an important up-coming cup clash. However, he realized that he would be unable to go along to the club's box office to buy the tickets because he would be abroad on holiday when they went on sale. Fearful that he would miss out, he asked his friend (who was not a football fan) to buy the tickets online, paying him back when he returned from holiday. The football fan enjoyed the game, watching his team win a hard-fought match, but it was his friend (who had no interest in football) who was subsequently contacted with club news and special offers as it was his name that had been recorded in the club's MkIS. This highlights the problem of not being able to recognize true customers because they do not interface with the organization's customer information recording systems.

Getting Customers to Identify Themselves

If the organization does not have sufficient information within its own records with which it can identify the customer, then it could always try to get the customer to identify themselves. This requires the customer to volunteer information (typically a name and address) to which the organization would not ordinarily have access. There are many ways in which this can be done; some of the more common ones are described below.

Competitions—usually requiring the customer to enter their name and contact details (such as postal address, e-mail address, or mobile phone number) in order to enter a prize draw. For instance, Tropicana, the fruit drink brand, has run prize draws for customers to win holidays. Customers are invited to tell Tropicana what their ideal holiday would be—relaxing on the beach, discovering and exploring new places, sports and activity-based or romantic city breaks—and then each day for a month a winner is drawn at random to receive their chosen holiday. In order to enter the competition, the customer has to register their e-mail address online and is also asked a number of questions about how frequently they buy fruit juice, which brands they usually buy, which types of juice they prefer, and from which retailers they usually buy their juice. With this kind of data, Tropicana is able to build up a picture of their customers and approach them directly with special offers that will be of specific interest to them.

Reward schemes—as discussed in the previous chapter, encouraging customers to carry loyalty, or reward cards can generate masses of useful data. By applying for the card the customer has to identify themselves and provide contact details in order to receive the reward. Unlike competitions, which identify the customer and provide a snapshot of their behaviour at any one time, the reward card identifies the customer and then tracks their behaviour on a continuous basis. One of the benefits of this to the organization is that they can not only identify which customers are spending more, but verify this by tracking their actual buying behaviour. Used judiciously the reward scheme can be a hugely powerful CRM tool, as Tesco have demonstrated.

Self-registration—requires the customer to identify themselves after the sale has been made in order to gain some benefit. Typical examples include registering for an extended guarantee to protect the product in use or registering to receive further product features. Virgin Mobile for instance is unable to identify which customers have bought its phones if they only use them on a pay-as-you-go basis, as there is no monthly contract. However, every new Virgin mobile comes with an invitation for customers to register their details. Virgin makes it clear what the benefits of registering are: to block the use of the phone if it is lost or stolen; to make it easier for customers to deal direct with Virgin in order to manage their accounts or top up their air time and also so that Virgin can send the customer updates on services and special offers. By combining the identity of the customer with their ongoing phone use, Virgin can develop individual CRM initiatives.

Subscriptions and season tickets—require customers to sign up for products and services in advance. In return the customer is guaranteed never to miss a copy of their favourite magazine or a ticket for the Cup Final should their team be lucky enough to get there. By signing up for these things, the customer is identifying themselves to the organization and thus paving the way for CRM. By contrast, the customer who buys her magazine every week at the newsagents or his match ticket every week at the box office will never be known to the organization.

Automatic payments—technology is enabling the cashless society to come a step closer and whereas customers paying in cash cannot usually be identified, those using other payment methods often can. Peppers and Rogers (2004) cite the example of Exxon Mobil, the fuel company, who issue customers signing up for their Speedpass campaign with special key rings. When the customer drives up to the petrol pump, a microchip within the key ring switches the pump on, records how much fuel is dispensed, and then automatically charges the customer's credit card. The customer is thus automatically identified whenever they fill up with petrol. London Transport System operate a pre-paid travel system called the Oyster card, which customers can use to travel on buses, tube trains, trams, and some national rail networks in London. The card can be automatically topped up either online or at a shop and the customer never has to worry about fumbling for small change when travelling. As the Oyster card is a smart card, it also captures details of the customer, both when the customer applies for the card and when they use it.

Linking Customer Identification with CRM

Peppers and Rogers (2004) suggest a number of customer identification activities that the organization must follow in order to implement an effective CRM system.

Define the customer's ID. The first of these is to decide exactly what will constitute the customer's identity. A name on its own is of little value as different customers can share the same name. A friend of the author was once amazed to find that over £20,000 had been transferred into his current account by his firm of solicitors. When he asked why, it transpired that the money should have gone to another client whose name he shared. If used, a name should be linked clearly with an address, telephone number, or postcode, although even then it is possible to have two members of the same household sharing a name (if they are father and son, for example).

One way to ensure correct identification is to give each individual customer an individual account number and then link this to their personal details such as name and address. Most banks, insurance companies, and utility suppliers ask customers to quote their account number in any correspondence, or write it on the back of cheques when paying bills. Although customers do not particularly associate themselves with a number, they are commonly used for identification purposes in CRM.

Link the customer's identity to all points of contact with the organization. One of the key objectives of CRM is to enable the organization to present a seamless face to the customer, no matter how many functional departments or operating divisions the customer has contact with. This means that the customer must be recognized at each and every point of contact, whether it be in person, by telephone, or online. These points of contact must also include enquiries, purchases, payments, and complaints. It may even include contacts made with overseas branches or operating divisions, e.g. banks or car hire companies. In practice this provides a major challenge to many organizations and requires considerable planning and investment in IT systems to pull off.

Barclay's Bank, for instance, offers its customer a wide range of financial services in addition to its core banking activities. These include the provision of credit cards, mortgages, pensions, and insurance policies, some of which are offered through subsidiary companies such as Barclaycard or the Woolwich. Each of these services operates independently, with separate policy statements and numbers, even for the same customer. However, at the touch of a button, Barclay's customer advisors are able to bring up all of an individual customer's dealings with the organization on a single computer screen. This not only gives the customer confidence that the organization knows what it is doing, it is also a valuable tool for cross-selling purposes.

Share the data electronically. That Barclay's is able to link its different operating divisions together like this is an example of how customer data is electronically shared. Not being able to share data in this way can lead to problems. The National Health Service faces a particularly big challenge as they must keep a close record on a patient's every medical complaint and treatment. One doctor might be able to do this, but when the patient visits different specialists for different medical conditions it starts to get complicated as each department can only diagnose and treat within its own specialist area and has somehow then to ensure that its records of the patient are shared with all other departments who might need them.

Sharing data means setting up organization-wide IT structures that are fully networked and able to transmit data in real time. This is a strategic initiative and requires the commitment of the whole organization from the top down. It cannot usually be implemented by one single department or operating division. Sales force automation is one result of electronic data-sharing as it enables the sales personnel in the field to be kept fully updated on a customer's current status. This is a huge leap forward in the management of customer relationships. Any salesperson who has ever taken an order from a customer not knowing that the customer's account is on hold due to non-payment of bills, or visited a customer to find that his colleague from a sister company visited the same customer that morning will testify.

Secure the data for customer privacy. The final area discussed by Peppers and Rogers regarding a customer's identity is to respect the customer's privacy. Thus, the data gathered should only be used within the organization and its availability restricted to those who really need it. This often presents a further challenge as it requires the creation of special access privileges to certain departments or members of staff instead of the easier blanket approach whereby the data can be seen by everyone inside the organization. Outside the organization customer details can often only be discussed with the customer themselves. This requires elaborate identity-checking techniques to ensure that the customer really is who they say they are. It can also create some frustrating situations whereby the customers' friends or family are not able intervene on their behalf. A large university in the Midlands found itself assailed by an irate student's father who was trying to find out his son's resubmitted coursework results. The student himself was backpacking across Australia but the university refused to divulge any information to the father.

Gathering Knowledge about Customer Behaviour

Once the customer has been identified as an individual, the next step is to track the frequency and the nature of their purchases and other contacts with the organization. Xu and Walton (2005) refer to this as behaviour modelling and suggest five types of customer behaviour which might be measured. These are purchasing behaviour, contact behaviour, response behaviour, retention behaviour, and migration behaviour.

Customer purchasing behaviour, monitoring what they have bought, how much they have bought, when they bought it, and how much they paid for it, is perhaps the most common form of CRM data to be gathered. Bradley (2007) refers to this as 'FRAC profiling'—frequency of use, recency of use, amount of use, and category of product being used. Not only is the collection of FRAC data relatively straightforward (because customer account numbers or loyalty schemes automatically monitor what customers have bought) it is also useful in developing **customer profiles**. The Tesco Clubcard is a typical example of being able to do this. Use of the card can reveal profiles such as:

> **Customer Profiles**
> a multi-dimensional picture of the customer based on his or her demographic characteristics and behaviour patterns

- life-stage and status (e.g. purchases of baby foods or children's products suggest a young family, purchase of lots of single-portion ready meals suggest someone who lives alone, etc.);

- attitudes (e.g. purchases of organic foods or 'Be Good To Yourself' products suggests someone who cares about what they eat);

- lifestyle (monitoring where and when the customer shops can suggest things about their lifestyle such as working patterns or free time).

When coupled with the identification factors already known about the customer such as name, age, gender, and postcode, a surprisingly detailed profile of the customer can be built up. From this it is relatively straightforward to develop targeted offers to individual customers.

Customer contact behaviour measures the frequency and type of contact that a customer has with the organization. There are two reasons why organizations might want to look at individual customers' contact behaviour. The first of these is so that they can recognize the customer's preferred method of contact, be it online, by telephone, post, or even in person, and thus design more personalized communications strategies. This is particularly true in B2B marketing situations where a good salesperson will know which customers can be dealt with online and which prefer a personal visit.

However, another reason why organizations are interested in customers' contact behaviour is that it enables them to distinguish between those who are more costly to deal with and those who are not. For instance, customers contacting their suppliers online might make things easier for the organization as they can be handled by an automated computer system. Conversely, customers requiring large amounts of personal assistance will cost the organization more as they rely on a member of staff to deal with them. 'High maintenance' customers or frequent complainers can be identified in this way, which as will be seen in Chapter 10, may well colour the organization's decisions on which customers they want to establish long-term relationships with.

Customer response behaviour measures the extent to which customers respond to sales and marketing approaches. As such they will also give the organization an idea of how worthwhile it is to try to build up a relationship with a particular customer. According to the old saying, there is no point in flogging a dead horse, and yet many companies continue to bombard customers with direct mail and messages, even though the customer never responds. This is wasteful practice. The best they can hope for is that sooner or later the customer will make an enquiry or buy something, but all too often the messages from the company become little more than wallpaper to the recipient and are ignored. At worse they can end up irritating the customer and driving them away.

Retention and migration behaviour is a measure of customer churn. We saw in Chapter 3 that excessive customer churn, or turnover, can be a drain on profits as the organization is constantly having to attract new customers to replace those who have left. By monitoring which customers remain and for how long, the organization can start to develop retention strategies to target those who are at risk of defecting. At the same time it is important for an organization to recognize its repeat customers, as these are more likely to form the core of long-term profitable relationships. Such customers can then be singled out for special treatment, such as rewards. Simply treating all customers as new runs the risk of alienating loyal existing customers as they can feel that their loyalty is either unrecognized, or worse, being taken for granted.

Additionally, by studying retention and defection behaviour, the organization can often identify longer term patterns in customer migration and segmentation. For example, Jaguar Cars in the USA became aware that its traditional customer base of conservative, older customers was moving away to newer brands such as Lexus. Jaguar's traditional customers were being replaced by young professionals who were more outgoing and individualistic in their lifestyles and values. One segment that typified these new customers was the affluent gay market of young professionals. Recognizing this trend, Jaguar targeted this group in its advertising and promotional campaigns.

Using Knowledge Strategically

We alluded earlier to the difference between operational and analytical knowledge. Much of the information described above in terms of identifying who the customer is and monitoring how they behave could be construed as analytical, in that it can help determine the organization's marketing strategy towards looking after existing customers and winning new customers. This is illustrated in Figure 5.3 below.

Loyal Customers are those who are strategically important to the organization. CRM systems can help identify such individuals, by looking at their size and spending power, together with their overall profitability. In this way the organization can calculate a customer's lifetime value based on their existing spending patterns. Clearly it would be in the organization's best interests to cultivate close, long-term relationships with these customers with the objective of ensuring that they are well looked after.

Similarly, existing customers who are *at risk* might be identified, based on their previous switching behaviour, level of repeat purchases, length of custom, and share of wallet. Depending on their overall profitability, the organization needs to take action here to shore up their support and try to turn them into loyal customers.

The Wish List represents customer segments that the organization would like to attract because they mirror the characteristics of existing key customers. Being able to use knowledge about prospective customers (as opposed to existing customers) highlights the importance of gathering non-transactional data, such as customer enquiries that did not result in a sale, or reasons for defection and also trying to find out about competitors' customers. From here the organization can determine who to regard as 'targets'.

Figure 5.3 Using knowledge to categorize customers

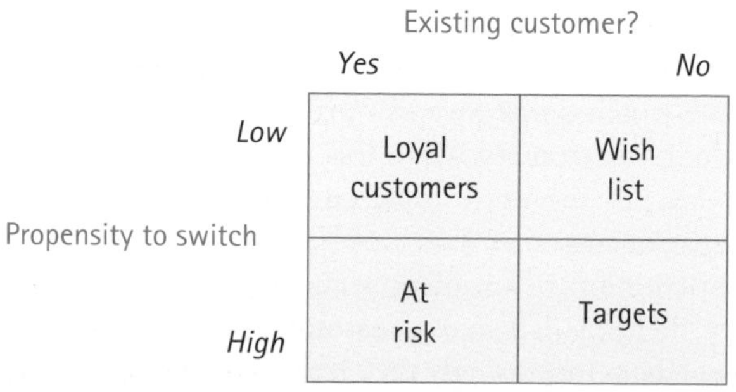

Targets are competitors' customers whose behaviour suggests that they can be persuaded to shift allegiance. Information on previous switching behaviour or satisfaction with present supplier might be useful here. Such customers will be the focus of an organization's new business targeting strategy.

The above examples demonstrate how analytical customer knowledge within a CRM system can include information not only on existing customers but also on prospective customers, defecting customers, and customers who are loyal to competitors. However, despite the strategic potential of such knowledge, Xu and Walton (2005) found that in practice most CRM systems are dominated by operational applications such as call centres and customer helplines.

Data Protection

As advances in IT have made it easier for organizations to gather, process, and disseminate more and more details about customers, concerns about individual privacy have grown. In the UK the 1998 Data Protection Act gives individuals the right to know what information is being held about them and imposes strict rules about how organizations can use this information. The Act is enforced by the Information Commissioner's Office (ICO), which has the power to prosecute companies or individuals who fail to protect personal information or make it available to third parties without the individual's prior agreement. The individual is further protected by schemes such as the Telephone Preference Service (TPS) and the Mailing Preference Service (MPS). These schemes enable the customer to opt out of unsolicited phone calls and mail-outs from companies using direct marketing techniques.

In effect these measures are giving control of the relationship back to the customer. By ticking a 'privacy box' stating that they do not wish to be contacted with further offers, or for their details to be shared with other companies, the customer is opting out of the relationship. Some believe that as privacy legislation gets even tougher, businesses will only be able to approach customers who have opted in, or given their permission to be contacted (Egan, 2004). See 'Permission Marketing' in Chapter 4.

However, the move towards more stringent privacy rules is not without its critics. Peppers and Rogers (2004) suggest that tougher European regulations to protect consumer privacy may threaten companies' growth prospects and be against the interests of the consumer. They argue that the collection and sharing of customer information, particularly in large global enterprises, is vital if these companies are to present a seamless, individualized service to each customer. They cite the example of an American airline which under Swedish privacy laws was prevented from storing data about its Swedish customers. With less information to hand it was unable to provide the same level of service to these customers as it was to its American customers where the use of customer data was less heavily regulated.

Aside from the irritation of unsolicited junk mail and spam, the rise in online fraud and identity theft has left many customers feeling vulnerable and protective about their personal data. Increasingly they feel that organizations have an obligation to use their personal data with integrity. Newell (2003) asserts that organizations which are seen to do this can claim to offer a differentiated service level—in other words handling a customer's personal data with respect—can add value to the relationship. As Newell is quick to point out, if a database is really working for the customer, then privacy would not be an issue. Some of the issues associated with the use of customers' personal data are outlined in Minicase 2, What's Coming Through your Door?

Minicase 2

What's Coming Through your Door?

According to a Direct Mail Information Service (DMIS) survey over 4 million items of personally addressed direct mail were sent to UK households in 2005, generating an estimated £27 billion worth of business. As an advertising medium, direct mail lies third only to the press and television in terms of annual spend. And yet to many householders direct mail is simply seen as 'junk'. The DMIS estimates that of all direct mail, 33% is thrown away unopened, another 22% is opened but not read, and the remaining 45% is opened and read. But direct mail is profitable. Around a third of the respondents to the DMIS survey said that they had responded to direct mail at least once in the previous 12 months, either by ordering products and services, making a charitable donation, requesting a catalogue, entering a competition or prize draw, or requesting more information.

The most prolific senders of direct mail were financial services organizations (banks, building societies, insurance companies, credit card providers, etc.) who accounted for 31% of total consumer mailings, followed by retailers (9.4%), charities (9.2%), utilities (6.1%), media (5.4%), and travel/tourism (5.3%). The government accounted for just 2.2% of direct mailings but enjoyed the highest response rate at nearly 25%. Other sectors achieving high responses were FMCG (15.8%), entertainment/leisure (15.6%), and pharmaceutical/health (12.8%). The lowest responses came from mailings by utility companies (3.2%) and the financial sector (3.8%), despite their massive spends. DMIS research suggests that the average cost of a consumer mailing is £44,133 with an average 326,029 mailings.

With so much at stake, the direct mail industry is keen to draw a distinction between legitimate mailings that are personally addressed and targeted at people who are likely to be interested, and random, or non-addressed mailings, usually in the form of leaflets and coupons. Unwanted, unread direct mail is simply a waste of resources and is an irritant to the customer. Indeed, such is the industry's concern over generating unwanted direct mail, that they fund the Mailing Preference Service (MPS) which allows people to opt out of receiving directly addressed advertising messages through the post.

Speaking in the *Sunday Times*, Experian Marketing Services' Lorcan Lynch stressed the need for a good database to support direct marketing: 'it is obvious that you will never get a response if you send the wrong information to the wrong people'. Mailing lists can come from a number of sources including an organization's own customer records, bought or rented from other organizations, or until recently the electoral register. This latter source has now been suspended following a High Court ruling that the supply of electoral register details to companies was a breach of human rights. The DMIS's research suggests that the highest responses come from 'warm' mailings, such as lists of previous customers, where there was already some connection between the organization and the recipient.

Questions

1. What are the benefits of direct mail: (a) to organizations; and (b) to consumers?

2. How can an organization ensure that its direct mail is relevant and of interest to recipients?

Sources:
The Letterbox Fact File 2006, Direct Mail Information Service
'Marketing: You've got mail—but its not junk, it's targeted', *Sunday Times*, 13 February 2005

Implementation Issues

As a result of its growing popularity CRM has become a big business. According to Andy Wood (2006) writing in *CRM Today*, two-thirds of UK companies are looking to CRM to drive their revenue growth and over 40% of top companies have appointed a senior head of CRM. Hundreds of CRM software applications are now available to help them implement CRM in their organizations and some contend that thanks to CRM the emphasis may have finally shifted from customer acquisition marketing to customer retention marketing (Wood, 2006).

CRM Software Applications

This diversity in software systems is carried through to the different types of CRM that they can perform. These include the following categories:

- customer service and support, including call-centre management and systems which enable customers to manage their own accounts without the involvement of service personnel (e.g. integrated telephony systems);
- communications support, including campaign management and multi-channel CRM (e.g. identifying which communications channels individual customers are most responsive to or prefer the organization to use);
- mobile CRM, including sales force automation, which enables distant users (e.g. field sales representatives) to use the system, often through wireless technology;
- personalization engines, which enable individually targeted offers to be made to customers (e.g. direct marketing);
- analytical CRM, which can be used to develop customer profiles, monitor trends and can be used for long-term planning purposes (e.g. data-mining);
- supplier or 'Business Relationship Marketing' systems, which although not directed at customers, can be linked in to CRM systems (e.g. loyalty schemes such as Nectar that are shared between a number of different partner suppliers).

Examples of prominent CRM software suppliers are described in Minicase 3, Examples of CRM Software. With such a wealth and diversity of CRM software available it is not surprising that many organizations have adopted CRM. What is surprising is how many of them have not had the success for which they hoped and this brings us to the final section of this chapter that looks at how easy—or otherwise—it is for an organization to implement CRM.

Minicase 3

Examples of CRM Software

Founded in California in 1987, PeopleSoft claims to be one of the biggest providers of CRM software in North America. One of its key selling points is its ability to customize its CRM applications to the needs of individual customers, thus making it more than just an 'off the shelf' solution. The company specializes in a number of market sectors including the energy industry, financial services, government departments, high technology sectors, and universities. Today PeopleSoft has grown so big that it has developed its own consultancy arm to help clients with CRM issues.

ProspectSoft is a UK-based operation concentrating on supplying CRM software to small and medium-sized enterprises (SMEs). Its programs are unusual because they can be integrated with existing accounting software such as Pegasus, Sage, or Exchequer in order to provide a seamless link between the firm's customer facing and back office operations. Additionally, the systems are modular, which means that they can be built up or added to in stages, thus enabling the firm to build up its CRM activities over time rather than going for a 'big bang' all at once. ProspectSoft offers a wide range of different applications including B2B and B2C (or a combination of both), customer help-desk management systems, call-centre management, mobile CRM, and integrated telephony systems.

Epicore CRM software solutions are aimed at 'mid-market' companies. They too offer modularized systems and claim to serve over 20,000 customers in 143 countries. Like PeopleSoft, Epicore offers supporting business consultancy services and full integration with other office-based systems—indeed, the company is a Microsoft Gold Partner in Europe (see Opening Case in Chapter 4).

Examples of other popular CRM software suppliers in the UK include Saratoga CRM; Onyx Customer Management; Microsoft Dynamics CRM; SuperOffice; and Goldmine.

Questions

1. Why might integration with other office software packages be significant for a company hoping to implement CRM?

2. What do you understand by the term 'off the shelf solution'? How practical do you think it would be for a firm to buy an 'off the shelf' CRM software package?

Sources:
CRM Today http://www.crm2day.com.news/crm accessed 30/08/07
Select CRM http://www.select-crm.co.uk accessed 15/08/07
PeopleSoft http://www.peoplesoft.com/corp/en/public_index.jsp accessed 17/02/08

CRM Implementation Problems

Despite the rush to adopt CRM systems, reports have shown that up to 75% of organizations do not achieve the benefits that they were expecting from their CRM and end up wasting their investment (Newell, 2003). According to *Marketing Direct Magazine*, of the £5.7 billion estimated to have been spent by European companies in 2001, nearly £4 billion was not used effectively (reproduced in Evans *et al.*, 2004). Various suggestions have been made for this high failure rate, most of which boil down into four broad areas:

- unsuited organizational culture and structure;
- ineffective management;
- unrealistic expectations;
- poor systems.

An organization's culture or structure can present a big stumbling block when implementing CRM systems because the system has to be integrated across a number of different functions and departments. For this reason, Woodcock *et al.* (2003) contend that larger organizations will find it more difficult to implement CRM than smaller ones, as more departments and more people are involved. Lack of commitment from staff, poor internal communication about the objectives of CRM, and poor staff training on the systems have all been blamed for the underperformance of some CRM systems.

Woodcock *et al.* suggest that CRM commitments and initiatives must be embedded into the culture of the organization rather than just being led by one champion within the company. However, they also point out that CRM designed by a committee can be equally fruitless as the organization risks going round in circles with plenty of talk but no action. Clearly, strong leadership is required if CRM is to succeed.

Ineffective management is a common theme when debating the reasons for CRM failure. Newell (2003) surmises that some managers lack a basic understanding of what CRM actually is. Some believe it is all about using technology to enable the organization to deal more efficiently with its customers—in other words how it can make things easier for the company rather than how it can add value for the customer. Many automated call centres have fallen into this trap and ended up alienating customers. Others believe that it is simply database marketing which can be used as a segmentation tool, missing the point that customer segments are aggregates, whereas CRM has the potential to operate at an individual level.

These misunderstandings are often manifested in the lack of supporting vision and an absence of an overarching customer strategy (Peppers and Rogers, 2004), which means that such managers will struggle to get the most out of CRM. Without an understanding of the full potential of CRM, planning for CRM becomes ineffective, with no clear goals or objectives to aim for.

If some managers do not fully understand the full potential of CRM, others have unrealistic expectations about what it can actually do. This is commonly manifested in the belief that CRM technology is a universal business panacea which will bring about a rapid and positive change in customer revenues and profitability for the organization. In other words, there is a belief that technology itself will do it all, rather than the people who work within the organization (Newell, 2003). Xu and Walton (2005) echo this, suggesting that integrating CRM should be about culture and processes rather than software and data flow. Integrating systems across the organization, training staff, and realigning existing business practices to work with the new systems requires commitment, thought, and planning. The belief that simply 'bolting' on some CRM software is a fast and straightforward route to success is a dangerous one.

This brings us to the final reason why many CRM systems fail—the software itself. Organizations attempting to develop CRM software applications in-house often end up with inadequate solutions that are simply extensions of their existing systems (e.g. sales order processing). With little or no analysis or intelligence gathering, they are unable to provide any real value to the business (Newell, 2003). As we have seen, there is a huge range of specialist CRM software suppliers who can provide standardized or tailor-made CRM solutions. However, Bull (2003) criticizes many organizations for not selecting software suppliers with more care and for under-budgeting for what they need. He argues that companies should negotiate with software suppliers to get the most appropriate and competitive system and preaches caution over what are often exaggerated claims of set-up times and operating efficiency.

Most commentators are agreed that strong leadership is a pre-requisite for successful CRM implementation. As Bull (2003) points out, CRM often involves a strategic change in terms of business processes and therefore requires a leader with vision and the ability to carry hearts and minds within the organization. It is important that CRM is not simply viewed as an IT project, but as something which is at the heart of the business. Data must be converted into knowledge that can be shared across those functions and partners who need it to meet the organization's objectives (Evans *et al.*, 2004). To this end, Bull suggests that a holistic approach should be taken, involving each department within the company at every level. Strong leadership, good internal communications, and an organizational philosophy which can support CRM are prerequisites to its successful implementation.

Chapter Summary

Customer Relationship Management (CRM) has been treated as a separate subject within the overall field of relationship marketing because it represents an easily recognizable and practical embodiment of customer-centric principles which most organizations can adopt. Although CRM can be viewed as a philosophy, it is philosophy that can be packaged (in the form of computer software) and sold, making it the closest thing that many organizations will come to relationship marketing. The two underlying principals of CRM are (a) that customer knowledge is valuable and can be used to develop specific customer strategies; and (b) that technology can be used to gather this knowledge and to manage subsequent customer relationships.

CRM technology enables the micromanagement of relationships by making it possible to recognize separate customers and treat them as individuals. Customer data is gathered from around the organization, from all customer touch points, which means that CRM must take an integrated approach, involving many different departments, functions, and operating divisions. The resultant data is fed into a central database where it can be accessed by different users from across the organization. CRM data can be used strategically (e.g. in identifying and targeting profitable customer profiles) or operationally, to ensure that the customer receives a seamless and efficient service (e.g. in managing a customer call centre).

A huge software industry has developed to enable firms to implement CRM. However, many do not achieve the success they expect, largely because of poor management (exemplified by unrealistic expectations and a general lack of understanding about what CRM actually is) or a poor fit with the organization's structure and culture (making integration difficult). With the manipulation of so much data, customer privacy has become an issue and organizations must work within strict data protection laws when storing and using customer data.

End of Chapter Case with Questions

Blyk—Tailored Advertising Via Your Phone?

From October 2007, making calls and sending texts on a mobile phone potentially become much cheaper for young people (aged 16–24) in the UK. This is because new mobile phone network operator Blyk launched its service offering free calls and texts in return for its users accepting directed advertising messages on their mobile phone handsets. Blyk's co-founder and Chief Executive, Pekka Ala-Pietila (ex President of Nokia) was confident that the service would catch on. Each customer signing up receives a free SIM card complete with 217 texts and 43 minutes of free air time to any UK network. Customers can top up themselves at 10p per text and 15p per minute, but it is unlikely that many would wish to do so as each month Blyk refills the SIM card free of charge. In effect, customers can enjoy free mobile phone use indefinitely.

In return for this, customers can expect to receive up to six adverts a day either from Blyk themselves, or from brands in which Blyk think the customer will be interested. This latter point is the key to Blyk's success. Ala-Pietila is keen to avoid the advertising messages being seen as junk or spam and the company therefore selects the message based on the likes and dislikes of each individual customer. In order to gauge this, each new customer signing up for the service is required to provide background details about themselves, such as age, sex, hobbies, interests, etc.

Blyk's intimate customer knowledge and its ability to target highly prospective customers with relevant offers make it an attractive medium for advertisers. This means that it can charge companies a premium rate for using its network, and it is this which pays for the free texts and airtime. Companies signed up include Coca Cola, L'Oréal, Buena Vista (part of the Disney Media Group), recruitment company Shepstone, and mobile gaming group I-day. Blyk has also signed a deal with the digital arm of Yell (the owner of Yellow Pages) to enable local advertisers to target people in their area with relevant messages and offers.

First Hop is the company providing the technology to run the advertising. They use the data they have in order to build up pictures of individual customers and match them to likely promoters. Customer profiles are further developed by monitoring their phone use, including Internet sites visited regularly and take-up of offers and promotions. Orange, the network provider behind the system, is very upbeat about its potential. Their own research suggests that customers are more than willing to interact with brands through their mobile phones. In a survey of 1,000 users, Orange found that over half would have no objection to seeing more advertising on their mobile phones, whilst only 6% were against the idea.

This is encouraging news to marketers who have struggled to keep up with the teenagers and young adults whose media preferences are constantly changing. This is a market which is often more receptive to social interaction on websites such as YouTube and Facebook than they are to traditional media such as television. So far, marketers have been slow to take up the challenges of these new media, but mobile phone advertising could be the way forward. The fact that Blyk is specifically aimed at 16–24-year-olds is significant because they are heavy users of mobile phones. They are also more accepting of the trade-off between free services and advertising, having grown up with the concept on Internet sites such as MySpace and Bebo.

The idea of mobile phone advertising is not new—easyJet's Stelios Haji-Ioannou has been toying with the idea for a while but has not yet found the right platform. In the USA, Virgin Mobile runs a service called Sugar Mama, which offers users free air time for every 'advertiser backed action' they take. This includes things like requesting more details, asking for a quote, etc. However, one mobile phone manufacturer is hoping to take the game to a whole new level. Motorola wants to monitor customers' calls and texts so that it can send them relevant advertising messages at the exact time they need them.

They claim that they have developed technology which will scan customers' text messages looking for key words which will alert companies to immediate marketing opportunities. If words like 'film' or 'movie' were picked up, for example, the customer could be sent an advert for a local cinema. GPS technology would enable the customer's exact location to be pinpointed, enabling highly location-specific messages to be sent. The technology is being further developed such that voice messages could also be scanned. Motorola admit that this would invoke big privacy issues, but claim that they would only scan a customer's messages with their prior permission and that this would most likely be in return for cheap rates or free air time such as with Blyk.

Despite this assurance, consumer privacy groups have deep concerns. Simon Davies, Director of Privacy International, summed it up: 'Phone companies may be talking about "opting in" to such schemes and providing customers with incentives to sign up, but down the line it is more likely that you will be penalized if you don't sign up'. Whatever the reality, there is no doubt that as technology advances the debate will grow in intensity.

Questions

1. What added value are the systems being offered by Blyk and (potentially) Motorola giving to customers?

2. Who stands to 'win' the most out of such arrangements?

3. To what extent can schemes such as these help to develop customer relationships?

4. What is the role of technology here?

Sources:
'Teens to get free mobile calls—with a catch', Richard Wray, *Guardian*, 26 March 2007
'Mobile phone firms plan to find out what you're talking about and tell advertisers', Elizabeth Judge, *Times*, 20 October 2007
http://www.blyk.co.uk accessed 02/11/07
http://www.theregister.co.uk accessed 06/11/07

Discussion Questions

1. Does it make sense to treat CRM as a distinct subject within the overall bounds of relationship marketing?

2. How might an organization using 'operational CRM' develop this into 'analytical CRM'?

3. What, if anything, does the study of 'Knowledge Management' have to do with CRM?

4. Is it possible to pursue CRM initiatives without technology?

5. Describe how a customer profile might be created through data-mining.

6. Other than the marketing department, suggest which other departments are likely to collect data that might be useful for CRM purposes.

7. Why is some direct marketing referred to as junk mail or spam? How can following the principles of CRM avoid this problem?

8. Think of all the organizations whose products and services you buy/consume. How many of them know your name? How can those that don't know your name find out?

9. Is knowing a customer's name and address enough to mount a CRM campaign? If not, what else might the organization need to do?

10. 'Data protection laws will limit the extent that organizations will be able to pursue CRM activities'. Discuss.

11. With so many software applications available, why do many organizations fail to find the success they expect with CRM?

12. What benefits does CRM bring to (a) the organization; (b) the customer?

Further Reading

Peppers, D. and Rogers, M. (2004) *Managing Customer Relationships. A Strategic Framework*, John Wiley & Sons, New Jersey.

Newell, F. (2003) *Why CRM Doesn't Work (How to win by letting customers manage the relationship)*, Kogan Page, London.

References

Bradley, N. (2007) *Marketing Research: Tools and Techniques*, Oxford University Press.

Bull, C. (2003) 'Strategic Issues in Customer Relationship Management (CRM) Implementation', *Business Process Management Journal*, 9(5), 592–602.

Christopher, M., Payne, A., and Ballantyne, D. (2002) *Relationship Marketing: Creating stakeholder value*, Butterworth Heinemann.

Drucker, P. (1996) 'The Information Executives Truly Need', *Harvard Business Review*, Jan.–Feb., 54–62.

Egan, J. (2004) *Relationship Marketing* (2nd edn), Pearson Education, Harlow.

Evans, M., O'Malley, L., and Patterson, M. (2004) *Exploring Direct & Customer Relationship Marketing* (2nd edn), Thomson Learning, London.

Gummesson, E. (1999) *Total Relationship Marketing. Rethinking Marketing Management: From 4Ps to 30Rs*, Butterworth Heinemann, Oxford.

Kotler, P. (2004) in **Peppers, D. and Rogers, M.,** *Managing Customer Relationships: A Strategic Framework*, John Wiley & Sons, New Jersey.

Newell, F. (2003) *Why CRM Doesn't Work (How to Win by Letting Customers Manage the Relationship)*, Kogan-Page, London.

Peppers, D. and Rogers, M. (2004) *Managing Customer Relationships: A Strategic Framework*, John Wiley & Sons, New Jersey.

Rodrigues, A. and Stone, M. (2002) in **Foss, B. and Stone, M.** (eds), *CRM in Financial Services*, Kogan Page, London.

Rowley, J. (2004) 'Partnering Paradigms? Knowledge Management and Relationship Marketing', **Industrial Management and Data Systems**, 104(2), 149–57.

Shultz, D., Tannenbaum, S., and Lauterborn, R. (1993) *The New Marketing Paradigm: Integrated Marketing Communications*, McGraw Hill Trade, New York.

Siboni, R. (2004) 'Get, Keep and Grow Customers in the 21st Century', in **Peppers, D. and Rogers, M.** (2004) *Managing Customer Relationships: A Strategic Framework*, John Wiley & Sons, New Jersey.

Wood, A. (2006) 'What did the CRM Industry focus on in the Year 2005?', **CRM Today**, 9 Jan.

Woodcock, N., Stone, M., and Foss, B. (2003) *The Customer Management Scorecard*, Kogan Page, London.

Xu, M. and Walton, J. (2005) 'Gaining Customer Knowledge through Analytical CRM', **Industrial Management & Data Systems**, 105(7), 955–71.

Websites

Business Link http://www.businesslink.gov.uk accessed 15/08/07

Investigation and Interpretation—Other Relationships

Electronic Relationships

Chapter Outline

Learning Outcomes

After reading this chapter you should be able to:

- appreciate the extent and nature of e-commerce;
- understand the implications of e-relationships;
- show how e-relationships can be used to develop B2B and B2C markets;
- determine the drivers and barriers to online shopping within a variety of retailing situations;
- suggest how trust can be developed in online relationships;
- demonstrate how e-relationships have led to customer empowerment.

Introduction

We saw in the previous chapter how organizations have been able to use information technology to find out more about their customers and get closer to them by adopting Customer Relationship Management (CRM) policies. This chapter takes a wider view of technology and relationships by considering how the rise of the Internet and electronic commerce has changed the way in which customers and organizations interact with each other. As all of this new technology is electronic, the prefix 'e' is generally adopted to describe any activity in this field (e.g. e-mail; e-communications; e-retailing; e-marketing; e-business, etc.).

e-Commerce

business which is conducted wholly or partly through an electronic medium

We thus begin by considering the extent of **e-commerce** and the implications this has had on traditional business structures and customer relationships. The idea of an 'e-relationship' might be considered something of a double-edged sword as on the one hand it brings together more customers and suppliers than ever before, but on the other hand eliminates any form of personal, face-to-face contact. For this reason, managing e-relationships has become a big challenge to many organizations, and those who get it right are often able to enjoy a considerable competitive advantage.

The chapter goes on to explore issues affecting the management of e-relationships in both B2B and B2C settings (including e-retailing—or e-shopping, depending on which side it is approached from), with particular emphasis on the challenge of building trust and commitment online. The chapter closes with a look at how customers are increasingly taking control of e-relationships and the implications of this for marketing managers.

Opening Case Study with Questions

Why Christmas Comes Early For Internet Retailers

According to the British Retail Consortium (BRC), Christmas 2007 was a disappointing time for the UK's High Street retailers who recorded their worst sales figures since 2004. Like-for-like figures across the sector stagnated in the run-up to Christmas compared to the previous year, with many shoppers holding back for bargains in the January sales. Interest rate rises, higher energy bills, falling house prices, and a general credit squeeze all led to shoppers tightening their belts in the final months of 2007. Faced with tough conditions, many retailers slashed their prices before Christmas—a risky tactic, as for many this is the period when they would normally expect to make most of their annual profit.

This contrasts sharply with figures released by the Office for National Statistics which showed that Christmas 2007 was the best ever for Internet retailers. The figures show that shoppers in the UK spent a whopping £15.2 billion on line during the final quarter of 2007. This represents an increase of 50% over the same period in 2006, which was itself the previous highest ever. In fact, Internet sales have been increasing every year since the late 1990s and now figure strongly in nearly every purchase category. In 2001, 22% of shoppers said that they would do some of their Christmas shopping online, a figure that had risen to 40% by 2005 (out-law.com). At the same time, as consumer confidence grows the value of items being bought over the Internet is increasing. Where once customers were content to buy books and CDs online, they are now splashing out on expensive electrical goods, such as washing machines and plasma screen televisions.

Traditionally, the busiest time for Internet shopping is lunchtime on the second Monday in December and 2007 did not disappoint. The Internet Measurement Research Group (IMRG), which represents Internet retailers, reported that at 1.09 p.m. on Monday 10 December, more money was spent online than had ever been spent before. Iggy Fanlo of price comparison website shopping.com explained why Mondays were so big for Internet shopping. 'People don't shop online over the weekend. They do their research offline, in the shops, and on Monday when they are back in the office they go online and compare prices.' Many people then wait until their lunch break before going online and placing their orders.

As a result, many High Street retailers managed to boost their seasonal performance through their online sales. Sales at Tesco.com and Tesco Direct were up 24% to £190 million over the Christmas period, whilst rivals Sainsbury's saw web sales rise by 40%. Department store Debenhams, saw one of the largest year-on-year on increases, with online sales up 85% in the four weeks to 5 January. Meanwhile Amazon, with no High Street shops to worry about, revealed that Christmas 2007 was its best ever, with online shoppers ordering 5.4 million items on 10 December alone.

Supporters of online shopping are quick to point out how easy it makes our lives. No fighting your way through the Christmas crowds to find the present you want, no driving round trying to find a parking space at the shopping mall, and no worrying about how you're going to find the time to fit everything in. *Times* reporter Sally Kinnes suggests that the Internet can even help you if you don't know what to buy. For instance, many men are notorious for not knowing what to get their wives or girlfriends, but by logging on to www.pressies4princesses.co.uk they can receive advice and guidance—including the top mistakes men make when buying for women. Similarly, by telling eBay's interactive present picker about your loved ones, it will suggest gifts that they might like. Buying for children can also be made easier by looking at www.toyretailersassociation.co.uk to find out what toys are in and what are out.

But it is not all good news for the Internet retailers. Many customers still worry about security and tend to stick with well-known traders. Others are concerned about whether they will receive their orders in time—in fact 20 December is usually the final day that online orders can be taken as it will be impossible to guarantee delivery before Christmas after this date. Those who leave their Christmas shopping too late will still have to dash to the shops. In previous years the big supermarkets have alerted their regular Internet customers to book early as online grocery orders surge in the period before Christmas. Failing to fulfil Christmas orders would be a 'PR disaster of heroic proportions' according to Ed Garner of retail consultancy TNS.

It seems clear, however, that online shopping continues to grow, the impact on traditional retailing channels could be far-reaching.

Questions

1. Describe the pros and cons from a customer's point of view of shopping online.

2. Do traditional 'bricks and mortar' retailers have any advantages over pure 'e-tailers' such as Amazon?

Sources:
'Why Christmas falls on 12 December' http://www.news.bbc.co.uk accessed 30/11/05
Sally Kinnes, 'Clickable Christmas' http://www.timesonline.co.uk accessed 04/11/07
'Festive sales at "three-year low"' http://www.news.bbc.co.uk accessed 15/01/08
IMRG Home News http://www.imrg.org accessed 17/01/08

Implications of e-Commerce for Relationships

It could be argued that the explosion of PC use and the accompanying rise of the Internet have brought about the biggest change in marketing relationships since the industrial revolution. The opening case shows how this is affecting the retail industry, but the impact goes further than this. In the developed world, it is rare to find anyone these days who does not have some sort of **e-relationship** with someone, be it an organization, a supplier, or groups of other individuals. This might be purely commercial (e.g. Internet banking or online shopping), it could be practical (e.g. online search engines or news channels), it could be operational (e.g. staff or student 'Intranet' sites), it could be recreational (e.g. Friends Reunited) or it could be personal (e.g. Facebook or Bebo). As a result there has been a scramble by organizations to capitalize on the opportunities raised by people's appetite for e-relationships.

> **e-Relationship**
> a relationship which is conducted wholly or partly through an electronic medium

Advantages of e-Relationships

From a purely commercial point of view, these opportunities arise through two main areas:

- reaching the customer;
- being better able to serve the customer.

Reaching the Customer

According to Newell (2000), the Internet is the most pervasive media channel the world has ever seen. He points out that it took radio 35 years to reach 50 million people and television 13 years, but it has taken the Internet just four years. Unlike radio and TV however, the Internet is interactive, meaning that businesses can not only reach huge numbers of customers with their offers, but those customers can respond immediately. Today it is estimated that over a billion people across the world have access to the Internet. Traditionally, countries with the highest Internet usage per head of population have included the Netherlands, the UK, Sweden, Canada, the USA, and Australia, all of whom came in at around 70% but the fastest growth in Internet usage is now taking place in the vast markets of China and India. The Chinese Internet Network Information Centre, Xinhua has reported that the number of Internet users in the country rose by 30% to over 132 million during 2006 (BBC News, 2006).

The implications to businesses of this reach can be seen in three broad areas. First. it has changed the basis of competition, because now, even small firms can compete in a global market with relatively little capital outlay. For example, Botham's cake shop in Whitby, UK now sells its cakes as far afield as Japan and the USA thanks to the Internet. This opening up of competition is of course a double-edged sword as it means that businesses that previously enjoyed a buoyant local market now find themselves under threat from any number of competitors around the world.

The second implication of the Internet's reach is that it has enabled customers in some markets to bypass traditional intermediaries and obtain products and services direct from the producer. This represents a fundamental shift in the structure of many markets and changing relationships between producers, intermediaries, and customers. Some of these issues are described in Minicase 1, which looks at the music industry, but other businesses could be affected too. Will people still go to the cinema to watch films if they can download them direct to their PCs? Will they still buy newspapers if they can get the news via their mobiles? Where will the profit come from for the producers of these goods and services?

Minicase 1

Shifting Relationships in the Music Business

The move to online music downloads is arguably the biggest shake-up the music business has ever seen, affecting the previously established relationships between music labels, retailers, musicians, and consumers alike. The development of music downloads has had a chequered history, as witnessed by the rise and fall and rise again of Napster. Developed in 1998 by 19-year-old college student Shawn Fanning, Napster was a file-sharing program which allowed users to transfer music files between each other. Songs downloaded in this way cost the user nothing and could be kept for ever. By December 2000 Napster had 20 million users, making it potentially the biggest repository of shared music in history. Increasingly aware of the revenue they were losing through this file-sharing, some of the big recording artists began to sue Napster for breach of copyright. Despite arguments that this breach was between users downloading music from each other and not from Napster itself, the courts ruled that Napster was illegal and in 2001 it was shut down.

Some have argued that suing Napster was a big mistake for the recording industry. Writing in the UK technical tabloid *The Inquirer*, Nick Farrell points out that with so many users, Napster could have provided the record companies with a huge database of online customers, had they chosen to work with them. Instead, when Napster closed, these users scattered to hundreds of smaller sites which made it impossible for the music industry to control them. Despite Napster's demise, its name remained synonymous with online music and as a result the company was bought out and relaunched as a legitimate business.

Today, the company offers a subscription service whereby customers pay a monthly fee and in return get the right to download on to their PC from the company's catalogue of four million music tracks on to their PC. Transferring tracks to another device such as an MP3 player costs extra and customers must keep paying the subscription or they will lose access to the songs. In effect they are 'renting' the music rather than 'owning' it. Napster's subscription model contrasts with the 'pay-per-track' model, typified for example by Apple's iTunes, where the customer buys each track, but is then allowed to keep it for good. With iTunes customers are currently charged £0.79 per track or £7.99 per album. Some companies charge less but have a more limited catalogue of music.

The big music labels are keen to ensure that they are fairly paid for the downloading and use of their music. As a result many will only make their music catalogues available with copy protection software known as digital rights management (DRM). DRM governs what customers can do with the tracks they download, in terms of how many CDs they can burn or how many playback devices they can download to. It also means that only authorized programs and portable players can use the songs; thus, for example, Napster users cannot play a track on an iPod. As a result customers are effectively locked into one system. DRM free songs are available (e.g. Apple's iTunes Plus) but these are more expensive and the choice of tracks is more limited as the music companies are more reluctant to release all of their music in this way for fear of piracy.

Whilst the industry argues about the best way to sell online music, traditional CD sales continue to decline and many High Street music retailers have struggled. In July 2007 Fopp went into administration, closing its 81 UK stores and making 700 staff redundant. In September of the same year Richard Branson sold his chain of 125 Virgin Megastores to a management team who rebranded them as Zavvi. However, what is interesting is that although sales of music CDs are down as a whole, this fall has not been matched by a corresponding increase in revenue from online downloads. Some in the industry have advocated a blanket licence to allow unlimited downloads free of the DRM-associated problems described above; but there is disagreement about what the customer should be charged for this. According to a report in IT journal *The Register*, even at 99 cents per song, some felt that this was too much for the average customer to fill an iPod but not enough to pay for the burden of a developing artist. As a result, the music industry is in a bit of dilemma—where are their future profits going to come from?

Questions

1. How has the onset of online downloads changed the relationship between the music companies, the online retailers, and the consumers themselves?

2. Compare and contrast the advantages and disadvantages for the consumer of buying music online and in a more traditional CD format.

3. How might traditional High Street retailers such as Zavvi and HMV ensure survival in the digital age?

Sources:
BBC h2g2: 'The Rise and Fall of Napster' http://www.bbc.co.uk/dna/h2g2/A741089 accessed 30/5/02
Farrell, N.,'Suing Napster was record industry's biggest blunder', *The Inquirer*, 13 March 2008
BBC News: 'Q & A: What is DRM?' http://news.bbc.co.uk/1/hi/technology accessed 02/04/07
BBC News: 'British CD sales drop 10% in 2007' http://news.bbc.co.uk/1/hi/entertainment accessed 09/07/07
Orlowski, A., 'iTunes sales "collapsing"', *The Register*, 12 November 2006

Other intermediaries who have suffered as a result of the direct reach of the Internet include travel agents. Many customers now book their flights directly with the airline, obtaining an e-ticket. They can also book hotels and even complete holiday packages directly, comparing locations, prices, and availability all online. Similarly, insurance brokers have found themselves out in the cold as customers find their best deals online. However, the Internet itself can create intermediaries.

Hollensen describes Internet intermediaries as hubs or portals because they bring together the suppliers of goods and services with potential customers. LastMinute.com is a good example as they look at the holidaymaker's requirements and then provide them with the options which most closely match these. If the holidaymaker is not sure what he or she wants, LastMinute.com enables them to browse amongst lots of different possibilities. As such, the electronic intermediary is providing the same thing as the High Street intermediary—it's just that they are able to reach more customers. Donaldson and O'Toole (2002) describe how new types of intermediary have been created by organizations that bundle our needs and wants on the Internet. Examples of these electronic intermediaries or hubs include iTunes (music), Facebook (social networking), Google (information), and Amazon (retailing).

The final implication of the Internet's reach is on the structure of businesses themselves. As Gummesson (2002) points out, if the organization is dealing with its customers online, then its personnel no longer have to be present in the location where the transaction takes place. This has led to many organizations streamlining their operations and reducing their costs. A good example is the banking industry. Many High Street branches have been closed in recent years as the big banks develop their Internet banking services. Online transactions such as electronic money transfer maximize value (Donaldson and O'Toole, 2002) by reducing overheads. However, this too can bring problems as many customers have reacted negatively to the impersonal nature of such business. We shall explore this area in greater depth shortly when we look at e-relationships in B2C markets.

Being Better able to Serve the Customer

The second big opportunity for businesses which e-commerce has thrown up is the ability to serve the customer in a better way. We noted in the last chapter how advances in technology have enabled organizations to gather information about the customer each time they visit a website, use a reward card, or make an electronic purchase. This has given rise to what Peppers and Rogers (2004) refer to as the 'Learning Organization', which is able to use knowledge about customers to create a competitive advantage by building intelligent profiles of the customer (Gordon, 1998). This is particularly true for companies serving mass markets where it was hitherto impossible to know each customer individually. As a result companies can not only develop the products and services that specific types of customer want, they can also personalize their offers to individuals.

This is, of course, one of the basic principles of CRM, which was discussed in the last chapter. As Gordon (1998) puts it, technology has put the word 'custom' back into 'customer' because each one can now be dealt with on an individual basis. This is neatly summed up by Newell (2000) when he quotes Jeff Bezoz, the founder of Amazon: 'We can make it your store, tailor-made for you. If we have 4.5 m customers we shouldn't have one store, we should have 4.5 m stores.'

Theoretically, then, e-commerce should allow the development of closer customer relations. It is clear how this might work in some B2B marketing situations where companies invest in computer-based technologies so that they can work more closely together. However, in B2C markets, it is less clear how inclined customers are to get closer to an organization through e-relationships. This leads to some negative implications of e-commerce for relationships.

Disadvantages of e-Relationships

A potential criticism of e-relationships is impersonality, because all business is done on a computer screen and the customer never gets to meet or even talk to a real human being. It was noted earlier that many businesses have been able to reduce their overheads and streamline their businesses by shifting their relationships with customers online. However, as Egan (2004) notes, it can be dangerous to assume that technology can effectively replace human relationships, particularly when the technology is aimed at increasing the efficiency of the organization rather than adding value for the customer.

If customers feel that they are being disadvantaged by being pushed towards an electronic relationship, they will resist. A good example of this is the automated call centre. Consumer group *Which?* (2006) claimed that customers using such call centres, were having to wait more than six minutes on average if they wished to speak to a human operator. They reported that in a survey of 1,000 people, almost 60% of them had changed to a different service provider in the previous year because of this. According to *Which?*, banks, utility companies, Internet providers, and telephone firms were the main culprits.

Such is the problem that American computer expert Paul English produced a 'cheat sheet' showing disgruntled customers how to bypass the automated call centres of hundreds of organizations in order to be put straight through to a human operator. In the UK, the West Midlands-based *Express and Star* newspaper reported in 2006 that these included:

- Vodaphone: press the zero key repeatedly, ignoring the 'invalid selection' message;
- NHS Direct: press the star key twice;
- British Gas: ignore all prompts and do not press anything, thus fooling the machine into thinking that you do not have a touch tone telephone.

Customer frustration at not being able to talk to a human is not just confined to automated call centres, however. Many banks have also found themselves in the firing line for closing down their High Street branches, thus denying customers the ability to visit their own branch to discuss their own financial affairs with their own bank manager. At least one bank, NatWest, has recognized this and has developed a strategy of re-opening local branches. This is underlined in their 'Another Way' advertising campaign, emphasizing the fact that unlike their competitors, their branches have not been turned into 'trendy wine bars' (Godson, 2005).

Marketplace

a physical place, such as a building, where people go to buy and sell things

The Nature of e-Relationships

Marketspace

a non-physical, Internet-based market where things are bought and sold electronically

Gummesson (2002) refers to the change in the way in which goods and services are bought and sold as the switch from physical **marketplace** to electronic **marketspace**. The difference between the two lies in their content, context, and infrastructure. In terms of content, when buying in the marketplace the product is present, when buying in marketspace, the product need not be present. Thus a customer buying a book in a shop such as Waterstone's (marketplace) can pick up the book and thumb

	From business	From consumer
To business	B2B	C2B
To consumer	B2C	C2C

Figure 6.1 Different e-Commerce markets

Source: Hollensen, *Marketing Management* (2003), Pearson Education Limited. Reproduced with the permission of Pearson Education

through it, whereas a customer buying a book on Amazon (marketspace) cannot. This does not mean that the customer is necessarily disadvantaged by shopping online as all of the information which is available to the customer in the shop (such as chapter content, size of the book, appearance of the book, alternative titles) is also available on the Internet. In marketspace, however, instead of the customer being present in the seller's shop, the customer can be anywhere—at home, in the office, on the train, even up a mountain, and there is no need for the customer and the seller to ever meet. This is the context which Gummesson talks about—the fact that in marketspace the interaction takes place on screen instead of face to face. Finally, the infrastructure is completely different between the two, as the marketplace requires a physical building, such as a shop, whereas the marketspace requires a computer network.

Of course these principles are nothing new. For years the characteristics of the marketspace have existed, only not through electronic means. In principle, home catalogue shopping is exactly the same as buying over the Internet, but the sheer scale, reach, and practicality of the Internet have created a marketspace far beyond the scope of mail order catalogues. To illustrate, Hollensen (2003) highlights four different e-commerce markets, along with examples, all of which have been profoundly affected or enabled by the Internet (Figure 6.1).

Students should be familiar with the concepts of business-to-business (B2B) and business-to-consumer (B2C) marketing relationships as they form the bedrock of any study of marketing. The impact of e-commerce has been enormous in both of these areas, whether it be through Electronic Data Interchange and Internet trade in B2B or the development of online shopping sites such as Amazon in B2C. We shall explore the extent of e-commerce in these areas later. For now, let us briefly examine two markets that are less frequently acknowledged in traditional marketing literature—consumer-to-consumer (C2C) and consumer-to-business (C2B)—both of which have been hugely enabled through e-relationships.

e-Relationships in C2C

The principle of a C2C market is nothing new—many people have at one time or another visited a car boot sale or used the small ads in local newspapers. These vehicles enable people to buy and sell items with other, like-minded individuals.

Traditionally they have been used these to get rid of things which were no longer wanted (usually at low prices) and to pick up things which were wanted at a bargain. The thrill of being able to make some money from something which was otherwise useless, coupled with the satisfaction in finding something of value at a much cheaper price than it might have cost in the shops, have made the C2C market an appealing and moreish place for many. The Internet has taken the scale of all this to a whole new level through the development of consumer auction sites such as eBay. See Minicase 2, eBay Comes of Age.

Minicase 2

eBay Comes of Age

Founded in 1995 by 28-year-old Pierre Omidyar, eBay has become one of the Internet's most iconic brands. The name derives from Omidyar's consultancy firm Echo Bay Technology Group where the entrepreneur had already made his name developing e-commerce solutions. The story that eBay was set up to allow Omidyar's fiancée to trade Pez sweet dispensers with fellow collectors has since been denied, but what is indisputable is the company's growth since then. In 2005 the BBC's *Money Programme* reported that eBay boasted over 100 million users, in over 30 countries including the USA, UK, Germany, India, Australia, Mexico, and China. Although many of these countries had their own branded sites, allowing users to trade with each other in local currencies, international trading between individuals in different countries became commonplace. eBay was floated on the stock market in 1998 making Omidyar a multimillionaire—a 2007 profile in *Get Inspired* estimated his wealth as $8.5bn.

eBay makes its money by charging users a listing fee and then a small percentage of the selling price when the product is sold. The company also owns the PayPal secure payment system, which can charge fees of its own. The site overcomes issues of trust between buyers and sellers by operating a rating system whereby users can view the transaction history of a buyer or seller and add their own rating according to their experience. Virtually anything can be traded over eBay although the company will not allow the sale of weapons, human body parts, drugs, or bootlegged items, amongst other things. Some of the more unusual things bought over eBay include Britney Spear's chewed gum (£140), the original Hollywood sign ($450,400) and a Volkswagen Golf previously owned by Joseph Cardinal Ratzinger before he was elected Pope Benedict XVI ($277,171).

Despite safeguards, eBay has been hit by concerns over security. In 2007, a report in the *Sunday Times* described how conmen were targeting the UK's 20 million eBay users by using stolen identities and fake secure payment sites. The company was reported to be 'working tirelessly' to detect and prevent such scams. Another potential issue was identified in a BBC news report, claiming that in the UK alone nearly 10,000 people earned all or some of their living from trading on eBay. The report highlighted the grey area between those who were buying and selling privately and those who were doing it professionally to supplement their income. The report concluded that the Inland Revenue would look at ways in which it could tax this income, by taxing eBay—a move which could well cause eBay to increase its fees to users.

> ## Questions
>
> 1. To what extent has eBay created a market where none existed before?
>
> 2. If eBay is all about C2C relationships, how can it be a business listed on the stock exchange?
>
> 3. Outline the advantages and disadvantages of C2C relationships as exemplified by eBay.
>
> Sources:
> 'Pierre Omidyar' (Profile) Get Inspired Business pioneers, 12 March 2007
> '"eBay" Money for Old Rope?', BBC *The Money Programme*, broadcast 25 February 2005
> 'Conmen hijack eBay user identities', *Sunday Times*, 21 October 2000

Now, millions of people all over the world can trade with each other and a whole new industry has been spawned—the online auction. According to the Office of Fair Trading (OFT), an estimated 79 million transactions took place on these online auction sites in 2005, with an overall value close to £2.8 billion. Such is the attraction of these sites that Hollensen (2003) describes them as a new form of entertainment, where buyers and sellers develop a sense of community which keeps them coming back for more. The lack of physical boundaries and the near inexhaustible supply of customers have enabled all kinds of consumer to take part, no matter where they are based or how esoteric their interests.

Such sites are understandably attractive in areas where large geographical distances separate the population, such as Canada, the USA, and Australia, where the nearest specialist store may be hundreds of miles away. However, they seem equally popular in the more densely populated countries of Europe, suggesting that their attraction lies in more than just convenience and does indeed involve some sort of social entertainment. The OFT (2007) suggests that 11% of time spent on the Internet in the UK is made up of visits to eBay. It would appear that these sites have not only acted as relationship enablers between customers but that customers have developed relationships with the sites themselves.

e-Relationships in C2B

C2B markets are a relatively recent phenomenon and have been largely enabled by the Internet. These operate along the lines of what Hollensen (2003) describes as a 'reverse auction'. Instead of the traditional business model where companies set the price and customers follow, in a C2B market customers propose a price and businesses can then bid to accept them, depending on how much they want the business. The more customers that are involved, the more the price is likely to be reduced and businesses have to be careful about what they can and cannot afford to do. Unlike C2C where items are likely to have a value which is subjective to an individual consumer (such as collectables), C2B markets operate around goods and services with mass market demand that are available from a variety of different suppliers. This includes things like car hire, hotels, airline seats, and insurance.

The Internet has helped because it can provide a focal point for customers to come together and set their prices. Websites such as Priceline.com and HedgeHog.com are examples of this. Priceline specializes in travel services such as airline tickets and car hire. Although it still offers a C2B vehicle, it has in recent years moved towards the more traditional B2C model where businesses present prices to customers. HedgeHog.com is geared towards organizational procurement and enables industrial customers to post up specifications of things they wish to buy. Suppliers can then compete against each other online to win the business. Clearly, the customer is in the driving seat because they initiate the transaction and all the bids from suppliers are live and can be seen by all those taking part in the auction.

The examples above show that e-commerce has changed the way in which business can be done and has opened up whole new markets. In doing so, it has ushered in new levels of competition and given the customer more power and greater choice than ever before. However, it is in the B2B and B2C markets where most organizations have had to come to terms with the impact of e-relationships and it is to these areas that we now turn.

e-Relationships in B2B

It could be said that e-commerce began in B2B marketing where companies would network their computers together so that they could quickly exchange large amounts of data between each other. Such arrangements enabled the adoption of lean production planning and just-in-time (JIT) supply chain management. They also helped companies to link their research departments, so that they could develop products together thus pooling resources and reducing the overall costs to both parties.

The sharing of data through networked computers is known as electronic data interchange or EDI and has become a powerful tool in the management of supply chain relationships. Suppliers and buyers using EDI have to work closely together to develop compatible systems, often requiring the investment of considerable capital to ensure their success. As a result, close, long-term relationships are formed between the two organizations. The benefits to both are clear. The supplier is able to tie in a customer over a long period of time (the investment that the customer has made in EDI will act as a switching barrier) while the customer is able to secure a long-term supply that is exactly tailored to their needs.

However, as the Internet became more prevalent, businesses began to undertake basic transaction functions with each other (such as ordering, invoicing, and payment) online, thus doing away with all of the traditional paperwork and documentation associated with such activities. For organizations handling large numbers of transactions, this represented a huge cost saving. For instance, the UK's National Health Service has reduced transaction costs by doing business electronically (NHS Shared Business Services, 2006). When one considers how many orders the NHS makes annually, from drugs and medical equipment, through to food for the canteen and stationery for the offices, it is clear that they are able to make huge savings on their operating costs by doing business electronically.

The implications for both supplier and customer organizations are profound. Not only can they reduce their overall transaction costs dramatically by doing business electronically; they may well find themselves excluded from the market altogether if they can't do business electronically. It therefore makes sense for organizations of all sizes to adopt the principles of e-business. As well as enabling the firm to compete in the first place, many argue that electronic interactions create relationships with customers and suppliers that are stronger than non-electronic ones (Rodgers *et al.*, 2002).

This picture is backed up by the research of Pavic *et al.* (2007), who suggest that the Internet is more than just a technology, that it can and should be used to manage customer and supplier relations and thus enhance business performance and success. However, they claim that many smaller businesses only use the Internet for sending e-mails and gathering information. In other words they are not using e-business to create value. Pavic *et al.* suggest that this is due to a number of reasons, including the business owner's attitude towards new technology, a lack of knowledge about how to use e-business to build an advantage, and a lack of financial resources required to develop an effective e-business system. This could be rather alarming if one accepts the argument of King and Clift (2000) that soon the prefix 'e' will be dropped from e-business, because all business will be conducted electronically.

Hollensen (2003) describes how the tools of e-business can add value at all levels of the buyer/seller transaction process. During the initial information search, buyers will need as much data as possible about what is available and at what terms, whereas suppliers will need to know as much as possible about what the buyer's precise requirements are. The Internet is an ideal tool through which to gather this data quickly and comprehensively. Rather than simple billboard sites, suppliers can provide websites that act as electronic catalogues. These not only provide detailed product information, but allow prospective buyers to configure product options by submitting their own specification requirements. Such websites allow personnel in the buying organization to download data that can be built into their own plans and used to seek internal approval for large or complex purchases.

Once the buyer has the required information, the next stage of the B2B buying process is negotiating with the supplier for the best deal. Internet-based information systems can add value here by ensuring that all parties in the negotiation process have access to the data they need in real time. Complex models and projections can be produced at the click of a mouse, enabling both parties to see the net value of any offering which is on the table. Sometimes buyers and sellers are brought together on a central 'hub' hosted by a third party. This is particularly common in commodity markets (oil, grain, rubber, ore, etc.) where the product is undifferentiated and can be traded unseen. Negotiation takes place through an 'aggregator', who then arranges the order fulfilment and it is possible that the buyer and seller never know each other's identities.

The third stage of the B2B buying process is the actual transaction itself. We have already seen how orders, invoices, and payments can all be made online, thus generating huge cost savings over paper-based systems. Other benefits of e-business at the transaction stage include the ability to track orders all the way through the system, including its process through the supplier's factory. Thus, a buyer can see at any one time where the product they have ordered is and when it will be delivered. Taken to a higher level, close cooperation between the buyer and the seller enables hugely efficient 'just in time' systems to be operated.

The final stage of the buying process is the post-purchase evaluation. This can range from a simple e-mail-based after-sales help service to complicated automated service systems. For instance many installations of capital equipment such as photocopiers, machine tools, heating, ventilation, or electronic security systems come with an on-board computer which can be connected directly back to the supplier's maintenance and service department. This will monitor the performance of the equipment in the customer's premises and allow the supplier to contact the customer when a service is due. Sometimes, the supplier can tell the customer that they have a fault with one of their machines before the customer even knows it! Service engineers in the field can be instantly updated about the status of a customer's machine before they even arrive. Such systems add value for the customer because they no longer have to worry about monitoring the service intervals of their equipment and experience less downtime. The supplier benefits because such systems tie the customer in and ensure an on-going relationship.

e-Relationships in B2C

It is clear that e-relationships have made a big impact on B2B, but it could be argued they have made an equal if not bigger impact in the B2C market. Just as in B2B, e-business can add value right the way through the customer's buying decision process in the B2C market (see Figure 6.2). It is important that organizations understand how they can develop their e-business systems to tap into this process in order to give themselves a competitive advantage.

Figure 6.2 e-Business and the purchasing decision process

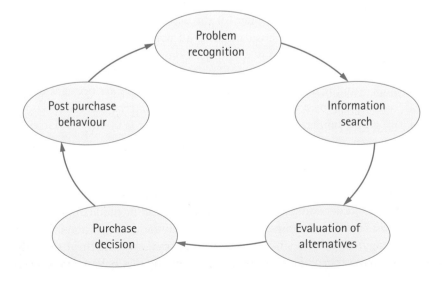

Problem Recognition

The first stage in the process might involve the customer having a problem in a negative sense (e.g. 'my car has broken down') or simply recognizing a need or desire (e.g. 'I fancy a holiday in the sun this year') In each case the customer begins to think about what they can buy that will solve their problem or fulfil their desire. Businesses can use e-relationships to pre-empt these needs and wants in a number of ways.

One way is to use their databases containing information relating to past customer behaviour to identify individuals who are likely to have a need at a particular time. For example, insurance companies can remind customers that their policies are due for renewal, a garage might advise that a customer's car is due for a service or an oil change, and an airline might send out details of flight offers, knowing what types of holiday a customer has previously booked. Alternatively, the organization might use the data they have to build up individual customer profiles which can then be used to predict what other products or services they might want. Amazon does this when it recommends books that you might like, based on your previous purchases. This is of course classic CRM as discussed in the last chapter.

Another way in which organizations might pre-empt customers' needs is what Peppers and Rogers (2004) refer to as *automatic replenishment*. Here the customer sets up their own usage and delivery schedules for things like groceries, regular medication, garden products, etc. In principle this is nothing different to traditional doorstop milk or newspaper deliveries. However, the Internet enables the whole process to be managed quickly and efficiently on line (no more notes tucked into milk bottles). An example of this is grocery company Abel & Cole who deliver fresh, organically grown fruit and vegetables. Customers can order boxes of products online, made up to their own specific requirements and which are then delivered direct to their doors. As well as fruit and vegetables, Abel & Cole also deliver milk, eggs, meat, fish, bread, and wine.

Peppers and Rogers point to a number of benefits to both suppliers and customers from this kind of system. From the supplier's point of view, they get to know their customers very closely, in terms of what they like, how frequently they buy, how much they buy, etc., thus enabling them to meet their customers' needs more exactly. As the customer comes to rely on the service a switching barrier is created and they are more likely to remain. Over time, trust is established which creates greater opportunities for cross-selling and also leads to an increased share of the customer's wallet. From the customer's point of view, they receive a service which is tailored to their exact requirements and have less worry about running out of the things they use regularly. It also relieves them of the chore of regular shopping trips and enables them to conduct their household management activities at times that suit them.

Information Search

Once a need is recognized, the customer may embark on some sort of information search to find out what products or services might fulfil the need, how much they will cost, where they can be obtained, etc. Here, the Internet really comes into its own with search engines such as Google able to scan masses of data in seconds. Just typing in something such as London Pet Shop throws up nearly half a million entries.

In some cases information overload can occur and the customer can have difficulty sifting through to find what they really need.

The first priority for businesses, therefore, is to make sure that customers can find them quickly and easily. One way of doing this is to try to ensure that their business comes out at or near the top of a search engine's listings. An alternative approach might be to obtain a web link on another organization's site. Clearly this will have to be negotiated and there will have to be benefits for both parties. Examples might include airline websites hosting links to car hire firms, or private hospitals hosting links to health insurance schemes. Finally, many third-party websites have been developed to hold details of products or services available in a particular area. Thus, a customer doing a Google search for a 'Manchester Airport Hotel' might be re-directed to HotelNet.co.uk which helps them narrow their search of type of hotel, exact location, and availability. In many ways these sites are the electronic version of the paper-based directories which businesses would pay to advertise in.

Evaluation of Alternatives

Once the list of alternatives is narrowed down, the Internet enables a quick and easy comparison to aid the customer's purchase decision. This could be informally through online communities, chat rooms, or Web logs set up by like-minded individuals who wish to share their experiences. For instance, Taiwanese students thinking about coming to the UK to do a degree can log onto chat sites to find out about what their peers are saying about studying in the UK, what the different universities are like, etc. Clearly, the UK universities would like to use these sites for marketing purposes, but to do so would destroy their value, as they would no longer be seen by students as being impartial. The best thing an organization can do is make sure that its service (to existing and potential customers) is exemplary, so that the customers themselves are happy to give positive referrals on informal chat sites.

In addition to these informal chat sites, the Internet has enabled the rise of more structured or formal sites where customers can objectively compare different products and services. Examples include Which.com, covering a wide range of consumer products and services and uSwitch where customers can find out which utility supplier offers the best deal for their needs. Online suppliers such as Amazon are also able to let customers tell each other what they thought about different books, etc. This is something that a traditional bricks-and-mortar shop would not easily be able to replicate.

Purchase

Within the consumer-buying process, one could argue that it is in the actual purchase itself where the Internet struggles the most. One reason is trust. When buying online, not only do customers have to trust that their payment details will be safe, they also have to trust that the product they have ordered will arrive safely and will meet their expectations (Harridge-March, 2006). Additionally, when buying online, in most cases the customer does not get the product immediately—they have to arrange for a physical delivery. We shall look at both these issues in more detail shortly, but one result is that some customers conduct their research online and then go to a real shop to buy the product. Alternatively, some shoppers assure themselves of the quality of a product first by visiting a real shop, and then go online to get the best deal. Both of these scenarios suggest that a retailer would be best served by having a physical High Street presence as well as an online retail site.

Post-purchase Behaviour

The Internet can add much value to the customer–supplier relationship at this stage of the buying process. For one thing it will be much easier for the supplier to contact the customer after an online transaction, in order to say thank you, check that everything is satisfactory, make further offers, etc. This is because they know who the customer is and have already started to find out something about them. This is the basis for the CRM initiatives we looked at in the last chapter. From the customer's standpoint, assuming that everything has been satisfactory, they know that they have found a good supplier with whom to do business. In this sense doing business online has brought the customer and the supplier closer together than would often be the case through a typical shop-based transaction.

The Move to Online Shopping

As a result of these advantages, more and more consumers have turned to online or *e-shopping* across a whole variety of products and services. This has led to some dire predictions about the future of the traditional bricks and mortar retailer. At the turn of the century, De Kare-Silver (2001) made his prediction that there would be a revolution in the way shopping took place and that within five to ten years many of the 'traditional' shops would cease to exist. He predicted that this revolution would hit nearly all retailing sectors, including supermarkets, banks, and cinemas. He based his predictions on the assertion that increasing numbers of customers now prefer to shop online and that it would only take a 15% drop in store traffic to make many UK stores unprofitable. This would result in an increasing number of empty shops which in turn would have a knock-on effect on other shops as fewer customers visited High Streets and shopping malls.

Others (e.g. Gilbert, 2003) have been more cautious, arguing that most retailers will simply develop Internet selling sites to run alongside their store-based operations (what some commentators have described as **clicks and mortar** operations). Certainly, many retailers have now gone down this route, with some (e.g. Next and Past Times) operating a multi-channel shopping approach consisting of physical shop, Internet site, and mail order catalogue. Perhaps the biggest immediate casualties will be those retailers who can offer neither the benefits of the Internet nor the physical shop in terms of customer relations—the mail order catalogue companies. In January 2008, the *Bradford Telegraph and Argus* announced that the catalogue company Empire Stores was to close with the loss of up to 850 jobs. Tesco is an example of an organization which has successfully combined the benefits of physical shopping in a real store, with the convenience of shopping online (see Minicase 3, 'You Shop. We Drop').

Clicks and mortar
a physical 'bricks and mortar' shop which also has an Internet-based sales operation

Minicase 3

'You Shop. We Drop.' The Tesco Online Shopping Experience

The principle of having groceries delivered by the shop directly to your door is nothing new as Granville's delivery bike in the hit television comedy *Open All Hours* demonstrates. However, the advent of Internet shopping gave the concept a whole new impetus as customers could now select, order, and pay for their groceries online and have them delivered to their home, all without leaving the house. As a result, supermarkets across the world have attempted (with mixed success) to take advantage of the opportunities. The one that appears to have come out on top is Tesco.com.

With 2007 profits of £124 and an estimated two-thirds of the UK's online grocery market (ZDNet.co) the success of Tesco.com has been attributed by some to its store-based order picking system. Under this system, customers' orders are fulfilled from their local Tesco branch. Pickers with specially adapted trolleys move up and down the supermarket aisles, mingling with store shoppers, to get the goods which the online customers have ordered. The trolleys are equipped with a touch screen display linked to the store's computer system, allowing the picker to scan the price of each item and record its sale. The display even directs the picker around an optimum route within the store in order to fulfil multiple orders at once. Customers pay the same price as they would at their local store (plus a delivery charge) and are familiar with what is available because many of them shop there from time to time in person. Tesco.com uses a fleet of local delivery vans to deliver the online orders within a two-hour window.

The in-store picking system contrasts with the alternative warehouse-based system adopted by Tesco's biggest rivals, Asda and Sainsbury's. Under the warehouse system orders are fulfilled from a large central location, from where they are transported to local delivery points. Critics of this system point to the huge, up-front investment costs needed to establish these warehouses. The beauty of Tesco's model, they argue, is that it taps into existing facilities and operations, thus making it a relatively low-risk strategy.

However, for organizations which don't have widespread existing networks of stores, the warehouse-based approach might be a way of competing. UK-based Waitrose (an arm of the John Lewis Partnership) invested £200 million into a warehouse-based operation called Ocado, serving online grocery customers in London and the south-east. The gamble appears to have paid off as Ocado is now generating profits. As the BBC's Peter Day reports, 'for all the vast costs and risk . . . it is far cheaper to invest millions in Ocado than to buy sites and get planning permission for the hundreds of stores that Waitrose needs to become a really big player in British groceries'.

Questions

1. How has Tesco leveraged its bricks-and-mortar operations in order to make a success of its online operations?

2. What are the risks and difficulties involved in going for a purely online, warehouse-based system such as Ocado?

3. How do online grocery sales add value for customers?

Sources:
'Tesco dominates internet shopping' http://www.zdnet.co.uk accessed 24/08/06
BBC News: 'Right up your street' http://news.bbc.co.uk accessed 09/08/05

Determining the Extent of Online Opportunities

With so many advantages to online selling it is not difficult to see why some have predicted the end of the traditional shop as we know it. Peppers and Rogers (2004) state that the two primary purposes of a shop are: (a) to provide a location for the physical storage of the product, and (b) to facilitate the exchange of information. In this sense the Internet can outdo the traditional shop as a retail channel because the customer is separated from the products she is buying at the point of purchase (hence no need for physical product stock) and the Internet can provide far more information than the average shop. However, they concede that there are a number of reasons why the traditional shop can still hold the advantage. These can be summarized into three broad areas: product factors, practical factors, and people factors. (See Figure 6.3.)

Product Factors

On the surface, some products are easier to sell online than others. For instance, anything that can be delivered in a digital format (music, film, photos, books, etc.) is likely to do well online (Hollensen, 2003) and we have already seen the decline of traditional record shops and photo processors. However, there are many products which benefit from being touched or experienced in some way before being purchased. Thus a customer may wish to test-drive a new car before buying it, try on a new pair of jeans to check the look and fit, squeeze a camembert cheese to see how ripe it is, or feel the weight of a piece of furniture to assess its solidity. De Kare-Silver (2001) suggests that a product's propensity to online selling depends to a certain degree on which of the five senses it appeals to. Thus, products which are sold on the basis of sight or sound alone can be sold online relatively easily, whereas those appealing to the senses of touch, taste, or smell cannot.

However, it is important to qualify this with a further observation. If the product is already established or well known to the customer, the need physically to experience it each time it is purchased is diminished. For example, it would be relatively easy to sell Chanel No. 5 perfume online because this is a well-known brand and most buyers will already know what it smells like, whereas a company launching

Figure 6.3 Will it sell online?

Product factors	Need to experience the product before purchase
Practical factors	Purchase, delivery, and fulfilment
People factors	Propensity to shop online

Source: De Kare-Silver, *eShock 2000* (2000), Palgrave Macmillan. Reproduced with permission of Palgrave Macmillan

a brand new perfume would most probably struggle to sell it online. De Kare-Silver goes on to suggest that products whose purchase is based on rational criteria, such as price or performance, lend themselves to online selling more than those whose purchase is perceived as complex, or where reassurance is required (e.g. needing to ask a salesperson's opinion about the look of an outfit). Additionally, products whose purchase is planned (as opposed to impulse or as a result of browsing) are more likely to sell online.

De Kare-Silver also argues that many shops have inadvertently taken away the emotional aspect of many products by packaging them up so that the customer cannot experience them properly in the store. For instance, fresh strawberries which are shrink-wrapped cannot be smelled and shirts which are sealed in plastic bags cannot be felt or tried on. In such scenarios the customer may as well buy online. The implications for bricks-and-mortar retailers seem to be that they can add value to the customer relationship by enabling them to experience the product in a way that they could not possibly do online. It is also important to use the face-to-face relationship to demonstrate products and reassure the customer.

Practical Factors

Although buying online can be seen as a highly convenient way of doing one's shopping, there is one area where it is less convenient and that is in the practical shipment of products between the supplier and the customer. Unless the customer's purchase can be transmitted digitally (e.g. software or music) it has to be physically delivered. This raises a number of issues which might reduce a customer's propensity to buy online and hand the advantage back to the traditional bricks-and-mortar shop.

First, there is usually a delivery charge to cover the cost of packing, postage, and insurance. This can make Internet purchases more expensive, or at least wipe out any price advantages found by shopping online. It is important, therefore, that the perceived benefits of buying online outweigh any additional costs incurred through delivery charges. From the organization's point of view, it might also be argued that delivery charges create higher value customers. This is because they are inclined to be less price-sensitive and they are more likely to order larger quantities in order to take advantage of bulk, or special delivery deals.

A second problem encountered by customers ordering things over the Internet is that they have to take delivery of them. For security reasons, many companies will only deliver to the address where the payment card is registered—usually the customer's home address. Furthermore someone usually has to be present to receive them and to sign for them. Missing a delivery means phoning up to arrange an alternative date and time, or a trek to the nearest distribution depot to pick up the parcel in person.

A third issue relates to the immediacy of ownership. Customers buying from a shop usually take possession of their purchases straight away, whereas those buying online have to wait for them to be delivered. Although delivery lead times today are relatively quick thanks to the efficiencies of modern carrier firms such as DHL, TNT, UPS, Fed-Ex, and Parcelforce, a customer who really needs something there and then will have to go to a shop to buy it.

A final practical problem of Internet shopping is what to do if the product which is bought is faulty or does not meet requirements. Unlike a shop where it can be taken back for a refund or replacement, things can be a bit more complicated with an online purchase. First, the customer would have to enter into a dialogue with the supplier. If they agreed to take the product back, the customer would either have to arrange for it to be collected by their courier or take it the Post Office to post it back themselves.

For these reasons Peppers and Rogers (2004) argue that Internet retailers must be prepared to develop flexible and innovative logistics models. They do, however, remind us that as the point of delivery is often the only human contact which the supplier has with the customer, delivery people who are customer-focused can help develop a learning relationship between the supplier and the customer.

People Factors

The final variable that will determine the extent to which products or services can be sold online will be the nature of the customers themselves. Simply put, some customers are more inclined to embrace e-relationships than others. De Kare-Silver (2001) suggests that a customer's propensity to shop online can be used as a segmentation tool. (See Figure 6.4.)

Convenience Shoppers have the greatest propensity for Internet shopping. He describes these as 'frenzied copers' who are too busy to go to the shops in person and value the ability to do everything online. A typical example would be the business-woman who does her grocery shopping online from her office computer.

Experimenters are happy to try out new things and will always be the first with the latest technology. They are likely to see Internet shopping as the future and will be quick to establish their custom there.

Value Shoppers are motivated by saving money and will generally believe that they can get things cheaper over the Internet. However, if it turns out that there is no saving, they are just as likely to go to a shop to make their purchases.

Figure 6.4 e-Segmentation

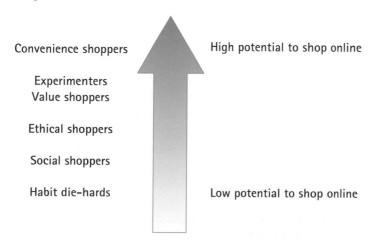

| Convenience shoppers | High potential to shop online |
| Experimenters |
| Value shoppers |
| Ethical shoppers |
| Social shoppers |
| Habit die-hards | Low potential to shop online |

Source: De Kare-Silver, *eShock 2000* (2000), Palgrave Macmillan. Reproduced with permission of Palgrave Macmillan

Ethical Shoppers are concerned about the larger issues surrounding their purchases and will buy from wherever offers the 'greenest' or most humane product solution. This might mean, for instance, that they prefer to buy things locally, rather than from a distant Internet supplier.

Social Shoppers enjoy the whole experience of physical shopping and their existence should not be underestimated. Buying over the Internet cannot replicate the experience of meeting up with friends on a Saturday afternoon, going round the shops, trying things on, stopping for a coffee, etc. For many, shopping is a social experience, which is why large malls such as the Trafford Centre and Meadowhall provide a plethora of restaurants, cafés, bars, cinemas, bowling alleys, and other leisure facilities.

Habit Die-Hards will have the lowest potential for electronic shopping as they are used to their ways and see no reason for change.

It must be recognized that these categories are not exclusive and that a customer can be a social shopper in some buying situations and a convenience shopper in others. A business must therefore determine what sorts of customer it has in its own particular situation before deciding whether to sell its products online. By using the above categories as segmentation tools, the organization can develop different marketing strategies to target particular segments as NatWest bank has done with their 'Another Way' campaign, which targets customers who prefer a face-to-face relationship with their bank.

Developing Trust Online

Perhaps one of the biggest challenges raised by electronic relationships is how to overcome customers' perceptions of risk. The mere act of doing business with anonymous trading partners can increase a customer's perceived risk and therefore reduce their propensity to shop online (Harridge-March, 2006). The level of perceived risk will vary from person to person and some people will be less risk-averse than others. In order to reduce perceived risk it is vital for organizations that rely on e-relationships to develop trust. Those doing so can generally enjoy high levels of customer loyalty, as from the customer's point of view, moving to another supplier would be a move into the unknown and therefore a risk.

The perceived risks of doing business online can derive from a number of areas, but commonly include fear of one's financial details being stolen, fear of the product not being as described, fear of one's privacy being abused (e.g. through unsolicited spam), and fear of contracting a computer virus. Chadwick (2001) proposes a number of things that can help to reduce customers' perceptions of risk when shopping online. These include branding, seals of approval, presentation, fulfillment, and technology.

A strong brand is generally seen to be a huge benefit when selling online (Dahr and Wittink, 2004) because customers will know what to expect and be more comfortable placing their trust in the online transaction. Establishing an online brand from scratch (as Amazon has done) is notoriously difficult because customers have nothing physical with which they can associate. The company therefore has to invest in high levels of publicity to position the brand. Once established, brand maintenance is critical to the online retailer because the brand will carry a large element of the trust that they will need to develop between themselves and the customer.

Brands that are already established through physical entities (e.g. Barclay's Bank, Marks & Spencer, Klick Photopoint, etc.) which then move their operations online will have an advantage over newer, purely web-based rivals who are unknown. However, Rowley (2004) reminds us of the importance of maintaining an integrated channel approach in order to preserve the brand value. In other words the same brand message should be communicated whether the customer is in a physical shop or buying online. Rowley suggests that this be achieved through consistency, in terms of logo, graphics, text and copy, colours, shapes, etc. as well as the product or service offer itself.

Providing 'seals of approval' is a further way of reducing the perceived risk of doing business on-line. Customers will need to be convinced that the offer is genuine and that they can buy with confidence. Without being able to demonstrate the product physically, online retailers can reassure customers by providing some sort of testimony. This might be from a respected third party (e.g. a consumer organization such as *Which?*) or from existing satisfied customers. Just as word of mouth can be a powerful referral tool off-line, so **word of mouse** can be equally, if not more important online (Harridge-March, 2006).

Word of mouse
product and service referrals that are passed from one party to another online

Customers will also need to be assured that their payment details are safe online. Fear of fraud is still a major barrier for many people who would otherwise do business over the Internet. Despite figures which suggest that there is more risk of having ones's credit card details stolen when using it over the telephone or in a restaurant (De Kare-Silver, 2001), the fear of online fraud persists. Companies can reduce these fears by investing in a trusted third-party payment system such as PayPal. Being well established, PayPal is already known to many customers and is a trusted way of doing business online. Using PayPal would therefore give an unknown Internet retailer a much higher perception of trust and legitimacy in the eyes of the customers. Whatever system they use, the online retailer must make explicit statements about the security of their sites, including prominent symbols and guarantees if they are to reassure the nervous customer (Harridge-March, 2006).

As well as branding and seals of approval, Chadwick (2001) suggests a number of other potential trust-building initiatives, most of which involve giving the customer a greater element of control over the transaction. For instance, after the online order has been placed, the customer will want to know that it has been received and is being dealt with. A quick e-mail message from the supplier is often enough to reassure the customer that everything is going through OK and also to say thank you. Such a message will immediately personalize what until now can have been a very sterile relationship. At this time the customer can be provided with a booking reference or 'e-ticket', thus providing them with something tangible as proof of their purchase. Furthermore the supplier can provide online tracking systems so that the customer can check at any one time where her product is and when it might be delivered.

Other examples of giving an element of control to the customer include allowing them to choose their preferred method of contact (e-mail, telephone, postal, etc.) or to opt in or out of future promotions and company contact. Additionally, the supplier can enable the customer to personalize the website (using headings such as 'my favourite . . .', etc.) or even provide tools to block against unwanted pop-up advertising. All of these things will help to engender a feeling of goodwill and go some way to developing trust and building a relationship between the supplier and the customer.

Once trust is established, the online seller can begin to use other tools to keep customers coming back to a website. Hollensen (2003) describes this as creating 'stickiness'—attracting customers to a site and then keeping them there. This can be achieved by giving people what they want. Using cookies to track customer's online behaviour can help build a picture of their likes and dislikes which can then be used to develop a personalized approach to each customer (CRM). At the same time the organization should invest in excellent technical systems so that the customer's online experience is smooth and hassle-free. With so much competition online, delays in connections or transactions will simply drive the customer to another website (Groucutt and Griseri, 2004). Finally, Hollensen suggests that organizations can create online communities where customers can share ideas and interact together. This is an area which opens up many possibilities for customer–supplier relationships but must be handled with care. Let us conclude this chapter with a consideration of the implications of online interactive communities for the customer–supplier relationship.

Managing Online Relationships

Gordon (1998) summarizes how communications between an organization and its customers can vary from a mass, blanket approach where all customers receive the same message, to an individual approach where the message is tailored to separate customers. At the same time, this communication can be either totally one-way, from the organization to the customer, or two-way, where the organization and the customer can interact. (See Figure 6.5.)

Figure 6.5 Different forms of communication

Communications Two-way	One-to-one talking	Intranets	Web logs (Blogging)
Communications One-way	Point-casting	Narrow-casting	Broadcasting
	Individual	Segmented market	Mass

Source: Based on Gordon, *Relationship Marketing* (1998), John Wiley & Sons. Reprinted with the kind permission of John Wiley & Sons Canada, Ltd, a subsidiary of John Wiley & Sons, Inc

Communicating With Customers

Much television, radio, or billboard advertising would fall into the category of *broadcasting*. It is a form of undifferentiated, one-way communication that has little to do with relationship marketing. As broadcasting becomes more targeted towards narrower segments it becomes *narrowcasting* (e.g. advertising in specialist magazines to particular groups of people) but it is still one-way. Taken to its extreme, narrowcasting could end up as *pointcasting* where one-way messages are sent to individual customers. This is not common in marketing, as most individual messages are designed to elicit a response and are therefore interactive, but it can happen with pop-up adverts or spam, for example.

Interactive marketing communications are nothing new. They are perhaps most associated with the one-to-one conversing that takes place between a salesperson and a customer, for example. Interaction in segmented markets, however, has largely been enabled by the Internet. Here, organizations are able to set up chat rooms or Intranet sites for groups of users or customers who share a common interest or need. Such sites are controlled by the organization and access to them is usually limited to customers or others who have registered their details and meet certain criteria. Most university students are familiar with such sites, as they are used by tutors to provide lecture notes and links to other learning materials. In addition they can be used interactively to facilitate discussion around the subject, provide feedback, and stimulate debate.

Many commercial organizations provide online chat rooms to add value for their customers. Examples include Amazon, where customers can exchange views about the latest book and film releases, Sainsbury.co.uk where they can swap ideas about food and lifestyles and the Manchester United FC official website where they can discuss the football season so far. By hosting the site themselves, and controlling access to them, companies are able to interact with tightly defined groups or segments of customers. Groucutt and Griseri (2004) stress the importance of developing a strong link between the online community and the brand, using Disney's FamilyFun.com bulletin board as an example. Here, parents can access a number of areas including activities and crafts, home and garden, parties, raising kids, recipes, travel, etc. Not only do such chat sites create a sense of community amongst customers, they also provide valuable information to the organization by telling them what sorts of things are important to their customers. In addition, the strong brand associations that are created through such sites raise the possibility of cross selling.

The final box on the matrix represents two-way, mass communication. For many years this box remained empty but it might now be suggested that **Web logs**, or 'blogging' have filled this space. In a world where everyone can be potentially connected to everyone else via the Internet, blogging is the latest phenomenon. A Web log, or blog, to give it its slang vernacular, is basically an electronic discussion board. Anyone with access to the Internet can set up a blog, which can then be accessed by any number of other Internet users, all of whom can add their own contributions, making this a truly interactive form of mass communication. Subjects covered by blogs can be anything from recipes to revolutions, cornflakes to conspiracy theories

Blog (Web log)
an Internet-based discussion site open to multiple users

and the range of opinions shared on these sites can be highly emotive and diverse (Groucutt and Griseri, 2004).

According to Groucutt and Griseri, there are a number of issues and problems surrounding these blogging sites. First, it can take time for a message to spread to all users of a blogsite. This is because the users have regularly to log on and many only visit the sites on an infrequent and casual basis. Additionally, the traffic generated on busy sites is so great that Internet service providers regularly have to purge the sites of excess material, thus only those who are logged on regularly will see everything. Even then, McClellan (1999) suggests that the vast majority logging on to a site will view but not take part in the discussion. Such people have earned themselves the unflattering nickname 'lurkers'. Finally, it is inevitable that some of these sites will attract views that are indecent, slanderous, or extreme and many will be policed by authorities trying to track down such contributors.

The rise of blogging has a number of implications for organizations:

- it can give voice to the dissatisfied customer;
- it can lead to 'brand hijack';
- it empowers the customer.

Dissatisfied Customers

We noted earlier that 'word of mouse' has become just as powerful a referral tool as word of mouth. In fact it should be taken very seriously by organizations because it has the potential to reach thousands, maybe even millions, of others and blogging is the ideal vehicle for it. For example, a colleague recently travelled by train on a journey he regularly makes. Unbeknownst to him, however, the train company had altered its pricing structure and the ticket which would previously have taken him six stops was now only valid for five. When confronted by the ticket collector, he was met by a lack of sympathy and issued with a penalty for travelling without a valid ticket. Although technically in the wrong, he felt that he had been treated unfairly and wrote a formal letter of complaint to the company. When he received no reply to his letter, his anger boiled over and he decided to set up a blogging site dedicated to criticizing the train company and its directors. Within a few weeks he had over 100 visitors to his site, most of whom joined in with complaints and horror stories about the company in question.

The fact that one disgruntled customer can gather together over a hundred like-minded individuals in just a few weeks should be of concern to the company. Not only are these people spreading negative word of mouth, the bigger the site becomes the more likely it will be picked up by Internet search engines and be accessed by customers looking for information about the company. As we shall see in the next chapter, the Internet has become a huge rallying point for people who have an axe to grind against an organization, with dedicated websites such as Tescopoly and McSpotlight. Some organizations have attempted to head off criticism by setting up their own discussion sites where controversial issues can be discussed. Groucutt and Griseri (2004) describe how oil company Shell has created an open forum on its website where interested parties can have their say on a number of controversial areas including energy use, the environment, and corporate responsibility.

Brand Hijack

Another potential problem faced by organizations through the use of blogging is a loss of control of their own brand, or as Wipperfürth (2005) describes it, **brand hijack**. Brand hijack can occur when a group of consumers exhibits such a passion for a product or a brand that they create a subculture around it (Cova and Pace, 2006). Such passions are similar to those which develop around cult-cars (such as the Volkswagen Beetle) or cult films and TV programmes (such as *Star Wars* or *Doctor Who*). The Internet can encourage such cults to thrive and the owners of the brands affected can struggle to keep control of their copyrighted materials. For example, Fox Broadcasting in the USA failed when it tried to limit the unofficial and free homepage sites set up by fans of its hit show *The Simpsons*, triggering instead an online boycott of its official merchandise (Donaldson and O'Toole, 2002). Harley Davidson took control of their cult fan base by setting up its own fan site—the Harley Owners Group (HOG).

But it is not just entertaining or aspirational brands such as Harley Davidson and *The Simpsons* that get hijacked. Ordinary fast-moving consumer goods brands are just as likely to become the objects of subcultures formed on the Internet. Examples include Marmite, Peperami, and Nutella, each of which has spawned online brand communities. In a study into the case of Nutella, Cova and Pace (2006) concluded that such behaviour was based on personal self-exhibition in front of other consumers rather than any intrinsic love of the brand. They suggest that the organization should play the role of 'non-intrusive enabler of these personal expressions'. Nevertheless the momentum created by these brand communities can be far-reaching. In 2007 Cadbury's relaunched Wispa, following an online campaign by die-hard fans who had turned the 1980s-based chocolate bar and its adverts into a cult brand.

> **Brand hijack**
> a sub-culture built around a brand over which the brand owner has little or no control

Customer Empowerment

It is difficult to imagine a medium other than the Internet that can enable so many customers to mobilize together so quickly and for so esoteric an issue as a chocolate bar. Companies and products have always had their share of obsessional admirers (and detractors) but in the past they have limited themselves to writing letters or perhaps making phone calls. As such they have been relatively easy for organizations to control, either by assuaging their feelings or ignoring them altogether. Now, however, when whole virtual communities start targeting an organization (for whatever reason), that organization has to sit up and take notice. Imagine the train company mentioned in the example earlier—what would they do if thousands, or even tens of thousands of unhappy customers joined the blog against them?

Electronic relationships have therefore empowered customers by giving them a large and powerful platform from which to make their voices heard. Some organizations attempt to harness this as impromptu market research (e.g. Cadbury's with Wispa). Others try to tap into it by starting their own word-of-mouth messages which they hope will be quickly spread around Internet users by e-mail. Usually these involve images, film clips, or spoof adverts which are so interesting or amusing that users will want to forward them on to their friends. Such marketing techniques are called **viral marketing** because they are infectious and can spread quickly (Kotler *et al.*, 2005).

Viral marketing can carry a number of benefits for the organization:

- It is a quick and inexpensive means of spreading a message. In effect it is getting your customers to do your marketing for you—this is classic referral marketing.

- Although originating from marketing companies, the messages carry a great deal of legitimacy because they are received from friends and are therefore more likely to be looked at and passed on.

- It can be a way of reaching customer segments which might otherwise be difficult to target. Younger people and teenagers in particular are less likely to be influenced through traditional advertising channels such as television or printed media, but more so by social networking avenues.

- Viral marketing campaigns are less constrained by censorship rules about what can or cannot be shown to a particular audience or before a particular watershed. Thus unfettered, viral marketers can be more creative in their use of imagery and language. This, too, adds a sense of legitimacy to many of the audiences at which they are targeted.

For these reasons, viral marketing has drawn a great deal of attention in marketing circles. However, there are risks involved in using viral marketing:

- It is difficult to control because its appeal is subjective rather than objective. Cadbury's could never have guessed that the Wispa bar would achieve cult status. The fact that it did was spontaneous and unpredictable. It is difficult therefore to design a viral marketing campaign and know how far it will go.

- It can draw criticisms to the brand if the message is too explicit or controversial. For example, Volkswagen strenuously denied that it had anything to do with an Internet advert which showed a suicide bomber unsuccessfully trying to blow up a Volkswagen Polo. Soft drink brand Tango also had to change its approach when its hugely successful 'You've been Tangoe'd' campaign led to a trend of children slapping each other in the playground.

- It can attract imitators who are more concerned with the artistic integrity of their adverts than they are with the brand message. Many budding media students or creative directors attempt to get themselves noticed by placing unofficial adverts on the Internet. Sometimes these can spread far and wide and be seen by millions, but the brand owner has no control over them. The Volkswagen advert mentioned above is thought to have originated in this way.

What is clear from all of the above is that blogs, Internet chat rooms, and virtual communities have opened up a whole host of opportunities and challenges for organizations. With so much potential power now falling into the hands of the customers, the onus is very much on the organization to know their customers like never before and provide products and services which are exemplary. Amazon is a good example of how this has been achieved in practice (see End of Chapter Case).

Chapter Summary

The rise of the Internet and e-commerce has changed the way in which customers and organizations interact. For many organizations this has brought opportunities, as they are able to reach more customers than ever before and serve them better by offering greater choice and convenience. However, it has also brought challenges in the form of increased competition and the management of an impersonal relationship with no face-to-face contact with the customer. Organizations that are able to overcome these challenges and take advantage of the opportunities can gain a significant competitive advantage.

Use of the Internet has changed the structures of many markets as more customers are now able to deal direct with a supplier instead of going through a middleman or intermediary. However, this has led to the rise of new types of electronic intermediary (or hub) such as eBay which supports a huge C2C market. Organizations wishing to develop e-relationships must overcome issues of trust, usually by reducing the customer's perceived levels of risk, and by adding value at each stage of the buying process. Ultimately, however, organizations must recognize that the Internet has empowered customers. Although some organizations have attempted to harness the potential of Web logs (blogs) and online communities, this is still a developing area and must be treated with caution.

End of Chapter Case with Questions

Amazon and its Development of Electronic Relationships

Established in 1995, Amazon.com has been one of the great success stories of the past 20 years. With a turnover in 2007 of almost $15 billion, profits of $655 million, and a brand value of $18 billion (Interbrand, 2007), its founder, Jeff Bezos, has reinvented not just the world of book retailing, but also the ways in which relationships between organizations and their customers are developed.

The Growth of the Business

Bezos was working as a hedge fund manager for a Wall Street bank and seemed destined for a fast-track corporate career when he came across a statistic which changed his life—usage of the Internet was growing at 2,300% per annum. Seeing this and recognizing the potential opportunities, Bezos reacted by quitting his job to concentrate on studying the factors needed to set up a successful Internet operation. From an initial list of 20 potential products, he narrowed the list down to two: music and books, both of which he felt had a competitive advantage for 'virtual' rather than physical selling.

In setting up the business, Bezos worked on two principles: the online store had to be customer-friendly and easy to navigate. He also recognized that there was little to be gained simply by replicating the traditional bricks-and-mortar store, but that the real potential lay instead, in providing a very different and enhanced customer experience, in which the problems typically associated with traditional book buying—such as getting to the store, searching for a title, waiting to be served, queuing to pay, waiting for out-of-stock books to be delivered, and paying for the physical facilities of the book store—were all removed.

By stripping out the activities and expenses that added little to the customer experience, the company was initially able to cut hardback book prices by 30% and paperback prices by 20%. Bezos recognized, however, that price by itself was not enough to drive long-term customer experiences or, more significantly, the development of long-term relationships. He therefore set out to build these in a variety of ways, but recognized from the outset that in developing relationships he was doing something that was very different from the norm. In most cases, relationships are developed over time as the result of face-to-face inter-action. Here, the relationship was being developed both at a distance and electronically.

Building Relationships

In many ways, Bezos's strategy for building relationships was deceptively straightforward and based on a combination of:

- the astute application of a new and rapidly growing technology to a product area that had high and demonstrably sustained—and sustainable—levels of demand;
- the creation of a virtual shopping experience which offered a personalized experience;
- an obsessive customer focus designed to ensure that the company constantly got closer to the customer and provided high levels of service;
- the use of technology to develop consumer profiles and consumer insights that became ever more detailed each time a customer dealt with the company;
- the adding of value at every stage of the process;
- ongoing innovation and excitement that was reflected in the company's move from books into music, consumer electronics, toys and games, clothes, kitchen and household goods;
- an emphasis on customer management and retention; and
- clear core value propositions (convenience, the size of the stock, selection, service, and price).

The Development of a Clear Value Proposition

From the outset, at the heart of the company's strategy there has been a deep-seated recognition that the new consumer searches for value and new experiences. Given this, the core proposition centres around two main areas:

- low cost and easy access that is designed to make the selecting of books both easy and fast; and
- the development of a value delivery network.

The notion of a value delivery network highlights the way in which players within the chain, and not just Amazon itself, are used to add value to the customer experience. This is done most obviously by customers providing reader reviews, authors who provide comments, and the personalization of the offer (customers indicate the types of book—either in terms of subjects or authors—they like to read. Having signed up for this, they then receive regular e-mails with reviews of the books that Amazon's editors feel will appeal to the customer).

Questions

1. In what ways did Amazon change the critical success factors for book selling? (Note: In thinking about this, you might usefully focus on the nature of the value that Amazon provides, what Amazon means to its customers, and how the company built relationships.)

2. What general issues emerge from the Amazon experience that other organizations might learn from?

© Professor Colin Gilligan (2007)

Source:
Vandermerve, S. and Taishoff, M. (1998) *Amazon.com: Marketing a new electronic go-between service provider*, European Case Clearing House.

Discussion Questions

1. What exactly is an 'e-relationship'?

2. Is there a role for intermediaries (middlemen) in the Internet age? Support your discussion with examples.

3. To what extent can e-relationships bring customers and suppliers closer together?

4. Discuss the advantages of e-relationships to (a) organizations and (b) customers. Who stands to gain the most?

5. Why has the Internet enabled a C2B market to evolve? Would this market structure work for all products and services?

6. How can doing business electronically reduce transaction costs?

7. How can an organization use e-relationships to pre-empt customer needs?

8. What future might the High Street (bricks-and-mortar) retailer have? Support your discussion with examples.

9. Use the three factors outlined in Figure 6.3 in this chapter to determine the opportunities for selling the following products and services online: a new car; a second hand car; a holiday; a house; a premium single malt whisky; a designer dress; grocery products.

10. Can doing business online be described as a 'virtual' experience? At what point, if any, do practical realities set in?

11. How might an organization reduce any perceived risk associated with e-relationships?

12. Is it possible for an organization to use Web logs for marketing purposes?

Further Reading

De Kare-Silver, M. (2001) *E-Shock: The New Rules*, Palgrave MacMillan, Basingstoke.

Groucutt, J. and Griseri, P. (2004) *Mastering E-business*, Palgrave MacMillan, Basingstoke.

Newell, F. (2000) *Loyalty.com: Customer Relationship Marketing in the New Era of the Internet*, McGraw Hill.

References

Chadwick, S. (2001) 'Communicating Trust in e-commerce Interactions', **Management Communication Quarterly**, 14(4), 653–8.

Cova, B. and Pace, S. (2006) 'Brand Community of Convenience Products: New forms of customer empowerment—the case 'my Nutella The Community', **European Journal of Marketing**, 40(9/10), 1087–105.

Dahr, R. and Wittink, D. (2004) 'The Online Store and the Role of Brand in Internet Shopping', in Peppers, D. and Rogers, M., *Managing Customer Relationships: A Strategic Framework*, John Wiley & Sons, New Jersey.

De Kare-Silver, M. (2001) *E-Shock: The New Rules*, Palgrave, Basingstoke.

Donaldson, B. and O'Toole, T. (2002) *Strategic Market Relationships*, John Wiley & Sons, Chichester.

Egan, J. (2004) *Relationship Marketing* (2nd edn), Pearson Education, Harlow.

Gilbert, D. (2003) *Retail Marketing Management* (2nd edn), Pearson Education, Harlow.

Godson, M. (2005) in **Doole, Lancaster and Lowe** (eds), *Understanding and Managing Customers*, Pearson Education, Harlow.

Gordon, I. (1998) *Relationship Marketing*, John Wiley & Sons, Canada.

Groucutt, J. and Griseri, P. (2004) *Mastering E-business*, Palgrave MacMillan, Basingstoke.

Gummesson, E. (2002) *Total Relationship Marketing. Rethinking Marketing Management: From 4Ps to 30Rs*, Butterworth Heinemann, Oxford.

Harridge-March, S. (2006) 'Can the Building of Trust Overcome Perceived Risk Online?', **Marketing Intelligence and Planning**, 24(7), 746–61.

Hollensen, S. (2003) *Marketing Management: A Relationship Approach*, Pearson Education, Harlow.

King, P. and Clift, J. (2000) *Time to Distinguish Between E-business and E-commerce*, www. pwcglobal.com accessed 13/03/08.

Kotler, P., Wong, V., Saunders, J., and Armstrong, G. (2005) *Principles of Marketing* (4th European edn), Pearson Education, Harlow.

McClellan, J. (1999) *The Guardian Guide to the Internet*, Fourth Estate, London.

Newell, F. (2000) *Loyalty.com: Customer relationship marketing in the new era of Internet marketing*, McGraw Hill Professional.

NHS Shared Business Services (2006) *FAQs for Submitting Invoices to NHS Shared Business Services via OB/0* accessed 02/01/08.

Office of Fair Trading (2007) *Internet Shopping: An OFT Market Study* accessed 02/01/08.

Pavic, S., Koh, S., Padmore, J., and Simpson, M. (2007) 'Could e-business Create a Competitive Advantage in UK SMEs?', **Benchmarking: An International Journal**, 14(3), 320–51.

Peppers, D. and Rogers, M. (2004) *Managing Customer Relationships: A Strategic Framework*, John Wiley & Sons, New Jersey.

Rodgers, J., Yen, D., and Chou, D. (2002) 'Developing e-business: A strategic approach', **Information Management and Computer Security**, 10(4), 84–92.

Rowley, J. (2004) 'Online Branding: The case of McDonald's', **British Food Journal**, 106(3), 228–37.

Wipperfürth, A. (2005) *Brand Hijack: Marketing without marketing*, Portfolio, New York.

Websites

Abel and Cole http://www.abel-cole.co.uk accessed 07/01/08

BBC News: 'China's internet users jump 30%' http://news.bbc.co.uk/1/hi/world/asia-pacific accessed 29/12/06

BBC News: 'Do small firms really need a website?' http://news.bbc.co.uk/1/hi/business accessed 21/11/07

DTI (Department of Trade and Industry): 'The Small Business Services: National Statistics' http://www.sbs.gov.uk accessed 2003

Express and Star Midlands Life, 'How to cheat that robot switchboard' http://www.expressandstar.com accessed 12/01/06

HedgeHog.com http://www.hedgehog.co/onlinereverseauctions.htm accessed 02/01/08

NHS Shared Business Services http://www.ob10.com/customers/NHS accessed 02/01/08

Office of Fair Trading http://www.oft.gov.uk/news/press/2007/155-07 accessed 02/01/08

Priceline.com http://www.priceline.co.uk accessed 02/01/08

Which?, 'Helpline hassle drives customers away' http://which.co.uk/reports_and_campaigns accessed 13/10/06

External Relationships

Chapter Outline

Learning Outcomes

After reading this chapter you should be able to:

- recognize what constitutes a stakeholder from the organization's viewpoint;

- appreciate why the effective management of external stakeholder relationships is important for the organization;

- understand how relationships with a variety of external stakeholders can be managed;

- determine which external relationships are likely to be most significant for any given organization;

- debate the extent to which the organization might need to embrace the principles of corporate social responsibility;

- demonstrate how relations with other organizations can enhance the overall customer relationship.

Introduction

So far in this book we have looked at relationships between suppliers and customers. For some this is where the subject of relationship marketing begins and ends—after all, is not the function of marketing to look after the customer, or *market*-facing aspects of the organization's activities? There are those, however, that take a broader view, and propose that relationship marketing should be concerned with the relationships which the organization has to manage with *all* of its stakeholders, whether or not they are directly involved in the market (Gummesson, 1987; Christopher *et al.*, 1991; Morgan and Hunt, 1994). This includes relationships with suppliers, which will be looked at in Chapter 8, and internal relationships within the organization, which form the basis of Chapter 9. In this chapter, however, we are going to examine relationships with stakeholders who are external to the organization and its market, but who can nevertheless affect its ability to do business effectively.

These relationships have been given various names by different theorists, each with a slightly different emphasis:

- Gummesson (1999) includes them under the heading 'Mega Relationships', *mega* from the Greek word meaning 'big' to reflect the fact that these relationships are often too large to be handled by the marketing department (or even one company) alone.

- Christopher *et al.* (1991) describe them as 'Influence Relationships' because of the way in which they can influence the central customer relationship.

- Morgan and Hunt (1994) use the term 'Lateral Partnerships' because they are neither downstream nor upstream of the organization (as customers and suppliers are), nor are they inside the organization (as employees are). They are therefore 'to the side of' or 'lateral' to the organization.

- Doyle (1995) takes a similar view, but simply describes them as 'External Partnerships'.

The exact make-up of who or what is included under the umbrella of external or mega relationships varies slightly depending on which model you are using. Gummesson, for instance, includes social and personal networks in his definition of mega relationships because of their ability to sway or influence the customer's buying behaviour. As we have already covered these in Chapter 2, we will confine our discussion here to a wider set of external relationships that are beyond the basic customer or supplier interface.

This leaves us with a potentially large and diverse group of stakeholders and other influencers with whom the business needs to manage a relationship. We thus begin with a consideration of who and what should be included in this group and why. The chapter then goes on to consider a number of different groups, each of whom can have a profound influence on the organization's market:

- governments and other authorities;
- financial institutions and lenders;

- pressure groups such as consumer organizations and environmentalists;
- the media;
- alliances and partnerships with other organizations.

The Opening Case introduces some of the issues that are raised in this chapter.

Opening Case Study with Questions

Tescopoly

In March 2008, supermarket giant Tesco completed a buy-out of three stores in the northern and western isles of Scotland. This move, according to the *Grocer* magazine, meant that the company now had a presence in every postcode area of the UK—except one. The HG postcode area of Harrogate in North Yorkshire was left in the unique position of being the only place in the UK not served by a Tesco store. At the time of writing, the company was exploring its options here, but local press was reporting a story of opposition from existing businesses and local residents who did not feel that they needed a Tesco.

The history of Tesco's rise to dominance over the UK supermarket sector has been well documented. The company is now said to control 30% of the UK grocery market and is expanding rapidly in non-food areas such as books, CDs, clothing, and home electrical products, all of which helped it towards record profits of over £2.5 billion in 2007. It is perhaps inevitable, therefore, that with this level of power and dominance, the company has attracted opposition from various parties who feel aggrieved or threatened by its actions. Until 2005 this opposition was fragmented amongst various small campaign groups and individuals but in June of that year some of these came together to form the web-based Tescopoly Alliance.

The Tescopoly website mimics Tesco's own by copying the company's corporate colours and typefaces and replacing the slogan 'every little helps' with 'every little hurts'. The alliance itself consists of a diverse range of groups each with a slightly different concern but brought together by their opposition to Tesco:

- Banana Link (concerned with ensuring that workers on banana plantations get a fair wage);
- Friends of the Earth (concerned with environmental impact of the way in which food is produced, transported, bought, and consumed);
- GMB London (concerned with workers' rights, both home and abroad);
- Labour Behind the Label (concerned with the exploitation of overseas labour markets);
- new economics foundation (nef) (concerned with the economic and social impacts of Tesco's dominance of the UK market);
- Small and Family Farms Alliance (concerned with protecting the interests of farmers who supply Tesco);
- War on Want (concerned with fighting global poverty and exploitation of overseas workers).

In addition to providing a rallying point for these groups and a mouthpiece from which they can get their message across, the Tescopoly website also provides a resource for local campaigners to share ideas and information. This section of the site contains links to further resources such as 'How to oppose a supermarket planning application', 'Planning Aid', and a 'Community Rights Resource Pack'. The site contains numerous links to news stories, not just about Tesco, but about all of the big retailing chains. In addition, when news stories about the big supermarkets break, the press may call upon Tescopoly for their comments if they want an opposing point of view. For example, a recent article in the *Times* quotes Rhys Morgan at Tescopoly describing Tesco's buy-out of Dobbies Garden Centres in Scotland as 'another nail in the coffin for consumer choice'.

So what impact is all of this having on Tesco? In an interview with the BBC, Richard Hyman, chairman of retail analysts Verdict summed it up: '. . . what they have to remember is that Tesco continues to deliver to its most important stakeholder—the customers'. 'The reason it has become very large is that it is more adept at knowing what customers want, and delivers it consistently every day in its stores.' Hyman goes on to point out that supermarkets are not in business to be philanthropic, but to 'discharge obligations'—among them to shareholders. But the argument that 'it's what the consumer wants' is described by Madeline Fuller writing for Tescopoly, as a 'clichéd response used every time retailers defend expansion'. 'It views individuals in only one sphere of life—as consumers. Yes we are all consumers, but we are many other things as well. We are residents, dog walkers, sportsmen and women, students, children . . . with different interests and concerns.'

Questions

1. Should Tesco be worried about Tescopoly? Support your answer with a reasoned argument.

2. How might Tesco manage its external relationships in order to answer the concerns of Tescopoly?

3. What other companies can you think of that attract the interests of pressure groups? How have they managed these?

Sources:
Tescopoly http://www.tescopoly.org accessed 22/05/08
'Dobbies falls to Tesco as supermarket forks out £155 million', *Times*, 9 June 2007
'Will protests hurt the Tesco brand?' http://www.news.bbc.co.uk accessed 24/06/05
'Tescopoly' by Madeline Fuller http://www.catalystmedia.org.uk accessed 22/05/08

A Note About Stakeholders

Before going on it is worth considering what we actually mean when we talk about an organization's 'stakeholders'. This is important because if we're considering stakeholder relationships we need to know where the boundaries are. According to Freeman and Reed (1983) the term **stakeholder** was first used by the Stanford Research Institute in 1963 to jointly describe customers, shareholders, suppliers, employees, financial lenders, and society in general. Since then the term 'stakeholder'

Stakeholder
anyone who can affect, or be affected by the actions of the organization

has generated much debate about just how wide a group an organization should consider its stakeholders to be.

A common mistake by students is to assume that a stakeholder is someone who has a financial stake in the business (e.g. a shareholder). This is an easy mistake to make as the words stakeholder and shareholder are very similar. However, accepting Freeman's (1984) wider definition that stakeholders consist of 'all those groups and individuals that can affect, or are affected by, the accomplishment of organizational purpose . . .', then a shareholder is just one type of stakeholder.

Some commentators have critically suggested that stakeholders comprise an infinite number of potential groups (Argenti, 1997) while others break these up into 'primary' stakeholders and 'secondary' stakeholders (Rivera-Camino, 2007) in the recognition that some will be more important to the organization than others. On this basis, Gummesson (1994) suggests that organizations need to work out which stakeholder relationships are most important and develop a mix of relationship strategies accordingly. For instance, relationships with the government will be important for an airline hoping to avoid more fuel taxes whereas, arguably, relationships with the local communities whom they overfly will be less so (because these communities do not have much power to affect the airline).

Dowling (2001) divides external stakeholders into two categories—normative groups and diffuse groups. **Normative groups** provide the authority for an organization to function and often have the power to withhold resources or block the actions that the organization wishes to take. Such stakeholders would include governments and other regulatory bodies, trade associations, professional associations, shareholders, and financiers. **Diffuse groups** are those that take an interest in the organization because they are concerned about protecting the rights of themselves or others. These stakeholders might include environmentalists, community and special interest groups, and campaigning journalists.

The acknowledgement that a wide group of stakeholder relationships needs to be addressed opens up a debate about who the organization is there to serve. Issues of corporate social responsibility (CSR) come to mind in the way in which the organization treats groups such as local communities, or environmentalists for instance. Lozano (2005) questions how success should be measured in an organization which is committed to stakeholder relationship management. Should it be by how well the relationships are managed? Or should it be by its overall corporate performance, i.e. how much money it makes? Payne *et al.* (2005) attempt to draw a line under these arguments by suggesting that effective management of all relevant stakeholder relationships can ultimately enhance the all-important customer relationship. For instance, if McDonald's addresses the concerns of the 'health food lobby', they can gain positive publicity and generate esteem in the eyes of their customers.

The pursuit of relationships with non-market stakeholders (i.e. those other than customers) might therefore be considered necessary if the organization is to serve its customers better. This might work in a number of ways:

- reassurance—we are a caring company and we do not harm the environment (for example, the Body Shop);

Normative groups
have the authority to regulate or control the actions of an organization

Diffuse groups
take an interest in an organization in order to protect the rights, interests, or beliefs of themselves or others

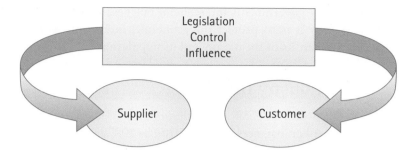

Figure 7.1 Who is the real customer?

- better value—we have lobbied to keep tax increases on our products to a minimum, so the customer pays less (for example, easyJet);
- superior products—our joint ventures and partnerships with other companies have enabled us to develop better products and offer greater choice (for example, Toyota/Peugeot-Citroën in the development of the Aygo/107/C1 model).

Who is the Real Customer?

Additionally, there is the possibility that although the customer wishes to buy from an organization, he or she must first seek permission or approval from a higher authority. In this case the organization has to forge a relationship at a higher level if it is to do business at the market level. Gummesson (1989, 1999) refers to this under the heading 'The real customer is not always found in the market place', reflecting the fact that someone behind the scenes is pulling the strings. (See Figure 7.1.) Such relationships clearly come under what Dowling (2001) would describe as *normative* (see above).

It is clear therefore that the organization must direct its relationship marketing activities to a number of external, non-market stakeholders if it is to serve its customers effectively. Let us now consider a number of relationships which fall into this category.

Relationships with Governments

All organizations are constrained to a greater or lesser extent by the intervention of national and international governments, usually in the form of legislation or taxation. This intervention can operate at a number of different levels and guises including local and regional authorities (e.g. the Greater London Authority), national government and its agencies (e.g. the Office of Fair Trading) and international alliances (e.g. NATO). Although organizations have to contend with their own domestic governments, those selling into foreign countries often come up against levels of government intervention far greater than they do at home. There are a number of reasons why governments intervene in business affairs, but aside from raising revenue, usually it is to protect the economic, industrial, social, cultural, military, or political interests of the nation and its population.

Economic and Industry Interests

Government actions to protect economic interests usually involve fiscal measures which affect businesses. For instance, before Christmas 2007 many UK retailers were pressing for a reduction in interest rates in order to boost consumer spending. Although interest rates are set by national financial institutions (the Bank of England in the UK), they are heavily influenced by government policy, hence the British Retail Consortium (BRC) was making representations to the Chancellor of the Exchequer. Government policy will also affect currency values and exchange rates. The long-running debate over whether Britain should adopt the euro as its currency has split businesses in the UK. Some see it as a positive move which would bring stability by removing exchange rate fluctuations, whereas others are opposed to it because the loss of economic policy independence could slow the economy and hurt their businesses. Organizations representing both views will lobby the government hard to get their views across.

The government's economic policy undoubtedly has an indirect impact on organizations, but it is also common for governments to intervene directly in business affairs by passing legislation which prohibits or limits certain business activities. An obvious example is the monopoly laws which are designed to enhance competition and thus protect consumer interests. A good example of this is the long-running disputes in the USA and Europe between Microsoft and anti-trust legislators (see Minicase 1, Microsoft versus the European Commission). In such situations, organizations need to pursue strong and positive relationships with governments to show that they are socially responsible enough to take on greater market shares.

Minicase 1

Microsoft versus the European Commission

Few competition court case rulings can have been as eagerly anticipated as the long-running dispute between Microsoft and the European Commission and when the verdict came in September 2007, it divided opinion for and against the company. The ruling went against Microsoft on all key points on the basis that the company had abused its dominant position in the computing world effectively by forcing out competitors and denying choice to consumers.

Microsoft is no stranger to such cases. In 2002 a landmark anti-trust case in the USA was settled by a consent decree under which the company agreed to share information with competitors to enable them to develop their own Microsoft compatible applications and operating platforms. In 2007, a Washington district judge approved an extension of the decree for a further two years after a group of ten states, including New York and California, argued that Microsoft's business practices were aggressively monopolistic and anti-competitive. In this case, the company agreed to comply fully with the decree.

The European case revolved around similar issues but was particularly hard fought by the company. Basically the issues boiled down to two things. First, the European Commission's competition watchdog was unhappy about the low levels of 'server interoperability' between Microsoft Windows and rival systems. The Commission accused Microsoft of withholding information from their competitors which would allow them to develop interoperability with Microsoft's products. This meant that computers running rival server operating systems, such as Linux, were not able to communicate properly with Windows and prevented the sharing of files and printers in offices. With the bulk of offices already running Microsoft Windows it was deemed by the Commission that this effectively excluded any competition.

The second issue involved media players which allowed users to play CDs and DVDs, or watch video files on websites. By bundling their own Windows Media Player together with the Microsoft Windows operating system, the Commission accused Microsoft of undermining the business of rivals such as Sun Microsystems and Real Networks. According to Thomas Vinje, a lawyer for the European Committee for Interoperable Systems, Microsoft's actions largely destroyed Real Networks' business at a time when most objective reviews rated Real's Real Player as a better product than Microsoft's Windows Media Player.

Microsoft strenuously denied these allegations, pointing out that it had a right to withhold information from competitors in order to protect its intellectual property. The company also defended its product bundling, claiming that many customers preferred all-inclusive software packages and did not want the hassle of having to download or buy everything separately. Despite this, an early European ruling in 2004 found Microsoft guilty of monopolistic practices and fined them €497 million. The company was also ordered to release key Windows interoperability protocols to rivals. Although it made some concessions to rivals, Microsoft refused to accept the EC ruling and took its case to the European Court of First Instance. The dispute dragged on for another three years, during which time Microsoft was fined a further €280.5 million for failing to comply with the original Directive. In September 2007 Microsoft finally lost its appeal and was fined a further €899 million, bringing its total fines to nearly €1.7 billion.

European Competition Commissioner Neelie Kroes commented that this was the first company in 50 years of EU competition policy to be fined for failure to comply with an antitrust order. For its part Microsoft said that it would not make any further appeals and would comply with the Commission's original rulings in full. What seems likely is that these rulings will have been watched with interest by other companies enjoying what might be considered to be 'dominant positions' within their industries.

Questions

1. Some have suggested that Microsoft was penalized for being successful. To what extent do you agree with this?

2. Suggest what companies such as Microsoft might do to mollify the attentions of governments.

3. How might the final consumer benefit from EC rulings and the fines imposed on Microsoft?

Sources:
'Judge sits on Microsoft for two more years', *The Register*, http://www.theregister.co.uk accessed 30/01/08
BBC News: 'EU fines Microsoft record $1.4bn', http://newvote.bbc.co.uk accessed 27/02/08

In international trade, many governments will act to protect the interests of their domestic industries. For example, the French government refused to lift the ban on imported British beef following the Bovine Spongiform Encephalopathy (BSE) outbreak, even months after the restrictions had been lifted. In the end it took a directive from the EC in Brussels and the threat of a heavy fine before it backed down. Sometimes, organizations can find themselves caught in the crossfire of international trade disputes which have nothing to do with them. Exporters of Scottish knitwear found this out to their cost when the US government slapped a hefty import tax on their products—in retaliation for an EU scheme which gave former colonies in the Caribbean special access to the European banana market!

Social, Environmental, and Cultural Interests

In addition to economic and industrial concerns, governments will also move to protect the social, environmental, and cultural interests of the country. Health and safety legislation means that products and services have to conform to strict guidelines, which can curtail an organization's activities. For example, firework manufacturers and importers hold their breath each year hoping that the government will not bow to growing public pressure from some quarters to ban them. The *Daily Telegraph* reported that German car manufacturers were up in arms over EC proposals to cut the permitted carbon emissions to 130 grams of carbon dioxide per kilometre by the year 2012. The UK brewing industry is becoming increasingly nervous that the government will impose massive tax increases to answer concerns over excessive 'binge drinking'. Meanwhile, in some countries (including the UK) manufacturers of confectionery, fast food, and fizzy drinks have had to contend with their products being labelled as 'junk food' and have been forbidden to advertise them on television before certain times that are known as 'watersheds'. It is estimated that UK legislation in this area could cost children's channels, such as Nickelodeon, up to 15% of their advertising revenue (BBC News, 2006).

Political and Military Interests

As if the above concerns weren't enough, organizations also have to contend with government intervention for political or military reasons. Gummesson (1999) points out that this is likely to be particularly true where the organization is supplying goods or services of an infrastructural nature, such as railway networks, telecommunication systems, or power stations. Following the invasion of Iraq in 2003, the US government made it clear that no French or German companies would be allowed to bid for contracts for the reconstruction of the country's infrastructure because their own countries' governments had refused to support the war. Government-imposed trade embargos against regimes to which they are opposed can also close off market opportunities for companies.

Lobbying
activities designed to influence governments or other authorities

Lobbying

The usual way in which organizations attempt to manage their relationships with governments is through lobbying. **Lobbying** is a form of public relations that has grown into a big business thanks to the scale of potential government intervention described above. Cutlip *et al.* (1994) define lobbying as 'the specialist part of public relations that builds and maintains relations with government primarily for the purpose of influencing legislation and regulation'. The actual term lobbying originates from nineteenth-century America when entrepreneurs and industrialists would gather in the lobby of the Congress house to try and get an opportunity to speak to the congressmen on their way in (Gummesson, 1999). Today, Washington remains a huge centre for lobbying, although some have reported that Brussels (as the political and administrative centre of the EC) has now overtaken it (Harris *et al.*, 1999).

Lobbying is a skilled and complex undertaking which often requires the right connections to people in high places. For this reason many lobbyists are often hired from public relations (PR) agencies that specialize in the field. Such is the demand that it is estimated that there are around 100,000 specialist lobbyists in the USA alone (Gummesson, 1999). It is important to recognize that lobbying is a legitimate and acceptable means of managing relationships with governments, although it is an area which must be handled with care by both politicians and businesses in order to avoid any suggestion of corruption.

Many organizations are simply too small to mount an effective lobby campaign on their own and therefore get together with other organizations in the same industry to pool resources. Sometimes this involves forming partnerships with competitors if it is in the interest of both to change government policy. For example, in the 1990s, leather goods retailer Gulliver's joined up with rivals to lobby the European parliament to reverse taxes on imported Chinese leather products. The taxes had been introduced to protect the high-class Italian and Spanish leather producers, but hit UK retailers who sold low-cost leather handbags, wallets, and purses which they imported from China. Very often, formal *trade associations* are developed to represent the interests of a whole industry. Examples include the Society of Independent Brewers, the BRC, the Society of Motor Manufacturers and Traders (SMMT), and the Direct Marketing Association (DMA).

Baines *et al.* (2004) remind us that only very large organizations who are constantly involved in political matters (e.g. Microsoft) might consider maintaining their own full-time, in-house lobbyists. However, they go on to say that it is not unusual to employ some sort of *Regulatory Affairs* department to handle specific regulatory bodies with which the organization is in constant contact. Examples of such bodies would include OFWAT, OFGAS, and OFTEL, which respectively monitor organizations in the water, power, and telecom industries, or the Advertising Standards Authority which regulates the advertising industry.

Relationships with Other Authorities

It is not just governments who fit the notion that the real customer is not always found in the marketplace. When discussing 'mega' relationships, Gummesson (1999) identifies other authorities and opinion leaders, who, although not customers themselves, have to be won over before the product or service can be offered to the market. These include professional bodies and industry councils.

Professional Bodies

Some market sectors are controlled to a great extent by the professional bodies or associations that operate in that sector. Gummesson (1999) cites the example of Healon, a specialist drug developed for use in eye surgery. The drug could only be sold to hospitals (the actual customer) once the world's top eye surgeons gave it their approval. Getting this approval required attracting the attention of the eye surgeons that, in the example Gummesson describes, involved a Minister of Health, an international ambassador, and the president of the pharmaceutical company. Clearly, this sort of relationship building is beyond the scope of the average sales and marketing department.

Industry Councils and Governing Bodies

Whereas professional bodies tend to wield informal, influential opinions, industry councils are more formal in what they permit. These bodies usually need to test or vet a product before they will allow it to be sold in the market. As such, they must be seen as *customers*, even though they are not buying or using the product themselves. One example is the Medicines and Healthcare Products Regulatory Agency (MHRA) which officially approves all new drugs and medicines before they can be bought by UK Health Authorities. Obviously this is to ensure that they are safe to use, but it can cause friction, particularly if a drug is already approved in one market (e.g. the USA) but not in another. In recent times there have been some high-profile cases of patients with life-threatening illnesses who are unable to obtain the drugs they want because the MHRA has not approved them. Even if they are approved, the bottleneck caused by putting them through the approval process can cause major delays in getting new products to the market. These sorts of relationships are usually handled in-house, as the organizations involved are used to managing them. In this sense they fall under the category of 'Regulatory Affairs PR' described by Baines *et al.* (2004) earlier.

Relationships with Lenders and Financial Bodies

On the surface, banks, investors, and other financial players have little to do with marketing as they are unlikely to be customers. However, the ability of these agencies to affect what the organization does, what it sells, to whom it sells, for what price it sells, etc. means that relationships in this area need to be taken very seriously too. From a marketing point of view, financial relationships break down into two broad and interconnected areas. The first is the need to attract and maintain investment in the company—in other words the need to sell the organization to the financial marketplace. The second area is the need for the organization to present a robust financial image to the outside world, so as to maintain the confidence of not just investors but also customers, employees, suppliers, and partners. Gummesson (1999) classes the first area as an internal relationship and the second as external, but because of the similarities in the way that both are handled by **financial PR**, we will consider both here as external.

Financial (corporate) PR
public relations aimed at investors and financiers

Investors and Shareholders

According to Reichheld (1996), it is just as important for an organization to attract loyal, long-term investors as it is to attract loyal long-term customers. He suggests that over the years churn (or turnover) amongst investors in American companies increased from a relatively stable 14% in 1960 to a more unsettling 52% by 1995. This compares unfavourably with Germany and Japan where Reichheld suggests levels of shareholder stability four times higher than those found in the USA. Long-term investors are desirable because they bring a level of stability to the organization, thus enabling the fulfilment of long-term business strategies. Gummesson and others have argued that this is important to the organization pursuing relationship marketing, because this in itself is a long-term strategy that requires vision and commitment. Family-owned enterprises, such as the Body Shop or IKEA, often provide this stability because the long-term strategy is based around the beliefs or visions of their founders. By contrast, short-term investors are more concerned with immediate return, which can make long-term planning difficult, if not impossible.

It can also be difficult for an organization to control what type of owners or investors it has, but Reichheld (1996) suggests that educating current investors is important. The loyalty of shareholders will be crucial in a takeover bid, so effective PR must be employed to cement a stronger relationship with them. Baines *et al.* (2004) suggest that a more personal relationship should be established with larger, institutional shareholders, involving one-to-one meetings, tours of the company, lunches with senior executives, etc.

Financial Analysts and Reporters

As well as managing owner and investor relationships, the organization must also be concerned with how its financial performance is judged by other stakeholders, as a loss of confidence can result in devastating consequences (see Minicase 2, Northern Rock in the Spotlight). Clearly, banks and other financial services organizations have to project a rock-steady image in order to reassure customers that their money is safe. In order to project an image of financial stability, organizations need to manage relationships with a number of stakeholders including financial analysts, credit-rating agencies, and the financial press. Financial analysts are usually independent organizations whose job it is to present information that will help investors, customers, suppliers, and potential partners decide how close they want to get to a particular organization. Baines *et al.* (2004) suggest that the accuracy of their reports will depend to some degree on the quality of the information they receive through an organization's PR sources.

Minicase 2

Northern Rock in the Spotlight

In September 2007, anyone turning on their televisions, or picking up a newspaper could not have avoided stories about the crisis at UK mortgage lender Northern Rock. Headlines such as 'Bank of England props up Northern Rock', 'Customers scramble to withdraw savings', and 'Northern Rock customers told not to panic', vied for the reader's attention on the news-stands. Television news channels beamed out pictures of long queues of customers waiting to take their money out of Northern Rock, for fear of losing their savings. Stories abounded of police having to control crowds and even of fights breaking out amongst desperate customers in some branches. Dozens of experts were interviewed about what this meant for savers and borrowers, what it meant for the British banking system, what it meant for the economy, etc.

The crisis began when it was revealed on the BBC that Northern Rock had approached the Bank of England for an emergency loan in order to meet its ongoing obligations. Unlike many other British mortgage lenders, who raise most of their funding from customer retail deposits, Northern Rock relied for most of its funding on inter-bank loans. Following the sub-prime lending crisis in America, banks were reluctant to lend money to each other for fear of inheriting bad debts within the system and as a result, inter-bank lending all but dried up. It was for these reasons that the European Central Bank had injected €94 billion of liquidity into the European banking system a month earlier. Now that Northern Rock had found that its usual source of funding was closed, it went to the Bank of England.

The BBC's Business Editor, Robert Peston said that Northern Rock's approach to the Bank of England did not mean that it was in danger of going bust and that there was no reason for customers to panic. However, customers did panic. Fearful that they would lose their life savings, thousands queued up outside Northern Rock's 75 branches across the country to take out their money. The *Times* quoted one man who had come down early to beat the crowds. He was concerned that Northern Rock might no longer be in existence so he closed his accounts. He agreed that if everyone did the same it would make Northern Rock's position even worse, but he didn't want to be 'the mug left without my savings'. As a result, on one day alone, it was estimated that about £1 billion was withdrawn by panicking customers and Northern Rock shares plummeted over 40% on the Stock Exchange. Such was the frenzy that the bank's website collapsed under the strain of Internet customers trying to access their accounts and its phone lines were jammed.

In a bid to stem the panic, reassurances flowed in from all sides. The Financial Services Authority (FSA) stressed that if they believed that Northern Rock was insolvent they would not allow it to remain open for business. Chancellor Alistair Darling moved to guarantee all deposits held at Northern Rock and told the general public that it was important that they should have confidence in the stability of the banking system. Chief Executive of the British Bankers Association, Angela Knight reiterated that people should calm down and refrain from making simplistic comments in what was a complex area and causing unnecessary concern. The bank itself took out a series of newspaper adverts assuring customers that although the bank had suffered troubled times, 'it will prevail and we will not let you down'.

By guaranteeing saver's deposits, the Chancellor's move served to stabilize the market and in the subsequent months Northern Rock was temporarily nationalized in order to protect savers and secure the best value for tax payers in the repayment of the loans that the bank had received. For those involved at the time, however, few will forget the sense of fear which gripped the UK banking market in September 2007.

Questions

1. Could media coverage be blamed in any way for what happened at Northern Rock?

2. To what extent (if any) should media coverage of corporate affairs be receptive to interests of a company or its customers?

3. What are the implications to organizations in the way in which they manage their relationships with the media?

Sources:
BBC News: 'Timeline: Northern Rock bank crisis', http://newsvote.bbc.co.uk accessed 20/03/08
'Northern Rock customers withdraw £1bn', *Daily Telegraph*, 16 September 2007
'Northern Rock savers rush to empty accounts', *Times*, 14 September, 2007

In addition to analysts, the financial press, or business media, will also take an interest in an organization's corporate affairs. We will be looking at media relationships later in this chapter, but the financial press deserves a separate mention, because of its specialist focus and its ability to transmit information about an organization's financial status to a much wider audience of stakeholders. This information falls into two main camps. The first is the straight reporting of share prices, profit figures, acquisitions, mergers, etc. This type of information is aimed at shareholders or investors who want to follow the performance of any particular stocks or shares. The data reported tends to be quantitative facts and figures and, in principle, is no different to the results and league tables found in the sports section of a newspaper.

However, a sports section of a newspaper will not just contain facts and figures; it will also include commentary, analysis, and speculation. The same is true of business reporting and it is in this area that organizations must take care to maintain good relationships with financial journalists and business editors. Baines *et al.* (2004) report that an in-house PR department can normally handle day-to-day financial relations through the annual report and accounts and the shareholder's Annual General Meeting (AGM). However, more specialized situations such as takeover bids, high-profile appointments or resignations, unexpected financial results or crises usually require the skills of a specialist corporate PR agency. Dowling (2001) notes that a skilled agency is usually better able to manage potentially adversarial relationships with journalists who are after a story.

For these reasons, financial PR has grown into a large and specialist sector of the PR industry. Individuals working in this field require sensitive communications skills, because a wrong word or impression can quickly send share prices tumbling and spark a crisis. In addition, they must have a highly detailed knowledge of financial regulations and all of the intricacies of the stock market, so that they can steer an organization's PR through potential problem areas. All of this puts them amongst the highest paid professionals in the PR industry (Wilson and Cameron, 2006). Managing financial relationships is therefore not cheap, but the stakes are so high that for most organizations—and particularly publicly owned corporations that are listed on the Stock Exchange—the price is worth paying.

Relationships with Pressure Groups and Publics

Perhaps the most diverse group of stakeholders with whom the organization must manage relationships is external pressure groups and publics. Dowling (2001) describes these as 'diffused groups', who take an interest in the organization when they are concerned about protecting a cause. As we shall see, these *causes* can range from defending international human rights to preserving the look of the local High Street and can sometimes have a major impact on an organization's operations and performance. Yet Dowling goes on to suggest that most corporate relationship-building strategies ignore these groups, preferring to concentrate on the more obvious stakeholder groups of customers and financial influencers.

Jones *et al.* (2006) remind us that the interest and intervention of external pressure groups into organizational affairs is nothing new. The Boston Tea Party in 1773, when hundreds of chests of tea were thrown into the harbour, was a public protest against the East India Company's favourable tax concessions. Nearly two hundred years later, Ralph Nader's one-man campaign against the big American motor manufacturers led to a huge public debate about whether car companies were putting profits before safety. Nader's book, *Unsafe at Any Speed* (1965) lambasted Chevrolet's revolutionary new Corvair model. He claimed that the Corvair's rear-engined design made the car unstable and likely to spin out of control or tip over, even at relatively minor speeds. Faced with a barrage of bad publicity and consumer mistrust, the Corvair never realized its full sales potential and was quietly withdrawn.

In a highly competitive marketplace, the impact of these groups can be enormously damaging. During the 1980s, Barclay's share of the lucrative student banking market dropped by 10% because it held business operations in apartheid-governed South Africa (Wilson and Cameron, 2006). Whether they like it or not, organizations have increasingly become the subject of public scrutiny and must learn to communicate effectively if they are to avoid censure. Christopher *et al.* (2002) describe how oil company Shell failed to do this, when they planned to dispose of the Brent Spar oil platform by sinking it in the North Sea. The resulting furore amongst environmentalists led to the picketing of Shell petrol stations across Europe and even firebomb attacks in some extreme cases. Like Chevrolet and Barclay's before them, Shell was eventually forced to do a U-turn and rethink its strategies.

In recent years the propensity for pressure groups and campaigners to exert influence over organizations has been elevated to a whole new level. We saw in the last chapter how virtual chat rooms, 'blogs', and online communities have enabled large and diverse groups of individuals to mobilize and quickly spread messages between each other. Levick (2004) describes this as a continuous war of attrition, which organizations must manage and keep on top of. In some cases high-profile websites have been created to target particular companies. Examples include Tescopoly (see Opening Case), Wal-Mart Watch (and now Asda Watch), and McSpotlight. Although Tescopoly purports to campaign against the growing power of all major supermarkets, its efforts are centred around Tesco, as witnessed by the parodied name and slogan ('every little hurts'), as well as the site content (Jones *et al.*, 2006).

To counter these attacks, organizations have had to manage their PR much more effectively and some have embraced CSR policies (Jones *et al.*, 2007). We shall look at examples of how they have done this as we go along, but first let us look at the sorts of external pressure groups and publics which the organization needs to address. These might be categorized as:

- consumer groups;
- environmentalists;
- human and animal rights activists;
- politically or ideologically motivated groups and individuals;
- local communities;
- public opinion leaders.

Consumer Groups

Although arguably part of the market and therefore covered under customer relationships, an organization will need to approach its relationships with organized consumer groups, differently from its everyday relationships with individual customers. For this reason, consumer groups have been categorized here as an external relationship.

Consumer groups are formed for a number of reasons, sometimes to fight for the rights of the customers of a particular organization and sometimes to represent the interests of a particular type of consumer. For example, real ale drinkers are represented by the Campaign for Real Ale (CAMRA). One might think that customer satisfaction would be one of an organization's priorities, but the fact that consumer groups exist at all suggests that some organizations or industries have an adversarial relationship with their customers. Typically, this occurs when the organization is perceived to have too much power and there are few alternatives available to the customer. Consumer groups can affect organizations in two ways: by an organized protest, such as a boycott, or over a longer period as a pressure group.

In January 2008, train operator First Great Western (FGW) found itself the target of an organized protest in the form of a fares strike by passengers protesting about overcrowded trains, elderly carriages, and soaring ticket prices. Organizers of the protest printed their own tickets, in the style of a FGW ticket but branded with the name 'Worst Late Western'. On the day of the protest, passengers were asked not to buy a genuine ticket, but to use one of the protest ones instead. The company threatened to take legal action against anyone not buying a proper ticket, but with so many passengers taking part in the action this proved difficult. Furthermore, the publicity that the fare strike generated forced the company into making a public statement justifying its ticket prices and explaining what it was doing to improve services and replace out-of-date rolling stock.

Organizations faced with consumer groups need to be proactive in the management of customer relations so that whatever grievance the customers have is not allowed to escalate into an organized protest that may attract damaging publicity. In some cases the organization can work with a consumer group to lend legitimacy to its products or services in the eyes of the customer. For example, many brewers of real ales use CAMRA's publicity materials and events to market themselves to real ale drinkers.

Environmentalists

Today, environmental issues are very much in the news, thanks to stories about global warming, the threatened extinction of wildlife, and increasing pollution in the land, sea, and atmosphere. As a result, organizations have come under increasing scrutiny from environmentalists who seek to draw attention to the damage they are doing and/or persuade them to change their ways. Jones *et al.* (2007) describe the environmental issues facing the big UK retailers, which include energy consumption, raw material sourcing and the transport of products, water usage, volume of packaging, genetically modified foods, and the use of chemicals. Some of them are attempting to address these issues by, for instance, encouraging customers to reuse bags, or labelling packaging that can be recycled.

Environmental campaign groups such as Greenpeace, Friends of the Earth, and the World Wildlife Fund have been around for many years now. As charities, they are well funded by their supporters and have the potential to generate much publicity. Recent targets include energy company Eon's plans to build a new coal-fired power station (the first in 30 years) and Japanese whalers in Antarctica. Hollensen (2003) describes how, instead of taking an adversarial approach to these groups, organizations can benefit from forming alliances with them. This will lend legitimacy to any green claims they make about their products or services and provide the organization with potentially positive publicity. Organizations might also be able to use the expertise of environmental groups to solve problems or develop better products.

Gummesson (1999) underlines the importance of green relationships by including them as one of his 30Rs—albeit as a customer relationship rather than an external one. As such, many organizations use green issues as a strategic platform from which to attract customers. Examples include the Body Shop and Ecover. However, some organizations are unable to avoid causing damage (real or perceived) to the environment and this puts them in the spotlight of campaigners. Airlines are an example of this—it is impossible to fly anywhere without burning large amounts of fossil fuel.

Similarly, car manufacturers come under fire, particularly those producing large 'gas-guzzling' vehicles.

Some organizations have attempted to deflect criticism by offsetting the harm they cause. Land Rover, for example, has launched a CO_2 offset programme, which, according to their website involves 'an integrated approach including investment in sustainable technologies and working with global conservation and humanitarian organisations'. Former UK airline Silverjet claimed to be the world's first carbon-neutral airline. Included in the ticket price was a 'mandatory carbon offset contribution, giving customers the opportunity to invest in a number of climate friendly projects around the world' (Silverjet press release, 2006). While it may never be possible to satisfy totally some of the more hard-line campaign groups, being seen to care can soften the potential damage with the customer market. By assuaging the guilt of consumers who know that air travel is bad for the environment, but still want their summer holiday in the sun, airlines are managing the green relationship.

Human and Animal Rights Activists

Further pressure can be put on organizations by groups who campaign for human or animal rights. Organizations which are seen to be transgressing or exploiting human rights cannot readily offset their actions and usually end up having to do a u-turn. Often, the bad publicity that is generated in such cases can be damaging to the brand image and sales. The exposure of sweat-shop conditions in some of Nike's overseas operations led to a fall in market share and a subsequent review of its subcontractors with a commitment to improve working conditions. Similarly, Wilson and Cameron (2006) describe how bra manufacturer Triumph was forced to close its factory in Burma after activists drew attention to human rights issues under the country's military dictatorship. Campaigners used images of a woman wearing a barbed wire bra with the slogan 'Support breasts, not dictators', a tactic that was sure to attract the attention of the press.

Animal rights activists can often be even more militant than human rights campaigners. Once again graphic images of animals in laboratories or intensive farming conditions are used to bring issues to the public's attention. Organizations likely to find themselves in the firing line are the manufacturers of drugs, cosmetics, and other household items which might have been tested on animals during their manufacture. Retailers selling animal-derived products might also be targeted. Fur coats are the obvious example, but even some butchers shops have come under pressure from some quarters (e.g. the Meat is Murder campaign). Finally, any organization seen to be treating animals cruelly needs to be aware of the interest they will attract from campaigners. This includes circuses, zoos, and aquariums, as well as farmers and livestock transporters.

In recent years some of these protests have turned violent and even companies not directly involved with animals have been intimidated. For example, building contractors working on a new animal-testing laboratory at the University of Oxford were physically threatened by animals rights extremists and forced to pull out of the job. PR commentators advise that organizations should not attempt to develop working relationships with anyone who is making threats (Wilson and Cameron, 2006). Winning the hearts and minds of the general public is usually more productive, as the university has attempted to do by highlighting the medical breakthroughs which can be made possible through such research. For many organizations it is enough to bypass animal rights groups with simple statements such as 'not tested on animals' on the products' packaging. Some do take the relationships a little further and make the whole principle of no cruelty to animals their unique selling point—the Body Shop is an obvious example of this.

Ideologically Motivated Groups

Ideologically motivated groups and individuals are similar to animal rights extremists in that they cannot be negotiated with. Their aim is to change the system and if an organization belongs to a system to which they are opposed, an adversarial relationship is inevitable. For example, anti-globalization advocates will target multi-national corporations (MNCs) such as banks, oil companies, and retailers. Prominent MNC brands such as McDonald's are often singled out for attack during demonstrations and protests. Sometimes it is the organization's customers who are targeted. For example, in 2007 a group calling itself the 'Alliance Against Urban 4x4s' dressed as crash test dummies and handed out leaflets to the drivers of these vehicles on London streets.

Once again, the advice from PR commentators to organizations faced with such protests tends to be don't get too involved and don't get emotional (Wilson and Cameron, 2006). McDonald's learned a hard lesson when they failed to heed this advice and took on two protestors who were handing out leaflets in the street entitled 'What's wrong with McDonalds—everything they don't want you to know'. The company sued the pair and in doing so generated a whirlwind of publicity and a huge upsurge in anti-McDonald's movements around the world. It could be argued that instead of taking on the protesters, PR aimed at a wider public would be more productive, as many of them will not necessarily share the extreme views of the campaigners.

Communities

Another category of pressure group with which an organization may need to manage relations is the local community. Issues here revolve around the impact, real or perceived, which the organization's operations make on the neighbourhood and the people who live and work there. A common obstacle faced by organizations wishing to develop or expand their operations is 'nimbyism' (from the acronym NIMBY, meaning 'not in my back yard'). Most people accept the need for airports, power stations, young offenders' institutions, new house-building, and mobile phone masts etc., but few of them would wish to see these situated near their homes. Very often, planning permission is only granted by the local authority following consultation with local residents, so it is important for organizations to win over the local community through reassurance and an open, honest approach.

Jones *et al.* (2007) suggest that a focus on being 'good neighbours' within the local community has become a part of the CSR of many big supermarkets. Often this involves putting something back into the community that will benefit everyone. For example, in gaining planning permission for a major new superstore in Sheffield, Tesco undertook to develop a riverside walkway and cycle way adjacent to their store. They also agreed to restrict deliveries and the unloading of lorries to the hours between 7 a.m. and 10 p.m., so as not to disturb local residents. However, in recent years the company has been accused of reneging on agreements and flouting planning laws (BBC News, 2006), claims which the supermarket is quick to address in its public statements.

Public Opinion Leaders

The final category of external pressure groups considered here does not in fact consist of groups at all, but high-profile individuals who can command public opinion. Their impact on an organization can be enormous, but is often indirect because they are concerned with a higher agenda. Consumerist Ralph Nader, for example, campaigned for automobile safety and the Chevrolet Corvair ended up in the crossfire. Similarly, TV chef Jamie Oliver campaigned for healthy school meals and in doing so publicly criticized the Turkey Twizzler (see Minicase 3, Jamie Oliver and the Turkey Twizzler). Sometimes the effect on organizations is favourable, as, for instance, when another TV chef, Delia Smith, put out a series on how to cook with eggs, in an attempt to inspire basic cooking skills. Following Delia's television series, sales of eggs rose by 1.3 million a day (BBC News, 1998). Conversely, politician Edwina Currie's attempts to educate the British public about the dangers of salmonella caused egg sales to plummet.

Minicase 3

Jamie Oliver and the Turkey Twizzler

Television chefs have come along way since Fanny Craddock showed viewers how to make traditional dishes such as roast beef and sherry trifle. For a start, there are a lot more of them today and as a result, rather than simply showing viewers how to cook something, each has taken a slightly different angle to the way in which they approach their subject. At the same time many of them have attempted to raise their public profiles, making them celebrities in their own right. Thus Gordon Ramsey helps failing restaurateurs to turn around their businesses (amid much profanity), Nigella Lawson shows viewers how they can easily and quickly prepare sumptuous dinner parties at home, and the Hairy Bikers tour the world, serving up local dishes with light-hearted banter.

One of the best-known TV chefs, Jamie Oliver, has used a number of different formats for his television shows. His Channel 4 show *Jamie's Kitchen* proved a hit with viewers when it took 15 unemployed young people and turned them into professional chefs. Following this success his next venture was to revolve around the food which children ate in school. In an interview in 2004, Oliver told the BBC, 'I've been concerned about what kids eat in school for some time now [and have] devoted most of the rest of 2004 to actually doing something about school food'.

The result was *Jamie's School Dinners*, a Channel 4 television series set in Kidbrooke School in Greenwich, south-east London. During the series Oliver attempted to turn the children away from foods he described as 'rubbish', such as pizza and chips. However, one product in particular was to receive the brunt of his criticism during the series and that was the 'Turkey Twizzler' produced by Norfolk company Bernard Matthews. Tests showed that the product contained 21.2% fat when cooked—double the recommended guidelines. As a result of this publicity, at least two of the big school catering companies, Scolarest and Sodexho, announced that they were dropping Turkey Twizzlers from their menus.

Bernard Matthews hit back at the criticisms. 'We have been unfairly treated over a turkey product, which is the least fatty of all meats. We were picked out by Jamie Oliver because everyone has heard of Bernard Matthews, yet we are a company that has been responding to health concerns for years and going down the low-fat route.' In the wake of the furore, the company reformulated the product to contain just 7% fat when cooked and in a statement said that it had no plans to withdraw it. Twelve months later their stance appeared to be justified as sales of the Turkey Twizzler were reported to be nearly one-third up on the previous year's figures.

Today Bernard Matthews continues to offer a range of children's products, including Golden Drummers and Turkey Dinosaurs and the company's website is keen to promote the nutritional content of all its products.

Questions

1. To what extent does a well-known brand name leave a company open to criticism from campaigners? What are the implications for organizations?

2. How much validity do the actions and statements of celebrities have? Illustrate your answer with examples.

3. How might a company criticized by a well-known personality best manage the publicity?

Sources:
BBC News: 'TV Chef Oliver returns to school', http://newsbbc.co.uk accessed 21/04/04
'Children keep gobbling Turkey Twizzlers', *Guardian*, 23 March 2005
Bernard Matthews http://buyersguide.co.uk/document/bernard_matthews accessed 20/03/08

Hollensen (2003) defines an opinion leader as a 'person within a reference group, who, because of special skills, knowledge, personality, or other characteristics, exerts influence on others'. Organizations have long sought to harness their influence, through, for example, the use of celebrities in advertising. However, convincing an opinion leader whose views conflict with the organization or its products can be impossible, and the company must use crisis or contingency PR to try and limit the damage. For example, when campaigning journalist Morgan Spurlock made his film *Super Size Me*, highlighting the ill effects he suffered through eating nothing but McDonald's burgers for 30 days, the company acted swiftly and decisively. They organized a number of interviews and news conferences pointing out that anyone eating as Spurlock had done would make themselves vulnerable to health damage and that this consumption was highly unrepresentative. McDonald's global nutritionist, Cathy Kapica, promoted the company's views on 'smart diet and exercise' and the organization briefed all of its franchisees so that they could handle media enquiries (Wilson and Cameron, 2006).

Relationship Strategies for Pressure Groups

The question of how far an organization should go to accommodate pressure groups depends to a large extent on how exposed it is and how much power the pressure group has. Rivera-Camino (2007), for example, points out that an organization's 'visibility' will play a major role in determining how much influence external pressure groups can bring to bear. Thus, organizations with famous brand names (e.g. McDonald's, British Airways, Land Rover, Citibank, Microsoft, etc.) are more likely to engage the attention of campaigners because they are in the public eye and will subsequently attract more publicity. As these organizations tend to be large and well-resourced, he argues that they are more likely to be proactive in their management of pressure-group relationships, e.g. by adopting environmental policies or engaging in green relationships.

An organization's size and performance can also make it a target. Tescopoly, for example, purports to campaign against the power of all big supermarkets, but as market leader, Tesco are clearly singled out in most of the campaign group's activities. According to Rivera-Camino, other factors which will play a part are the organization's proximity to the final consumer, with those at the end of the supply chain much more exposed than those who are further back. Thus, Nike is more likely to take the blame for sweatshop conditions in overseas factories than are its suppliers and subcontractors who are actually running the factories. Additionally, organizations whose pollution can be readily seen will attract attention more than those whose pollution goes unnoticed. For example, power stations are an easy target because their pollution can be seen, while the thousands of smaller factories which also pump out harmful emissions tend to go unnoticed. Clearly, organizations which are more visible in these ways will need to plan their relationship strategies with pressure groups much more carefully.

An organization might elect to follow one of two possible strategies when handling relationships with pressure groups:

- go it alone—whereby the organization bypasses the pressure group and develops its own CSR agenda to deflect potential criticism and appeal to a wider public;
- actively seek working relationships with the pressure group in order to gain positive publicity and possible competitive advantage.

Corporate Social Responsibility

In a study of UK retailers, Jones *et al.* (2007) described **Corporate Social Responsibility (CSR)** as integrating environmental, social, and economic factors into the organization's strategies and operations. As such, CSR can be seen as a means of

Corporate Social Responsibility
an organization's wider responsibilities to society in general

managing relationships with a number of stakeholders, both external and internal (Baines *et al.*, 2004). However, the issue of CSR has sparked debate amongst many observers, some of whom see it conflicting with traditional marketing. The *Ethical Corporation* (a global publication aimed at educating businesses about ethical issues), for example, has suggested that it might be difficult for CSR and marketing to meet the same objectives (Ethical Corporation, 2005). The argument is that looking after the environment and appeasing social groups will simply divert effort and resources away from profitably satisfying customers. However, Jones *et al.* (2007) point out that others have taken the opposite view and described CSR as corporate advertising which is aimed at consumers, with the objective of increasing sales.

We saw in earlier chapters that one of the underlying principles of relationship marketing is that a 'win–win' situation can be achieved, whereby no one in the relationship is disadvantaged. It is therefore perhaps useful to take a middle view of CSR. Yes, organizations will pursue CSR initiatives in order to gain consumer support (Maignan and Ferrell, 2001), but at the same time the initiatives that they are pursuing will be of benefit to a greater society. Sometimes an organization's philanthropy can help to mitigate the situation when things go wrong. Dowling (2001), for example, describes how although oil company Shell was fined following an oil spillage in the Mersey Estuary, the judge was moved to limit the extent of the fine because of the company's outstanding conservation record and generous support of the arts.

Whatever the reason, there is evidence that many organizations are now incorporating CSR into their business plans. For instance, both Shell and Tesco produce annual CSR reports, while Sainsbury's has no less than six board-level directors responsible for CSR issues (Jones *et al.*, 2007). At a grass-roots level, Tesco promotes a number of initiatives to customers, including the re-use of carrier bags, the provision of recycling facilities, the opening of 'energy-efficient' stores, the labelling of 'green' products, and working with the British Red Cross to address the theme of 'crisis care in your neighbourhood'. All of these initiatives are described in a leaflet distributed to Clubcard holders in 2006 and would appear to undermine some of the criticisms made by Tescopoly.

Sometimes, however, pursuing a CSR policy can backfire on an organization, particularly if it seen to be hypocritical or commercially motivated. For example, in 2006, Cadbury's ran a promotion whereby children could collect tokens from chocolate bars and exchange them for school sports equipment. Critics lambasted Cadbury's, suggesting that the healthy ideals promoted by the scheme were at odds with the company's chocolate-based products. One newspaper calculated that a child would need to consume 90 bars of chocolate to get a netball, or 2,730 to get a cricket set (www.foodcomm.org). In the face of this bad publicity, Cadbury's quietly withdrew the scheme. The implications appear to be that any sort of CSR initiative must have resonance with the organization's overall activities and must be seen clearly to address any negative connotations of the company or its products.

Working with Pressure Groups

As an alternative to going it alone in an attempt to by-pass, head off, or even confront the pressure groups, an organization can actively embrace the groups and work with them. We have already seen that this can bring benefits of credibility and expert knowledge and in some cases be used as a differentiation tool. The Body Shop and Traidcraft are good examples of this. However, meeting the objectives of a profitable business and keeping these groups on side at the same time can be a challenge. Wilson and Cameron (2006) describe several things that an organization wishing to work with pressure groups must do:

- avoid working with groups whose primary motivation is to gain publicity for the cause rather than to develop a workable solution (i.e. ensure common goals exist);

- maintain an open and honest relationship so that nothing inside the organization is hidden from the pressure group (i.e. build up trust);

- be seen to be taking actions in support of the ideals upheld by the organization and the pressure group (i.e. avoid rhetoric and empty promises).

Relationships with the Mass Media

Many of the things that we have already discussed in this chapter involve the media, because this is the vehicle through which, intentionally or unintentionally, much of the organization's non-customer communications is transmitted. By media we refer here to third-party, mass-reporting organs such as newspapers, journals, television, and radio channels. As such, although the organization has directly to manage its relationships with external pressure groups, investors, governments, etc., it also has to manage a relationship with the mass media. To underline the importance of mass-media relationships, Gummesson (1999) includes them as one of his 30Rs. He further asserts that because the media is part of society, they are above the market itself (i.e. they are not customers or suppliers) and should therefore be classed as a 'mega relationship'.

Managing Media Relationships

The problem with trying to manage relationships with the mass media is that there is an inherent goal conflict between the two parties (Cutlip *et al.*, 1994). The organization wants to see positive things reported which will reflect well on it and its products. After all, as Gummesson (1999) points out, good publicity is akin to free advertising and is likely to carry a lot more weight than traditional advertising, because it is seen as being unbiased. However, the media will only want to report on stories that are newsworthy or are of interest to their audience. This can bring them into conflict with the organization, particularly when things go wrong. Managing media relationships will entail working with journalists and editors, so the first thing that the organization must do is recognize the different types. Generally speaking, these can be broken down into:

- news reporters/editors, who will take an interest in the organization if a story breaks;

- investigative journalists, who will seek to uncover some truth about the organization. Sometimes these individuals can be freelance (i.e. not connected with a particular newspaper or TV channel);
- professional sector journalists and commentators, who only report on specialist areas. This might include the financial press (discussed earlier in this chapter) and also people such as motoring journalists or food critics.

Baines *et al.* (2004) assert that the organization must take a proactive approach to the media, by developing long-term, open, and trusting relationships with journalists and editors. This means giving them access to information and making senior management available for interview. It might entail providing products (e.g. a new car for a motoring journalist to test), market data, or the results of research. Long-term, close relationships with journalists are important, because if they know you personally they are more likely to take care to ensure accuracy in what they report and be more sympathetic in their style.

Crisis PR

One of the biggest tests of an organization's relationships with the mass media is what happens when critical or unexpected incidents occur. Corporate history is littered with crises which have engulfed organizations and taken over the headline news. Typical examples include oil spillages, air crashes, and food contamination scares. In such scenarios, Dowling (2001) reports that the media will have three basic questions:

- What happened?
- Why?
- What are you going to do about it?

The way in which the organization handles these questions can potentially make or break its future (Gummesson, 1999). It is important, therefore, that it is prepared by having some sort of **crisis or contingency PR** strategy in place. In order to do this, Dowling suggests that the organization should conduct a risk analysis, to identify various potential crisis scenarios and draft a broad media response to each. Staff should be briefed about how to handle media enquiries and usually a central point of contact for the media is assigned. Dealing with the media in situations such as these is a skilled job and many organizations rely on experienced PR agencies that specialize in this field. In either case, if long-term, open relationships have already been established with the media, it can be easier to manage the scramble of interest following an unexpected event.

Gummesson (1999) reminds us that some organizations try to create positive events which will attract favourable publicity. He calls these 'pseudo' events, because they are attempting to manufacture news stories where otherwise there wouldn't have been any. Events such as film premieres are good examples, as they will capture the public's interest and attract much media coverage. However, the average company might find it more difficult to generate media interest in their product launches, new shop openings, or name changes. One way of attracting media attention is to use a celebrity to launch a new product, or open a new shop. However, as Gummesson

Crisis (contingency) PR
used by an organization to manage its image when things go unexpectedly wrong

points out, this can be a fruitless exercise as the media interest is likely to be focused on the celebrity and not on the company staging the event.

Charismatic Business Leaders

One personality who can attract interest in the organization, however, is a charismatic business leader. Over the years Richard Branson has maintained a constant media presence though charity events, record-breaking stunts, and even an appearance on the hit comedy show *Friends* (see the End of Chapter Case). His relationship with the media has given his Virgin group of companies a ready mouthpiece that many of his rivals lack. Other examples include Bill Gates of Microsoft, who has given $5 billion in donations to charity, the late Anita Roddick of the Body Shop who promoted a number of environmental causes, and Alan Sugar, whose television show *The Apprentice* has created an image of shrewd, down-to-earth, business professionalism around his companies. However, it can work both ways and there have been cases where a business leader's handling of media relations can be disastrous for the organization. One of the best-known examples is Gerald Ratner, owner of a High Street chain of jewellery shops. In a speech to the Institute of Directors in 1991 he famously described the products his shops were selling as 'total crap'. Despite protestations that his comments had been taken out of context, the media had a field day and overnight his business was ruined.

Alliance/Partner Relationships

The final type of external relationship that can influence customer markets exists between the organization and its partners, i.e. those other organizations with which it works in order to serve its own customers more effectively. Ordinarily this might include relationships with suppliers and distributors, but as this is such a big area, it will be considered separately in the next chapter. Here we will concentrate on the challenges thrown up by managing relationships through alliances, partnerships, joint ventures, and other working arrangements into which the organization might enter. These are often referred to as 'collaborations' and usually come about when two or more organizations are able to bring together complementary skills, capabilities, functions, or products to improve organizational competitiveness and enhance customer value. Such collaborations are classed by Gummesson (1999) as 'mega' relationships, because they are usually handled at a strategic corporate level above the everyday customer market.

The idea of complementary relationships between organizations, with each bringing a different skill, and each deriving a benefit from the partnership, clearly fits the 'win–win' ideal of relationship marketing. For example, DIY chain Homebase originally came about through a partnership between UK supermarket Sainsbury's and Belgian DIY retailer GB-Inno-BM. Sainsbury's wanted to expand into the DIY sector but had no expertise in this area, while the Belgian company wanted to expand into the UK market of which it had no knowledge. Together, however, the two organizations were able to jointly realize their goals. With advancing technology, shorter product

	Internal	External
Informal	Tacit agreements	Business networks
Formal	Trade associations and alliances	Joint ventures agreements and alliances

Figure 7.2 Types of collaboration

development cycles, increasing globalization, and ever more demanding customers, such collaborations allow organizations to keep up and remain competitive.

As well as engendering 'win–win' solutions, organizational collaborations also fit neatly into other aspects of relationship marketing. Gordon (1998), for example, describes how technology has enabled the greater flow of data between organizations and facilitated collaborations. This is very much along the lines of the electronic relationships (through EDI or the Internet) which we discussed in the last chapter. Similarly, Ford *et al.* (1998) consider these relationships in terms of networks, stressing that each organization must assess and develop those relationships which tie in with their overall aims.

Collaborations can be categorized as being *internal* to an industry (i.e. between organizations operating in the same industry or sector) and *external* to the industry (Egan, 2004). Additionally, collaborations may also be classed as formal and informal. As a result, these can be plotted onto a four-box matrix to illustrate four distinct groupings. (See Figure 7.2.)

Tacit Agreements

Gummesson (1999) observes that in some industries tacit, or unspoken agreements and alliances develop through a rule or consensus which means that all industry members behave in the same way. For example French wine producers have stuck with the *Appellation d'Origine Contrôlée* system to guarantee quality. In the UK, the house-building industry has traditionally closed down for two weeks in December/ January, newspapers were historically divided into broadsheets or tabloids, and retailers opened and closed at the same times each day. Gummesson argues that this can hold companies back if they uphold the past at the expense of the future, and that innovation can mean breaking away from the tacit alliances and going it alone. Clearly this has already happened in some of the examples given above.

Sometimes, however, tacit agreements can lead to price-fixing or other restrictive practices which are designed to protect the profits of those involved. Such alliances are often referred to as cartels and in most markets they are illegal. However, their existence can be difficult to prove as they are agreements between individuals, made in private and with no written record. Such is their prevalence in some areas that

Gummesson includes them as one of his 30Rs—R17, the Criminal Network. Whether legal or not, tacit alliances are usually the result of industry networking.

Trade Associations and Alliances

Very often, formal agreements are made between organizations operating in an industry. Sometimes this can involve developing working relationships with competitors, where the objective is to protect or further the interests of the industry as a whole. For example, the Timber Trades Federation (TTF) was formed to promote the interests of joinery manufacturers. Although normally fierce rivals, all the companies were under pressure from environmentalists who were opposed to their use of timber. Pooling their resources, the TTF set out to reassure public opinion by promoting the ethical behaviour of its members and highlighting the sustainability of their timber sources. Other examples include smaller companies who have banded together to pool marketing resources. Sunkist began as an amalgam of California orange growers who wanted to reach a wider audience. Kerrygold did the same thing for Irish dairy farmers.

Combining resources in order to give greater value for the customer is another common reason for formal alliances. One of the best examples of this is in the airline industry where many organizations have combined their frequent flyer schemes so that customers can continue to accumulate rewards even if they don't always fly on the same airline. For example, One World Alliance brings together British Airways, American Airlines, Cathay Pacific, Finnair, Iberia, Japan Airlines, Lan Airlines, Malév, Qantas, and Royal Jordanian. Usually, airlines getting together in this way tend not to compete directly on the same routes, although inevitably some overlap does occur. The Nectar reward card (see Chapter 4) is a similar example, this time illustrating an alliance between a number of high-profile retailers.

Business Networks

Business networks are an example of the informal alliances and agreements that exist between organizations across different industries—Japanese Keiretsus are an example of this. The significance of business networks is covered in more detail in Chapter 2, but it is worth noting here that these can lead to unpredictability, when individual relationships become part of a much bigger, interrelated portfolio of relationships (Ford *et al.*, 1998). They can also make doing business in a market difficult if a company is are not part of the informal network.

Joint Ventures and Alliances

Formal alliances between organizations that complement each other can take a number of forms:

- **Formal Partnerships**—whereby two organizations remain independent but trade resources or know-how, such that each can develop their business. For example, in the 1980s and 90s Honda gained access to the UK car market through its partnership with Rover, while Rover gained access to valuable new model designs.

- **Joint Ventures**—whereby two or more organizations create a separate, jointly owned enterprise. For example the original Smart car was the result of a joint venture between Swatch and Daimler-Benz.

- **Consortia**—similar to joint ventures, but more of a network than a one-to-one relationship. Consortia are usually found in large construction or engineering projects (such as the NASA Space Shuttle) which one organization alone cannot undertake. Organizations working in these areas are usually experienced in managing such relationships (Hollensen, 2003).

- **Licensing Agreements**—whereby complementary brands or products can be sold or promoted together. For example, Disney products are used as promotions in McDonald's, while toy car company Corgi is famous for its James Bond models.

- **Co-marketing, or co-branding**—where two distinct marketing messages or brands are put together to boost both of them. For example, in recent years many organizations have issued 'affinity credit cards', often combining a credit card issuer with a charity (e.g. MasterCard and World Wildlife Fund).

- **Management Contracts**—whereby one organization is contracted to perform some or all of the operations of another. For example, UK rail operator Railtrack has management contracts with companies such as Jarvis, who maintain the rail network.

Managing relations between collaborating organizations presents challenges at a number of levels. Gummesson (1999) suggests that a short-term approach in order to get quick results will not pay off, and that alliances should be managed as strategic, long-term initiatives. When describing how organizations might manage alliance relationships, he draws an analogy with the advice that a marriage counsellor might give: 'choose your partner carefully, invest in a win–win relationship, stay attractive to your partner, develop a sound economy and search for a division of labour which works for all parties'. Issues of management must be agreed in advance (e.g. who is responsible for resolving problems which might arise, when neither party is in absolute control?) and each organization must be able to exercise patience and understanding.

Collaborations between international organizations can be the most challenging, particularly when they involve different national cultures. In a study of relations between Japanese and American firms, Voss *et al.* (2006) concluded that an organization's cultural sensitivity played a key part in determining the success of the alliance. In other words, the more an organization is willing to learn about other cultures and tailor its approach accordingly, the more likely it is that trust will be established and the alliance will work. This may sound obvious, but is not always easy to achieve when international cultures are ingrained. Hofstede (1991), for example, describes how the Japanese and Chinese see themselves in terms of a group (collectivism) as opposed to Americans who see themselves as individuals. These principles colour the way in which organizations from these respective countries are run.

Chapter Summary

Although customer relationships will be the focus of most relationship marketing strategies, all organizations will be influenced to a greater or lesser extent by other stakeholders who can affect what goes on in the marketplace. A wider study of relationship marketing therefore considers how effective management of relationships with 'external' stakeholders can enable the organization to serve its customers better. These external relationships include the way in which the organization works with governments and other regulatory bodies, investors, pressure groups, the mass media, and partner organizations. Although external relationships are traditionally handled through PR, the elevated position of some of these stakeholders means that relationship management has to take place at a level above the average marketing department.

Organizations must therefore determine which external relationships are going to be the most significant for them by, for instance, considering the power and influence of each stakeholder group. Relationships with stakeholders who can prevent the organization doing business (e.g. governments) must be handled with care, as without them there is no market. Managing relationships with influential stakeholders can sometimes create a conflict with the way in which an organization may wish to serve its customers—when, for example, issues of CSR appear to contradict the firm's marketing objectives. Ideally, the organization should seek a win–win situation that not only placates external stakeholders, but also generates good publicity at a customer level. Organizations finding themselves particularly in the public eye should develop proactive strategies to manage stakeholder relationships in order to protect themselves in the all-important customer market.

End of Chapter Case with Questions

Richard Branson—Master Publicist

Walk into a pub and ask people to name the boss of British Airways and perhaps some of them will know that it is Willie Walsh. Ask them then to name the boss of Virgin and the chances are that more of them will be able to answer 'Richard Branson'. This is because Branson has consistently gone out of his way to attract publicity and by linking his personal image with a successful brand name he has become arguably one of Britain's best-known businessmen. With his Virgin empire now embracing planes, trains, financial products, mobile phones, the media, and holidays, his personal fortune is estimated to be over £3 billion.

Born in 1950, Branson's first business venture was selling mail-order records through the *Student Magazine* he was publishing. In 1971 he opened his first Virgin record shop in Oxford Street, London and went on to develop the Virgin Record Label. The name 'Virgin' reputedly came about after one of the girls working on his student magazine quipped 'we're all virgins at business'. Since then the Virgin group has expanded into air travel (1984), holidays (1985), publishing (1991), radio (1993), cola (1994), wedding dresses (1996), railways (1996), cosmetics (1997), mobile phones (1999), and media (2007) as well as many other avenues. Although many of the ventures have been sold over the years, by 2007 it was estimated that there were around 200 different Virgin companies operating in 30 different countries and employing over 25,000 people.

Part and parcel of Branson's business philosophy is to use publicity to create brand equity around the Virgin name. Over the years this has involved a number of 'stunts' and other publicity-generating activities. In 1986 Branson's boat, *Virgin Atlantic Challenger II* crossed the Atlantic in the fastest ever recorded time and the following year he did the same thing in his hot-air balloon, *Virgin Atlantic Flyer*. Other daredevil stunts have included a balloon crossing of the Atlantic and the fastest ever crossing of the English Channel in an amphibious vehicle in 2004 to mark the twentieth anniversary of the Virgin Atlantic plane service. Branson has also posed in a wedding dress to launch Virgin Bride and driven a tank through Times Square to fire at a Coca Cola sign to publicize the launch of his own cola drink. More serious activities have included the setting up of charitable foundations and being one of the first on the scene of a Virgin train crash in 2007 to comfort victims and talk to the press.

All of this publicity has enabled Branson to pursue what he calls a 'branded venture capital' approach to enter new businesses. Basically this means that wealthy partners provide the bulk of the cash for new deals, while the Virgin brand is exchanged for a controlling interest in the enterprise. Thus, when Virgin Mobile merged with media provider NTL, the group was named Virgin Media and Branson became the largest shareholder. In return NTL got a more saleable brand name with which to revive its fortunes.

Questions

1. How has Richard Branson's personal profile helped the Virgin Group?

2. Is Branson's approach viable for all organizations? Support your answer with examples.

Sources:
'About Virgin' http://www.virgin.com/AboutVirgin/RichardBranson accessed 23/05/08
'Richard Branson, so who is the Virgin airline king?' http://www.millservices.co.uk accessed 23/05/08
BBC News: 'Profile: Richard Branson', http://newsvote.bbc.co.uk accessed 26/11/07

Discussion Questions

1. From an organization's point of view, what is a stakeholder? Why is there such a debate around the subject?

2. Why should the study of marketing be concerned with stakeholder relationships?

3. Describe who would normally undertake lobbying and for what reason.

4. What does Gummesson mean when he says that 'the real customer is not always found in the market'?

5. How might investors and other financial influencers affect an organization's relationships with its customers?

6. Why is financial PR such a specialist job?

7. Describe the various motives of different pressure groups who might be opposed to McDonald's. To what extent do McDonald's customers share these motives?

8. Should an organization work with pressure groups? If not, how can they limit the impact of their campaigns?

9. Why might there be potential for conflict in relationships between organizations and the mass media?

10. Describe the different types of PR that an organization might need to manage. At which stakeholders are these aimed?

11. What is 'corporate social responsibility' (CSR)? Is CSR compatible with marketing?

12. What are the challenges in managing relationships with partner organizations? How might the success of these relationships be of benefit to customers? Give examples.

Further Reading

Baines, P., Egan, J., and Jefkins, F. (2004) *Public Relations: Contemporary Issues and Techniques*, Elsevier Butterworth-Heinemann, Oxford.

Jones, P., Comfort, D., and Hillier, D. (2007) 'What's in store? Retail marketing and corporate social responsibility', **Marketing Intelligence & Planning**, 25(1), 17–30.

Gummesson, E. (1999) *Total Relationship Marketing. Rethinking Marketing Management: From 4Ps to 30Rs*, Butterworth Heinemann, Oxford.

References

Argenti, J. (1997) 'Stakeholders: the case against', **Long Range Planning**, 30(3), 442–5.

Baines, P., Egan, J., and Jefkins, F. (2004) *Public Relations: Contemporary Issues and Techniques*, Elsevier Butterworth-Heinemann, Oxford.

Christopher, M., Payne, A., and Ballantyne, D. (1991) *Relationship Marketing: Bringing quality, customer service and marketing together*, Butterworth-Heinemann, Oxford.

Christopher, M., Payne, A., and Ballantyne, D. (2002) *Relationship Marketing: Creating stakeholder value*, Butterworth-Heinemann, Oxford.

Cutlip, S., Center, A., and Broom, G. (1994) *Effective Public Relations* (7th edn), Prentice Hall, Englewood Cliffs, NJ.

Dowling, G. (2001) *Creating Corporate Reputations: Identity, image and performance*, Oxford University Press.

Doyle, P. (1995) 'Marketing in the New Millennium', **European Journal of Marketing**, 29, 23–41.

Egan, J. (2004) *Relationship Marketing* (2nd edn), Pearson Education, Harlow.

Ethical Corporation (2005) 'How to Communicate your Corporate Values to Consumers', available at www.ethicalcorp.com/consumer accessed 18/02/08

Ford, D., Gadde, L., Håkansson, H., Lundgren, A., Snehota, I., Turnbull, P., and Wilson, D. (1998) *Managing Business Relationships*, John Wiley & Sons, Chichester.

Freeman, R. (1984) *Strategic Management: A stakeholder approach*, Pitman, Boston, MA.

Freeman, R. and Reed, D. (1983) 'Stockholders and Stakeholders: A new perspective on corporate governance', *California Management Review*, 25(3), 88–106.

Gordon, I. (1998) *Relationship Marketing*, John Wiley & Sons, Ontario.

Gummesson, E. (1987) 'The New Marketing—Developing Long Term Interactive Relationships', *Long Range Planning*, 20(4), 10–20.

Gummesson, E. (1989), 'Nine Lessons on Service Quality', *Total Quality Management*, Feb., 82–90.

Gummesson, E. (1994) 'Making Relationship Marketing Operational', *International Journal of Service Industry Management*, 5(5), 5–20.

Gummesson, E. (1999) *Total Relationship Marketing. Rethinking Marketing Management: From 4Ps to 30Rs*, Butterworth Heinemann, Oxford.

Harris, P., Gardner, H., and Vetter, N. (1999) ' "Goods over God" Lobbying and Political Marketing: A case study of the campaign by the Shopping Hours Reform Council to change Sunday trading laws in Britain', in Newman, B. (ed.), *Handbook of Political Marketing*, Sage Publications, London.

Hofstede, G. (1991) *Cultures and Organizations: Software of the Mind*, McGraw-Hill, London.

Hollensen, S. (2003) *Marketing Management, A Relationship Approach*, Pearson Education, Harlow.

Jones, P., Comfort, D., and Hillier, D. (2006) 'Anti-corporate Retailer Campaigns on the Internet', *International Journal of Retail & Distribution Management*, 34(12), 882–91.

Jones, P., Comfort, D., and Hillier, D. (2007) 'What's in store? Retail Marketing and Corporate Social Responsibility', *Marketing Intelligence & Planning*, 25(1), 17–30.

Levick, R. (2004) 'A Virtual Omnipresent Enemy: Defending clients against Internet blog attacks', *Levick Strategic Communications*, available at www.levick.com accessed 17/01/08.

Lozano, J. (2005) 'Towards the Relational Corporation: From managing stakeholder relationships to building stakeholder relationships (waiting for Copernicus)', *Corporate Governance*, 5(2), 60–77.

Maignan, I. and Ferrell, O. (2001) 'Corporate Citizenship as a Marketing Instrument', *European Journal of Marketing*, 35(3/4), 457–84.

Morgan, R. and Hunt, S. (1994) 'The Commitment–Trust Theory of Relationship Marketing', *Journal of Marketing*, 58 (Oct.), 20–38.

Nader, R. (1965) *Unsafe at Any Speed*, Grossman Publishers, New York.

Payne, A., Ballantyne, D., and Christopher, M. (2005) 'A Stakeholder Approach to Relationship Marketing Strategy', *European Journal of Marketing*, 39(7/8), 855–71.

Reichheld, F. (1996) *The Loyalty Effect*, Harvard Business School Press, Boston, MA.

Rivera-Camino, J. (2007) 'Re-evaluating Green Marketing Strategy: A stakeholder perspective', *European Journal of Marketing*, 41(11/12), 1328–58.

Voss, K., Johnson, J., and Cullen, J. (2006) 'Relational Exchange in US–Japanese Marketing Strategic Alliances', *International Marketing Review*, 23(6), 610–35.

Wilson, D. and Cameron, G. (2006) *Public Relations: Strategies and Tactics*, Pearson Education, Boston, MA.

Websites

'Delia's golden eggs' http://www.bbc.co.uk/1/hi/entertainment/216737.stm accessed 18/11/98

'Junk food ad ban "shocks" firms'
http://www.bbc.co.uk/1/hi/business/6157708.stm accessed 17/11/06

'Tesco breaching planning laws' http://www.bbc.co.uk/1/hi/uk/5261844.stm accessed 18/08/06

'Cadbury wants children to eat two million kg of fat—to get fit!'
http://www.foodcomm.org/parentsjury/cadbury_03.htm accessed 17/02/08
http://www.landrover.co.uk/gb/en/Company/Sustainability/ourplanet accessed 17/01/08
http://www.flysilverjetcom/Press-release-2006-11-26.aspx accessed 17/02/08

'German car giants pressure EU over emissions' http://www.telegraph.co.uk accessed 08/08/07

Supplier Relations

Chapter Outline

Learning Outcomes

After reading this chapter you should be able to:

- understand the various contexts of supplier relationships;

- differentiate between different types of suppliers;

- recognize the difference between supply chains and distribution channels;

- evaluate the contribution of supplier relationships to strategic success;

- relate the principles of supplier relationships to relationship marketing;

- acknowledge the potential limits to supplier relationship theory.

The costs and risks of marketing attach to whole processes rather than to particular transactions: many of them are common to a great part, and some even to the whole, of the affairs of a business.

(Marshall, 1920: 179)

Introduction

The significance of supplier relations within the marketing context has tended to be a bit of a Cinderella subject. Whilst increasing attention has been paid to the importance of suppliers for sustained competitive success in a range of other discipline areas, marketing has tended to focus more on the downstream components of the supply chain, i.e. **distribution channels** and, of course, customers. Notions and research into supplier relationships has almost exclusively been informed by the subject domain of Operations Management. A key exception to this, however, has been the work of the Industrial Marketing and Purchasing Group (IMP) (see, for example, Ford (2002) and Håkansson *et al.* (2004), who see suppliers and, specifically, relationships with suppliers, as being key to the successful marketing effort. An additional perspective that has also made a considerable contribution to the wider view that supplier relations are of strategic significance is the work contained within the field of Industrial Economics and Organization Studies, and especially, Strategic Management informed by such perspectives.

> **Distribution channels**
> the downstream components of a supply chain

Whilst a clear logic as to the importance of supplier relations has emerged over the last couple of decades, why should it be of concern to marketers? This chapter attempts to address this question by drawing on a range of concepts and perspectives found not only within the relationship marketing body of knowledge, but also from these wider domains. In order to explore the significance and impact of supplier relationships it is first useful to gain a clear overview of the key construct governing the production and passage of goods until they create ultimate customer value—the supply chain.

Why does marketing need to pay attention to suppliers and have relationships with them? In order to address this question it is important to have a clear understanding of what a supply chain is and the difference between a supply chain and a distribution channel.

Opening Case Study with Questions

Supplier Relationships at Dell

Dell is a global brand in IT and personal computers and has drawn much attention owing to its phenomenal success. The annual turnover exceeds $40 billion p.a.—not bad for a company that was only started in 1984. They currently ship an average of 140,000 PC systems per day. Two key strategies have been identified as driving this success: the 'direct business model' and 'virtual integration'.

Dell Direct Business Model

The Dell Direct Business Model should be familiar to any student of Marketing. At its heart lies the concept of disintermediation. Typically, producers of PCs, e.g. IBM Lenovo, Packard Bell, Compaq, Fujitsu Siemens, rely heavily on re-sellers such as specialized PC retailers, general electrical retailers and department stores. Dell, on the other hand, always sought to offer its products directly to the consumer via direct marketing. The key communication channels that Dell uses in order to achieve this include its website and direct response advertising, both backed up by call centres. Put simply the Dell Direct Business Model is a form of direct marketing. The rationale for using this model, in Dell's case, was that if it could get PCs to the customer cheaper than its competitors, it would be successful. It's important to note, however, that anyone can offer a product at a cheaper price—to be successful two key criteria need to be addressed: first, that the cheaper price still affords a profit (i.e. contributes to a surplus after costs); and second, that customers rarely go by price alone: customers will assess the quality of the offering and if there is comparable (or better) quality, may then be influenced by the cheaper price.

'Most important, the direct business model has allowed us to leverage our relationships with both suppliers and customers to such an extent that I believe it's fair to think of our companies as being virtually integrated. That allows us to focus on where we add value and to build a much larger firm much more quickly.' (Michael Dell quoted in Magretta, 1998: 74)

Virtual Integration

This term has been used a lot over the last decade or so and actually refers to a number of quite different things. In Dell's case virtual integration refers specifically to their strategy of only directly producing what they have to—that where they have a core competence—and using the resources contained within their supply chain to contribute the rest. This is then supported by a range of collaborative relationships which effectively glue the supply chain together. With so much activity outsourced to the supply chain it is essential that appropriate governance mechanisms are in place to ensure that the right supply and the right products are in the right place at the right time in order to satisfy customer demand.

Virtual integration is more than just a mechanism for coordinating activity, however. Through working collaboratively with suppliers, economies can be secured, risk can be reduced, and innovation can be fostered.

Partnering with Panel Display Makers

'Dell might need 20 million flat panel displays, and some years there will be more demand than supply. Other years, there will be more supply than demand. A few companies are making multibillion-dollar investments in the manufacture of these displays. So we cook up a little deal where the supplier agrees to meet 25% of our volume requirements for displays, and because of the long-term commitment we make to them, we'll get our displays year in year out, even when there's more demand than supply. The supplier effectively becomes our partner. They assign their engineers to our design team, and we start to treat them as if they were part of the company.' (Michael Dell, op. cit.: 75)

Shipping

Dell does not make any of the display panels for its PCs. Instead it uses a number of companies, some very well-known brands in their own right, to produce Dell own-brand displays (and VDU monitors). By developing close relationships with these suppliers and their logistics suppliers' shipping costs can be dramatically reduced. This cost is reduced by two key factors. First, display products are not actually delivered to Dell—if you order a Dell PC system, the monitor or display that come with it has never actually been touched by Dell as it has come directly from the producer. Second, by outsourcing shipping to logistics experts, Dell can capture both the economies of scale and economies of expertise that will reside in such practice.

In America, for example, Dell will tell its logistics supplier (e.g. Airborne Express or UPS) to collect 10,000 PCs a day and simultaneously collect 10,000 monitors from the Sony plant in Mexico. The logistics supplier will then match up the PC system to the corresponding monitor and ship directly to the customer. Clearly this can only work with the very sophisticated uses of data and information exchange between all parties. Clearly also, this cannot work if all the parties do not have a close and collaborative relationship with each other.

Questions

1. Do you think Dell computers would be as competitively priced if they used more traditional production/distribution techniques?

2. Close relationships with suppliers can reduce costs; how else do you think such relationships could benefit end customers?

3. Do you think the coordination illustrated in the shipping example could be achieved if Dell and its supplier did not have collaborative relationships?

Sources:
Magretta, J. (1998), 'The Power of Virtual Integration: An Interview with Dell Computer's Michael Dell' (1998) *Harvard Business Review*, Mar.–Apr., 73–84
Dell corporate website—
http://www1.euro.dell.com/content/topics/global.aspx/corp/soulofdell/en/index?c=uk&tl=en&ts=corp&~ck=mn accessed 30/10/07
http://www1.euro.dell.com/content/topics/global.aspx/corp/sup_diversity/en/index?c=uk&tl=en&ts=corp&~section=001 accessed 30/10/07

Different Views of Supply Chains

Supply chains and **supply chain management (SCM)** are typical of those terms that are much cited but actually little understood. The key reason for this is that there are several different definitions and perspectives as to what they actually are and of what they consist. In exploring these different views, a range of key perspectives and issues can be introduced.

Supply chain management
the concept of managing a supply chain as a whole, rather than as separate components

External Supply Chain

Supply chains are often considered, and popularized, as rather simple—linear—flows of materials, components, semi-finished products, to the final production of a product and its ultimate consumption. This is often referred to as the external chain view, and is presented in Figure 8.1.

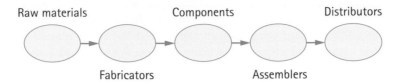

Figure 8.1 The external supply chain

As can be seen from the diagram, each organization that comprises the chain performs a different set of activities and tasks. Theoretically, all of these activities can be performed by one organization: this is referred to as vertical integration. This form of organization was relatively popular in large manufacturing firms from post-industrialization. However, over the years this form of organization has become less prevalent for a number of reasons and is only really suited to a narrow range of supply contexts. For example, supply chains concerned with the production of relatively simple products or commodities would be those most likely to be using such an approach.

Minicase 1

Vertical Integration at FMC

The Ford Motor Company (FMC) were in many ways the pioneers of modern mass production, especially when in 1910 they opened their new Highland Park near Detroit to build thousands of the iconic Ford Model T. The design of this factory set a precedent for virtually all mass production factories that followed—it was the first to have an assembly line. Whilst the production process was new, paradoxically the factory was also an extreme example of work organization—vertical integration. This economics term is used to describe where the ownership of the processes needed to produce products lies. A vertically integrated firm is one that owns many of the processes and steps needed to make a product. The Highland Park plant did not have any deliveries of subassemblies or finished components of any sort—everything was physically produced in the factory. Wire was delivered and made into fastenings, and even rubber compound was delivered and made—in the factory—into the tyres that ultimately the Model Ts would drive away on. Relationships with suppliers in this orthodoxy were not really important other than to ensure that the raw and basic materials supplied were of acceptable quality and the right price.

> **Vertical integration**
> whereby two or more of the activities within a linear supply chain are performed by the same organization

Questions

1. What are the key advantages of the Highland Park approach to vehicle production?

2. What sort of additional benefits could more collaborative relationships with suppliers provide for Ford or its ultimate customers?

3. What were the key reasons for producing as much as possible in-house?

Sources:
http://www.ford.com/about-ford/heritage accessed 30/10/07
Wilson, J. M. (1995), 'Henry Ford's just-in-time system', *International Journal of Operations & Production Management*, 15(12), 59–75

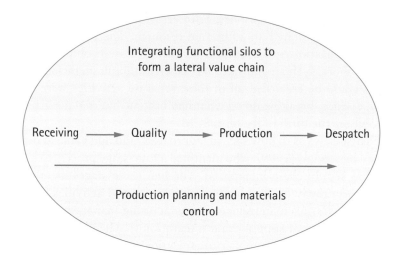

Figure 8.2 The internal supply chain

However, Harland (1996) usefully identifies that in addition to this external supply chain, there are three other views of supply chains prevalent in the literature: internal supply chains, dyadic supply chains, and network supply chains. Over the past few years another view of supply chains has also emerged—the e-supply chain.

Internal Supply Chains

The origins of the term SCM go back to the early and mid-1980s (Oliver and Webber, 1982) when there was great interest in increasing efficiency in the movement of production components and finished goods. As can be seen from Figure 8.2, production components and the information that accompanied them passed through different departments, each with its own objectives and reporting structures. The receiving, or goods-in, department was concerned with ensuring that what was delivered was of the right quantity and type and corresponded to what was actually ordered (i.e. that the delivery note corresponded to the purchase order), and that there were no obvious problems, such as damaged cartons, etc. Until all of these checks had been made, goods received were essentially in quarantine.

The components would then be released and move into the control of production where they would be coded and stored until needed in the production process. At any point throughout this process the quality department could be making various checks to ensure that the components were of the correct quality—samples were taken and measured and various quality techniques were used, such as statistical quality control, etc.

When the components had been turned into finished products they would then be under the control of the despatch department who would organize distribution to customers. If the company was operating a quality control system, there would be further quality checks of the finished product. Whilst all of these activities occur for good reasons it is clear that there is an amount of duplication of effort, for example repeated storage or checking episodes. Further, running each of these procedures and departments necessitated an additional resource. The passage of components from input to output took time as each department released components to the next department. In short, such an approach has inherent inbuilt inefficiencies.

Efficiencies could be created if all of these separate activities were centrally coordinated, in essence, breaking down what had become internal departmental silos. In so doing, we see the birth of the term SCM.

One of the first views as to how such an approach could add value to organizations was suggested by Stevens (1989), who identified a four-stage process to achieve what he described as supply chain integration. The first three stages identified the progressive movement away from individual procedures and activities to a functional integration (e.g. materials management, manufacturing management, and distribution). The fourth stage of supply chain integration is when this **internal supply chain** is interlinked with the supplier organization and customer organization. In essence this forms an external supply chain as outlined previously and discussed in the following section.

This form of SCM still exists today but has become integrated with production planning and scheduling techniques, most often IT facilitated and driven. The passage of components through the company is now often managed by materials requirements planning (MRP) systems. More sophisticated systems also take account of the various resources required at each stage of the production process—these are known as manufacturing resource planning or MRPII, and more latterly enterprise resource planning (ERP). With the advent of increasingly sophisticated information and communication technologies (e.g. the Internet), such systems now span organizational boundaries and are further discussed in Chapter 6. Such real-time information-enabled supply chains, and the software that facilitates them, have become a separate definition of supply chains in their own right and have spawned a large and lucrative supply chain software industry.

Using the internal supply chain as a means to identify value-adding activities within the organization gives rise to the idea of 'internal customers' and, hence, 'internal suppliers'. These issues are explored further in the following chapter.

Internal supply chain

the movement within an organization of production components and finished goods and the information which accompanies them

External Linear Supply Chains

The success of the internal SCM approach begged a simple question: if such efficiencies could be gained internally, what efficiencies could be gained if each supplier utilized this approach and the whole supply chain was coordinated in some way?

Conceptually the external chain approach is similar to the internal chain in that it is about breaking down silos—the internal chain silo is the functional department, whereas the external chain silo is the whole supplier (or customer) company. Conceptually, however, there are also major differences between these two views. It is relatively simple for a company to organize or reorganize what happens within its boundaries—it owns and controls these—but how can a range of companies be organized, controlled, and managed? This issue has perhaps caused the most debate and research within the area of SCM. No consensus has been reached, nor can be reached as the context of the supply situation varies from supply chain to supply chain and what might work in one context may be disastrous in another.

As mentioned in the introduction, this linear view of supply chains is rather simple, but there are historical reasons for this. Most of the research undertaken in the area of SCM has been conducted in the automotive and electronics industry sectors. In many ways these sectors are very similar in that: lead companies (typically the brand owner or 'original equipment manufacturer' (OEM)) are very powerful, often the most powerful players in the supply chain; these sectors are characterized by very large production volumes; similarly, there is a high degree of production stability over the life cycle of the product (about six months for PCs, longer for home electronics, and about six years (with a mid-cycle revamp) for motor cars). Another important historical reason for the development of this view is that it represents a westernized interpretation of the production and supply practices of Japanese manufacturers.

External supply chains in the automotive and electronics sectors look very different from what is presented in Figure 8.1. It is impossible for a car producer to still behave in a vertically integrated way because of the increasing number of component parts that comprise finished products and the increasing complexity embedded in many of these parts. A single company does not have the expert resources to manage such a range of different supply internally, nor can it bear the transaction costs associated with dealing with large numbers of suppliers. An effective way in which to manage both of these problems is to outsource whole elements of supply.

For example, car makers used to produce car seats as these were an integral element of the car. This necessitated transacting with a range of suppliers such as: fabric, foam, wire, thread, metal tubes, fixings, plastic components, etc. All of these components had to be managed, stored, and financed (and bear the risk associated with doing this). Whilst car seats are an important element of a car—should they be considered integral to the brand, or an essential requirement that needs to be resourced internally? If so, what would be the opportunity cost of doing this?

Minicase 2

Car Seats

How many components make up a car seat? A basic seat will have a metal and wire frame, some sort of covering, some sort of padding, runners, and fittings to attach it to the floor, a variety of fastenings and thread to hold it all together, some moulded plastic components, and some springs. More advanced car seats will also contain airbag mechanisms, electrical adjustment controls and motors, heating elements, and even massage systems. Assuming that each of these components is uniform and supplied each by one supplier, that's over ten suppliers and a range of different varieties of each of the component. This all has to be ordered and stored. Furthermore it all has to be produced and then assembled into the car itself.

Whilst car seats are obviously important parts of a car, unless you are of a non-average size or shape or have a bad back, the car seat is unlikely to influence your choice of new car.

Also, to what extent are the materials, technologies, and processes associated with the car seat similar to other materials, technologies, and processes used to produce a car? If asked what are the core elements that define a car (apart from branding) most people are likely to answer: the car body, its engine, and other key mechanical elements. Car producers are therefore better off focusing on a narrower range of activities that more specifically address the core values of the product. As well as being peripheral to the core values, the number of suppliers of car seat components adds significant cost. Multiple transactions with multiple suppliers carries a heavy transaction cost (the cost of making the order and subsequent expediting, management, and ultimately payment). Similarly, in getting someone else to produce the car seats, the car maker can concentrate its limited resources into the areas that are more strategically important. Finally, in outsourcing the production of car seats, car makers can benefit from the economies of scale that such suppliers can elicit, as well as securing the expertise of such suppliers—car seats are their business.

Questions

1. Reducing the number of transactions can reduce the cost—how can external transaction costs (i.e. with suppliers) be compared to internal transaction costs (i.e. the cost of using your own department); what metrics and data could be used for such a comparison?

2. There are a number of benefits to buying systems rather than manufacturing them one-self. What are more important, the reduction in cost of the system, or the potential addition of greater innovation?

3. If car seats were traditionally made by the car makers themselves, from where do car seat makers come and where do they get their expertise?

Source: Author

Instead of designing car seats and, producing, buying, and managing all the necessary supply, car makers now outsource the whole component—or system—as such 'whole' components have become known. Other examples of common 'systems' include the interior facia, engine management systems, gear boxes, and, depending on the manufacturer, suspension systems and engines. This form of supply chain management is known as *systems integration*, and the supply chains that result are shown in Figure 8.3.

In the above diagram the car maker, or OEM example, is dealing with five key suppliers (i.e. systems integrators). If they were a vertically integrated company, they would have to deal with hundreds or even thousands of suppliers. This reduction in the number of suppliers with whom companies now deal is referred to as supply base rationalization, and has been a growing phenomenon over the past couple of decades. It is also interesting to note how each of the systems integrators' supply chains look in terms of the number of actor links. This can be seen from two perspectives. First, there are the number of linear connections e.g. A and D have three; B and C have four. These are referred to as tiers or echelons. Second, some of the

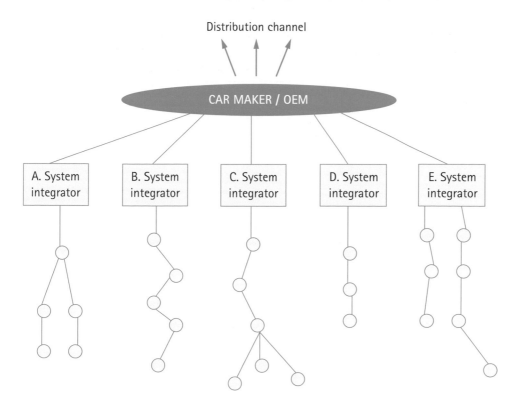

Figure 8.3 A systems integration view of supply chains

systems' integrators are supplied by more than one chain or chains which converge at lower echelons. The reality of supply chains is indeed far more complicated than the usual linear supply chain outlined in Figure 8.1.

The trend towards supply base rationalization is driven by both push and pull factors. Push factors have largely been covered previously in terms of the costs associated with vertical integration and managing and transacting with a large supply base. Another key push factor is the drive towards cost reduction. It may seem counter-intuitive to consider that buying in a component can be cheaper than producing it internally—indeed, buying in components carry additional transaction costs (e.g. the cost of sourcing supply; the cost of negotiation; the cost of contracting and payment, etc.). However, costs can be significantly reduced by using the supply chain in two key ways. First, suppliers concentrate on producing large numbers of what they are specialists in and can therefore benefit from economies of scale such as production run scaling or reduced process from their own suppliers because of the large quantities bought. The second way in which costs can be reduced is via economies of scope. The suppliers' expertise is concentrated on a narrower range of activities than the buyer, thus giving them greater opportunities to innovate in terms of design or production (e.g. design to reduce costs and produce more efficiently).

Table 8.1 Different attributes of component supply and systems integration

Typical component supplier	Systems integrator
large numbers	few numbers
low complexity	high complexity
easy switching	difficult to switch
low unit cost	high unit cost
low life cycle cost	high life cycle cost
low risk	high risk
little need for knowledge	greater need for knowledge
little need for innovation	greater need for innovation
transactive	relational

Pull factors are becoming increasingly important in many supply contexts. Two key pull factors include innovation and knowledge, i.e. the buying company wants to draw on the suppliers' knowledge and innovation in order to produce better, rather than just cheaper, products (or produce products better). Drawing innovation from the supply chain is increasingly embedded within commercial contracts and the ways in which organizations interact with each other. For example, historically, manufacturers would produce detailed specification documents defining exactly what they wanted. This was then embedded in the contracts they issued to suppliers to ensure that the specifications were met, or remedies were in place should they not be met. Increasingly, however, we are seeing new types of specification and contracting. Instead of detailed specifications, buyers are using 'performance specifications'. The same sort of specification is also often seen in service contexts. For example, the 'performance specification' is written in the form of a 'service level agreement' where the buyer stipulates what it wants the service to achieve, e.g. process so many in-coming calls per hour, etc. Buyers are focusing on components achieving specific performance objectives rather than what they are made out of, etc. Innovation is also increasingly sought via non-contractual means, discussed later in this chapter.

Whether supply base rationalization is the result of push factors or pull factors, it places new demands on the management of supplier relationships. What is being supplied by a systems integrator differs significantly from that of a typical component supplier, as can be seen from Table 8.1.

As suggested above, the nature of the relationship between an OEM and its systems integrators will also be very different, whether based on more open specifications and contracts or other forms of relational communication and governance.

Dyadic Supply Chains

When discussing supply chains many researchers and commentators limit their view to the interplay between the buying organizations and the supplying organization. Whilst this is a rather limited definition of supply chains, it can make a powerful unit of analysis for looking at relationships with wider views of supply chains. This has already been illustrated in the previous discussion of system suppliers, for example. Similarly, dyadic relations also exist within the wider network views of supply chains as noted in Chapter 2 (business networks), and will be explored further in the next section on supply networks.

One of the key differences between organizational purchasing and consumer buying behaviour is that the former is often reliant on a range of people usually referred to (in the B2B literature) as a **Decision Making Unit** (DMU), typically constituting initiators, deciders, buyers, influencers, users, and gatekeepers (Webster and Wind, 1972). It is impractical for a single representative of the selling organization effectively to interact with the whole DMU; they usually would not have the range of skills, expertise, information, and authority to do so in any case. Effective relations between organizations therefore require a range of interactions between a range of different people, not unlike those illustrated previously in Chapter 2 (Figure 2.5). Effective dyadic relationships need an effective inter-organizational interface to ensure that such interactions are enabled and timely. This is perhaps quite different from what might have been considered to be the 'traditional' view of inter-organizational interaction, often characterized by sequential 'point-to-point', i.e. buyer to seller, negotiation. Relations based on such limited interfaces can be stifled by inefficient and ineffective information flow: inefficient in that the buyer/supplier interface may not have the capacity to convey all the information required in a timely manner; and ineffective in that information from the range of people involved, at arms length (e.g. designers, finance, etc.) may be distorted or missed. The buyers and sellers may, inadvertently, act as a form of gatekeeper; thus, that other people in key areas may not be able to make effective contributions to the relationship. For example, the supplier's design team may not fully understand the reason why the buying company needs specific modifications. If they knew the reasons for this, they may be in a position to translate such requirements elsewhere and thus add greater value to the relationship. Interaction between individuals also increases the chance of passing on tacit knowledge (see following section p. 255), which can also add to the relationship value. For example, in closer relationships, buyers are more likely to describe the 'why' rather than just the 'what'. This enables suppliers to better address the needs of the customer.

Understanding the importance of relationships occurring between people in different organizations is significant because, put simply, organizations do not have relationships with other organizations, it is the people within them that do. This people element has already been explored in Chapter 2.

Organizational relationships, whether with suppliers or buyers, may take different forms. It is worth going back to basics in terms of conceptualizing exactly what a relationship is. At its simplest an organizational or institutional relationship is a form of **governance**. It is a way to set expectations as to the behaviour of each party, and allied to this, what the rewards or sanctions of such behaviours are. Governance can, of course, be established via legal mechanisms, i.e. **contracts**, but increasingly it is being argued that there are greater benefits (in appropriate circumstances) to employing relational (non-legalistic) forms of governance. Both forms of

Decision Making Unit
the range of individuals within an organization who have an input into the purchase decision

Governance
formal or informal 'policing' of the behaviour of each party in the relationship

Contract
a legal agreement between parties

governance set out expectations for each party and both will probably contain rewards and sanctions for good or under performance. Both forms of governance will carry a set-up cost, so why are firms moving more towards relationships than contracts as their preferred governance mechanism?

Minicase 3

Partnership Sourcing: Anti-competitive?

Partnership Sourcing Limited (PSL) was formed in 1990 as a joint establishment between the Confederation of British Industry (CBI) and the Department of Trade and Industry (now BERR). It was originally based in the CBI's headquarter offices at Centre Point, London.

PSL was formed with a clear mandate—to promote the use of more collaborative relations with suppliers throughout the UK economy. The reason for this is simple—collaboration increases competitiveness. Collaborative relations are not just for large multinationals, but critically, SMEs are encouraged to adopt 'partnership' practices. Similarly, PSL seeks to encourage public sector bodies to adopt partnership principles where possible. Full partnerships are not always possible within the public sector due to a stringent European-wide free market philosophy throughout the EU member states with laws and statutes to ensure free trade. Collaborative relations are seen by many, especially the public sector, to be anticompetitive and therefore inferior to free market or 'transactive' relations. The argument for the latter is that free market competition drives innovative solutions and cost reduction more so than collaboration. However, the public sector is gradually adopting some partnership approaches. All public sector tenders, by law, have to be advertised throughout the EU states, thus ensuring initial use of the free market. However, when a supplier has been selected via these competitive means (i.e. tenders and bidding), partnerships can be developed over a defined period of time, thus accruing some of the key benefits of collaboration.

Source: http://www.pslcbi.com accessed 20/11/07

No matter how well written, a contract has two key problems. First, it can never take account of all eventualities because these may not be known. Is it possible, for example, to specify in a contract that the supplier must supply some form of innovation that neither party can specify that has something to do with their primary product or the use of their primary product? For this, and other reasons, there is always a risk of what is known as contract failure. Relationships, of course, can fail also. Mari Sako, based on seminal research, identified a key commonality between contracts and relationships—trust. In studying automotive supply chains in Japan, Sako (1992) identified three different types of trust as presented in Table 8.2.

Obligational contracting
contracting between parties that is fundamentally informed by good will and trust

This analysis of trust gave rise to what became known as **obligational contracting**, i.e. contracting between parties that was fundamentally informed by goodwill trust. Obligational contracting is just another term for relationship.

There is an interesting parallel here between external contracting (i.e. suppliers) and internal contracting (i.e. employees). All employees have contracts of employment

Table 8.2 Three types of trust

Type of trust	Buyer perspective	Supplier perspective
Contractual trust	Basically not trusted to perform the task effectively so must use the safeguard of a contract to ensure remedies, should there be failure. This may be based on perception of supplier-firm expertise or experience, or experience of poor past performance or behaviour of the supplier. It could be based on having a lack of knowledge regarding the supplier. May use the supplier again, may not—no explicit commitment.	This might just be a one-off order so want to keep investment (financial or otherwise) and costs to a minimum. Aim to satisfy the customer's most basic requirements. No point trying to do anything else (e.g. 'delight' the customer) as there is no guarantee of future business. Will we be paid for this work? Will we be paid on time? Is the customer displaying nuisance tendencies, e.g. keep changing their mind, poor communication, unrealistic demands/expectations, etc.
Competence trust	Trust that the supplier does have the necessary skills and expertise to perform the task. Perhaps based on prior experience or interactions indicating the supplier's intent, attitude, culture, professionalism, etc. May be based on reputation or knowledge of other customers served. May be based on external accreditation (e.g. quality marks).	Confidence that payment terms will be adhered to. May be a customer keen to keep (e.g. reputation of supplying this customer). Indications of potential future business opportunities. As such can perhaps invest more in the supply situation as possibility of future payback. Customer behaving in a professional manner. e.g. clear communication, realistic demands. Possibility of being a 'preferred supplier'.
Goodwill trust	Complete confidence that the supplier will meet all their requirements. These requirements may be explicit *and* implicit. Confidence that the supplier will do all it can to satisfy the customer in terms of both quality of product and the service. Good source of technical knowledge and innovation. Could exploit this in other areas.	Is a preferred supplier—a first port of call. Know future order requirements and changes well in advance so can plan well ahead. This is good for general business and not just the relationship with that particular customer. May get valuable market or technological insights, e.g. trends and shifts in customer markets.

by law. However, as is well documented in the organizational behaviour literature, such contracts do not provide a complete incentive for sustained maximum performance, nor a disincentive for poor performance (unless marked). This is another example of 'contract failure', but in this case organizational behaviour has presented a potential solution in the form of the **psychological contract** (Schein, 1965). Whilst the basic rules of work are bound within the contract of employment, the way in which work is done is developed over time with reference to the way the employee feels they are treated fairly, group culture, and normative behaviours. All of these points are hard to articulate unanimously and instead are learnt over time. Employee commitment and performance can be managed and improved by various interventions such as formal appraisals, ad hoc (positive) feedback, and continuous personal development. All of this is clearly going to be a difficult or easy range of tasks depending on the quality of the employee in the first place, i.e. how effective the recruitment process was, and how accurate and realistic the job description and personal specification are.

> **Psychological contract**
>
> expected behaviours from each party based on understanding, trust, and mutual respect

There are clearly very interesting parallels here with supply relationships. Suppliers will perform better if they are the right supplier in the first place i.e. that the buyer has an effective sourcing policy and that the supplier is not misrepresenting its own capability. Similarly, the job description and person specification are mechanisms for setting down clear expectations as to what tasks need to be done and what sort of skills and competence the employee needs in order to do this. Again, to what extent do customers think of their suppliers in this way. Similarly if employee performance falls below expectations, usually some form of personal development activity (e.g. training) will be provided to ensure an improved performance rather than summary dismissal. Is this the case in supply relationships? All too often, customers are seduced by the lowest cost denominator rather than the value maximizer multiplier and are all too quick to terminate relationships if there are signs that they are falling below par. The costs of developing a supplier need to be compared with the costs of seeking and securing a new supplier. In many cases the former can work out as the best option if only considered.

It seems logical that whilst minimum levels of performance can be achieved via explicit contracts, better levels of performance can be achieved via other means. This begs a rather simple, yet profound question: is doing the bare minimum enough to ensure sustained competitive advantage? This question is equally valid from both a supplier and buyer perspective—relationships are, after all, two-way streets.

Supply Networks

Business networks in general have already been discussed in Chapter 2. Whilst drawing on this area, supply networks also introduce other dimensions, and perspectives, as to the working and rationale for B2B interactions.

As the name suggests, networks can be complicated interconnections between numerous organizations. Unlike the other three views of supply chains, networks can also involve horizontal as well as vertical relationships. This horizontal dimension is

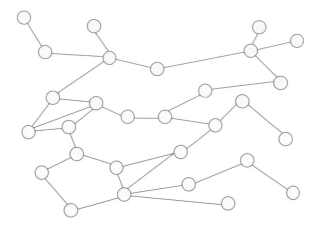

Figure 8.4 Networks

particularly important if technological innovation is key to the supply chain's success as such innovation can come from non-supplier sources, e.g. universities. Members of these networks are therefore not limited to just 'buyers' and 'suppliers'. For example, they could also include supplier associations, financiers, banks, research institutes, the media, and even local government agencies—as well as buyers and suppliers.

Supply networks can be viewed from three perspectives: industrial marketing and purchasing (IMP) group, geographical and innovative systems, and ephemeral.

Industrial Marketing and Purchasing (IMP)

Perspectives as to supplier networks have already been partially discussed in Chapter 2. The IMP Group identifies networks as being comprised of three elements: actors, activities, and resources. One party could possess just one of these elements whilst another may hold all three (permanently or temporarily). The key issue here is that the tasks and resources needed to produce products that ultimately satisfy increasingly demanding customers do not necessarily have to reside under the ownership of one firm, or be permanently embedded within a durable/rigid supply chain. These three key elements have essentially been conceptually disaggregated from firm or supply chain ownership and control. Instead they are present within a wider network and can be drawn upon through various interactions between the actors in the network as and when needed. The Dell case study presents an excellent example of this view. The key resources are not owned by Dell, who, instead, concentrate their activity on managing the network and developing the brand. In many ways this IMP view draws on the other views of networks discussed below.

Geographical Networks

Geographical networks have been studied extensively in other discipline areas such as economic geography but have recently passed squarely into the business and

Geographical network
networks of organizations that create and disseminate innovation within a specific geographic location

Table 8.3 Characteristics of Keiretsus and Supplier Associations

Supplier perspective	Buyer perspective
Single customer	Single source of supply
Co-located (within 2 miles)	Supplier development
JIT deliveries (e.g. every 15 mins)	Supplier prizes
Part of joint team with customer	Probably hold some form of equity stake
Part of the customer's new product development process	in the supplier

management domain, largely as a result of the work of Porter (1990) in extending ideas of 'clusters'. Clusters, 'regional innovation systems' (Marshall, 1890), and 'innovative milieux (Crevoisier, 1993) are networks of organizations, some of which will comprise of 'traditional' supply chains and customer–supplier relationships, and institutions (universities, public sector bodies) that create and disseminate innovation within a specific location, thus making that location well known for its particular activity. Players typically develop expertise in specific technologies or sectors which, over time, develop a supply chain infrastructure to support such industry. Some good examples of such clusters include Silicon Valley (Saxenian, 1994), Third Italy (Piore and Sabel, 1984), and Motor Sport Valley in Oxfordshire (Hendry and Pinch, 2000).

At a microscale such networks have been studied in specific relation to individual supply chains. The most common view of this is the **Keiretsu** or 'supplier association'. Keiretsu's were noticed in Japan (Dyer, 1996) as innovative forms of supply chain organization within the automotive and electronics sectors. Due to the success of this form of supply chain organization it was mimicked in the West in the form of what came to be known as 'supplier associations' (Hines and Rich, 1998). Characteristics of Keiretsus can be seen in Table 3.

Keiretsu
long-term operational and personal relationships between organizations in Japan

Ephemeral Networks

Ephemeral networks include some element of organizing for innovation in terms of seeking a short-duration relationship with a supplier (horizontal or vertical) for a specific aspect of the innovative development. However, ephemeral networks equally are comprised of many potentially transactive relationships. In certain sectors suppliers are largely undifferentiated from one another (e.g. the supply of photocopier paper) and the switching costs are relatively low. In cases such as this, buyers can play off supplier against supplier to drive down costs, i.e. there is an explicit competitive pressure exerted by the buyers. Supply chains can reconfigure quickly as new or alternate suppliers are selected at particular points in time. Just as from a marketing perspective customer networks are not really referred to as they are considered to be a market, an ephemeral supplier network is the outcome of a competitive supplier market characterized by either/or low switching costs and short-term demand for innovation or other services.

Ephemeral network
numerous short-term or one-off relationships characterized by transaction marketing features

Supply Chains and Distribution Channels

Passage of goods from company to company is a concept well known within marketing, even though supply chains and SCM may not be quite so well known.

A simple way to consider the differences between the four views of SCM as proposed by Harland (1996) is that each has a different unit of analysis, i.e. the organizations itself; a whole linear supply chain; the dyadic relationship between two parties within the supply chain; and the network of enduring and ephemeral relationships that comprise a supply network.

Distribution channels tend to focus on the movement of the finished product only. A key difference between supply chains and distribution channels is the way in which value is created. In supply chains the value is created primarily through the transformation of the physical product, i.e. raw materials are refined; they are fabricated into components; they are made into semi-finished products; they are assembled into finished products. In distribution channels the only 'transformation' of the product is in terms of its location and pack size. Value in distribution channels is primarily a function of movement as there are no further changes to the physical properties of the product. In some cases there can be interesting trade-offs between the inherent value of a product and its distribution. Of course a collection of components is inherently less valuable than a finished product. This is illustrated in Figure 8.5.

It is easy to see why marketing attention has tended to focus on distribution channels rather than supply chains. Choices need to be made in order to determine which distribution channels can effectively and efficiently serve the markets of the product. Branding and marketing communications become increasingly important in making an attractive buying proposition to customers. Customers, on the whole, tend to be not particularly interested in the make-up of the products they buy. There are

Figure 8.5 Supply chain versus distribution channel

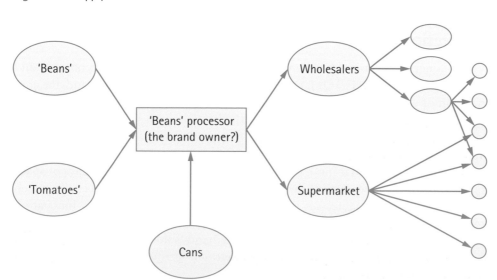

exceptions to this, and perhaps there is a trend that customers are becoming increasingly interested in what makes up their products and how (and where) they are produced; for example, in assurances that products are grown in organic ways or produced ethically. This latter point is another key reason why marketing needs to pay greater attention to the supply chain than in previous times.

The Strategic Imperative

Unlike the industrial era that gave rise to mass production where firms tended to aim for the benefits of vertical integration, firms today seek other benefits which are largely derived from outside of their boundaries. Notions of supply chains and the practices that have evolved to manage these are a direct response to this. From a marketing perspective the difference between the industrial era and today's post-Fordist or even postmodern era can be summed up by seeing how markets themselves have changed. Industrial markets were characterized as being homogeneous in that demand was relatively undifferentiated. Returning to the Ford Model T case, Ford produced one style of car famously in one colour. At the time there wasn't a demand for various different styles of car with different engines and trims. Customers had a relatively simple need—cheap and practical motoring. Vertical integration was the perfect means to satisfy this need. Nowadays however, customer needs are far more complex, even contradictory. The value derived from products has extended beyond the 'basic' or 'core' product and resides increasingly in the additional product attributes of 'extension' and 'augmentation' (see Kotler, 2000). Markets today are characterized by many different needs and wants and hence demands; markets today are heterogeneous. To satisfy such needs and wants, products need to be differentiated. This can take the form of physical product differentiation, e.g. my product has more features or is more attractive than yours; or differentiation in terms of the service offered. In a supplier context such differentiation increasingly takes the form of the quality of the actual supplier relationship, i.e. what (additional) value it can produce.

Innovation

Whilst concepts such as SCM (and a range of other operational techniques and philosophies, such as JIT, TQM, etc.) are a means of affecting such demand, the contribution of supplier relationships has never been more important. The importance of innovation has been referred to consistently throughout this chapter, so it is worth pointing out explicitly from a marketing perspective why innovation is now so important. Products are inherently more complex—even simple domestic products use electronics that are far more powerful than those used in the early days of space travel. Customers are ever more rapacious and acute. Customers seek benefits which at once signal a belonging, yet simultaneously define distinctiveness. Innovation stems from both the very products themselves, but also the way in which the potential benefits of such products are communicated and 'sold' and the development of as yet unknown products and technologies that will satisfy needs and wants which do not currently exist.

It is too big a job for most companies to be experts in all of these areas; they now need fundamentally to rely on innovative collaborations from within the supply chain and the wider network; and such innovation needs to be captured in meaningful ways. Typical transactive supplier relations are not conducive to the passage of innovation as transactions, by definition, can be undertaken by any party willing to seek, and pay for, the benefit. As well as satisfying more demanding customers, firms have to do this in a distinctive way such that other firms cannot satisfy their customers to the same extent. Such differentiation could be embedded within the very product itself, or it could revolve around the messages of the brand which they have developed. Firms need to seek innovation from the supply chain in ways which exclude such innovations from their competitors. If buyers have good relations with their suppliers and mutually satisfactory exchange can be sustained, this can help lock in innovation to that supply relationship. On the other hand, if a mutually satisfactory exchange cannot be maintained, such innovation is likely to find its way to competing buyers.

Knowledge

Knowledge is also posited in westernized economies as being the driver of innovation—both in terms of fostering it and exploiting it. Collaborative supply relationships are an essential tool in the passage of knowledge through a supply chain. Knowledge essentially takes two forms: codified knowledge and tacit knowledge (Nonaka and Takeuchi, 1995). **Codified knowledge,** by definition, is easily transferable, it can be packaged and easily communicated. In short, such knowledge can be a commodity that can be bought and sold or hired. This type of knowledge therefore does not really present a key source of sustained competitive advantage as the competitors can have access to it. **Tacit knowledge,** on the other hand, is 'sticky', and hard to transfer. It cannot be packaged and its transfer is slow and experiential. The passage of tacit knowledge is much more likely to occur in collaborative relationships as these have built up over time and there are routines and architectures in place that comprise the relationships that foster the transfer of knowledge.

Collaborative supply relationships are therefore essential for competitive success in all but the most commodified of markets.

Codified knowledge can be easily 'packaged' and traded as a commodity, thus generally available to all

Tacit knowledge embedded within a specific individual or organization and transferable only in close, long-term collaborations

Minicase 4

A Factory Shopping Mall

I was lucky enough to have the opportunity to interview a senior manager at the Jaguar factory in Castle Bromwich as part of a research project. On entering the factory and being directed to the interview location, I was faced with a walk down quite a long corridor which had what looked like lots of neon signs all along the walls. On getting closer, it became apparent that these signs were actually the logos and brand names of lots of suppliers to Jaguar. They were like a long row of mini shops in a shopping mall. Intrigued, I looked through the windows as I walked along and saw a hive of activity in each 'shop'. Often Jaguar staff were in the shop—they had distinctive uniforms. On reaching my destination I asked the interviewee what this set up was all about. He responded that they were the key suppliers to the factory and some years ago had all been invited to set up offices there. What was the point of that, I asked. It saves a lot of time to-ing and fro-ing between sites, but more importantly it: (a) integrates the suppliers more fully with the realities of the operations at the Jaguar factory so that the suppliers can design out factors that would become production issues had they just had their usual supply meetings; and (b) it develops personal relationships between Jaguar and its suppliers. Relationships are essentially between people and not organizations.

Questions

1. What other benefits of co-locating suppliers on site might occur?

2. What could be some of the problems associated with developing collaborative relationships with suppliers at the design stage?

3. How could you effectively manage co-located staff?

Source: Author

Applying Supplier Relationships

A strategic perspective has been taken in looking at the impact of supplier relations on sustained competitive success, but of course, the reality is slightly more complicated.

The Supply Context

Supply can be categorized according to what purpose it serves. This chapter has assumed the perspective of strategic supply, i.e. components and goods that are essential to the competitive success of the enterprise. For the average company approximately one-fifth of its purchasing spend is on non-strategic items (e.g. photocopy paper, consumables, etc.). Intuition might suggest therefore that a transactional relationship might be a better use of the firm's resources as the competition of the market can be used to determine the best supply sources rather than time-consuming investment in collaborative relations. This may be so, but operational and efficiency gains, rather than strategic gains, can also accrue from collaborative relations. For example, rather than devote management time to the ordering, stock taking, allocation, etc. of consumable items, could firms not 'outsource' such management to suppliers? Indeed they are increasingly doing this. Instead of spending valuable management resources on non-strategic activity, such management capacity can be freed up and refocused on managing supply and suppliers that are of strategic significance.

Basic marketing principles can be applied to the supply market to help achieve the right balance of operational efficiency versus strategic effectiveness. Just as customer markets can be categorized, or segmented, so too can supplier markets. The Pareto Principle applies in both cases—80% of profit will come from 20% of customers, so most management attention should be focused on the profitable customers or developing the marginal customers into more profitable customers. Similarly, in the supply market, suppliers can be segmented according to the amount of bought out spend they receive (perhaps a useful proxy for strategic significance); switchability of their products; quality of service and supply, etc.

Close supplier relationships are not inherently 'better' than the use of transactive market forces. What is important is that the right type of supply relationship is fostered and developed according to the particular market context involved. If the core business revolves around basic commodities and there are plenty of competing suppliers, perhaps transactive relations might be the most appropriate. Then again, knowledge and innovation can effect and transform even the most basic of products.

Power Contexts

Another key issue in terms of applying supplier relationships is the use (or abuse) of power in commercial relationships. Power was referred to earlier in relation to lead companies (typically OEMs or brand owners), i.e. the companies within the supply chain that tend to hold the most power. Power, whilst a complex issue with many differing perspectives, is usually regarded as the ability of one company to influence (the actions) of another. In commercial terms power is usually thought of as being economic—larger companies are typically more powerful than smaller companies. More precisely, rather than power being a function of firm size per se, it is more useful to compare the proportion of supply and purchase between two firms. For example, a company which buys the majority of the production from a supplier will usually be seen by the supplier as being in a position of power—if it wants something (even perhaps unreasonably) it is likely to get it.

Power is not just a function of size or proportion of turnover. A useful taxonomy of power was developed by French and Raven (1959) who identified five power bases. Whilst originally conceived as inter-personal mechanisms (i.e. between people rather than between organizations), they nevertheless can provide a useful insight into supplier (and customer) relations:

Legitimate Power is based on formal authority. In a supply context such authority could emanate from contracts; and from a classical marketing rhetoric, the customer is, of course, always right. If a delivery is late, the buyer has a legitimate right to complain!

Referent Power refers to an ability to attract loyalty from others. Applied in a supply context, a supplier may have developed a relationship with a buyer over a long period resulting in high levels of goodwill trust. Suppliers are therefore likely to act on the demands of buyers as they will be viewed as being to their benefit (either in the immediate or longer term).

Expert Power (including Information Power), as the name suggests, is where one party has a particular expertise, or (access to) information that the other party does not. A supplier may have proprietary processes or materials which cannot be accessed elsewhere. A buyer may have access to particular markets or distribution channels (through geographical rights or good relationships with key retailers, for example). A simple way to apply the notion of expert power in a supply relationship is to compare it to dependency situations where buyers, or suppliers, have little or no choice (e.g. a monopoly or use of patented design).

Reward Power is the ability on one party to give some form of return or incentive. In many supply situations products will have a long life cycle (including updates and continuous development). An obvious form of reward would therefore be the promise of future business. In some respects the reward in this case is the promise of a sustained business relationship. Some supply situations cannot make such promises. Limited life projects (as compared with continuous production), for example. However, there could be the promise of using the same supplier if a similar project materializes in the future.

Coercive Power is in many respects the opposite of reward power—instead of rewarding good behaviour, there will be a sanction for bad behaviour.

As supplier (and customer) relationships are complex, it is perhaps obvious that all of the above types of power can exist in the same relationship at different times according to the relationship life cycle or discrete events within it. However, when analysing power in supply relations three key themes emerge: the degree of control; the degree of dependence; and the culture and atmosphere of the relationship.

In terms of control, the use of different types of power can be seen as intrinsic elements of the governance mechanisms outlined previously in this chapter, i.e. contract and different degrees of relationship trust. A buyer will quite naturally expect to receive their deliveries for when they have ordered them. Late deliveries can cause production stoppages in upstream supply chains and stock-outs downstream—clearly a situation which is not desirable, especially in recent years when there has been a considerable move away from keeping stock items. How can buyers control this? As part of the chosen relationships mechanism (contract/trust) power can provide incentives to prevent this from happening or subsequent sanctions to reduce it from happening in the future.

The degree of dependence of the buyer and supplier is also a key theme. In some situations buyers and suppliers will be entirely independent of one another (i.e. a true competitive market situation). In other circumstances buyers and suppliers may be mutually dependent. This latter point is becoming increasingly significant with the inexorable shift away from vertically integrated organization. As outlined previously with regard to systems integrators, for example, car assemblers are dependent on these key suppliers as it would be very difficult (indeed impossible in the short term) to find alternative supply arrangements, should the relationship disintegrate.

Some buying companies take an interesting and perhaps counter-intuitive view of dependence in their supply relationships. Bosch, for example, will only do business with a supplier if it amounts to a specified percentage or less of the suppliers' turnover. This is to minimize dependence, both in terms of reducing the likelihood of the supplier becoming over-dependent on Bosch; and to minimize the risk to Bosch of being over-dependent on a particular supplier (i.e. they multi-source supply). This is an entirely different perspective to the one taken by VW, discussed in the End of Chapter Case. Here suppliers have to commit a significant investment such that buyer and supplier become mutually dependent. Interestingly, both of these very different perspectives display a degree of commitment to the supply relationship. In the latter example, commitment to the relationship derives directly from the significant financial investment placed in it. The former example perhaps illustrates an ethical commitment to the supplier in that Bosch do not see suppliers' over-reliance as being a moral situation.

The prevailing culture or atmosphere (Håkansson, 2002) of the relationship also influences the use of power and governance mechanisms. Some organizations are naturally open and cooperative, others might tend to operate on a very secretive basis. Some companies, for example, may not fully share basic information such as sales/supply forecasts and see cost reduction as primarily a result of 'good negotiation'. Other companies, on the other hand, see cost reduction as emanating from a clear sharing of information such that economies and efficiencies can be built into the supply relationship. Neither perspective is right or wrong; again the context of the supply situation is critical, but this does illustrate the role that power (e.g. information power) can be seen as being an additional variable within the supply context.

A final point on power concerns brands specifically. Physical products are not the only things that pass through supply chains and distribution channels—communication also passes either way. Brand owners can attempt to circumvent the power of the distributors by creating demand from consumers directly. This is a mainstream marketing ploy for most of the major fast-moving consumer good (FMCG) producers. Direct communications with customers via advertising or sales promotions (from in-store displays, to 'BOGOFs', etc.) are all mechanisms to stimulate consumer demand. Such demand should then 'pull' the brands through the distribution channel. In most FMCG cases this is a far more (though expensive) use of limited marketing budgets than 'pushing' brands through the distribution channel via sales and trade shows. Occasionally, surprising examples of brand-derived pull demand emerges. Perhaps the most celebrated example is Intel and their strapline 'Intel Inside'. Most consumers of PCs really didn't care what make of chip was powering their PC . . . until the Intel advertising campaign.

Service Contexts

The distinction between physical products and intangible services has not been explicitly made when discussing the supply context as all products, in reality, comprise elements of tangibility and intangibility. Similarly, the distinction between 'physical product' and 'service product' is rather arbitrary. When purchasing physical products, service elements have been embedded in the creation of the physical product. This notion has been widely discussed recently with the development of what has become known as **service-dominant logic** (Lusch et al., 2007).

Perhaps a simple way to differentiate physical and service products is to focus not on the product itself, but the contract (or relational governance mechanism) which

Service-dominant logic
the service elements relating to a product before, during, and after its purchase

supports the product. With physical products, the 'contract' revolves around passage of ownership and therefore will concern itself with entities. With service products, on the other hand, the 'contract' does not revolve around passage of ownership but rather, rights of access. Another distinction between service and physical product contracts are that the former exist between organizations, whereas the latter exist between organizations and people. Even the most basic commodity products will not add value unless supported by a service infrastructure from taking purchase orders to delivery. The same principles of SCM and supplier relations therefore apply also in a service context. If there is a desire to treat services differently to physical products perhaps then brands should be treated separately from products—brands are, after all, intangible, aren't they?

Minicase 5

Automatic Retail Supply

Retailers, especially today's supermarkets, carry thousands of lines of products from a huge number of suppliers. Even large suppliers such as Heinz will only account for a tiny fraction of the sales and supply cost to the supermarket. Collaborative relationships come in many forms and can have a primary focus on different objectives. The key driver for some relationships may be cost reduction; for others, seeking innovation from the supplier.

In an increasing number of cases, retailers are developing relationships with suppliers based on technological efficiency as the key driver. Some supermarkets have directly linked key suppliers to their electronic point-of-sale (EPOS) systems. Information of sales of products is sent in real time to the supplier automatically. When a certain level of sales has been reached, this triggers a stock replenishment request—again all automatically. This system can clearly significantly reduce transaction costs and inventory management for the supermarket. It has additional benefits for suppliers also. Instead of receiving weekly orders, selected suppliers can now see actual sales figures of their products in real time. This can help suppliers better to plan the production schedules as sales forecasting will be more accurate.

In some cases this system has been extended even further. As well as doing all of the above, the system will also trigger an electronic funds transfer (EFT) from the supermarket to the supplier, i.e. the system can now automatically pay the supplier.

Questions

1. For what other business contexts would this system be suitable?

2. Can you see any disadvantages in using an increasingly automatic order-replenishment-pay system?

3. Even though this system is a form of collaboration between supermarkets and some of their suppliers, do you think supermarkets could benefit from other forms of more collaborative relationship with their suppliers?

Source: Author

Relationship Portfolios

Most successful companies will in reality be operating a range of different supply relationship strategies as determined by the industry and context in which they operate. Some relationships will be invested in and developed, as potential mutual gain can be accommodated. In other cases there will be little or no gain from collaboration. There are clearly a range of other types of relationship that can be developed, based on whatever criteria firms might wish to apply—degree of supply risk, supply contribution to profit (short term or long term), inimitability of supply (or the service of that supply), etc. For example, a simple metaphor can be used to describe the difference between collaborative and non-collaborative (or transactive) relationships—cake. In this example the cake represents the total profit of the exchange available to both parties, i.e. buyer and supplier. In a non-collaborative exchange both parties will be fighting for the biggest slice of the profit cake. In more collaborative relationships both parties will agree the size of their 'slice' and work together to increase the total size of the cake. Whilst in the former example, the hard negotiation of a buyer may mean it ends up with the largest slice of the profit cake, in the latter example, it may end up with a smaller slice, but from a bigger cake. If there is really no scope to increase the size of the cake, perhaps a more transactive approach would be the most appropriate—though many supply chain theorists would argue that collaboration can still increase efficiency and hence reduce costs.

Supply chain strategy should determine what type of relationship ultimately produces the greatest value for the customer and hence the wider organizational stakeholders. Supplier relationships are mechanisms for harnessing and transferring value. The type of relationship employed should therefore be determined by what the ultimate customers, and stakeholders, see as being of value.

Chapter Summary

Supplier relationships come in many different forms. At one extreme there can be a very loose relationship which is characterized by market competition. At the other extreme are deeply collaborative relationships where all the actors, in many respects, seem to act as one organization. There is no absolute 'right' form of relationship—this is determined by the specific context in which the supply situation resides.

There has, however, been a noticeable move towards a greater use of collaborative supply relationships, and this move has been positively encouraged by organizations such as Partnership Sourcing Ltd, for example. The reason for this is logical: the delivery of value to customers is an increasingly complex business. Many products now contain new technologies, more complexity; and the environment in which customers are served is more complex. There is global competition, more readily available information on most things, and generally higher levels of competition. Ultimately it is the customers themselves who have become more demanding and less likely to give loyalty to suppliers who do not meet their exact needs and requirements.

There are many faces to collaborative relationships—some will be primarily concerned with cost reduction and the creation of greater efficiencies. Other relationships are more concerned with harnessing the more strategic resources that reside within supply chains, such as knowledge and innovation. The choice of the most appropriate supply relationship is therefore a function of what a company wants to achieve through such a relationship: the objective should not be to develop a collaborative relationship for its own sake.

Whilst there may well be a good rationale for the development of a collaborative supplier relationship, all parties to the relationship need to share the same objectives. In a dyadic situation, one party, for example, may simply not possess the necessary cultural fit to operate in a collaborative way. Similarly, in a lean linear supply chain, the desire of the majority of the chain actors to collaborate may be hampered by just one actor within it.

Collaborative supplier relationships should not be seen as being the 'easy' or 'soft' option. They require resources to ensure that the best partners have been identified and they need constant maintenance. For some companies the 'easiest' option is simply to use the market forces.

In reality most companies will usually operate a range of relationships with their suppliers—perhaps unknowingly. The development of a portfolio of relationships seems a sensible approach to take as naturally some suppliers will be of strategic importance (for a variety of reasons), whilst others will not. In many ways such an approach could be seen to benefit from applying basic marketing principles—in reverse: just as there are customer markets, so too are their supplier markets. Of course, both of these elements contribute to the ultimate *market*. Marketing as an academic subject and practical discipline, however, has tended to focus almost exclusively on just the customer market. The customer market cannot function effectively, nor be managing in any meaningful way without also focusing on the supplier market, without which no market would exist.

End of Chapter Case with Questions

The Ultimate Factory? The Ultimate Supplier Relationships?

Volkswagon truck and bus division opened its new plant in Resende, Brazil in 1995. This was an experimental plant that was quite unlike any other high-volume manufacturing plant anywhere in the world. It may seem strange to realize that out of the 1,500 workers at the plant, VW do not employee any production floor staff at all. The plant produces about 30,000 buses and trucks each year, comprising of 17 different truck models and three different bus models, mostly for export to the USA and Europe—it is not a small factory by any undertaking.

One of the innovations introduced by this plant was the development of a chassis that could be used interchangeably for buses and trucks. Until then buses and trucks used different chassis, necessitating separate production units. However, the biggest innovation in this plant was the development of a production system which became known as 'modular production'.

The production of the trucks and buses basically comprises of six key modules as follows, with the 'suppliers' bracketed:

- production and assembly of the cabin (Delga and Tamet);
- painting the cabin (Eisenmann);

- steering and electric work (VDO);

- interior trim (VDO);

- assembly of the frame, wheels, and tyres (collaboration between Iochpe-Maxion, Borlen and Bridgestone);

- production and assembly of axles and suspension (Rockwell);

- preparation and assembly of engines and transmissions (MWM and Cummins).

The suppliers, in this case, actually do a lot more than simply supply the systems (i.e. act as systems integrators). These suppliers actually, collectively, assemble the whole truck/bus. This was accommodated by a cleverly designed production line which was based around each of the key supply systems. Most of the suppliers developed satellite plants to produce the whole system or core elements of the system ahead of full integration at the VW plant. These plants were all situated within a couple of miles' radius of the main plant to facilitate unimpeded 15-minute deliveries throughout the day.

VW staff did not get involved in any of the production processes but were obviously keen to ensure the quality of their product. As such, when each system was incorporated, VW quality staff would sign off the system, allowing it to progress to the next stage of the production process, these staff being named 'maestros'. Out of the 1,500 staff, only 200 were VW employees. As well as overseeing the quality of the production process the bulk of the staff were concerned with administering the relationships within the factory and product design and marketing. Interestingly VW had essentially absolved itself (legally) from the usual problems and issues of managing a large pool of labour as they were all employed directly by the suppliers.

The organization of production in this way calls for deeply collaborative relationships with suppliers. What this case also illustrates is that the suppliers themselves need to be deeply collaborative with each other in order to coodinate production.

Questions

1. Could these collaborative relationships go even deeper? In what way?

2. To what extent do you think that buyer–supplier relationships and associated governance mechanisms (e.g. contracts) are a substitute for employing labour directly?

3. If customers are aware that the brand owner is not actually producing the brand, does this harm associate brand values?

Sources:

http://www.vwgroupsupply.com

Marx, R., Zilbovicius, M., and Salerno, M. (1997) 'The modular consortium in a new VW truck plant in Brazil: new forms of assembler and supplier relationship', *Integrated Manufacturing Systems*, 8(5), 292–8

De P. Abreu, A., Benyon, H., and Ramalho, J. R. (2000) "The Dream Factory": VW's modular production system in Resende, Brazil, *Work, Employment & Society*, 14(2), 265–82

http://www.youtube.com/—search for 'volkswagon constellation' accessed 17/11/07

Discussion Questions

1. Evaluate the notion that collaborative supplier relationships are the best way of achieving competitive success.

2. To what extent do different perspectives of supply chains add to the understanding of the term 'supply chain management'?

3. What are the key differences in terms of how value is added between a supply chain and a distribution channel?

4. Why should organizations move from rigid departmental structures to more horizontal structures?

5. How does the type of product affect choice between collaborative or adversarial supplier relationships?

6. What benefits are there to an organization in having fewer rather than more suppliers?

7. Discuss the differences between a component supplier and a systems integrator. How could a component supplier become a systems integrator?

8. Who are the key personnel from buyer and supplier organizations that enable successful transactions?

9. Outline the three different types of trust. Should goodwill trust be accompanied by a contract?

10. Why are knowledge and innovation important when discussing supplier relationships?

11. Does the use of power in supplier relationships have a positive or negative effect?

12. Are collaborative supplier relationships appropriate to service products? What benefits could they bring?

Further Reading

Brennan, R., Canning, L., and McDowell, R. (2007) Business to Business Marketing, Sage, London.

Forrester, Jay Wright (1961) *Industrial Dynamics*, MIT Press.

Granovetter, M. (1985), 'Economic Action and Social Structure: The Problem of Embeddedness', *American Journal of Sociology*, 91(Nov.), 481–510.

Halldorsson, A., Kotzab, H., Mikkola, J. H., and Skjoett-Larsen, T. (2007) 'Complementary theories to supply chain management', **Supply Chain Management: An International Journal**, 12(4), 284–96.

Handfield, R.B., Ragatz, G.L., Petersen, K.J., and Monczka, R.M. (1999) 'Involving suppliers in new product development', *California Management Review*, 42, 59–82.

Larson, P.D. and Halldorsson, A. (2004) 'Logistics versus supply chain management: an international survey', **International Journal of Logistics: Research & Application**, 7(1), 17–31.

Lusch, R.F. and Vargo, S.L. (2006) 'Service-dominant logic: reactions, reflections and refinements', *Marketing Theory*, 6(3), 281–8.

Spekman, R.E., Kamauff, J.W., and Myhr, N. (1998) 'An empirical investigation into supply chain management: A perspective on partnerships', *International Journal of Physical Distribution and Logistics Management*, 28, 630–50.

Tempelmeier, H. (2006). *Inventory Management in Supply Networks—Problems, Models, Solutions*, Books on Demand, Norstedt.

Webster, F.E. and Wind, Y. (1972) 'A general model for understanding organizational buying behavior', *Journal of Marketing*, 36(2), 12–19.

Wilson, D. (1999) *Organizational Marketing*, Thomson, London.

References

De P. Abreu, A., Benyon, H., and Ramalho, J. R. (2000) '"The Dream Factory": VW's modular production system in Resende, Brazil', *Work, Employment & Society*, 14(2), 265–82.

Crevoisier, O. (1993) 'Spatial Shifts and the Emergence of Innovative Milieux: The case of the Jura region between 1960 and 1990', *Environment and Planning C: Government and Policy*, 11(4), 419–30.

Dyer, J. (1996) 'How Chrysler Created an American Keiretsu', *Harvard Business Review*, 74(4), 42–53.

Ford, D. (ed.) (2002) *Understanding Business Marketing and Purchasing*, Thomson, London.

French, J. R. P. and Raven, B. H. (1959) 'The Bases of Social Power', in Cartwright, D. (ed.), *Studies in Social Power*, University of Michigan, Ann Arbor, MI, pp. 150–67.

Håkansson, H., Harrison, D., and Waluszewski, A. (2004) *Rethinking Marketing: Developing a new understanding of markets*, Wiley, Chichester.

Håkansson, H. (ed.) (2002) *International Marketing and Purchasing of Industrial Goods: An interaction approach*, John Wiley & Sons, Chichester.

Harland, C. M. (1996) 'Supply Chain Management: Relationships, chains and networks', *British Journal of Management*, 7, S63–S80.

Henry, N. and Pinch, S. (2000) 'Spatialising Knowledge: Placing the knowledge community of Motor Sport Valley', *Geoforum*, 31(2), 191–208.

Hines, P. and Rich, N. (1998) 'Outsourcing Competitive Advantage: The use of supplier associations', *International Journal of Physical Distribution & Logistics Management*, 28(7).

Kotler, P. *et al.* (2000) *Marketing Management*, Prentice Hall, London.

Lusch, R. F., Vargo, S. L., and O'Brien, M. (2007) 'Competing Through Service: Insights from service-dominant logic', *Journal of Retailing*, 83(1), 5–18.

Magretta, J. (1998) 'The Power of Virtual Integration: An interview with Dell Computer's Michael Dell', *Harvard Business Review*, Mar.–Apr., 73–84.

Marshall, A. (1890) *Principles of Economics*, Macmillan, London.

Marshall, A. (1920) *Industry and Trade*, Macmillan, London.

Marx, R., Zilbovicius, M., and Salerno, M. (1997) 'The Modular Consortium in a New VW Truck Plant in Brazil: New forms of assembler and supplier relationship', *Integrated Manufacturing Systems*, 8(5), 292–8.

Nonaka, I. and Takeuchi, H. (1995) *The Knowledge-creating Company: How Japanese companies create the dynamics of innovation*, Oxford University Press, New York.

Oliver, R. K. and Webber, M. D. (1982) 'Supply-chain Management: Logistics catches up with strategy', in Christopher, M. (ed.), *Logistics: The strategic issues*, Chapman and Hall, London, pp. 63–75.

Piore, M. J. and Sabel, C. F. (1984) *The Second Industrial Divide*, Basic Books, New York.

Porter, M. (1990) *The Competitive Advantage of Nations*, The Free Press, New York.

Sako, M. (1992) *Prices, Quality, and Trust: Inter-firm relations in Britain and Japan*, Cambridge University Press.

Saxenian, A. (1994) *Regional Advantage: Culture and competition in Silicon Valley and Route 128*, Harvard University Press, Cambridge, MA.

Schein, E. H. (1965) *Organisational Psychology*, Prentice-Hall Inc, New Jersey.

Stevens, G. C. (1989) 'Integrating the Supply Chain', *International Journal of Physical Distribution and Materials Management*, 19(8), 3–8.

Webster, F. E. Jr and Wind, Y. (1972) *Organizational Buying Behavior*, Prentice-Hall, Englewood Cliffs, NJ.

Wilson, J. M. (1995) 'Henry Ford's Just-in-time system', *International Journal of Operations & Production Management*, 15(12), 59–75.

Internal Relationships

Chapter Outline

Learning Outcomes

After reading this chapter you should be able to:

- recognize the different types of relationship within the organization that might be of relevance to a study of relationship marketing;

- appreciate the ways in which the management of internal relationships might impact upon the organization's ability to serve the external market;

- understand the limitations of trying to impose external marketing tools and tactics to the internal market;

- critically assess the means by which an organization might try to engender a customer-focused ethos amongst employees;

- debate the extent that internal relationships are the responsibility of the marketing department;

- demonstrate the significance of organizational structure and culture in the management of internal relationships.

Introduction

We have already seen that a broader study of relationship marketing needs to consider more than just the customer–supplier relationship. Chapter 7 looked at how the organization's relationship with external stakeholders might impact upon its business, while the last chapter discussed how the effective management of supply chain relationships can enhance the experience of the final customer. In this chapter we are going to examine the management of relationships in another area which although not constituting part of the customer market, can nevertheless affect the way in which the organization can serve its customers. This area is often referred to as the 'internal market' and covers the large, but potentially hazy, area of 'internal marketing', or put more simply, relationships with, and between employees.

We have to be careful here, as we are now at the limits of what might normally be classed as marketing. Managing employee relationships sounds very much like employee relations which is, and always has been, a central role of an organization's Human Resources (HR) department. What must be made clear here, however, is that as marketers we are concerned with the way in which internal relationships can impact upon the external market. As Clark (2000) reminds us, employees usually represent the People 'P' in the 7Ps of marketing and as such are becoming an increasingly important means of differentiation in the quest for competitive advantage. Marketing must therefore take an interest in what goes on inside the organization, as well as outside.

While the need for internal or employee relationships is generally accepted amongst relationship marketing theorists, the approach to the subject differs:

Nano relationships

Gummesson's term for internal relationships

- Gummesson (2002) broadly categorizes these under the heading **Nano Relationships**, *nano* from the Greek word meaning 'dwarf', or 'small' to reflect the fact that they exist below the market proper because they are inside the organization. In this sense they are the opposite of 'mega' (or external) relationships which exist above the market. Gummesson asserts that these relationships are part of the fabric of the organization being found in its structure, systems, and processes. As such they support relationships with customers and relationships with the 'mega' influencers discussed in Chapter 7.

- Christopher *et al.* (1991) describe them as 'Internal Markets' covering relationships with employees and also 'Recruitment Markets' covering relationships with potential employees. These markets comprise no less than two of their Six Markets Model.

- Morgan and Hunt (1994) and Doyle (1995) use the term 'Internal Partnerships', comprising relationships between the organization and its employees, relationships between functional departments within the organization, and relationships between strategic business units (SBUs) within the organization.

Just as we discovered when looking at external relationships, the exact make-up of who or what is covered under the term internal relationships varies, depending on which model one is using. Gummesson, for example, includes relationships with the external providers of marketing services under this heading, as well as relationships with owners and financiers. As we have already covered these elsewhere in this book, we shall confine our discussion here to those individuals or departments who are inside the organization, but whose actions can impact directly or indirectly on to the external market.

This still leaves us with a potentially vast area to cover, particularly if we accept the assertion of Gummesson and others that internal relationships involve the structure and culture of the organization. Once again, it seems that the study of relationship marketing is taking us over and above the remit of the average organization's marketing department. We therefore begin this chapter by determining the scope of internal relationships within the context of relationship marketing, with the objective of applying a meaningful structure to the subject. This leads us to a consideration of two broad areas:

- the concept of the internal customer;
- the way in which employees affect the perceptions and experiences of external customers.

Each of these areas is divided into further subsets for ease of study. The chapter closes by exploring what in practice, the management of internal relationships for relationship marketing purposes might involve. This includes a consideration of the age-old question—HRM or marketing? The Opening Case, although fictional, illustrates how internal interactions affect the day-to-day running of an organization.

Opening Case Study with Questions

Midhampton University—A Day in the Life . . .

Although fictional, the following narrative is intended to reflect the reality of working in a large organization based around different departments and functions. Like any big organization Midhampton University relies on a wide range of staff in many different areas in order to help it function effectively. The vignettes below focus on five distinct areas, seen through the eyes of the people who work there: the Marketing Manager, the Lecturer, the Library Supervisor, the IT Technician, and the Course Administrator.

Emma—the Marketing Manager

Emma's mind was focused on one thing: ensuring that the forthcoming university Open Day planned for this Saturday ran smoothly. Although she had booked the rooms in advance, a last-minute increase in the number of visitors expected had meant that she had had to ask Room Bookings to secure a larger suite of rooms. This had provoked a particularly irate response from one professor who had been forced to move a lecture he was running for part-time students to a different building. The catering manageress had also grumbled about being asked to provide extra staff at a weekend at short notice, but at least the IT guys were happy. They were paid extra for working weekends. Now all Emma had to do was persuade the various course tutors to come in and talk about their subject areas. . . .

Jane—the Lecturer

Jane was having a bad day. The tutor of the previous class had overrun and all her students were forced to wait in the corridor until the room became free. She cursed the previous tutor even more when she finally got into the classroom as he had not cleaned the white board and had shut down the PC and projector. She particularly hated having to get the classroom PCs and projectors up and running. The two machines never seemed to 'talk' to each other and she had been forced to call the IT Department on more than one occasion, wasting yet more valuable class time. Now she had returned to her office, she found that the Marketing Department was asking for volunteers at this Saturday's Open Day. This was the day she had planned to finish marking the student's coursework, as the Course Admin team needed to input the marks the following Monday to meet the deadline for the next Subject Board. Sighing, she picked up the phone and began to dial. . . .

Carl—the Library Supervisor

Carl's day had begun early as he wanted to brief his staff about the forthcoming Open Day before the library became busy with students. A couple of the team were on long-term sick leave and he had had to ask the HR Department to allow him to hire in external temporary replacements. However, this was not at the forefront of his mind this morning. He was in a particularly good mood because the budget request he had submitted to the Finance Department had been approved in full and he was now able to buy in a large amount of new textbooks for the next academic year. Carl relied on lecturers telling him what books they had put on their reading lists for students and had found in the past that this information was not always easy to obtain. Before worrying about this, however, he was off to a meeting with the IT Department to discuss the implementation of a new online system for staff and students to access electronic books and journals. He remembered the confusion when the current system had been introduced two years ago. . . .

Jim—IT Technician

Jim was in his element. A delivery of new web cams had arrived this morning and the team were busy preparing them for booking out by lecturers for use in recording student presentations and other activities. He expected that he would have to arrange briefing sessions to explain to the staff how they worked. Experience told him that these sessions would be patchily attended. The lecturers in particular never seemed to have the time to attend and then they ended up ringing the IT Department for help when they couldn't make something work. At least Carl in the library would listen; he was always keen to harness whatever new technology could offer. His thoughts were broken by a shout from across the room: 'Facilities just reported that work men have cut through a cable in the new Arts building—student Intranet is down. . . .'

Mani—Course Administrator

At last! Mani breathed a sigh of relief when the last of the postgraduate coursework marks came in from the course leader. He was now able to put together a sample for the external examiner and get things moving for next week's Subject Board. He could also make arrangements to get the student's marks and feedback up on the student Intranet—hopefully this would prevent the constant stream of e-mails and phone calls he had been receiving over the last two weeks. But as he scanned the list of names he realized that not all the students would be going forward. Only that morning, the Finance Department had sent him a list of students who still had outstanding fees to pay. They were trying to arrange payment terms with these students but until something was worked out Mani had to withhold their marks. He was also awaiting confirmation from Student Services about two students who had not submitted work owing to personal circumstances. Logging on to the Intranet he was stopped in his tracks—'the site you are seeking is temporarily unavailable' . . .

Questions

1. Discuss how each of the operational areas above affect the experience of students.

2. Do the individuals described above share the same priorities?

3. How might the actions of one department in the above examples prevent another from doings its job effectively?

4. How might internal communications in such a large organization be managed?

Source: Author

The Scope of Internal Marketing

We noted above that use of the term internal, or employee, relations suggested a very wide area, some of which would not normally be covered by marketing. For the purpose of relationship marketing, the term **internal marketing** is usually applied to internal relationship activities designed to improve the overall effectiveness of the organization in the external market. In this sense, studies of internal marketing have contributed to the wider development of relationship marketing itself. However, as we shall see, there is disagreement over what exactly internal marketing is or how it should be conducted. In order to put the subject into some sort of perspective, it is useful to trace the development of internal marketing as a concept in its own right.

Internal marketing
a marketing-like approach applied internally to improve the overall effectiveness of the organization in external markets

The Development of Internal Marketing

The concept of internal marketing is widely attributed to Berry *et al.* (1976) who first raised its potential as an enabler of service quality in retail organizations. Berry later developed his theories around internal marketing based on the notion that the organization could only serve its external customers well (i.e. operate efficiently), if all of its internal employees were satisfied and working well together. Put simply, happy employees lead to happy customers! Research by Schneider (1980) and others into the retail banking industry in America certainly seemed to support this idea. In order to achieve high levels of employee satisfaction, Berry suggested that the organization treated its employees as customers and the concept of the 'internal customer' was born.

The idea that employees could be viewed as customers was later developed into the notion that the organization could use internal marketing to sell its mission, objectives, directions, and strategies to employees, in order to get their buy-in (e.g. Piercy and Morgan, 1991). In other words it could be used as a strategy implementation or change management tool. Despite criticisms that these concepts go beyond the scope of marketing, Ballantyne (2003) and others maintain that employees can be seen both as internal customers and internal suppliers. Just as in the external market, the way in which relationships are managed in these internal exchanges can add value to the exchange and enhance overall performance.

At the same time a slightly different approach to internal marketing was being taken by Grönroos (1990) and others, based around making employees more customer-oriented. This line of thinking did not advocate the treatment of employees themselves as customers (Ahmed and Rafiq, 2002), but nevertheless recognized that the organization had to manage employee relationships in such a way that the needs of the external customer were effectively met. This line of thinking stems very much from the interaction that many employees have with customers and the way in which the entire customer experience could be enhanced by the way in which they were treated by employees. Clearly this has more resonance in service industries such as supermarkets, airlines, hotels, or banks, where customers are more likely to come into contact with the organization's employees. However, it can also apply to the service elements of manufacturing organizations where employees in areas such as invoicing, delivery or after-sales support can interact with customers.

It could be argued, therefore, that there are two broad approaches to internal marketing:

- employees as internal customers and suppliers;
- employees being externally customer orientated.

There are similarities between the two approaches. Both can be used strategically to give the organization a competitive advantage, both stress the need to motivate employees by applying 'marketing-like' techniques, both of them form a distinct part of a wider study of relationship marketing because of their ability to impact (directly or indirectly) on the final market. This enables Ahmed and Rafiq (2002) to provide us with a useful definition of internal marketing: 'a marketing-like approach directed at motivating employees for implementing and integrating organizational strategies towards customer orientation'.

It is important, however, to recognize the subtle differences between the two approaches, as these will help us to develop a framework through which to understand internal marketing relationships further. These are summarized in Figure 9.1 and can also be seen in practice in the Opening Case at the beginning of this chapter.

Within these two broad internal marketing areas, studies of relationship marketing can be broken down into further subheadings, each of which reflect a slightly different angle and require different approaches to internal relationship marketing (see Figure 9.2). Let us now look at each of these areas in more detail.

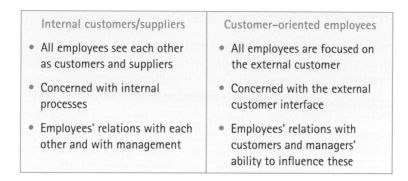

Internal customers/suppliers	Customer-oriented employees
• All employees see each other as customers and suppliers	• All employees are focused on the external customer
• Concerned with internal processes	• Concerned with the external customer interface
• Employees' relations with each other and with management	• Employees' relations with customers and managers' ability to influence these

Figure 9.1 Differences between two approaches to internal marketing

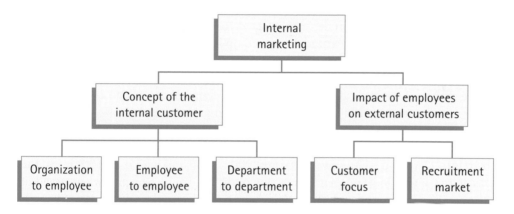

Figure 9.2 Internal marketing relationships

The Concept of the Internal Customer

Internal customer
a concept whereby employees are looked upon as customers—of each other and of the organization itself

The idea that the employees of an organization can be classed as customers themselves, suggests that an internal market exists that is some sort of 'mini' version of the external market. Gummesson (2002) goes so far as to assert that this internal or 'nano' market shares the characteristics of a full market economy, complete with customers and suppliers all interacting with each other inside the organization. For these reasons, he suggests that marketing management principles originally developed for external marketing purposes should also be used for internal marketing. In order to see how this might work in practice, we can sub-divide internal customer relationships into three distinct areas:

- employees as customers of the organization;
- employees as suppliers and customers of each other;
- internal departments or operating units as suppliers and customers of each other.

Employees as Customers of the Organization

Sometimes, in the concentration of designing strategies focusing on the external customer, it is easy to assume that everyone in the organization automatically knows what the company is trying to achieve and will pull together to help get there. While employees might be familiar with their organization's mission statement, outlining the aims and values of the company, these are often couched in very broad terms and cannot always convey specific strategic directions—particularly in times of change.

For example, some years ago UK retail chain Swift's was keen to update its image. The company had been successful selling a wide range of small leather goods, handbags, briefcases, and luggage, but was experiencing a stagnation in sales, particularly in the key fashion sector of handbags. Market research suggested that Swift's had an outdated and unfashionable image compared to newer rivals such as Next and Accessorize, and so the company set out to revitalize itself. After a lengthy search a new brand name, L'Attitude, was selected to replace Swift's. Extensive research indicated that the name L'Attitude conjured up images of fashion, style, and quality amongst the company's target customers.

A design company was then set on to come up with a whole new look for the shops in line with the L'Attitude ideal. This involved the design of a new logo and shop fascia, along with interior store layout, new carpets, fittings, fixtures, lighting, and staff uniforms. Even the background *muzak* was changed to reflect the new image. A rolling programme was then devised to refurbish each of the existing Swift's stores and turn them into L'Attitudes. At upwards of £60,000 a shop and with over 100 shops, this was no mean feat. Imagine then the reaction of the Managing Director, when attending the opening of the very first L'Attitude, when he overheard the sales assistant happily telling a customer 'Of course we're still Swift's—it's just a name change . . .'

What Swift's had failed to do was sell the reason why they were making the change to all of their staff. The word 'sell' is used here because staff have to buy into the change if they are to make it work. When Jan Carlzon turned around Scandinavia Air Services, he issued *all* of the organization's employees with a little red book called *Let's Get In There and Fight* outlining his objectives for the company and showing employees how they fitted into these (Carlzon, 1987). The result was a surge in energy from SAS's 20,000 employees as each of them united in achieving the organization's goals (see End of Chapter Case on p. 30 in Chapter 1).

Sometimes an organization will try to engender a corporate philosophy within the workforce by adopting a company song or standard uniform (even for the senior executives) to reflect the 'company spirit'. Such policies are common in Japanese enterprises where, culturally, a collective sense of belonging is the norm. When such practices have been adopted by western companies they have met with mixed success. Writing in the *Financial Times*, columnist Lucy Kellaway describes the Shell company song, *Growing and Winning*, set to the tune of former charity song *We Are The World*:

> we are the best,
> we are all winners,
> we are the ones who have made a change
> we've grown the business.

Shell are not alone—Wal-Mart, GE Healthcare, and accountants KPMG have also adopted corporate anthems in the past to reflect their visions and values. More down to earth are the policies adopted by Nissan in Sunderland when they brought Japanese company values to a British workforce. This included every employee being salaried as opposed to being paid on hourly rates, no clocking in or out, an employee sickness benefit scheme, and private medical insurance for all. Additionally, all employees including senior management used the same canteen (Basu and Miroshnik, 1999). The results were impressive as Nissan achieved productivity rates previously unheard of in UK car workers.

Another approach is for top management to lead by example. At furniture retailer IKEA for example, 'anti bureaucracy weeks' were introduced where senior managers from the corporate head office went to work in the stores (Gummesson, 2002). In the past, it has been reported that despite his success and wealth, owner and founder of IKEA, Ingvar Kamprad, echoed the organization's sentiments of frugality and efficiency by driving to work in a Nissan Primera each morning. Meanwhile, employees of US-based office supplies manufacturer 3M are each allowed up to 15% of their working time to research and develop new products—whether or not they work in product development. This policy reinforces to all of them the organizational ethos of advancement through innovation.

Bringing the Tools of Marketing Inside the Organization

Initiatives such as those described above can work well in communicating the values of the organization to employees, but companies are increasingly relying on internal marketing to carry through organizational change. In order to do this, some have argued that the traditional tools of external marketing should be brought inside the organization. For example, Morgan (2004) describes how the 7Ps of service marketing can be applied to an internal marketing programme in order to establish a new IT system within an organization:

- The 'Product' is the IT plan itself and the values, attitudes, and behaviours that are required to implement it.

- The 'Price' is the opportunity cost of what employees might do if they did not divert resources and energy into implementing the IT project.

- The 'Promotion' is the internal communication that the organization uses to tell employees about the new system.

- The 'Place' concerns the timing and delivery of the project.

- The 'People' are those tasked with rolling out the new system—answering the questions of employees, bringing them up to speed, etc.

- The 'Process' relates to how the new IT system is integrated into the organization's existing systems and procedures (e.g. staff training, hand-over of responsibilities, etc.).

- The 'Physical Evidence' must convey what Morgan describes as 'a tangible feel of something new and substantive'. This might include a new software interface when employees log in, or perhaps a detailed operating manual.

However, just as this traditional 'tool-box' approach has attracted criticism in external marketing, so it has when applied to internal markets. In a study of UK retail banks, Papasolomou-Doukakis and Kitchen (2004) describe these traditional internal marketing approaches as mere 'window-dressing', presenting the trappings of marketing but with little relevance or impact insofar as employees are concerned. These views are echoed by Ballantyne (2003), who asserts that the quality of relationships within the organization will determine how far knowledge exchange and learning can take place. In other words he is arguing that the principles of relationship marketing are better suited to internal marketing than those of straightforward traditional marketing.

The idea of treating employees as customers has also come in for criticism from those who believe that the conditions inside an organization do not duplicate those in the external market, and that the tools of external marketing are therefore inappropriate. For example, in the external market customers would usually have a choice of products or services and would be free to decide whether or not they wished to buy any of them. In the internal market, employees rarely have a choice about what they are being offered by the organization (e.g. working with a new computer system or brand name) and they are usually forced to accept it, whether or not they like it. In this sense, the purpose of internal marketing is to persuade them that this is a good thing, so that they are happy to support it.

Some people also have a problem in viewing employees as customers because it suggests that the employee should enjoy the same sovereignty as the external customer—after all, is the customer not king? Problems can arise when the organization cannot simultaneously meet the needs of both external and internal customers. For example, a waitress in a pub might not wish to work late shifts, but if the customer demand is there, she may have little choice. For these reasons Ahmed and Rafiq (2002) suggest that the term 'internal customer' should be used with care when it is applied to the relationship between the organization and its employees. However, when one views employees as suppliers and customers of each other, a whole new picture emerges and it is to this area that we now turn.

Employees as Customers of Each Other

The view that employees within an organization exist to serve each other (as well as the external market) stems from Total Quality Management (TQM) theory and focuses on the way in which all the individual and functional departments within an organization work smoothly together in order to raise the quality of the final product or service before it is offered to the market. Thus, every employee performs a task which then enables someone else in the organization to do their job. In this way, every employee becomes a customer and/or a supplier of another employee. It is easy to think of the idea of internal customers and suppliers as a car production line in a factory. As the car moves down the line, each assembly worker fits a part which enables the next person down the line to fit their part and so on until the finished car rolls off the line. If anyone on the line does not do their job properly, the next person cannot do their job and eventually the line grinds to a halt.

In reality, the concept of internal customers and suppliers extends much further than a production line, as it involves every process in the organization, from manufacturing to marketing and purchasing to personnel (see Opening Case). The idea that every process leads on to another underlies the slogan 'the next process is your customer' which was coined by one of the originators of TQM thinking, Kaoru Ishikawa, back in the 1950s. Problems arise when individuals get stuck in a 'silo' mentality, concerned only with their own objectives or targets. Gummesson (2002) illustrates this when describing the situation at Chrysler before Lee Iacocca took control. Here, the factory and the sales people were not communicating with each other, so the factory kept on producing cars that the sales people had not asked for and could not sell.

It is sometimes all too easy for people within an organization to see no further than their own job. Many people spend a long time training for what they do and then over time become experts in their jobs. Universities are full of people studying accounting, marketing, engineering and other specialist subjects and many of the students on these courses will hope to go on and follow a career in these areas. In many organizations, particularly larger ones, this entails joining a functional department—the accounting department, the marketing department, the engineering department, and so on. Problems can arise when these departments turn into 'silos', which are self contained, self-absorbed, and inward looking.

Sometimes the strength of identity held by these functions can turn separate departments into adversaries pulling against each other. For example the Marketing staff in one large organization referred to their counterparts in Finance as 'penny pinching bean counters, afraid to spend money' while the Finance staff had an equally unflattering opinion of the marketing people; 'frivolous egotists, content to waste money'. As Gummesson points out, marketing literature itself may to be blame for some of this by talking about marketing orientation and production orientation as rights and wrongs. Gummesson and others are keen to assert that internal marketing, in the sense of departments seeing themselves as customers of each other, will help to break down some of these functional barriers and make the overall organization more effective.

The thinking of internal relationship marketing is that every employee inside an organization should recognize that they have customers to serve—both inside and outside the organization. Effective communication and interaction is very much along the lines of TQM thinking, which aims to make organizations more effective by concentrating on the processes between functions rather than the functions themselves. No matter how good an individual department is, its overall impact will be limited unless the things it does mesh together with the things which other departments do. In this sense, TQM is not so much about this 'doing things right' as 'doing the right thing'. Gummesson observes that that sometimes means functional departments working very closely together at early stages of product or service development. For example, the department responsible for cleaning within an organization could be involved in the early stages of building design and layout, in order to make cleaning easier when the building goes into use.

There are a number of advantages in pursuing these internal relationships. They enable everyone in the organization to see what their role is and how they contribute to the overall performance of the organization. They also create natural feedback, as employees who can see the big picture will be able to come up with suggestions as to how processes might be improved. As such, employees feel valued and their morale improves. Gummesson claims that this concept is simple and easy to implement and yet it can be a powerful strategic tool, as Jan Carlzon proved at Scandinavia Air Services.

From Value Chain to Value Constellation

The concept of the internal customer brings to mind the Value Chain thinking that was popularized by Michael Porter in the 1980s. Porter's value chain purported that the core functions within an organization such as R&D, manufacturing, and marketing formed part of a continuous process, adding value at each stage and ensuring that the final product or service met the customer's requirements. Gummesson, however, criticizes the value chain, because it gives the impression that these core functions must be performed in a given order one after the other. He suggests that these functions should be simultaneous, not sequential, thus giving rise to a 'value star', or 'value constellation' rather than a sequential chain.

The 'value constellation' puts the emphasis on combining separate functions to meet a single overall need. A simple analogy is the military task force which brings together a number of army, air force, and naval operating divisions under one command to achieve a specific military objective (such as storming an enemy beachhead). Although the different divisions will have their own operating and command structures, these are subsumed for the time being until the job has been done. In organizational terms these task forces are usually called 'project groups' and these too are cross-functional, often involving the suspension of traditional, hierarchical lines of management in favour of a more matrix-like structure. A common example of such projects is new product development. The following Minicase outlines a typical new product development (NPD) process, highlighting the complexity of managing such a project.

Minicase 1

New Product Development Involving the Whole Organization

STAGE 1—IDEA SCREENING

1.1	Register idea	*NPD Manager*
1.2	Estimate sales potential	*NPD Manager*

Brief Report to the Board—Proceed/Not Proceed

STAGE 2—FULL APPRAISAL

2.1	Market analysis	*Marketing Analysts*
2.2	Identify site of manufacture	*NPD Manager/SBU Directors*
2.3	Identify distribution channels	*Logistics Director*
2.4	Estimate development time/cost	*NPD Manager*
2.5	Estimate manufacturing costs	*SBU Directors/Cost Accountants*
2.6	Estimate sales and marketing costs	*Marketing Director/Sales Director*
2.7	Projected 24-month return	*Sales Analysts/Financial Accountants*
2.8	Identify special requirements	*Operations Director/Technical Manager*

Full Report to the Board—Proceed/Abort/Hold

STAGE 3—PHYSICAL DEVELOPMENT

3.3	Design Product	*Technical Department/Draftsman*
3.4	Source materials/components	*Purchasing Department*
3.5	Build prototype	*Factory/SBU Manager*
3.4	Determine packaging	*Technical Department/Marketing*
3.5	File copyright patents	*Legal Department*
3.6	Structural/health and safety tests	*Technical Department*
3.7	Prepare warehousing/distribution	*Logistics Managers*
3.8	Design promotional literature/POS	*Marketing Department*
3.9	Set launch date	*Sales Director/Marketing Director*

STAGE 4—REAPPRAISAL

4.1	Is the project on time and budget?	*NPD Manager*
4.2	Has the market shifted?	*Marketing Analysts*

Full Report to the Board—Proceed/Abort/Hold

STAGE 5—PRE-LAUNCH

5.1	Set prices	*Marketing Dept/Finance Dept*
5.2	Name product	*Marketing Department*
5.3	Set up in online order on system	*Sales Department*
5.4	Order materials/components, etc.	*Purchasing Department*
5.5	Produce usage instructions	*Marketing Department*
5.6	Tool up and commence manufacture	*Production Manager*
5.7	Photograph product	*Marketing Department*
5.8	Commission advertising and PR	*Marketing Department*
5.9	Brief internal staff	*Marketing Department*
5.10	Brief key customers	*Sales Department*
5.11	Build up pre-launch stock	*Logistics Department*

Launch

STAGE 6—POST-LAUNCH ASSESSMENT

6.1	Monitor sales	*Sales Department*
6.2	Rectify teething problems	*Production Managers*
6.3	Actual costs against budget	*Finance Department*

Feedback report to the Board

Questions

1. How many different functional interfaces within a new product development project can you identify from the above table?

2. What sort of organizational structure might best be able to cope with this?

3. What difficulties might arise in trying to manage such a project?

4. Is being based in the Marketing Department the best location for a New Product Development Manager? Where else might the position be better based?

In this way a wide number of organizational employees can become both customers and suppliers within a complex internal network. The value of these networks for the organization depends on how well they communicate and interact with each other. Problems can arise where one party places a higher value on the interaction than another (e.g. a factory manager might not attach the same importance to putting through a new product prototype than a marketing manager might). The way in which these interactions are managed make up the processes which glue an organization together and underpin the principles of TQM. In an effort to take on board these principles, some organizations have undertaken business process re-engineering (BPR), which dismantles existing organizational structures and starts again from scratch, building the business up around processes rather than functions (Gummesson, 2002).

While strategies such as BPR can be seen as extreme and perhaps lie outside the boundaries of marketing thinking, they do reflect the concept of the internal customer. A more literal example of internal customers and suppliers can be found, however, when external market mechanisms are reproduced inside the organization and it is to this area that we turn next.

External Market Mechanisms Inside the Organization

Gummesson (1988, 2002) draws our attention to a final aspect of internal customer thinking when he reminds us that many organizations create internal markets complete with buyers, sellers, and regulators. This is because they structure themselves around internal profit and cost centres in an attempt to introduce efficiency at an operational level. These internal centres are often restricted to buying from and selling to each other rather than being allowed to go to the open market, hence a 'mini' market is created inside the organization. The difference between a profit centre and a cost centre is that the former is expected to make a profit on its operations whereas the latter is expected to operate within certain cost boundaries.

The move towards internal profit and cost centres is a result of the growing size of many organizations. Mergers and acquisitions, consolidations, and supply chain integration have all contributed to fewer, but larger organizations in many market sectors (e.g. the automotive industry, steel, mining, aircraft and ship-building, FMCGs, the media, retailing, hotels and leisure). In order to maintain management efficiency, many of these large corporations are divided up into smaller operating divisions or strategic business units (SBUs) with their own profit and loss responsibility. Sometimes an SBU is set up specifically to supply other SBUs within the organization. For example, in the 1990s Britain's biggest joinery manufacturer, the John Carr Group specifically acquired a glass producer called Abbseal to supply the Group's door and window manufacturing divisions with sealed glass units. Although an internal supplier to the Group, Abbseal was an independent SBU in its own right, retaining responsibility for its own profit or loss.

Similarly, many large organizations have gone through a phase of decentralization, whereby individual functions or departments are given a level of autonomy, including the control of their own finances. When these departments work for each other (as was described in the previous section when we looked at internal customers) an overhead is charged to the 'receiving' department to cover the costs of the 'supplying' department. For example, within most universities the teaching departments are expected to pay a transfer fee to the Estates or Facilities department whose rooms they are using to deliver the teaching. They are also expected to pay a charge to the IT department for use of technical equipment and if they hold a cheese and wine reception for students, they must provide the catering department with a cost code, so that they can be charged accordingly.

Gummesson (2002) argues that the calculation of an internal price, transfer fee, charge, or overhead, indicates that market principles have been let into the organization. In this sense then, the term 'internal customer' is literally true, because one department or SBU buys something from another one. However, one should not assume that the concept of the free market exists between internal customers and suppliers or that the principles of external marketing can so easily be applied inside the organization. Often the internal customers have no choice but to buy from the internal supplier. Continuing with the university example above, the teaching department would be expected to conduct its classes in university-owned accommodation (i.e. it would need to pay a transfer fee or overhead to the Estates department). Only in exceptional circumstances would they be allowed to go outside the university, e.g. to a hotel, to look for teaching rooms.

This leads to a closed and very controlled market, involving what Gummesson describes as a triad, or three-way relationship between the two profit centres and the central organization's corporate management. The goal of the corporate management is to ensure that the organization as a whole makes a profit, but a suboptimal overall performance might result if an internal supplier is trying to get as high a price as possible from an internal customer. As a result, the task of setting internal prices has become a vexed issue and many argue that some sort of intervention by central management is necessary if organizational performance as a whole is to be maximized. Accepting this, Gummesson draws an analogy to external markets where central management is the government who can set rules that limit free trade. This suggests that the relationship between internal departments and central management might be based on influence and lobbying, with each internal department trying to ensure favourable trading conditions for themselves. Once again, internal networks and relationships will come into play.

Another analogy might be that relationships between internal suppliers and buyers reflect those in an external supply chain. We saw in the last chapter how it is not always possible for everyone in a supply chain to maximize their profits, and that sometimes a trade-off has to take place if the overall supply chain is to offer the best experience to the final customer. Perhaps the same is true of large organizations which operate separate profit centres. In this case, the relationships between the supplying and buying departments need to reflect an acceptance that the organization's final customers are the ones that count.

We have seen then, that the idea of the internal customer is a broad concept that can embrace a number of different areas. So far these have involved relationships and networks which stretch across the organization, sometimes impacting on the organizational structure itself. In this sense, therefore, they are way above what might be considered the remit of the average marketing department. Let us now turn to an area a bit closer to home—that of aligning employees to serve the customer better.

Impact of Employees on External Customers

In the struggle to differentiate themselves from one another, many organizations have turned to personal service and the quality of the interaction that customers experience when using their products and services. As such, aligning the thoughts and actions of employees towards the external customer has become an increasingly important objective for them. Such sentiments are echoed in the oft-heard mantras 'remember [it's the customer] who pays your wages' and 'the customer is king'. Clark (2000) reminds us that one of the objectives of internal marketing is to enable staff to work together across functional boundaries, such that the organization is working with one overall objective in mind—customer satisfaction—instead of numerous departmental objectives. We have already covered cross-functional relationships when we looked at the concept of internal customers and suppliers earlier. What we have not yet examined is how managing internal relationships actually maps on to the customer experience.

In this sense, employees may be viewed as 'ambassadors' of the organization, particularly where they have a direct interface with customers. From the customer's perspective, these interfaces can be seen as 'moments of truth' and come to define the organization (Carlzon, 1987). It could therefore be argued that one of the jobs of internal marketing is to ensure that employees have the right attitude, knowledge, and resources to serve the customer effectively. Some employees are set on specifically to work in marketing or sales, in which case their core job is customer-focused. There are many others, however, who do not work in the marketing or sales departments and yet can still affect how customers experience the organization. For example, the core job of a switchboard operator is to put callers through, but the way in which he or she talks to a customer can make a huge difference. Gummesson therefore makes a distinction between what he calls **full-time marketers** (**FTMs**), whose actual job lies in marketing and sales and **part-time marketers** (**PTMs**), encompassing all others in the organization.

While the idea of FTMs and PTMs is useful in acknowledging that all employees have a customer responsibility, it does not consider the extent of customer contact that a PTM might have. The receptionist mentioned above can spend most of her day talking to customers whereas someone working in the factory may never have any kind of interaction with customers. Additionally, it is not always straightforward to distinguish between sales and non-sales personnel. For example, can the person who serves burgers in McDonald's be considered a salesperson? For these reasons it is useful to consider Judd's (1987) categorization of employee roles as they relate to customers. This is based around how involved the employee is with customer service and marketing activities and how frequently they interact with customers (see Figure 9.3).

Contactors are those employees whose core job it is to interact with customers, see that they are looked after and serve them well. This would include people such as supermarket check-out staff, airline cabin crew, waiters and waitresses, as well as full-time sales executives. Although not all of these people work directly in sales or marketing, their impact on the customer is crucial.

Full-time marketer

someone who is employed in a sales or marketing role

Part-time marketer

someone who is not employed in a sales or marketing role but who might nevertheless affect the customer's overall experience

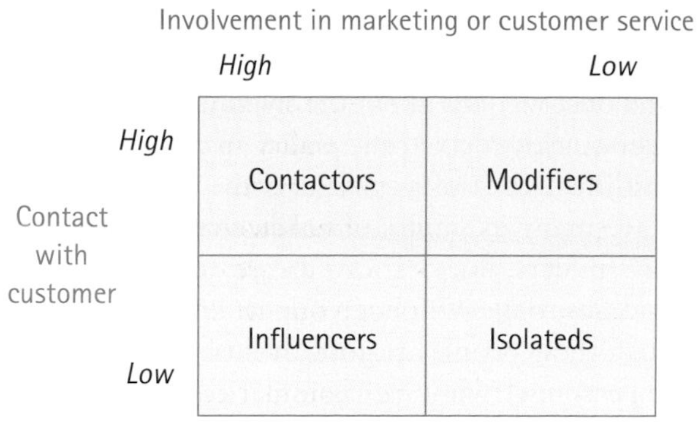

Involvement in marketing or customer service

	High	Low
High / Contact with customer	Contactors	Modifiers
Low	Influencers	Isolateds

Figure 9.3 Categorizing customer–influencing employees

Source: Reprinted from Judd (1987) 'Differentiate with the 5th P: People', *Industrial Marketing Management* 16(4), 7, with kind permission from Elsevier.

Influencers are people who are directly employed in marketing but don't necessarily have any contact with customers. This might include designers, copy writers, desk researchers, marketing planners, advertising and PR executives, and even marketing managers. In fact, it may come as a surprise how few people who work in the average organization's marketing department actually get to interact with real customers. Gummesson alludes to this when he suggests that an organization which has very close relationships with its customers should not need to undertake market research, because it will know the answers already! Nevertheless, despite their lack of customer contact, one would hope that full-time marketing staff do understand their markets. What is without doubt is that the things they do will have a direct influence on the customer.

Modifiers form an important group from an internal marketing prospect because although they interact with customers, their core role does not lie in marketing or customer service. As such their customer awareness skills may need to be developed. Modifiers can include a potentially huge group of people, from bus drivers to librarians, cleaners to airline pilots, all of whom can contribute to the customer's 'moment of truth'. What they say and do can materially affect whether the customer comes back to that organization or not.

For example, a few years ago a novice passenger who was very nervous about flying took an internal flight between Brisbane and Sydney in Australia. The cabin crew (*contactors*) performed their duties in the usual customer-focused way, but it was the aircraft pilots (*modifiers*) that really put the passenger at ease. As the aircraft levelled out following a rather bumpy ascent, they came over the intercom with the following discourse:

1st Pilot: 'G'day folks and welcome to Flight 234 out of Brisbane to Sydney. My name's Brian . . .'

2nd Pilot: 'and I'm Dave!'

Together: 'and we're the boys at the pointy end today.'

The announcement went on in this light-hearted and jocular manner for several more minutes and continued on-and-off throughout the flight with jokes, insights about Sydney life, and observations about the swimming conditions at Bondi Beach. The nervous passenger quickly relaxed and ended up enjoying the flight so much that he returned to that airline many times again over the years.

Conversely there are many examples of academics who are brilliant researchers but have no time for students, doctors who are thoroughly competent but have no 'bedside manner', and librarians with huge subject knowledge but no patience with enquirers. Even though these people are good at their jobs, if a competing organization has equivalent personnel who *are* customer-centric and the customer has a choice, then it becomes a marketing issue. For this reason, internal marketing is often particularly aimed at personnel who might be classed as modifiers.

Isolateds are classed as those employees who have little or no customer contact and no direct influence over marketing or customer service. This would include many support functions within an organization such as purchasing, human resources, IT support, and finance, as well as some core operational activities such as manufacturing. It is important for these employees to be customer aware, and to work together to make the whole organization more customer-focused. When looking at 'isolateds' the concept of the internal customer and the internal supplier makes sense.

Managing Relations with Customer-facing Employees

It would seem, then, that if the organization is intent on differentiating itself through customer service, it should concentrate its internal marketing activities onto the *contactors* and *modifiers* who interact with customers. In order to do this, Clark (2000) suggests that employees be segmented according to their level of customer contact. Thus, those on the front-line of customer service delivery can be singled out for special training or reward. This idea is echoed by Gordon (1998), who advocates that the organization should identify which employees are in a position to add the most value for the customer and assess their performance accordingly. In this way the organization can develop training programmes to close any knowledge gaps which might be identified. This will also give the organization the opportunity to perhaps move some employees to 'back-room' operations if it is deemed that they are unsuited to interfacing directly with customers.

Once it has recognized which internal roles will be important in adding value for the customer, there are a number of things which an organization can do to ensure that the employees in those roles carry the right message. These basically boil down to the following activities:

- 'smile campaigns';
- reward and recognition;
- training and personal development;
- employee empowerment and involvement;
- recruitment and selection.

'Smile Campaigns'

Perhaps one of the more contentious elements of internal marketing thinking is what Payne *et al.* (1995) refer to as the **smile campaign**. Basically this is an attempt to make sure that all customer-facing employees behave in a certain way when interacting with customers. The principles of this lie at the roots of service marketing because it is a way of reducing the variability by which customers experience a service. One of the big differences between products and services is that, whereas a product can be standardized such that each and every one is exactly the same, this is not always possible in the delivery of a service—largely because humans are involved. People delivering services will to a certain extent be susceptible to their own moods and emotions. The restaurant waiter whose girlfriend has just dumped him is going to find it harder to behave in the same way as his colleague whose wife has just given birth to their first child.

Smile campaign
an attempt to ensure that all customer-facing employees behave in a certain way when interacting with customers

The objective of introducing standardized codes of behaviour is therefore to ensure that customers are treated in a pleasant and efficient way by all staff at all times, thus reducing the potential for variability. Furthermore, by adopting a controlled approach to customer interaction, the organization is sending out a message about its values and identity. In this sense staff behaviour becomes as much a part of the brand as the corporate logo. For example, all the staff working in Disney theme parks are taught to consider themselves on-stage or off-stage. On stage they are in the public eye and are expected to behave as if they were in a show, even if they are just serving burgers or sweeping the litter (Gummesson, 2002).

Many service organizations thus adopted 'smile campaigns', requiring all staff to smile at customers or send them on their way with a 'thank you, have nice day!' Ogbonna and Wilkinson (1990) argue that such initiatives attempt to go deeper than just the surface, behavioural approach of the employee. Rather, they are an attempt by the organization to instil in employees the meanings, values, and assumptions which underlie this behaviour. But while some organizations such as Disney appear to have found success with this approach, others have been criticized for using 'smile campaigns' as bolt-on, quick-fix solutions. Christopher *et al.* (1991) describe many of them as 'cosmetic attempts to improve the appearance of the customer interface' which do nothing to address the real question of how the organization can support or empower front-line staff to serve the customer better.

In a study of UK supermarkets, Ogbonna and Wilkinson describe some of the problems of trying to apply a standardized approach to the customer interface. One checkout operator describes herself as being a good actress (suggesting that the genuine underlying values or customer ethos have not necessarily been taken on board). Another checkout operator runs into problems with a customer's wife, who mistakes the smiling approach to her husband as flirting! Meanwhile a third operator complains that 'you can't smile at someone who's calling you a stupid bitch'. Ogbonna and Wilkinson note that in some instances, the checkout operators are monitored and anyone not showing the required demeanour is called into a room for a 'chat'. They thus conclude that enforcing a standard of behaviour under threat of sanction does not embed in employees a sense of organizational values and that there are clear limits to how far the organization can go to instil a customer ethos.

Reward and Recognition

An alternative to coercing staff to behave nicely to customers is to reward them for it. Thus, passengers on a bus might be asked to vote for their 'bus driver of the month', guests in a hotel might be asked in their check-out questionnaire if any particular staff deserve a 'special mention', and drinkers in a pub might see an 'employee of the month' certificate proudly displayed behind the bar. Sometimes these results are gained not from customer votes, but through the use of 'mystery shoppers'. A mystery shopper is usually employed by a research agency and will pose as a real customer in order to evaluate how good the service is.

In the 1990s, shoe repair chain Mister Minit used mystery shoppers extensively. Working to a 27-point questionnaire, they rated all aspects of the service experience, from how they were greeted to the quality of the shoe repair itself. The results were used to reward top-performing staff with holidays and other prizes, alongside a big mention in the organization's magazine. Conversely, the results also enabled the company to pinpoint poorly performing staff and to take remedial action where necessary.

Training and Personal Development

If 'smile campaigns' are to have any real value, they must be backed up by a deeper commitment from the organization to staff development. Disney has shown that an underlying set of values can be engendered to a certain extent by investing in staff training and development (see Minicase 2, Learning the Disney Way). However, Clark (2000) recognizes that many front-line, customer-serving staff are low-paid and unskilled. This is epitomized in the slang term 'McJob', meaning a low-paid, unfulfilling job with few prospects, only undertaken as a stop gap or for transient reasons. The term derives from McDonald's, which, like many fast-food, catering, and retail outlets, employs large numbers of relatively low-paid people in customer-facing positions. McDonald's has fought hard to refute this image by emphasizing the value of its staff and the prospects which it offers. The company's commitment to staff is therefore backed up by rigorous training programmes.

Minicase 2

Learning the Disney Way

Millions of people every year enjoy the 'magic' of a Disney theme park, but how many of them pause to consider how this fun and fantasy experience has been developed and maintained so consistently over the years? Bringing the 'magic' to life relies upon the enthusiasm, hospitality, and professionalism of Disney's employees, each of whom is provided with training at the organization's own university.

Whilst the idea of a Disney University (complete with a coat of arms featuring Mickey Mouse's ears) may provoke sniggers in some areas, the organization takes its staff development and support very seriously indeed. Part and parcel of the training programmes is to imbue the theme park employees (referred to as 'Cast Members') with the values, traditions, and standards which lie behind the Disney experience. Writing on the website Mouse Planet, one cast member describes how this was done. 'We were told that we put on a show for our customers'; 'we don't wear "uniforms", we wear "costumes"'; 'visitors to Disneyland are "guests", not "customers"'. He goes on to describe how employees are taught to act their parts with the right body language, to smile (not just with the mouth), never to cross their arms, lean or sit whilst 'on-stage', never to point with less than two fingers and never to act preoccupied, annoyed, or bored. 'After a while, these terminologies seep into your bloodstream and infuse your cells; they become second nature.'

But Disney's objectives went further than just training its employees how to behave in a theme park. Through the Disney Institute they offered a range of specialized training programmes designed to allow employees to upgrade their skills and acquire new knowledge. For example, a leadership programme focused on areas such as 'leveraging personal strengths', 'uplifting', 'empowering', and 'inspiring' fellow employees and bridging the gap between 'dreaming' and 'doing'. Inspired by their success the Disney Institute began offering tailored programmes to external organizations. An article in *Education & Training* magazine describes how the US health care sector was one of the first to come to Disney. They wanted to learn more about Disney's approach to respect, service, and responsiveness.

Disney is not alone in developing its own university. As more organizations come to realize that developing people is the key to their future, they are becoming keener to take control of their executive training. This trend is seen most clearly in the USA, where 'corporate universities' are relatively common. McDonald's Hamburger University in Oak Brook, Illinois boasts 30 resident professors and has churned out 50,000 graduates since its inception in 1961. Other examples include the Ford Heavy Truck University in Detroit, the Intel University in Santa Clara, Sun Microsystems 'Sun U', and Apple's University in Cupertino, California. In the UK, GEC has long had it own college in Dunchurch, which it now uses to offer training to employees of other organizations too.

Although the growth of these 'corporate universities' has been treated with disdain amongst some traditional academics, it would appear that the demand for specifically tailored degree courses is growing. In 2008 it was announced that Buckinghamshire New University had validated a course in Selling Beds.

Questions

1. When there are plenty of traditional universities, why do organizations feel the need to develop their own?

2. To what extent might the skills and knowledge imparted by the 'corporate universities' be transferable?

3. Some have accused Disney's induction programme for new employees as 'brain washing'. Is this a justified criticism? Develop a reasoned argument to support your view.

Sources:
'Cast Place: For and by Disney employees past and present' http://www.mouseplanet.com accessed 17/03/08
Hong Kong Disneyland Briefing Paper, Tourism Commission, November 1999
'Can your college compete with the magic of Disney?' (1998) *Education and Training*, 40(4), 151–2
Crainer, S., 'Corporate views of university' http://www.managmentskills .co.uk/articles/univer.htm accessed 17/03/08

Many organizations are now recognizing that even staff who are not employed in marketing or sales jobs need to be conversant with customer service principles. As a result, they are sending staff on external training courses or developing their own courses. In 2008, the UK government announced a move to allow employers the right to award their own qualifications which would be nationally accredited vocational equivalents of A levels and GCSEs—in other words the qualifications would be officially recognized outside the organization, just like a college qualification or university degree. Among the first companies to sign up to the idea were McDonald's, FlyBe, and Network Rail. Investing like this in staff not only helps to develop the right skills; it also demonstrates a commitment and a sense of value in the employee over and above the gloss of simply telling them to smile at customers.

Empowerment and Involvement

Employee empowerment

allowing employees to make decisions without recourse to higher management

In addition to training and development, organizations must also provide their staff with the necessary resources to serve the customer properly. Often this will entail **empowering the employee** to take decisions and sort out customers' problems quickly and efficiently without having to recourse to a higher authority. In order to decide how much empowerment to give an employee, Ahmed and Rafiq (2002) propose that the complexity and range of the customer needs is taken into account, alongside that of the tasks needed to fulfil these needs.

Complex customer needs would include situations where a tailored solution is required. This might range from a diner in a restaurant asking for something which is not on the standard menu (e.g. fish with mashed potatoes instead of chips) right through to an organizational buyer requiring a bespoke computer software package. Such situations require high levels of routine discretion from the employee (i.e. the waitress is able to accept non-standard orders off the menu and the sales executive is able to offer a pricing deal for the bespoke computer package). The task complexity will depend on the degree of technology involved and the nature of the product itself. For example, if the restaurant's computerized till was unable to accept a non-standard menu combination, the waitress might not know how much to charge the customer. Likewise, the computer software package might be so detailed that the salesperson has to refer it all back to the design department for costing.

Empowering employees is not cheap. Ahmed and Rafiq (2002) remind us that it will increase the scope of the job and may well lead to demands for more pay to take into account the increased responsibility. They also point out that it might slow down service delivery as the employee tries to individualize the service for each customer. In addition, there is a risk that employees may give away too much when trying to compensate dissatisfied customers or even that they may discriminate between customers when deciding to whom to give better service.

As a result of these potential costs, Ahmed and Rafiq propose that the organization thinks in terms of 'zones of empowerment'. Safe (green) zones are those where the employee is routinely expected to take decisions independently. The potential cost to the organization of a wrong decision here is not great. Low-risk (amber) zones are those where the employee is given some routine discretion but also the option to consult their manager where necessary. High-risk (red) zones are those where the employee must consult their manager before making a decision. Naturally it is in the interests of customers for the organization to have as many green zones as possible, but because of the potential costs involved, the organization must strike a balance between green, amber, and red.

Potential for Employee Conflict

The above sections on empowerment, reward training, and coercion all suggest that the employee is not naturally customer-focused and that this somehow needs to be engendered in them by the organization. There are a number of studies, however, that suggest that employees do want to please customers but are often prevented from doing so by organizational constraints. In a major study into the US retail banking sector, Schneider (1980) noted that employees were often judged against mechanistic, internal targets (such as speed of service or number of errors made) rather than how much goodwill they generated with customers. When discussing managers in service organizations, Schneider distinguishes between what he calls 'service enthusiasts' and 'service bureaucrats'. Service enthusiasts recognize the importance of personal relationships when dealing with customers and a more flexible approach to rules and regulations. For example, a bus driver may delay setting off for a couple of minutes to allow passengers who are running for the bus to catch it. Service bureaucrats, on the other hand, lay more emphasis on the rigid application of organizational rules and operating procedures. Here, the bus driver would be instructed to set off at the exact second his timetable demanded, and leave behind anyone running for the bus.

Schneider argues that many customer facing employees have a strong inclination to please people and make the customer happy. When organizational rules or structures get in the way of this it can lead to stress and frustration and even the desire to resign and find a better job. Going back to the bus example, passengers of a large northern bus company noticed a sudden change in the punctuality of the service. Instead of turning up at 5.35 p.m. as it had for years, the bus always seemed to be running 25 minutes late. The passengers complained bitterly to the driver, who shared their frustrations. He explained that his managers had asked him to take a new route which added an extra 20 minutes to his journey, but that they would not change the timetable to reflect this. When asked if he would convey the passengers' disapproval back to the management, he sighed and said that the drivers had all complained about the new service but to no avail. He concluded that if the managers wouldn't listen to the drivers, they certainly wouldn't listen to the customers.

The message seems to be that with the right support, customer-facing employees can add much value to the customer. But put obstacles in their way and the opposite happens. Customer service employees who feel that they have to meet conflicting demands between their managers and the customers end up feeling stressed. Thus, as Schneider concludes, employee and customer perceptions of the organization and the service quality being offered are positively related. Put simply, happy employees equal happy customers, unhappy employees equal unhappy customers.

The Recruitment Market

In recent years the UK has experienced a shift in the demographic make-up of the population that has seen the proportion of older and retired people rise significantly in comparison with younger people. In the USA the Bureau of Labor and Statistics has estimated that by 2012 there will be 165 million jobs to fill, but only 162 million workers available to fill them (Extended Retail Solutions, 2008). As a result, Christopher *et al.* (1991) suggest that people are becoming the scarcest resource that an organization has. Simply finding people to fill vacancies has become a major challenge in some industries.

At the same time employee turnover has become much higher. Whereas in the past people might have expected to go into a job for life, this is often no longer the case. Ever increasing competition, the decline and consolidation of traditional industries, and the introduction of market forces to many previously 'safe' professions (e.g. teachers, civil service, health workers) has eroded the loyalty that might once have existed between organizations and their employees. As a result, many people now accept that they will switch employers and maybe even change careers several times during their working lives. Younger people especially are likely to move between organizations as they seek out the most advantageous job ladder (Beardwell and Holden, 2004). For organizations relying on staff to deliver good customer service, finding the right employees and hanging on to them has become a priority and some have begun to look in new directions (see Minicase 3, Never Too Old To Work*).*

Minicase 3

Never Too Old To Work

For many years now it has been illegal for an employer to discriminate between job applicants on the basis of gender or ethnicity. However, until relatively recently it was perfectly normal to see job adverts asking for a 'dynamic *young* individual' or stipulating a maximum age of 30 or 35. According to the National Institute of Economic and Social Research (NIESR), this was particularly the case in newer industries such as IT, media, or advertising. The NIESR believed that much of this ageism was down to typical stereotypes of older workers, such as an inability to adapt to new technology, being difficult to train, stuck in their ways and unambitious. In addition, older people were less likely to have a degree—in the 1970s only around 6% of people went to university compared to 40% today.

Such was the problem of ageism in the workplace that in October 2006 the UK government passed legislation making it illegal to discriminate against existing employees or job applicants on the basis of their age so long as they were under the age of 65. Whilst the Trades Union Council does not expect that this will lead to a revolutionary change overnight, they do believe that a slow cultural change is taking place in the way that older workers are viewed by employers. Many are coming to recognize the benefits that older workers can bring by consequence of their experience and knowledge.

For example, at the tourist village of Portmeirion in North Wales, older workers who live locally are valued because they are more likely to speak Welsh, something that personnel manager Gareth Evans is keen to promote: 'Americans and people from other countries love hearing people speaking Welsh—it's part of the reason they come'. Evans also finds that older workers, with more experience of life, find it easy to strike up conversations with the visitors—more so than with 'somebody who has just left school and hasn't seen much of the world'. In addition the older workers tend to be more 'dependable' and 'conscientious about time keeping'.

Tourism Partnership North Wales is not alone in its praise for older workers. DIY store B & Q has for many years adopted a policy of recruiting people of all ages. Their stated aim is to get the best person for the job—young people with new skills and older people with life experience and knowledge of DIY. According to government agency Age Positive, around 22% of B & Q's 37,000 workforce are aged 50 or above (in 2006, Sidney Prior, aged 91, became their oldest employee). One store, in Macclesfield, was staffed entirely by people over 50. Research there found that profits were 18% higher than average whilst staff turnover was six times lower. In addition, there was 39% less absenteeism and 59% less stock shrinkage. Tellingly, customer perception of the service also improved.

Other companies have been following B & Q's lead. For example, supermarket Sainsbury's launched a campaign to attract an extra 10,000 'mature' workers. Asda offered its 'Asda Goldies' flexible hours and other benefits in recognition that the Goldies helped to train and settle younger staff and were also appreciated by customers. Many organizations have now introduced flexible retirement options for their employees, allowing them to stay on after 65 if they wish to continue working. Among them are the Nationwide Building Society, Marks & Spencer, Royal Bank of Scotland, BT, and many universities. It seems that in some industries at least, life really does begin at 60.

Questions

1. What do many of the organizations mentioned above have in common which makes employing older staff an attractive option?

2. How might an organization that is happy to employ older staff get this message across?

3. What are the advantages of employing older workers?

Sources:
'How UK "turned its back" on older workers' http://news.bbc.co.uk accessed 24/09/06
'Silver workforce test for tourism' http://news.bbc.co.uk accessed 22/03/06
'Case Study B&Q' http://www.agepositive.gov.uk accessed 17/03/08
'Second careers and third age: you're only as old as your new job'
    http://www.guardian.co.uk/business accessed 19/01/06

Christopher *et al.* (1991) estimate that annual employee turnover is as high as 150% in some service industries. The cost of this turnover to organizations can be massive due to:

- the lost output of employees who have left and the resulting disruption to the business and its customers;
- the strain on remaining employees who have temporarily to cover the work;

- the financial costs of recruitment and selection, including placing job adverts, holding interviews and other assessment exercises, and the time of staff involved in these;
- the costs of training new staff and the reduced output during this period.

Christopher *et al.* quote estimates suggesting that the cost of replacing an employee might be 50% of their annual salary. In this sense we can draw a parallel with the costs of customer acquisition and retention outlined by Reichheld (1996) and discussed in Chapter 3. For these reasons Reichheld points out that *employee* retention can be just as important as *customer* retention. This view is echoed by Beardwell and Holden (2004), who suggest that fostering long-term employment relationships can help to create switching barriers which reduce the mobility of workers between organizations.

Even if the organization manages to hang on to its staff, finding the right kind of employee in the first place can be difficult. We have already seen that many customer-facing jobs are seen as low-paid and relatively menial (the McJob syndrome) and yet the type of person who does the job can make all the difference as far as the final customer is concerned. We have also seen that employees who buy into the organization's overall ethos or objectives can create a positive customer-focused dynamic. For these reasons, Christopher *et al.* (1991) suggest that companies should base their selection on candidates' psychological characteristics, rather than technical skills which can be taught later. In other words the candidate has to fit the organization and the organization has to fit the candidate.

Finding the right person in this way can be difficult because it entails finding out what sort of a personality a candidate has. While it has been reported in the past that graphology (the study of handwriting) and even astrology (horoscopes) have been used to determine a candidate's personality, in practice, organizations usually use more scientifically proven and reliable tests. In their study of UK supermarkets, Ogbonna and Wilkinson (1990) observed the use of psychometric profiling, occupational testing, and the reliance on managers to spot suitable candidates through personal interviewing. Christopher *et al.* report that Southwest Airlines in the USA has developed its own psychometric profiling test, based on its internal studies of the most successful and least successful roles in the organization.

Finally, an organization might need to 'sell' itself at a higher level in order to attract staff who are internationally recognized or are leaders in their field. For example, a hospital will wish to attract the finest consultants and surgeons, a TV company the most popular presenters, and a university the most distinguished professors. The employment of such people will enhance the organization's overall standing in its own marketplace and enable it to attract the right type of customers more easily.

For these reasons, Christopher *et al.* (1991) include recruitment as a separate market within their Six Markets Model. In this sense it is just as important for the organization to project itself to potential employees as it is to external customers. In order to attract the right type of staff, companies often develop close working relationships with third parties that can act as recruitment supply channels. These include recruitment specialists, executive search agencies, the careers offices of schools, colleges and universities, and also university placement departments. In addition, the power of word of mouth and business networking should not be under-estimated here.

Managing Internal Marketing Relationships

It can be seen from the preceding sections that internal marketing is a potentially large and diverse area. From a relationship marketing viewpoint it is important to distinguish between what is and what is not marketing in the sense that managing internal relationships will help to make the organization more competitive in the external marketplace. Clearly, some aspects of managing internal relationships will fall under the responsibility of the HR department. As these do not fall within the scope of this book, we must therefore be clear about where the distinction lies. Of the remaining issues, some might be classed as 'operational', in which case they would normally be undertaken by the organization's Marketing department, whilst others might be seen as 'strategic', in that they involve long-term planning and are handled at the top of the organization. Let us end this chapter by looking at these three areas in turn.

The HR/Marketing Boundary

The question about whether internal relationships should be considered an HR or a marketing issue can be a vexed one. Indeed, Ahmed and Rafiq (2002) are quick to draw a comparison between a marketer's definition of internal marketing and an HR commentator's definition of HRM:

> Internal marketing is attracting, developing, motivating and retaining qualified employees, through job products that satisfy their needs. (Berry and Parasuraman, 1991)

> Human resource management is concerned with the set of decisions and policies through which the organizations attract, recruit and motivate, reward and develop their employees. (Willman, 1989)

The issue appears to revolve around the extent to which the organization relies upon customer contact personnel to further its business. For example, Ahmed and Rafiq (2002) suggest that where the service which the employee provides forms a major part of the product being offered (e.g. a hairdressing salon), then marketing needs to be as closely involved in staff recruitment and selection as HR. Such views have, however, led to criticisms that marketing as a functional area of the organization is trying to spread its influence too far (Papasolomou-Doukakis and Kitchen, 2004).

We must be careful, therefore, to distinguish between what is a core service (e.g. cutting the customer's hair) and what is a differentiating service (e.g. being friendly and chatty with the customer while you're doing it). It could be argued that recruiting people with the right core skills (i.e. qualifications and experience in hair dressing) is the role of HR, while ensuring that they have a good customer disposition is the role of marketing. This would certainly lend support to suggestions that marketing should not only be involved in recruitment and selection, but also in employee training and motivation systems. In this area, Ahmed and Rafiq suggest that a useful distinction between marketing and HR is that marketing does not have the coercive powers over employees that HR does (i.e. it does not have the ability to fire people in other parts of the organization). It would seem therefore that HR and marketing should work closely together if the overall objectives of the organization are to be met.

Operational Aspects of Internal Marketing

In practice, internal marketing is usually handled through communications within the organization. Baines *et al.* (2004) refer to this as internal public relations and separate it into three headings:

- **Upward communications** from employee to management, so that the employee feels involved in marketing and customer care decisions. For example, when Swift's set about finding a new name, all the staff were invited to submit suggestions. The eventual choice, L'Attitude, originated from one of the junior buyers of the organization. Ogbonna and Wilkinson (1990) cite how some organizations also operate 'customer care committees' where customer-facing personnel can make suggestions about how the customer experience can be improved. As a result of this, one supermarket chain introduced child-changing facilities into its stores.

- **Sideways communications** from employee to employee. The aim of these is to enable staff to network with each other and thus work more effectively together. Typical examples include the staff news sections of internal journals announcing details of new starters and retirees, staff who have had babies, got married, or perhaps passed away in retirement. Often staff can place classified adverts if they wish to sell things, or organize social events. In such a way, employees are encouraged to feel that they are part of a team, or family where everybody knows each other and helps each other out.

- **Downwards communications** from management to employee. This would include news about what the organization is doing, how it is performing, etc. As well as company newsletters and magazines, this would also include policy documents, staff handbooks, and organizational mission statements. Ogbonna and Wilkinson (op. cit.) describe how one of the supermarkets in their study placed posters at all entrances to the shop floor reading 'Smile—You're On Stage!' Clearly, downward communications reflect a hierarchical top-down approach which can provoke cynicism if not well handled. The introduction of staff Intranet systems has helped in this area, because they are interactive and thus more conducive to the development of a two-way relationship.

Organizational Structure and Culture

Some commentators have likened the downward communication described above as the internal equivalent of transaction marketing (e.g. Ballantyne, 2003). They argue that for internal marketing to generate any real benefits, a long-term, relationship-building approach should be undertaken whereby knowledge is created through interaction rather than simply transferred from one part of the organization to the other. Developing such an approach represents a more strategic approach, which can require a culture shift within the organization.

Clark (2000) demonstrates how many organizations are run as hierarchical pyramids, with the management at the top filtering down information, rules, values, and procedures to those below them. Very often in such structures, the employees right at the bottom of the pyramid are those in the front-line of customer service—the checkout operators, waiters, bank clerks, etc. Clark suggests that the pyramid should be inverted such that these people become the most important in the organization and that instead of telling them what to do and think, the management asks 'what can I do to help you do your job better?' In many ways this sums up the idea of the internal customer and the internal supplier. If internal marketing is run along these lines, then the whole organization might truly become customer-focused, but in accepting this, one must also accept that the concept of internal marketing is too big to be handled by one department alone.

Chapter Summary

The issue of managing internal relationships can be divided into two broad areas:

- the concept of the internal customer, whereby the employees of the organization are seen as suppliers and customers of each other;

- the notion that employees themselves will colour the external customer's experience of the organization and should therefore be managed as a marketing resource.

The acceptance of internal customer thinking acknowledges that marketing principles which are usually applied in the external market may be brought within the organization. Emphasis has been placed on managing the processes through which different organizational functions interact with each other, and this is something which may impact on the organizational structure itself. In this sense managing internal relationships becomes an organization-wide issue.

The impact of employees on external customers has led some to distinguish between 'full-time marketers' and 'part-time marketers' in the recognition that all employees are significant in some way for the final service delivery. Ensuring that customer-facing staff carry the right message can be achieved through rewards, training, empowerment, recruitment, and even coercion. Whilst accepting that employees can affect the marketing effectiveness of the organization, there is debate about where marketing ends and HRM begins.

Many of the issues that have been raised in this chapter are brought to life in the End of Chapter Case, which looks at how one organization has made a success out of managing internal relationships.

End of Chapter Case with Questions

Cobblers Enjoy Their Jobs More Than Most

Think of a great place to work and a number of things might spring to mind. Perhaps for an airline, or a holiday firm, travelling the world and seeing the sights. Maybe a food or film critic, being wined and dined and attending premieres, or perhaps you'd rather be a test driver with Porsche or Ferrari. It may come as a surprise then to learn that shoe repair chain Timpson has consistently appeared in the *Sunday Times*' list of Best Companies to Work For in the UK.

Timpson is a family business, run by John Timpson, great grandson of William Timpson, who began selling shoes in 1865 and moved into shoe repair in 1903. John Timpson has been running the company as a family business again, since he bought it back from the retailing conglomerate Hanson in 1983, where it had been under-performing. One of Timpson's first moves was to divest the shoe-retailing operation and concentrate on shoe repairs and key cutting. Despite the stagnant nature of this market sector, during the last 20 years Timpson has increased turnover to nearly £100 million and at the same time boosted profits from £500,000 to £12 million. With around 600 shops in the UK and Ireland, Timpson is now a clear market leader in its field.

John Timpson is under no doubt about what has led to the success of the business. It all revolves around what he calls 'upside down management'. In an interview in the *Sunday Telegraph* in 2003, Timpson summed up this philosophy: 'We've got to be terribly nice to our customers. We don't advertise. So we've got to look after the people who look after the cus-tomers.' This means trusting employees and giving them, within reason, the right to do what they want. Thus, shop managers can set their own prices and come up with their own pro-motions. Employees can control their own training and the company head office near Stockport is described as a 'facilitator', there to help the shops work better rather than just handing down rules. In this way Timpson describes how employees are given the 'freedom and the space to get on and show how good they are'.

This 'upside down management' approach is backed up by open communications and an employee-oriented organizational culture. John Timpson and his son James spend two days of every week visiting the shops (he reckons he gets round 500 a year) and talking to staff. A weekly newsletter is circulated telling employees how the shops are doing and featuring a piece from Timpson himself, alongside stories and pictures from individual shops. Timpson is keen to separate the administrative and legislative aspects of HR from the 'people' role. As such the company employs a 'people person' whose job is the support and social welfare of the staff. The people person represents the company at weddings and funerals and organ-izes employee holiday homes and retirement functions.

Timpson is adamant that success is about employing the right people and then looking after them. As such Timpson employees can enjoy a number of perks. They all benefit from a final salary pension scheme and bonuses based on experience. They also get a day off on their birthday and use of the company's corporate season ticket for Manchester City (Timpson has been a life-long supporter) as well as access to Timpson's Harley Street doctor. Each year, employees are invited to a barbeque at John Timpson's mansion in Cheshire and also have the opportunity to use the company's holiday homes free of charge. The company spends £3 million a year on staff training and Timpson himself writes the cartoon-based training manuals and other books, all subtitled *The Timpson Way*.

Although the company encountered a few difficulties following its takeover of Minit shoe repair shops in 2003, employee turnover is relatively low and there are a high number of long-serving employees. Indeed, according to the *Sunday Times*' Best Companies to Work For survey, despite their modest salaries, more than half of Timpson's employees say that they are in their dream job. So who needs to be a Ferrari test driver?

Questions

1. What are the benefits of Timpson's 'upside down management' approach?

2. Could any organization adopt this policy? What are the risks?

3. What relevance does all of this have for marketing?

Sources:
'Timpson: the eccentric cobbler', *Sunday Telegraph*, 30 March 2003
Profile of John Timpson, *Director Magazine*, 08/07
'The Sunday Times 100 Best Companies to Work For', 2 March 2003
'What has HR ever done for John Timpson?', *Human Resources Magazine*, 1 September 2004

Discussion Questions

1. What are the issues in determining the scope of internal marketing?

2. Taking an organization of your choice, describe how the concept of the internal customer might be applied.

3. What are the possible limitations in thinking of employees as customers?

4. Why might the concept of the internal customer be linked with the thinking behind TQM?

5. How far does an 'internal market' created by internal profit and cost centres reflect the realities of the external market?

6. Discuss how Judd's categorization of employee roles (Figure 9.3) might apply to the following: car mechanic, salesperson, nurse, cleaner, managing director, computer programmer, policeman, newsreader, postman, HR manager.

7. What are the implications of managing internal relations with the above job categories?

8. What are the problems associated with trying to standardize a level of customer service?

9. How might an organization ensure that its front-line staff convey the right message to the customer?

10. What do Christopher *et al.* mean when they talk about the 'recruitment market'? In this 'market' who is marketing what to whom?

11. Describe the different functions typically carried out by an organization's marketing department and its HR department. When might the two overlap?

12. How might organizational structure encourage or hinder internal marketing?

Further Reading

Ahmed, P. and Rafiq, M. (2002) *Internal Marketing: Tools and Concepts for Customer-Focused Management*, Butterworth Heinemann, Oxford.

Gummesson, E. (2002) *Total Relationship Marketing. Rethinking Marketing Management: From 4Ps to 30Rs* (2nd edn), Butterworth Heinemann, Oxford.

Papasolamou-Doukakis, I. and Kitchen, P. (2004) 'Internal Marketing in UK Banks: Conceptual legitimacy or window dressing?', *International Journal of Bank Marketing*, 22(6), 421–52.

References

Ahmed, P. and Rafiq, M. (2002) *Internal Marketing: Tools and Concepts for Customer-Focused Management*, Butterworth Heinemann, Oxford.

Baines, P, Egan, J., and Jefkins, F. (2004) *Public Relations: Contemporary Issues and Techniques*, Elsevier Butterworth-Heinemann, Oxford.

Ballantyne, D. (2003) 'A Relationship-mediated Theory of Internal Marketing', *European Journal of Marketing*, 37(90), 1242–60.

Beardwell, I. and Holden, L. (2004) *Human Resource Management: A Contemporary Approach* (4th edn), Pitman Publishing, London.

Basu, D. and Miroshnik, V. (1999) 'Strategic Human Resource Management of Japanese Multinationals. A Case Study of Japanese Multinational Companies in the UK', *The Journal of Management Development*, 18(9), 714–32.

Berry, L., Hensel, J., and Burke, M. (1976) 'Improving Retailer Capability for Effective Consumerism Response', *Journal of Retailing*, 52(3), 3–14.

Berry, L. and Parasuraman, A. (1991) *Marketing Services: Competing through Quality*, The Free Press, New York.

Carlzon, J. (1987) *Moments of Truth*, Ballinger, New York.

Christopher, M., Payne, A., and Ballantyne, D. (1991) *Relationship Marketing: Bringing quality, customer service and marketing together*, Butterworth–Heinemann, Oxford.

Clark, M. (2000) 'Customer Service, People and Processes', in *Marketing Management: A relationship marketing perspective*, Cranfield School of Management, Macmillan Press, Basingstoke.

Doyle, P. (1995) 'Marketing in the new millennium', *European Journal of Marketing*, 29, 23–41.

Gordon, I. (1998) *Relationship Marketing*, John Wiley & Sons, Canada.

Grönroos, C. (1990) *Service Management and Marketing*, Lexington/Macmillan, New York.

Gummesson, E. (1987) 'The New Marketing—Developing Long Term Interactive Relationships', *Long Range Planning*, 20(4), 10–20.

Gummesson, E. (2002) *Total Relationship Marketing. Rethinking Marketing Management: From 4Ps to 30Rs* (2nd edn), Butterworth Heinemann, Oxford.

Judd, V. (1987) 'Differentiate with Fifth P: People', *Industrial Marketing Management*, 16, 241–7.

Kellaway, L. (2006) 'A Distinct Lack of Value from This Year's Top Twaddlists', *Financial Times*, 17 December, 15.30.

Morgan, R. (2004) 'Business Agility and Internal Marketing', *European Business Review*, 16(5), 464–72.

Morgan, R. and Hunt, S. (1994) 'The Commitment-Trust Theory of Relationship Marketing', *Journal of Marketing*, 58 (Oct.), 20–38.

Ogbonna, E. and Wilkinson, B. (1990) 'Corporate Strategy and Corporate Culture: The view from the checkout', *Personnel Review*, 19(4), 9–15.

Papasolamou-Doukakis, I. and Kitchen, P. (2004) 'Internal Marketing in UK Banks: Conceptual legitimacy or window dressing?', *International Journal of Bank Marketing*, 22(6), 421–52.

Payne, A., Christopher, C., Clark, M., and Peck, H. (1995) *Relationship Marketing for Competitive Advantage*, Butterworth Heinemann, Oxford.

Piercy, N. and Morgan, N. (1991) 'Internal Marketing—The Missing Half of the Marketing Programme', *Long Range Planning*, 24(2), 82–93.

Reichheld, F. (1996) *The Quest for Loyalty*, Harvard Business School Publishing Corporation.

Schneider, B. (1980) 'The Service Organization: Climate is crucial', in Payne, A, Christopher, M., Clark, M., and Peck, H. (eds), *Relationship Marketing for Competitive Advantage*, Butterworth Heinemann, Oxford.

Willman, P. (1989) 'Human Resource Management in the Service Sector', in Jones, P. (ed.), *Management in Service Industries*, Piton, London.

Websites

Extended Retail Solutions, 'The Silver Lining at Borders'
http://www.extendedretail.com/pastissue/article.asp?art=269287&issue=188
accessed 17/03/08

PART
4

Implications—For
Organizations and the
Future

The Management of Relationships

Chapter Outline

Learning Outcomes

After reading this chapter you should be able to:

- recognize situations where relationship marketing might be more appropriate than transaction marketing and suggest an optimum balance between the two;

- critically assess which relationships an organization might choose to develop;

- understand how different organizational structures and systems can aid or hinder the implementation of a relationship marketing strategy;

- apply models such as the 'Spectrum of Behaviour' to determine an optimum relationship approach within a given situation;

- appreciate the significance of return on relationships and how this might be calculated.

Introduction

So far in this book we have covered a number of ideas and theories about what relationship marketing is and how it works. We have seen that the organization is surrounded by relationships, not just with customers but with many other stakeholders, both internal and external. We have explored the concepts of business networks, loyalty and retention, and also seen how managing information about customers and others can help the organization to forge closer links with its markets. The examples and illustrations have shown how many companies have used the principles of relationship marketing to create a competitive advantage. Not surprisingly, the proponents of relationship marketing (such as Gummesson, Grönroos, Christopher, Reichheld, etc.) believe that this is a major departure for marketing thinking, or as Gummesson (2002) puts it a 'paradigm shift'.

But we have also seen that traditional, transaction marketing still has a part to play, particularly when customers are primarily motivated by price, or have no interest in a relationship. Even when a relationship strategy might be appropriate, we noted in Chapter 3 that customer acquisition (as opposed to customer retention) still remains a dominant policy in many areas, often for cultural or historical reasons (Maister, 1989). Furthermore, it was acknowledged in Chapter 5 that companies who do seek to implement some sort of relationship marketing initiative, e.g. through a Customer Relationship Management (CRM) software package, sometimes don't get the results they are looking for because they fail to appreciate the strategic implications of relationship marketing (Newell, 2003).

The purpose of this chapter is therefore to consider the practicalities of adopting and implementing a relationship marketing strategy. The chapter is structured around a broad marketing planning cycle involving:

- evaluating the extent to which a relationship strategy is appropriate;
- choosing which relationships to develop;
- organizing for relationships;
- implementing a relationship strategy;
- monitoring the effectiveness of relationships.

We shall see that developing and maintaining strong relationships requires an approach which is both dynamic and firmly rooted within the overall marketing strategy of the organization. As such, planning for relationship marketing becomes an ongoing cycle to keep customers and others involved and loyal. This is illustrated in Figure 10.1.

Evaluation—To What Extent is a Relationship Strategy Appropriate?

Throughout this book, a distinction has been drawn between the concept of relationship marketing that, amongst other things, is focused on customer retention and transaction marketing, which is more concerned with customer attraction and acquisition. One might be forgiven, therefore, for believing that these approaches

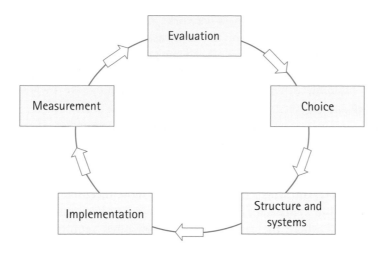

Figure 10.1 Planning for relationship marketing

represent two opposing alternatives between which the organization must choose. In practice, however, most organizations will find themselves with a mixture of new and retained customers and will, therefore, have to adopt some sort of balance between relationship-based strategies and those that are transaction-oriented. The question then becomes 'how far should an organization take its relationship-based strategies and what should the balance be?' To try and answer this question, we can look at two broad considerations—the nature of the customers themselves and the characteristics of the product or service. In practice, organizations might also consider a third area—the relative costs and benefits of attracting or retaining customers. Such is the significance of calculating return on relationships (ROR) that we shall be considering this area separately towards the end of this chapter, which will bring us round in a full circle.

Customer Considerations

Do They Want a Relationship?

Just as in a marriage, a relationship should be beneficial for both parties if it is to have any chance of success. If the customer cannot see any value in a relationship, then it can be fruitless for the organization to try and pursue one. In consumer marketing this can be a big issue, as there is often no reason why the customer should need to interact with the supplier once the initial transaction has taken place (unless there is cause for complaint while the product is in use). This is just as true of fast-moving consumer goods (FMCGs) such as dog food and cornflakes as it is for bigger purchases, such as cars or even houses (how many Ford drivers need to have a 'relationship' with Ford?, How many home-owners give a second thought to the housebuilder once they've moved in?). If they have any kind of relationship, before or after the sale, it is with the intermediary who sold them the product.

Organizations attempting to implement relationship marketing for their own ends, without considering what their customers want, might be setting themselves up for disappointment. Even in business networks, Gummesson (2002) points out that it is not enough for an organization to simply ask 'what's in it for us?' They should also be asking 'what's in it for the other members of the network too' as the outcomes of different relationships are interdependent. Before committing to long-term relationship-building strategies, therefore, it is important to take a wider view of the mutual benefits which the relationship will bring.

Timescales

Bund-Jackson (1985) argues that the time horizon over which customers view their purchases will affect their propensity to enter into relationships with a supplier. Generally speaking, the longer the timescale, the more receptive the customers will be to a relationship approach. This is typified in many business-to-business (B2B) buying situations where the buying organization often requires a tailored offer (e.g. in terms of product design, payment terms, delivery, installation, staff training, service back up, etc.). From the buying organization's point of view, finding a suitable supplier and setting up a deal takes time. Often, there is more than one person involved in both the buying and selling organizations and so links are made at a number of different levels and functions (this principle is behind Gummesson's description of the many-headed customer and the many-headed seller). To break all these and start again with a different supplier every time a purchase is made would take too long, which is why most buyers in these circumstances will be happy to find the right supplier and form a relationship with them. This explains why many B2B purchases are made on a contract basis. Once the contract is set up, the buying organization is free to concentrate on its own core business without having to worry about supplies.

In such situations it is worth the supplier investing up front in a relationship because they know that hopefully it will be long-lasting. By contrast, the customer that sees his or her purchases over a short time horizon is less likely to be interested in a relationship. This explains why many suppliers in business-to-customer (B2C) markets still rely on transaction marketing to shift their products, particularly FMCGs, as the customer sees no need to take a long-term perspective. If the customer has to make some sort of longer term commitment (e.g. through a contract or service agreement) then they are likely to be more receptive to relationship approaches. In these purchase situations, customers will seek reassurance that they have chosen the right supplier and expect products and services tailored more closely to their requirements in return for their commitment. This can be seen in digital TV or broadband services, or even in simple doorstep milk deliveries. It is no coincidence that longer term relationships tend to be associated with the purchase of services—as we have already noted, service marketing (along with B2B marketing) has been held up as an antecedent of relationship marketing.

Types of Loyalty

When evaluating their customers, organizations should be questioning what type of loyalty they have—spurious, latent, sustainable—and the extent that inertia is keeping customers loyal (Dick and Basu, 1994). As we saw in Chapter 4, attempting to build relationships in situations of spurious loyalty can be problematic, as the customer is usually open to a better offer if received. In addition, the organization should also evaluate the extent to which it has a 'trust brand' or a 'relationship brand'. For many years the owners of the Mini brand (BMC and later British Leyland) had no idea how involved customers had become with the Mini. They even refused to supply vehicles for the making of the 1969 film *The Italian Job*, a movie that made a star out of the little car. When Hollywood came to remake the film 34 years later, the new owners of the brand, BMW, did not make the same mistake.

Marketplace Dynamics

Finally, when considering customers, it is prudent to bear in mind that nothing stays the same for ever. We are living in a dynamic world where changes in lifestyle, technology and competition have all led to consumers who are more demanding and expectant than ever before. Organizations that have relied on an established loyal customer base can no longer afford to take this for granted as Marks & Spencer found out to its cost. It is vitally important, therefore, that an organization constantly evaluates its current customer relationships in terms of how it is perceived by the customer. Part and parcel of this will be to determine exactly who the customers are and what is important to them. As organizations strive to move their customers up the loyalty ladder, they can be sure that competitive action and inertia will push them back down again.

After evaluation, organizations can use customer loyalty as a segmentation base for their marketing strategy. It will not be possible or profitable to move every customer up the loyalty ladder and the organization must recognize which customers will stop where on the ladder. Customers can be divided into relationship seekers and exploiters, those who are loyal and those who are promiscuous. The organization can then decide which groups to target and where best to invest in relationship marketing strategies. For instance some retailers, acknowledging the spurious nature of customer loyalty in their market sectors, have concentrated on high-profile promotions (e.g. Somerfield Saver Card), whilst others have gone for more sustainable relationship-building (e.g. Boots Advantage Card).

Product Considerations

In addition to evaluating its customer characteristics, the organization should also consider the extent to which the product or service that it is selling is conducive to relationship-building. To an extent we alluded to this when talking about the time-scales over which a customer views a purchase, but other considerations including the way in which the product is experienced and its position on the product life cycle, will also affect the organization's propensity to pursue relationship marketing strategies.

How the Product is Experienced

When discussing customer loyalty and retention, Rosenberg and Czepiel (1984) suggest that products vary, depending on how easy it is for customers to quantify the differences between them. Where the performance or image of a product can be judged objectively against competitors, they argue that the organization should work on retaining its customers (i.e. pursue strategies that are more relationship-based). For example, some car brands can be seen to have distinct competencies which their rivals do not possess—BMW (sporting performance, engineering excellence), Mercedes-Benz (solidity, longevity, gravitas), Honda (reliability, dependability). Branding is the tool which organizations often use to develop relationships in these circumstances, as is clearly illustrated by designer brands where the relationship between the brand and its user tends to be very close. Even fast moving consumer goods have attempted to differentiate themselves in this way. Thus, Head and Shoulders shampoo claims to eliminate dandruff, Benecol claims to cut cholesterol, Duracel claims to last longer than other batteries, and Ronseal does 'exactly what it says on the tin'. Rosenberg and Czepiel refer to such products as developing customer retention around objective superiorities.

Conversely, products which are experienced in a more subjective way, i.e. where performance differences are not so readily apparent, tend to struggle in the relationship stakes. Petrol is an obvious example of this (see Minicase 2 in Chapter 4), but others typically include mainstream brands of beer, some makes of car, low-cost airlines, insurance, banks, and many FMCG products. Here Rosenberg and Czepiel suggest that brand-switching occurs as customers have no reason to stay with a particular brand. In such circumstances a transaction marketing-based strategy would seem to be more appropriate. It could be argued that in B2B markets, this type of subjective evaluation and brand-switching is less common because the purchase decision-making has to be taken in a more controlled and qualified way. In other words, B2B buying decision-making tends to be more objective and thus more conducive to a relationship approach.

Life Cycle

Product life cycle

used to determine appropriate marketing strategies at different stages of a product's life—introduction, growth, maturity, and decline

The **product life cycle** (PLC) is a well-established strategic evaluation concept used in marketing to help determine product strategy and resource allocation. Plotting the sales of a product or brand over time, the PLC is usually depicted as an S-shaped curve made up of four distinct phases: introduction; growth; maturity; and decline (see Figure 10.2).

Figure 10.2 The product life cycle

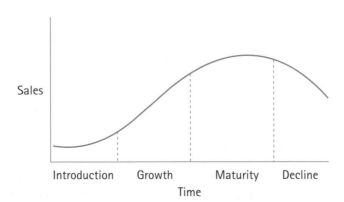

Kotler (2000) notes that the curve can apply to generic product categories (e.g. cars or newspapers), product forms (e.g. four-wheel-drive SUVs or broadsheets), or individual brands (e.g. Land Rover Freelander or *Daily Telegraph*). Different life cycles tend to apply within these groups. Thus, the current model of the Land Rover Freelander might have a life of six or seven years before it is replaced by a new model, whereas the SUV form of vehicle itself has already lasted for around 30 years, and the generic category of cars themselves is well over 100 years old and still going strong. It could also be argued that the curve can apply to companies or organizations. As history has shown, many follow a growth, maturity, and eventual decline stage. Naturally, the length of time over which the product life cycle will apply to different products, brands or companies will vary considerably. For example, fashions might come and go very quickly, whereas brands such as Coca Cola and Kellogg's have endured for decades and show no signs of decline.

Hollensen (2003) reminds us not to assume that the PLC is an inevitable process which can be taken for granted. By taking various marketing actions, the organization can manipulate the cycle to ensure that the introduction stage quickly moves into rapid growth and that the decline stage is put off for as long as possible. Clearly, it seems logical to apply transaction marketing in the introduction and growth stages when new customers are needed, and relationship strategies in the maturity stage, when existing customers need to be encouraged to remain, in order to stave off decline. In fact, it could be argued that relationship strategies should kick in shortly after the introduction stage and operate alongside transaction strategies. This would follow the principles of the Ladder of Loyalty, by turning customers into repeat buyers and then into loyal supporters and advocates. However, it is important to get the balance right. Going after too many repeat purchasers in the early stages may stifle the growth of the product as a rapid influx of new buyers is needed here (Rosenberg and Czepiel, 1984). Conversely, spending too much time trying to attract new customers at the maturity and decline stages suggests a misdirection of resources away from keeping customers. Such an approach might be likened to continually filling a leaky bucket instead of plugging the holes to stop the water escaping in the first place.

It was noted above that companies themselves can go through the stages of the PLC. It could therefore be argued that relationships developed at a higher level (e.g. with the company or parent brand that is in the mature stage) will lessen the need to attract new customers when individual new products are introduced. Thus, companies such as BMW or Harley Davidson do not necessarily have to worry about transaction marketing every time a new model is launched, because they have already established longer term relationships with customers that will carry through to their newer products.

Rosenberg and Czepiel (1984) concede that, in practice, most organizations will end up with a mix of new and retained customers, and that the above considerations will merely help to determine the proportions of each in the overall customer portfolio. As a result, they propose that the organization develops two distinct marketing mixes, one for acquiring new customers and one for existing loyal customers. The acquisition mix will naturally include elements of traditional 4Ps marketing while the retention mix will follow the loyalty-building initiatives discussed in Chapter 4. To this end, permission marketing and CRM can both play a part in determining how far to pursue relationship building.

Choice of Relationships

The previous section compared the appropriateness of relationship or transaction-based strategies in different situations. However, once the decision has been made to pursue a relationship approach, the organization faces a further question—which relationships to pursue? It is not unusual for a business to experience some element of the **Pareto rule**, whereby 80% of the profit comes from just 20% of the customers (Donaldson and O'Toole, 2002). It follows, therefore, that an organization should selectively manage its relationships in order to maximize its profits. This will involve identifying what Stone and others (2000) have termed 'good' and 'bad' customers and developing a portfolio of relationships in order to balance risk (both present and future) and plan resource allocation accordingly.

> **Pareto rule**
>
> reflects a generally observed imbalance whereby 80% of return comes from just 20% of the customer base

Managing 'Good' and 'Bad' Customers

It may seem paradoxical to talk about 'bad' customers but Stone *et al.*'s (2002) description is based upon the principle that different customers generate different amounts of profit and that by serving some of them, the organization might even be losing money. However, if the organization chooses not to serve a particular type of customer, they must be careful how they handle this, particularly if it means getting rid of existing customers. Halifax Bank of Scotland found this out to their cost when they left a flip-chart outside one of their offices which had been used for staff-training purposes. Under the heading 'We Don't Want. . . .' the flip chart listed a number of customer groups which presumably the bank found unprofitable to serve. These included businesses that dealt in coinage, taxi drivers, small shop-keepers, market traders, and window cleaners. The resulting furore when the chart was leaked to the press caused embarrassment for the bank and handed a publicity coup to their competitors who were quick to claim that they welcomed such customers (Bartram, 2002).

According to Gamble *et al.* (2003) 'good' customers generally share a number of characteristics. To begin with, they have a high net value after taking into account the costs of serving them (including relationship costs). For example, gas and electricity companies generally prefer their customers to pay monthly by direct debit rather than quarterly by cheque, because it costs them less in paperwork and they don't have to rely on the customer remembering to send in their payment. They also benefit from the money being in their bank account more quickly and over a longer period. As a result, some utility companies have started applying a surcharge to customers who don't pay by direct debit, whilst others have offered discounts to those who do.

In addition, the 'good' customer will be higher up the Ladder of Loyalty, perhaps at advocate level, recommending the product to others and remaining stable and predictable over a long period. In this sense they will deliver the increased profitability of long-term customers described by Reichheld (see Figure 3.1 in Chapter 3).

Customers who are punctual and reliable, with both their orders and their payments also represent a big benefit. This is particularly so in B2B markets where late, last-minute orders can be costly to serve and delayed settlement of accounts can cause major cash flow problems. Finally, Gamble *et al.* describe 'good' customers as being responsive to marketing communications that are relevant to them, enabling the development of long-term relationships.

Naturally, 'bad' customers are described by Gamble *et al.* as exhibiting the opposite characteristics. Stone *et al.* (2000) summarize the 'bad' customer under several broad headings:

- **Fraudulent.** No business wants fraudulent customers, but some businesses are more exposed than others (e.g. those who sell to consumers on credit and insurance companies who have to guard against bogus claims).

- **Irresponsible.** Customers who waste time (e.g. by asking for quotations when they have no intention of buying), 'don't play by the rules' (e.g. by returning clothes to a shop as being the wrong size or colour when in fact they have already worn them), or cause nuisance to others (e.g. rowdy hotel guests) can all end up costing the organization money. For this reason many hotel chains in places such as Blackpool, Dublin, and Prague do not accept any bookings of three or more single-sex parties.

- **Persistent complainers.** Complaints which are justified should be taken seriously by the organization as they can help to repair or cement a relationship if handled well. However, Stone *et al.* suggest that some customers make frequent complaints which are not justified. Such customers might be motivated by the hope of some compensation, or may just have nothing better to do. Handling customers who are frequent complainers can be a big draw on the organization's time and resources.

- **Transitional.** Customers who are going through periods of change (e.g. in B2B, companies with cash-flow problems or undergoing takeovers) might be seen as risky to deal with. For example, a few years ago it was reported that some mortgage lenders refused loans to applicants who were employed by the Austin Rover group. The lenders took the attitude that the company was likely to close in the near future and the applicant would be made redundant. A similar thing happened recently when credit card provider Egg decided that up to 7% of its customers posed an unacceptably high risk (see Minicase 1, Egg Cracks Down on 'High-Risk' Customers).

Minicase 1

Egg Cracks Down on 'High-Risk' Customers

When UK credit card provider Egg announced that it was going to cancel the cards of 7% of its customers, the headlines were less than flattering. The BBC's 'No sunny side for Egg customers' and 'Egg complaints come to the boil' were typical of the press coverage which the move prompted.

The bad headlines were perhaps uncharacteristic for a company that had developed a major brand from scratch which within ten years had become the world's biggest pure online bank (according to the company's own publicity). Launched in 1998 the Egg credit card appeared to break the mould of the more traditional credit card, with its Internet base and competitive rates, and by early 2008 was estimated to have around 2.3 million customers in the UK. Although originally owned by Prudential, Egg was sold in 2007 to the giant US-based Citigroup for £575 million in a move which appeared to fit well with Citigroup's position as one of the largest credit card issuers in the world.

However, in 2007 the banking sector was running into difficult times due to what became known as the 'sub-prime lending crisis'. Basically, when times were good, some lenders had made credit a little too easy for borrowers to get hold of, by offering unsecured or risky loans in their scramble to win business. When things slowed down, the high levels of unsecured debts made the world's financial markets uneasy and in some cases led to a loss of consumer confidence (as witnessed at Bear Stearns and Northern Rock). As one of the world's leading banks, the crisis left Citigroup particularly exposed to bad debts and as a result they began to look round for means of stemming losses by reducing risks.

Having just acquired the Egg credit card business, Citigroup undertook a review of customers to identify those who represented a higher risk profile. The company then wrote to 161,000 customers in February 2008, notifying them that their credit cards would be withdrawn within 35 days. However, it soon transpired that even customers with perfectly good credit ratings had been included in the cancellation. The BBC's online *Business News Channel* was 'deluged' with messages from angry customers with perfect credit histories. They believed that their cards had been cancelled because they managed their money properly, did not overspend, and paid off their balances in full each month—in other words they did not generate much profit for the bank through interest payments.

Egg maintained that these customers represented a deteriorating credit profile 'regardless of their current status' and that as such they did not feel it appropriate to lend money to them. This stance was supported by Angela Knight of the British Banking Association who claimed that Egg's move was 'a sensible way of doing business'. Nevertheless, other banks were quick to distance themselves from Egg's actions. MBNA, Barclaycard, HBOS, Capital One, and First Direct all stated that they were not going to follow suit.

Whether or not Egg's actions were driven by a desire to reduce risk and get rid of unprofitable customers at the same time is still a source of speculation in the press. What cannot be denied, however, is the amount of negative publicity the move generated.

Questions

1. Do organizations have a right to get rid of customers they do not want? Support your argument with examples from different sectors.

2. How might a credit company go about dealing with less profitable customers without generating bad publicity?

Sources:
'Egg customer anger at credit move' http://news.bbc.co.uk accessed 02/02/08
'No sunny side for Egg customers' http://news.bbc.co.uk accessed 27/02/08
'Banks won't scramble to follow Egg's lead' http://www.guardian.co.uk/money accessed 10/02/08
'A bit about Egg' http://www.egg.com accessed 20/05/08

As a result of this distinction between 'good' and 'bad' customers, Stone *et al.* (2000) have argued that the organization should choose its relationships carefully. This will require a calculation of the costs involved in serving a particular customer, or group of customers and perhaps segmenting the market accordingly in terms of the offer made to each group. Customers who are difficult or less profitable to serve should be avoided, or charged at a different rate (e.g. surcharges for small orders, delayed payments, etc.). Law *et al.* (2003) suggest that organizations might decide to 'outsource' unprofitable customers to other organizations so as to achieve a more favourable cost structure. For example, a haulage company might subcontract small, local loads to a company that is more suited to handle them. In this way, the organization can try to ensure that it is developing relationships with the right kind of customer.

Developing a Portfolio of Relationships

By looking at relationships individually, it is possible to develop a portfolio of customer and other stakeholder relationships (Donaldson and O'Toole, 2002). Just as a portfolio of shares helps to spread risks, with a mixture of high-risk, high-return alongside low-risk more stable investments, so a portfolio of relationships can help to maintain a balance and protect against being overexposed in any one area (McDonald and Woodburn, 2007). In order to develop a portfolio, it is important to identify different categories of relationship. As we have seen above, one way is to consider the economic contribution that the relationship makes to the organization. However, Donaldson and O'Toole go on to suggest that the stage of the relationship and the nature of the relationship itself can also be used to ensure a balanced portfolio.

Stage of Relationship

Similar to a product life cycle, Donaldson and O'Toole and others have suggested that a relationship will go through a number of different stages over time. In the *initial* stage the two parties are still getting to know each other. At this stage the emphasis is on identifying common ground and developing trust in each other. For the supplier this may involve a relatively high level of investment in time and resources, with little initial payback. Once it has been established that the two parties can gain from a relationship, the next stage involves *building* the links between them. In B2C markets this equates to customers becoming more than simply a 'repeat' buyer and moving above the middle of the Ladder of Loyalty. In B2B terms, it may mean the setting up of joint systems where the two organizations can work together more closely. Although investment by the supplier remains high, at this stage of the relationship the benefits start to kick in for both parties.

By now, if the relationship is working for both sides it can move into a third phase whereby it is extended to all areas of the of the supplier's or customer's business. At this stage, the two parties are very close and operating at what Bund Jackson (1985) describes as the 'lost for good' end of the Spectrum of Behaviour ('lost for good' in the sense that no other supplier can get a look in). The final stage of the relationship can go one of two ways. If it is consolidated, for example through joint investment in new product development or supply chain integration, then the relationship might endure over a long term. On the Ladder of Loyalty this represents the final rung—that of partner. The alternative is a decline in the relationship leading to a possible dissolution.

Nature of the Relationship

To maintain a healthy balance, Donaldson and O'Toole suggest that the organization includes relationships from different stages of this cycle, so that at any one time new relationships are coming up to replace those which might be ending. However, they also suggest that the relationships themselves can be divided into four different types, depending on the volume of business generated by the relationship (the 'action' component) and the closeness of the two parties (the 'belief' component). Closeness can be thought of in terms of trust, knowledge of each other, and shared values. Plotting these dimensions on a four-box matrix results in four categories of relationship that are not dissimilar to the four types of product described in the Boston Consultancy Group matrix (Stars, Cash Cows, Question Marks, and Dogs) when relative attractiveness and potential are combined.

Close relationship
characterized by high volumes of business and a high degree of trust and belief between the two parties

Close relationships are characterized by high volumes of business between the two parties and a high degree of belief in each other. Here, the two partners co-operate for mutual advantage and understand each other enough to be flexible when responding to each other's needs. Donaldson and O'Toole describe how such relationships tend to endure over long time horizons. In this sense they are more likely to be at the 'consolidated' stage of the relationship life cycle. Examples of this might include the relationships which a car manufacturer has with its suppliers in order to enable joint product development and 'just in time' supply chain management. These relationships are critical to both partners and as such, care should be taken to maintain them and manage them for maximum value.

Recurrent relationship
characterized by low volumes of business but a high degree of trust and belief

Recurrent relationships are those which are high on trust and belief between the two parties, but relatively low on actual volumes of business. Such situations might occur where one of the parties (either the supplier or the buyer) is simply not big enough to meet all the needs of the other. Alternatively it could be that one or both of the parties is simply not interested in getting too close to one partner. As Little and Marandi (2003) point out, this is typified in many B2C relationships where the consumer likes and trusts a brand, but still prefers the option of being able to shop around. In such situations, the organization might be best advised to maintain the trust and belief elements of the relationship, but concentrate close relationship-building efforts on partners who are more receptive to a close relationship.

Dominant partner relationship
characterized by high volumes of business but a low degree of trust and belief

Dominant partner relationships are the opposite of *recurrent* ones in that the belief or trust element between the parties is relatively low and yet the volumes of business are high. This is usually because one of the parties (either the supplier or the buyer) is reliant on the other. If the reliant partner wishes the relationship to continue, they must meet the demands of the dominant partner—the alternative is to end the relationship. Examples of this can be seen in many retail supply chains, where the buyer (often a large supermarket or chain) has power over suppliers (see Minicase 2, Avent and Mothercare).

Discrete relationships are the final category, representing those where both the belief and action components are low. Here there are few, if any, ties between the two parties and the relationship is dominated by opportunism. As Donaldson and O'Toole observe, such relationships are only relationships in the sense that the two parties come together to do business. If such relationships are at an early stage of development, there might be a possibility to move them on to a closer footing, but the organization must be clear about the likelihood of this before investing large amounts of resources.

> **Discrete relationship**
> characterized by low volumes of business and a lwo degree of trust and belief

Minicase 2

Avent and Mothercare

As a brand leader in baby-feeding bottles and a history of innovative design, Avent is a natural supply partner for Mothercare, one of the UK's leading retailers of maternity and baby products. Both companies have been highly successful in their own right. Avent began life as an arm of the Cannon Rubber Company and under the leadership of its entrepreneurial boss, Edward Atkin, quickly developed into a state-of-the-art manufacturer of baby feeding products. By 2007 exports accounted for 80% of its £109 million sales (*Real Business*) and the company had won several Queens Awards, including five for Enterprise and one each for International Trade and Innovation. Similarly, Mothercare, founded nearly 50 years ago and with over 230 UK shops and a growing number of franchised stores overseas has become a familiar name in the supply of parenting products.

Despite stiff competition from the Far East, Avent has remained a major supplier for Mothercare, but over the years the relationship has shifted, reflecting the sometimes tough trading conditions which both companies have had to weather. *Financial Times* journalist Richard Gourlay describes how until the mid-1990s Avent would make weekly deliveries to Mothercare's warehouse in Wellingborough, where the products were then repackaged by a separate contractor to be sent out to each of the Mothercare stores. However, faced with rising competition from supermarkets and other outlets, Mothercare was keen to reduce its overheads and therefore made the change to a 'stockless warehouse' system.

Although a 'stockless warehouse' might sound like an oxymoron, in reality it meant that Mothercare no longer had to use a separate contractor to manage its packaging. Instead, Avent was asked to carry the stock for Mothercare and use the retailer's own EPOS systems to package up the goods and bar code them for Mothercare's individual stores. This move inevitably meant that Avent had to invest in sophisticated stock management systems that would interface with Mothercare's own systems.

Avent's MD, Edward Atkin, was resigned to the move, describing it as an example of the relentless pressure that big customers were able to put on smaller suppliers: 'It's the only game in town—if you don't play you are out of business'. However, in implementing the new system, Mothercare reduced the number of its suppliers from around 300 to just 130 and those that remained enjoyed a more closely integrated relationship with the company.

Questions

1. Is a dominant partnership relationship such as that described above a good thing?

2. How does the final consumer benefit?

3. What are the longer term implications of such a relationship?

Sources:
Gourlay, R. (1997) 'It's a big boys' game,' *Financial Times Marketing Case Book*, Pitman.
'I'll have what Edward and Celia Atkin are having', *Real Business*, 30 August 2007.
http://www.mothercare.co.uk accessed 21/05/08
http://www.avent.com.uk accessed 21/05/08

A portfolio can therefore include a potentially wide range of relationships in terms of overall value, stage of development, and type. Understanding the make-up of this portfolio and managing it for an optimum balance will help the organization to allocate resources effectively and maximize the value of its relationships over an extended period of time. As a relationship moves through the different stages of development, its value and nature will change, so it is important that relationship portfolio management is seen as an ongoing process and not just a one-off 'snapshot' exercise. One of the more common manifestations of relationship portfolio management in B2B markets applies directly to customer relationships, and this is known as 'key account management'.

Key Account Management

Key account management

individually managing a select number of the most profitable customers to protect and maintain their custom

The notion of **key account management** springs directly from the Pareto principle whereby 80% of the business comes from just 20% of the customers. It follows, therefore, that in organizations where this applies, the few customers who provide most of the business should be given special attention to protect and maintain their custom. This simple principle underlies what some would argue is a strategic management approach to selectively develop long-term, mutually beneficial partnerships between organizations (McDonald and Woodburn, 2007). We have used a number of key words here:

- **Strategic**—key accounts will be of strategic importance to the supplying organization and key account management should be planned at the highest level.
- **Selective**—the organization must develop a range of criteria by which to recognize and select key accounts. We shall consider this in more detail shortly, but it is fair to say that key accounts must represent a significant proportion of the organization's business.
- **Long-term**—key account management is not just about looking after those relationships which are currently important to the organization; it is also about identifying and developing those which have the potential to be key accounts in the future.

- **Mutually beneficial**—although key account management is usually instigated by the supplying organization, success depends upon its ability to bring strategic advantages to both the parties involved. Indeed, the efficiency of the whole supply chain can be enhanced by the close cooperation of the parties (Donaldson and O'Toole, 2002).

Describing key account management as a strategic approach acknowledges that it is more than just a sales function; rather, it consists of a number of links between the organizations at various different levels and across various different functions. For example, supplying a key account is often more than just managing a transaction. It could well involve close links between the two organizations' technical operations, manufacturing and finance departments, as well as the sales and purchasing functions. They might well involve senior board members of each organization playing golf together. In this sense key account management mirrors 'the many-headed customer and the many-headed supplier' described by Gummesson (1987) in his early essays into relationship marketing. It also echoes the significance of personal and business networks which we discussed in Chapter 2.

McDonald and Woodburn (2007) advise that the selection of key customers should be done with care. Key account management involves a considerable investment of the organization's financial resources and manpower, and once a customer has been given the status of key account, it is not always easy to backtrack. It is not enough simply to draw a line around the biggest customers or those placing the highest orders and assume that these are the key accounts. McDonald and Woodburn suggest that the selection process should begin by deciding how many key accounts the organization can realistically manage. They recommend something between 5 and 75 and counsel against having too many for fear of diluting the benefits which can be afforded. This is because the whole point of key account management is that they be managed individually, not en masse, and the more there are, the more difficult this will be.

'Hard' performance measurements such as overall profitability (both current and future) should be taken into account together with 'softer' criteria such as the compatibility of the organizations and the quality of the relationship between them. While the hard, quantitative selection criteria will determine the profit potential of the relationship, the softer more qualitative criteria could well determine the likelihood of the relationship working. To this end Millman and Wilson (1996) suggest that the strategic fit of the organizations is important. Things such as aligned corporate goals, complementary strengths, and resource synergies (being able to combine resources to achieve greater mutual efficiencies) will all help to determine if a key account approach is appropriate. As effective key account management relies on the mutual cooperation of both parties, these views of strategic fit must be held by both organizations.

The types of activity undertaken under key account management will vary as each relationship is unique. However, Little and Marandi (2003) make the interesting observation that most descriptions of key account activities involve adding value for the customer rather than cutting the price. Typically this would include enhancing the service quality being offered. Thus, a supplier might offer key customers quicker order turnaround, flexible delivery, and a dedicated member of staff to manage administration of the customer's orders and after-sales service. As intimated above, it is likely that key accounts would receive some form of customization, perhaps in the form of a bespoke product, packaging, or promotional literature. Sharing their resources such as research and development, technical expertise, logistics handling, market information, or even personnel is another way in which the supplier can add value for their key accounts. All of this will require clear and open communications between the two parties, including joint planning of business activities—an activity which in itself can strengthen the relationship further (Ryals, 2000).

Ongoing key account management will require the continuous monitoring of the initial selection criteria against performance, to ensure that the portfolio of key accounts remains valid. McDonald and Woodburn have observed that some portfolios include customers who should not be there, either because the relationship is not being reciprocated or because their performance against the selection criteria was overrated. A regular review of all customers should therefore take place with promotion to, or relegation from, key account status in mind.

Structures and Systems for Relationship Marketing

Be it CRM, key account management, external relationships or internal relationships, it would appear that to implement these effectively, an organization-wide approach is required. This may require an element of organizational restructuring to ensure structural integration of the strategies, as opposed to just bolting them on as an addendum to the marketing department. For instance, Tesco's Clubcard forms part of the company's strategy and has been instrumental in developing market share and position and the brand extension into new, unrelated markets. Indeed, the acceptance that relationship marketing is bigger than just one functional department has been stressed throughout this book. Ryals (2000) summarizes the themes of this approach as follows:

- being customer-focused instead of product-focused;
- a commitment throughout the organization to deliver customer value;
- identification of the core processes within the value chain;
- acceptance of cross-functional collaboration and the need to work with other organizations;
- a willingness to reorganize if necessary in order to achieve this.

Contrasting Organizational Structures

Ryals and others observed that the traditional organizational structure, which is based around functions, can be a hindrance when it comes to implementing relationship marketing. The traditional structure is characterized by a series of hierarchies,

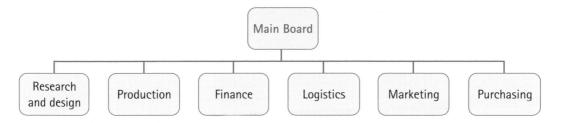

Figure 10.3 Organizational structure based around functions

with the Chief Executive or Managing Director at the top and a command structure, or Board of Directors below them. Underneath the command structure, each of the organization's functions is run as a separate division or department. This is shown in Figure 10.3.

There are advantages to this structure. It is logical and transparent. Everyone knows their place in the organization and there are clear lines of progression. With the emphasis on individual functions, a degree of specialist skill can be built up in each area (e.g. the organization can hire a specialist Finance Director or a specialist HR Manager). This divisional structure tends to be good at dealing with stable or predictable business environments, as it relates to the external market in a very formal and structured way (Donaldson and O'Toole, 2002). However, in dynamic markets with changing customer characteristics and unpredictable competitors, its rigidity can hold it back. For example, when Dell entered the home PC market with its direct supply model, established competitors such as Hewlett Packard and IBM found it difficult to hit back. Dell's loose structure, relying on partner organizations to do its manufacturing and assembly, enabled it to deal with customers directly, offering them customized solutions. With their more rigid, divisionalized structures based around R&D, manufacturing, marketing, and distribution, Dell's competitors were unable to match them.

One way of escaping the rigid divisional structure is to adopt a matrix structure where instead of being hierarchical, the organization splits its structure across two dimensions—typically, products and markets. Figure 10.4 shows how a matrix structure might look for a large building products manufacturer. Such structures tend to be decentralized, in that responsibility for big functional areas such as marketing, HR, or finance tends to be devolved to the different operating departments.

An advantage of the matrix structure is that information can flow sideways, rather than from top to bottom as it does in a hierarchical structure. As a result the 'silo' mentality of the strictly function-based structure can be broken down and the organization can be more customer-focused (Ryals, 2000). However, the matrix structure can bring with it problems of control. There is a risk that some jobs may be overlooked altogether, or done twice if the communication is not up to scratch. As Ryals points out, the bigger and more diverse the market being served, the more complicated the matrix becomes.

As a result, she suggests that neither the functional structure nor the matrix structure is ideally suited to relationship marketing. The rigid lines of authority found in

		Product divisions		
		Softwood joinery	Hardwood joinery	uPVC products
Markets	Builders' merchants			
	DIY chains			
	Housebuilders			

Figure 10.4 Organizational structure based around a matrix

the typical divisional structure inhibit the cross-functional collaboration needed for things like key account management or internal marketing, while the complexity of the matrix structure can be confusing for the customer and make the development of close relationships difficult. Instead, many writers agree that some sort of structure is needed that emphasizes the links between organizations, customers, and other partners. It is argued that these links represent processes which add value for all parties. Donaldson and O'Toole (2002) have therefore suggested a structure akin to overlapping circles. Each circle represents an organizational function or external partner, including customers, who create value by interacting together.

Key Processes

The idea of value being created by the processes which take place between internal functions, rather than the actual functions themselves is encapsulated in the value chain which we discussed in Chapter 9. As we saw in that chapter, Gummesson (2002) suggests that instead of thinking along the lines of a linear chain, it might be more appropriate to consider a 'value constellation' or 'star' to reflect the fact that process value added is ongoing, without beginning or end. In this sense his ideas mirror the overlapping circles suggested by Donaldson and O'Toole. What all of these ideas have in common is that the customer is an integral part of the value added process. In other words it is necessary to establish a 'co-creative' environment whereby customer interaction helps drive the organization's product development, pricing and communication (Law *et al.*, 2003). This can be seen at Amazon where customer involvement is a key part of the overall service offering, or at Dell, where customers 'build their own computer' and have it delivered directly to their home.

If an organization is to concentrate on its processes rather than its functions, then it needs to recognize what its core processes are. According to Ryals (2000), these should be the areas in which the business has high relative strengths and are fundamental to building a competitive advantage. From here, other processes can if necessary be outsourced to partners, allowing all parties to concentrate on what they are good at. To go back to the Dell example, their core process is the interaction they have with the customer, allowing the customization of the product and service offer. The other activities needed to deliver this can then be designed around the core offer. Thus the design and manufacture of components, the configuration of the customer's chosen product, and the delivery to the customer's home are all outsourced to Dell's partners for whom they represent core activities.

Of course, there are risks associated with outsourcing to partners. For example, many High Street banks now offer packages of services which include the provision of insurance and other financial services. As insurance is not usually one of the banks' core activities, it is usually outsourced to a partner for whom it is a core activity. However, trouble can ensue if the outsourced service does not come up to the customer's expectations. For example, a customer who had a poor experience when trying to make a travel insurance claim not only lambasted the insurance company, he also closed his bank account which had provided the insurance. For these reasons Donaldson and O'Toole (2002) stress the need for tightly integrated operating relationships between value chain partners. They argue that these should be characterized by transparency, openness, and long-term commitment.

To manage core processes, whether outsourced or not, requires skills and knowledge associated with cross-functional working. To this end Christopher *et al.* (2002) suggest that the McKinsey 'Seven S Model' provides a useful base. The seven Ss in the model refer to:

- structure—the operating lines along which the organization is run;
- strategy—the actions taken to move the organization in a particular direction;
- systems—the operating procedures within the organization;
- skills—the unique competencies and capabilities which are embedded within the organization;
- staff—types of people employed by the organization;
- style—the 'personality' of the organization as shaped by its history, culture, and symbols;
- shared values (sometimes referred to as 'super ordinate goals')—the commonly held values and aspirations of all the organization's members.

The first three—structure, strategy, and systems—are sometimes referred to as the 'hard' elements of the Seven S framework as they provide the rigid base on which the organization operates. However, it is the remaining four—skills, staff, style, and shared values—the 'soft' elements, which often determine how well the organization can adapt to the cross functionality of relationship marketing. The shared values in particular are described by Christopher *et al.* as the 'glue' which binds the organization together. If the organization is to become 'customer focused' instead of 'product focused', then this must be reflected in the shared values held within.

Implementing Relationship Marketing

Assuming that the appropriate structures and systems are there, the organization can go about implementing its relationship marketing strategies. However, even at this stage, the organization has decisions to make about the type of approach it will adopt. We have already seen that the choice between out-and-out relationship marketing or full-blown transaction marketing is not always distinct and that in practice some sort of mix between transaction strategies and relationship strategies will be required. Nowhere is this better illustrated than in the **Spectrum of Behaviour** described by Barbara Bund-Jackson (1985).

Spectrum of Behaviour

Bund-Jackson's model describing a range of customers between 'always a share' (appropriate for transaction marketing) and 'lost for good' (appropriate for relationship marketing)

When we talk about a 'spectrum' many people will think about the range of colours which are observed when light is refracted. These are the colours of the rai bow and are always seen in a progressive sequence—red, orange, yellow, green, blue, indigo, and violet. Bund-Jackson's spectrum also describes a range or sequence, but here the range falls between what she calls 'lost for good' customers at one end and those who are 'always a share' at the other (see Figure 10.5).

In this sense 'lost for good' means that a customer is so closely tied to an existing supplier that they are very unlikely ever to move. For an organization trying to win their business they are lost for good. Of course, for the organization that already has them, they might be described as 'theirs for good'. It they do leave, it will be at least as hard to win them back as it was to win them in the first place. In this situation Bund-Jackson argues that a relationship-marketing approach is appropriate. On the other hand, 'always a share' customers are those who will be happy to spread their business around, always seeking out the best offer or cheapest price or simply seeking variety. It is suggested that these situations are better suited to transaction marketing. However, by accepting that there are many positions in between these extremes, she describes how customers will fall closer to one end or the other, largely depending on how easy it is for them to move between suppliers. Interestingly, she also argues that customers do not necessarily stay at the same position on the spectrum. They can be moved up or down the line, either by the actions of the suppliers or through their own investment actions.

Customers towards the 'lost for good' end of the spectrum are often there because the switching costs of transferring their business to an alternative supplier are relatively high. These 'switching costs' may entail either a real monetary expenditure or an unacceptable level of inconvenience. For example, mortgage customers wishing

Always-a-share

Lost-for-good

Figure 10.5 The spectrum of behaviour

to switch to another supplier will often be faced with an early repayment fee on the account that they are closing. B2B customers who integrate their processes closely with suppliers (e.g. for JIT) are also likely to incur some cost if they wish to switch their business. Similarly, where switching the business would require a lengthy tendering process, or the retraining of staff, for example, businesses may conclude that it is too much trouble to keep chopping and changing supplier. In such instances they are more likely to accept a long-term relationship with their supplier.

From a supplier's perspective this presents them with two possible courses of action. First, they can attempt to move their customers further towards the 'lost for good' end by investing in things that will discourage them from flitting regularly between different suppliers. For example, joinery company John Carr produced a detailed catalogue of their products that was used by builders when selecting the exact size and type of door or window frame they needed for a job. John Carr's key customers, the large builders' merchants, were provided with a customized version of this catalogue, overprinted with their own name, thus providing them with a comprehensive selling tool that they could use with their own customers, the builders. (It did of course mean that by using the catalogue, the merchants had to sell John Carr products.) Similarly, many ice cream and soft drinks manufacturers provide shops and catering outlets with branded fridges and vending machines in exchange for an exclusivity deal, and banks bundle together lots of financial products and services under one deal. Although this might represent a good deal for the customer, it does mean that if they wish to switch their account they end up having to re-arrange a whole host of insurances and investments.

On the other hand, the supplier may wish to move customers back towards the 'always a share' end of the spectrum if it will give them a chance to win the business from their competitors. This means that they will have to dismantle or remove the switching barriers which are keeping customers 'lost for good'. For example, a mortgage company may offer to pay the fees which the customer may incur by switching from one mortgage provider to another. Alternatively an industrial supplier might invest in software which enables compatibility between different operating systems. For many years it was impossible to run Apple Macs and PCs together, so a business was locked into one system or the other. Software developments have removed some of these barriers by, for example, enabling businesses and individuals to install Microsoft Windows software on Apple Macs.

However, it is not just suppliers who can move customers along the spectrum—customers can attempt to move themselves, particularly if they do not wish to be tied to a particular supplier. Thus, a shopkeeper might buy his own soft drinks fridges, instead of taking one from one of the big brands and then being tied to that supplier. Similarly, a transport company might invest in its own vehicle-servicing facilities so that it can buy different types of lorries and not be tied into a service arrangement with one particular manufacturer. Sometimes the dynamics of the market itself will move customers along the spectrum. For example, a local oil supplier who normally relies on stable customer relationships based on historical ties and service values, might find that its customers move further back toward the always-a-share end of the spectrum in times of high price rises.

According to Bund-Jackson, suppliers can use the spectrum to diagnose a customer's behaviour by analysing their switching costs and then selecting a marketing approach which will move them to a desired position. Likewise, other theorists advocate the use of their frameworks to determine the actual relationship approach. Thus Gummesson (2002) suggests using the 30Rs as a checklist, with the inclusion of relationship marketing-based goals not only in the marketing plan, but also in the broader organizational plan (recognizing the strategic significance of relationships and also their cross-functional implications). He suggests that these relationship-marketing-based goals be based on the returns that the organization is likely to enjoy as a result of their relationships (e.g. customer retention, share of wallet, etc.) on top of the more traditional measures such as sales volume and market share. Christopher *et al.* (2002) take a similar view, describing how organizations should develop relationship objectives and value propositions based around each of the areas in their Six Markets Model. The End of Chapter Case considers how the National Centre for Popular Music might have used the Six Markets Model in this way.

Monitoring and Control of Relationships

Finally, working on the premise that if *you can't measure it, you can't manage it*, regular stock must be taken of how well an organization's relationship marketing strategies are working. Herein lies a potential difficulty, however, because while it is straightforward enough to measure things such as sales and market share, it is less easy to measure the effectiveness of relationships. This is partly due to the long time-frames associated with relationships—e.g. Reichheld (1994) talks about the value of customer retention in terms of net present value, meaning that value is being measured against potential future returns that have not yet been realized. It is also partly due to the very subjective nature of relationships. To illustrate this point, in a recent BBC television edition of *The Money Programme*, a young woman claimed that she had over 250 friends, based on those who were signed up to her Facebook site. Even if all of these people were indeed the lady's friends, it is unlikely that the level of their friendship would be equal. Sometimes, one only finds out how close a friend is when things are not going so well. Applying these thoughts to a business context, organizations should therefore be asking how strong are our relationships and what value are they giving us?

To continue the personal analogy, it should also be recognized that over time some friendships grow and others wane. While some people are lucky enough to have friendships lasting from their school days, many early friendships will have withered away. In practice most people will probably have a mixture of friends, old and new. In business terms this reflects the dynamic nature of relationships, with customers moving both ways along the spectrum of behaviour, either due to market forces or the actions of rival suppliers. It is therefore important to monitor continuously the effectiveness of the organizational relationship strategy, in order to take remedial action if necessary. Little and Marandi (2003) suggest that this monitoring and control be broken down into three elements: relationship facilitators, relationship features, and relationship returns.

Measuring Factors Which Enable the Relationship

Relationship facilitators are those things that determine whether a relationship is possible in the first place. Satisfaction, trust, and quality will all play a part here. However, as we saw in Chapter 4 these factors alone are not enough to guarantee loyalty. These things are what might be described as 'hygiene' factors. Customers have a right to expect to be satisfied (who buys a product or service expecting not to be satisfied?). They have a right to be able to trust the organization (often they are protected by legal safeguards against unscrupulous trading) and they have a right to expect a certain level of quality (particularly where multiple suppliers are continually raising the benchmark). It could be said then that these are the minimum entry points on which customer retention and, ultimately, close relationships can be established. It is therefore important to measure performance in these areas through satisfaction surveys, customer complaints analysis or quality control systems because without them, it can be difficult to establish and maintain relationships.

There are instances, however, where relationships persist even when the above factors are not present. Gummesson (2002) describes how dissatisfied customers do not necessarily take their business elsewhere, but remain as 'ticking time bombs' spreading dissent and costing the organization money through constant complaints or giving negative referrals to other potential customers. Such customers may remain through their own inertia or because they are locked in by a contract or prior agreement. For example, a customer of a major health spa chain became dissatisfied with the service and quality she was receiving. Complaints to the management fell on deaf ears and, trapped into a 12-month contract, the customer told others of her experiences. By her own admission, she estimated that she had put off at least three potential new customers from joining the spa and with an annual membership fee of £640, the lost revenue quickly mounted up. Such is the damage that they can inflict, that these types of customer have been labelled 'terrorists' (Kelly, 2005). If this happens, it is important for the organization to find out what is causing the dissatisfaction and either put it right or effect a swift and amicable exit for the customer.

Measuring Factors Which Describe the Relationship

The next stage of monitoring and controlling relationships is to try to ascertain the depth and quality of the relationship. Here, the organization is faced with a number of potential measures ranging from those which may be considered 'hard', such as retention rates, length of relationship, and share of the customer's overall business (sometimes known as 'share of wallet') and the 'softer' dimensions, such as the customer's commitment and genuine affection for the brand or company. In Chapter 4 it was pointed out that the 'hard' dimensions sometimes classed as 'behavioural' were relatively easy to measure because they could be expressed in numbers. For example, the organization can cross-reference regular measurements in the following areas:

- number of active customers (e.g. some studies suggest that 25% of Nectar customers are using their cards less than four times a year);
- number of loyal customers, as demonstrated by repeat business and customer retention (but be careful not to confuse loyalty with inertia);
- defection rates—the opposite of retention: as Gummesson (2002) points out, if a customer is lost, then their whole future profit potential goes with them;
- revenue per customer—it makes sense to concentrate loyalty-building programmes on those customers who are spending the most. This is what British Airways did when they aimed their frequent flyer programmes at the lucrative business traveller market.

Christopher *et al.* (2002) point out that similar performance metrics can also be applied to other stakeholder relationships, e.g.:

- supply chain relationships—cost reductions, number of returns, speed to market, etc.;
- internal relationships—employee retention, satisfaction, and performance;
- external relationships—shareholder churn, publicity value, number of external partnerships, etc.

The softer dimensions, sometimes referred to as 'attitudinal' are much more difficult to measure because they cannot usually be expressed numerically. Being close to the customer, as for example in a key customer relationship can help here, as personal and social networks can give a better insight into the real nature of the relationship. Other indicators may also be used, such as how customers interact with the brand or the company or how readily they respond to the organization's advances. For example, Harley Davidson can clearly see the strength of their customer relationships through the activities of the Harley Owners Group.

By measuring the above 'hard' and 'soft' factors on a regular basis, the organization can get a picture of whether of not it is succeeding in actually establishing and developing relationships. However, given that at the end of the day, relationship marketing is a business strategy, the bottom line of whether it is working or not will be financial outcomes and the impact on overall profitability. To this end the ultimate measure of relationship success must be one of return on relationships.

Measuring the Return On Relationships

Return on relationship

the long-term financial worth of relationships

Gummesson (2002) strongly advocates that **return on relationships** should be an integral part of the organization's profit and loss account. Abbreviating it to ROR, he puts it on a par with return on investment (ROI) and return on capital employed (ROCE). His definition of ROR is: 'the long-term net financial outcome caused by the establishment and maintenance of an organization's network of relationships'.

Although studies by Reichheld and others have suggested that long-term, retained customers are generally more profitable than new ones, it should not be forgotten that establishing and maintaining a long-term relationship will require investment and ongoing costs. Typical investment costs might include those associated with restructuring the business to achieve compatibility of systems up and down the supply chain (see, for example, Minicase 2, Avent Baby Bottles). They may involve investments in staff in order to improve the customer experience in service environments or the implementation of key account management. We saw in Chapter 5 how the costs of even the most basic CRM software management systems were coming in at thousands of pounds and the implementation of major schemes such as the Tesco Clubcard and the Nectar card running into many millions of pounds. Expenditure on maintenance of a relationship will involve things such as ongoing brand support, public relations, and regular contact with the customer. It is only right, therefore, that some attempt is made to calculate the return of the relationships against these costs in order to establish whether or not a profit is being made.

However, applying the broad brush approach of simply subtracting overall costs from overall sales revenue does not acknowledge a point that we made earlier in this chapter—that some customers are worth more than others. It follows, therefore, that the relationship costs of serving individual customers, or at least specific *types* of customer, should be broken down. This is akin to the principals of activity-based costing (ABC) in financial management. Under ABC, instead of applying overheads equally to all activities, a calculation is made of what proportion of overhead each activity actually uses and thus a cost is allocated accordingly. Companies adopting ABC have sometimes been surprised to find that products that they previously thought were profitable were actually losing money and vice versa. In calculating return on relationships, therefore, Gummesson stresses the need to be aware of unprofitable customers hiding amongst the profitable. This reflects the Pareto 80:20 rule discussed earlier.

Gummesson (2002) is also keen to stress the need to establish a sound basis for estimates. He is particularly critical of measuring results purely in immediate financial terms, claiming that these abolish vision and leadership. As an example he cites a chain of shops in Eire called Superquinn. They found that introducing children's playrooms left their mothers free to browse and shop for longer and helped to promote return visits. However, while the cost of the playrooms was evident, it was impossible to put an exact figure on how much the playrooms were worth in terms of increased customer spend and loyalty. Conversely, having sweets at the checkout generated hard, short-term cash flow, but was the cause of aggravation between parents and children who were pestering for the sweets. In these instances it is possible that parents might have avoided the shops because of the sweets, but it is impossible to put a figure on this.

In the same way, the value of a relationship is not always easy to calculate, but it can make a huge difference to the bottom line. For these reasons, Gummesson is at pains to point out that the value of an organization's relationships should be acknowledged in the organization's financial accounting systems. This reflects the thinking behind the Balanced Scorecard (Kaplan and Norton, 1992) which we discussed in Chapter 3. Here the two traditional measures of organizational performance—Financial and Operational—are balanced against two new measures—Customer Satisfaction and Organizational Innovation and Improvement. This sort of thinking can be seen in many company valuations which now include an element of 'goodwill' to reflect the significance of the relationships and networks from which the company benefits.

Ongoing monitoring and control of relationships brings us back in a circle to deciding to what extent a relationship strategy is needed, and so the cycle starts again. In this way the organization can continue to manage its relationship marketing strategies effectively.

Chapter Summary

The implementation and management of marketing relationships can be seen as a dynamic and ongoing process which should reflect the organization's business environment. It should not be assumed that a relationship approach is necessarily the best strategy in every circumstance. Organizations need to understand the expectations of its customers in terms of the timescales with which they view the purchase and level of involvement with which they are comfortable. Factors such as the way in which the product is experienced, and its position on the product life cycle will help to determine whether a transaction or a relationship approach is most appropriate. In practice, many organizations will end up with a mix of potential new customers and retain existing ones, thus requiring two different marketing approaches to appeal to each. The challenge for the organization, therefore, becomes how to achieve an optimal balance between the two.

When developing customer relationships, it is important that the organization differentiates between different types of customer. Over the long term some will be more profitable than others and it makes sense to allocate resources accordingly. Key account management is an example of how organizations might proactively manage a portfolio of relationships to ensure a good long-term balance. Managing relationships requires an integrated approach across the whole organization so it is important that the organization's structures and systems are able to support this. In general, structures which are based around processes are better able to cope with an organization-wide relationship approach than are those which are based around separate functions.

The cost-effectiveness of managing ongoing relationships must be taken into account in order to ensure that an optimal balance is maintained. Gummesson (2002) proposes that a new financial measure—*return on relationships*—be added to the organization's accounting procedures in order to reflect this. The value of relationships is not always easy to calculate as it should include 'softer' elements such as goodwill as well as hard financial measures.

End of Chapter Case with Questions

Could a Relationship Approach have Saved the National Centre for Popular Music?

Students at Sheffield Hallam University have reason to be proud of their Student's Union building. The building was designed by architect Nigel Coates (the man behind the Body Zone at the London Dome) and instantly became an iconic city landmark, known locally as 'the steel kettles'. But it was never intended that it should end up as a Student Union bar, for its original purpose was to house the National Centre for Popular Music (NCPM). With its traditional industries of steel and coal in decline, Sheffield's move towards a more cultural-based economy made sense and the NCPM was an ideal reflection of these aspirations. The idea for the NCPM was borne out of the city's pop music heritage, based on bands such as Heaven 17, the Human League, and Pulp as well as a plethora of 'indy' groups feeding a thriving music scene.

The NCPM was thus devised as a visitor attraction based around a museum of pop music. Although the idea came from local enthusiasts, it was only made possible by lottery money made available through a grant from the Arts Council. Once the grant had been secured, a board of management was appointed, consisting of local musicians and long-term exponents of Sheffield's musical scene. They came up with some organic ideas about what the content of the museum should be, with advice from 'music academics and exhibition designers'. Management consultants Coopers and Lybrand projected visitor numbers of around 400,000 a year, based on just 1% of the 35 million people living within a 75-mile radius of the museum coming to see it.

The NCPM opened its doors in March 1999 at a cost of £11.35 million in lottery money. However, once the opening fanfare died down, it quickly became apparent that the venture was not living up to expectations. From the first day, visitor numbers were only a fraction of what had been predicted. To make matters worse, local people who had been were spreading a story of disappointment and poor value for money. Furthermore, stories began appearing in the press that the venue was in trouble. The problem seemed to lie in the content of the museum, which one *Guardian* journalist described as 'dumbed down and deeply patronising'. He was referring to a section where visitors could try out musical instruments by beating a drum or blowing a horn to hear what sound they made. Another section of the museum featured a large collection of dolls dressed as various pop stars from the past.

Even the board members themselves were not impressed. In subsequent interviews one confessed that the centre lacked the 'oomph' she was expecting whilst another described the atmosphere within as being like a 'morgue'. With little revenue from paying customers and no bail-out from the Arts Council, the centre was forced to rely on visits by school parties to make ends meet. This proved too much for many of the 'hands on' exhibits. Soon many of them ceased to work any more and there was no money available to repair them. Within three months of opening, the NCPM was in crisis and having to make people redundant and the feeling amongst those that remained was described as one of a 'sense of doom'.

The redundancies and resignations continued and by November 1999, just eight months after opening, the NCPM was placed in the hands of receivers, Price Waterhouse Coopers. Only 66,000 of the projected 400,000 visitors had materialized. The exhibits were soon dismantled and removed and for a while the building was rented to local music promoters to hold club nights. Ironically these proved to be successful and with hindsight many of the board members believed that the centre should have been a combination of a live music venue and a museum from the start.

On the question of who was to blame for the failure, the board members felt that they were not the right people to have been left to manage the centre as none of them knew anything about visitor attractions—they were for the most part musicians! Neither the consultants who had advised them, nor the Arts Council who provided the funding would comment and the building was eventually taken over by Sheffield Hallam University as their new Student's Union.

Questions

1. Apply each of the six markets described by Christopher *et al.* (customer market, referral market, influence market, supplier and alliance market, recruitment market, and internal market) to the situation described above.

2. How might these markets have been managed to achieve a better result for the NCPM?

Sources:
Based on 'Pop goes the museum' featured on *Architecture Today*, BBC TV, first shown 2002.
'Arts Council naivety led to waste of lotto's £33m', *Times*, 2 May 2003

Discussion Questions

1. Why is planning for relationship marketing an ongoing process? What sort of things might cause the plan to change from year to year?

2. Is a relationship approach always the most appropriate for a B2B situation? Give examples within a B2B setting where a transaction-based approach might be considered.

3. It could be considered that Kellogg's Corn Flakes are at the mature stage of the product life cycle. To what extent, then, is Kellogg's practising relationship marketing?

4. Are 'bad' customers not worth pursuing? Support your answer with examples.

5. How could having a 'portfolio' of relationships benefit an organization?

6. How might you counter the argument of someone who tells you that selecting key accounts is a quick and straightforward process?

7. What could a customer who is classed as a 'key account' expect to get out of the relationship?

8. Why might a divisionalized, hierarchical, organizational structure struggle to adopt the principles of relationship marketing?

9. Apply the McKinsey 7S framework to an organization of your choice and suggest how the 'soft' elements (style, skills, staff, and shared values) could enable a relationship approach.

10. What is the significance of identifying 'core processes'? How might an organization use this knowledge to add value for customers?

11. Consider where on Bund-Jackson's Spectrum of Behaviour suppliers of the following products and services might be:
    - office consumables (stationery, etc.);
    - photo copying machines;
    - fleet delivery vans;
    - airline caterers;
    - home insurance policies.

    For those you consider to be at the 'lost for good' end suggest how a rival supplier might move them back along the spectrum in order to win the business. For those at the 'always a share' end, suggest how a supplier might move them in the opposite direction in order to retain the business.

12. What are the challenges in trying to measure 'return on relationships'?

Further Reading

McDonald, M. and Woodburn, D. (2007) *Key Account Management: The Definitive Guide* (2nd edn), Elsevier, Oxford.

Bund-Jackson, B. (1985) 'Build Customer Relationships that Last', **Harvard Business Review**, Nov.–Dec., 120–8.

Stone, M., Chalder, M., and Gamble, P. (2000) 'Managing Good and Bad Customers in Practice', **Journal of Database Marketing**, 7(4), 356–80.

Gummesson, E. (2002) *Total Relationship Marketing. Rethinking Marketing Management: From 4Ps to 30Rs* (2nd edn), Butterworth Heinemann, Oxford.

References

Bartram, P. (2002) 'The Good, the Bad and the Unprofitable', **Marketing Business**, July/Aug.

Bund-Jackson, B. (1985) 'Build Customer Relationships That Last', **Harvard Business Review**, Nov.–Dec., 120–8.

Christopher, M., Payne, A., and Ballantyne, D. (2002) *Relationship Marketing: Creating Stakeholder Value*, Butterworth–Heinemann, Oxford.

Dick, A. and Basu, K. (1994) 'Customer Loyalty: Towards an integrated framework', **Journal of the Academy of Marketing Science**, 22(2), 99–113.

Donaldson, B. and O'Toole, T. (2002) *Strategic Market Relationships: From strategy to implementation*, John Wiley & Sons, Chichester.

Gamble, P., Stone, M., Woodcock, N., and Foss, B. (2003) *Up Close and Personal* (2nd edn), Kogan Page, London.

Gummesson, E. (1987) 'The New Marketing—Developing Long Term Interactive Relationships', **Long Range Planning**, 20(4), 10–20.

Gummesson, E. (2002) *Total Relationship Marketing. Rethinking Marketing Management: From 4Ps to 30Rs* (2nd edn), Butterworth–Heinemann, Oxford.

Hollensen, S. (2003) *Marketing Management: A Relationship Approach*, Pearson Education, Harlow.

Kaplan, R. and Norton, D. (1992) 'The Balanced Scorecard Approach—Measures that Drive Performance', **Harvard Business Review**, Jan.–Feb., 71–9.

Kelly, S. (2005) in Doole, I., Lancaster, P., and Lowe, R. (eds), *Understanding and Managing Customers*, Pearson Education Ltd, Harlow.

Kotler, P. (2000) *Marketing Management*, Prentice Hall, New Jersey.

Law, M., Lau, T., and Wong, Y. (2003) 'From Customer Relationship Management to Customer Managed Relationship: Unravelling the paradox with a co-creative perspective', **Marketing Intelligence and Planning**, 21(1), 51–60.

Little, E. and Marandi, E. (2003) *Relationship Marketing Management*, Thomson Learning, London.

Maister, D. (1989) 'Marketing to Existing Clients', **Journal of Management Consultancy**, 5(2), 25–32.

McDonald, M. and Woodburn, D. (2007) *Key Account Management: The Definitive Guide* (2nd edn), Elsevier, Oxford.

Millman, A. and Wilson, K. (1996) 'Developing Key Account Management Competencies', **Journal of Marketing Practice: Applied Marketing Science**, 2(2), 7–22.

Newell, F. (2003) *Why CRM Doesn't Work (How to win by letting Customers Manage the Relationship)*, Kogan-Page, London.

Reichheld, F. (1994) 'Loyalty and the Renaissance of Marketing', **Journal of Marketing Management**, 2(4), 10–21.

Rosenberg, L. and Czepiel, J. (1984) 'A Marketing Approach for Customer Retention', in **Payne, A, Christopher, M., Clark, M., and Peck, H.** (eds), *Relationship Marketing for Competitive Advantage*, Butterworth–Heinemann, Oxford.

Ryals, L. (2000) in *Marketing Management: A Relationship Marketing Perspective*, Cranfield School of Management, Macmillan Press Ltd.

Stone, M., Chalder, M., and Gamble, P. (2000) 'Managing Good and Bad Customers in Practice', **Journal of Database Marketing**, 7(4), 356–80.

The Future of Relationship Marketing

Chapter Outline

Learning Outcomes

After reading this chapter you should be able to:

- understand the context of relationship marketing in the twenty-first century;
- critically evaluate key Web 2.0 impacts on firms;
- evaluate the significance of customer metrics and organizational issues within a relationship driven approach;
- consider the extent to which relationship marketing represents a paradigm shift within the overall field of marketing;
- apply your knowledge to the case studies in the chapter.

Introduction

Relationship marketing (RM) is a relatively modern concept which is being adopted by marketing practitioners and theorists. Hunt (1994) referred to relationship marketing as 'all marketing efforts directed at establishing, developing, and maintaining successful relational exchanges'. This reflects the longer term focus of RM, and the need to plan and evaluate relationship activity carefully. This has led some to a reliance on databases and Customer Relationship Management (CRM) systems, but true RM is a strategic concept which is accepted throughout the organization as being of crucial financial relevance.

Many changes took place during the 1990s including the increasing power of the customer, partly due to world oversupply of goods, and partly due to the transparency provided by the Internet. 'Individuals began to assert themselves more strongly as customers, and particularly, as users. They were no longer willing to be part of the vague so- called mass market somewhere down the distribution trail, accepting what business would produce most efficiently' (Vandermerwe, 1995). As Buttle (2004) argued 'What used to delight customers a year ago is only likely to satisfy them today'. The real concern for companies in the twenty-first century is that writers such as Reichheld (1996) have proven conclusively that up to 60% of customers who state they are 'satisfied' will defect within one year. Satisfaction is merely an expected starting point; the real relationship issues start from there.

There are various interpretations of the term 'relationship marketing'. Some emphasize technology such as CRM and database management systems, but Hunt (1994) stressed that it was a strategic business concept of corporate wide scope and relevance. Within this conceptual framework, however, are a series of highly relevant tools and constructs. This broad approach is now the general starting point for a more detailed evaluation of RM. The concept of RM has already come a long way in a relatively short period of time. In this final chapter we now consider some of the issues which might affect its future direction.

The Significance of New Technology

Technology is constantly evolving. Search engine optimization is now routine for many companies who are desperate to achieve high URL listings on search engines such as Google to avoid being unknown to the Internet-trained audience. Zineldin (2000) pointed out that IT has a significant effect on market communications, supplier relations and interactions, and stakeholder integration. For example, one could cite the use of an Extranet to allow a named third party access to a company information system using password controls. **Blogs** and video clips, user-generated content, and a heavy reliance on networking are increasingly characterizing companies' interactive communications with their customers. The company Eat Natural took this one step further: in a recent advertisement in the *Sunday Times* they took out an advertising page and simply stated 'What do you want us to put here? Send your ideas to our website'. This is a classic example of relationship-driven integrated marketing communications.

Blog (Web log)
an individual's own website set-up used to record their feelings, attitudes, descriptions, or general commentary about a particular subject

Twenty-first Century Business Trends

In 2008, a survey by the Economist intelligence Unit (EIU) of 141 senior international business executives ranked the so-called 'second coming of the Web' sixth out of the top ten global mega-trends in business-to-business (B2B) marketing. Indeed, the top ten mega-trend list is worth considering here as it reflects many of the issues relevant to RM:

- Thought leadership becomes a priority. Internal relationships networks (see Chapter 9) will facilitate the creation and spread of knowledge and innovation within organizations.

- B2B marketing develops in scope. As supply chains and partnerships become more complex, and targeting key decision-makers in a value chain becomes a key priority, managing relationships across entire supply chains will be critical (see Chapter 8).

- Integrated marketing becomes the norm. Maximizing returns on marketing expenditure and measuring cost effectiveness is both possible and crucial, and campaigns will be global in thought and decision but with regional interpretation in content and media. As we saw in Chapter 10, return on relationships can become an integral part of an organization's accounting procedures.

- Emerging markets move to the centre stage—not just India and China, but parts of Africa and the Middle and Far East as well as Russia and Brazil. Successful organizations will be those who can develop and tap into relationships across different cultures (see Chapter 2).

- Knowledge management comes of age. Intelligence systems, instant access to latest research findings, and use of **Web 2.0** tools will become crucial.

- The second coming of the Web. Web 2.0 initiatives such as blogs, microsites, webcasts, and digital channel use, with search engine optimization and other Web metrics are changing the way in which organizations interact with their customers. As we saw in Chapter 6, these have the potential to empower customers and affect the way in which marketing relationships are managed.

> **Web 2.0**
> a perceived second generation of the Internet which is based around networking, collaboration, and sharing between users

- A new conference model (tying conferences to thought leadership themes and positions.) This will enable more productive lateral relationships with partners and other organizations (see Chapter 7).

- The growing influence of advertising agencies. (Integrating elements of trend 6, and aligning general advertising and PR with thought leadership initiatives.) This once again reflects the importance of supply chain and partner relationships, thus allowing the organization to concentrate on its core activities.

- B2B purchasing decisions become more complex. As we saw in Chapter 2, relationships and networks have always been important in B2B trading. As companies come to terms with intra-organizational complexity, the need for appropriate responses to external dynamics and change, and attempts at a more entrepreneurial approach, B2B purchasing decisions will become even more complex.

- The ROI (return on investment) model. According to the survey, in five years' time 89% of the executives said they would measure the return on thought leadership approaches. This integrates the use of several of the tools mentioned under mega-trend 6.

(Adapted from EIU, 2008)

It is very interesting to compare this with a KPMG report *Rethinking the Business Model* conducted in 2005. In this report, the emergence of new technology and related initiatives was ranked by 336 senior international decision-makers as the second most important factor causing their companies to change the business model between 2005 and 2008 (KPMG, 2006). Emerging market expansion was rated as the number one choice, and the driver for this was the growing challenges and opportunities presented to companies in an increasingly globalized world. This factor was also driving companies to use technologies such as Web 2.0 in an imaginative and cost-efficient way to enhance the value of their relationships with customers and other stakeholders. RM is the broad approach, but the optimum use and development of enabling technologies in a globalized, highly competitive, rapidly changing world is a major success factor.

In answer to the question: 'which of the following issues will require your company to make the biggest change to its business model over the next five years?' The key factors cited by the respondents in the KPMG report were:

- expansion of emerging markets (39%);
- emergence of new technology (38%);
- changing customer requirements/buying habits;
- increased competition from established competitors;
- regulatory changes;
- increased competition from new entrants;
- offshoring and outsourcing;
- industry consolidation;
- commoditization;
- trade liberalization;
- rising oil/raw material prices;
- pressures to improve corporate governance;
- population ageing;
- pressures on corporate finance(pension fund liabilities, downgrades to credit ratings, etc.);
- increased focus on corporate social responsibility;
- other (not specified);
- rising interest rates.

(KPMG, 2006)

Significantly, the emergence of new technology was seen as a major commercial opportunity by 43.5% of the sample, and as a major threat by only 2.1% of them (KPMG, 2006). From this it is possible to make two broad observations:

First, that the acquisition and development of the latest technology and associated capabilities is seen as crucially important in a strategic sense by key decision-makers in international businesses; second, that it can be inferred from the surveys that companies that are slow to adapt to the possibilities that Web 2.0 can offer could suffer a major competitive disadvantage in the next few years.

Web 2.0

One could argue that this approach is extremely relevant in the globalized world of integrated communications, and a battery of attempts at social networking as a means of developing preferred relationships. Web 2.0 refers to the enhanced capabilities of Web applications in the twenty-first century, particularly when integrated with e-media techniques. Common initiatives will include webcasts, microsites, and blogs, which enable marketers to reach wider audiences and engage in stakeholder dialogue at a relatively low cost. Allied to this, the interactivity of digital channels gives an organization the opportunity to build an online community and collaborate with its target audiences. With the availability of low-priced Web metrics such as search engine optimization, it is relatively straightforward for companies to track the effectiveness of e-media marketing campaigns. One only has to note the growth of price comparison websites to see how these tools can be extremely important. Perhaps the real key for marketing executives is the chance to engage in a genuine and ongoing two-way dialogue with key customers, allowing those customers to send in user-generated content which is both informative and credible.

In this respect, an evaluation of the EIU 2008 global megatrend survey shows that the next three to five years are predicted to see a major growth in Web 2.0 use and e-media techniques:

- 35% of the sample used **podcasts** now, but 53% are expected to do so in the next 3–5 years.
- 38% used audio or video **webcasts** now, but 50% are expected to do so in the next 3–5 years.
- 34% used **intranets** now, but 49% are expected to in the next 3–5 years.
- Interactive forum use is set to rise from 27% to 48% in that period.
- **Microsite** use is predicted to rise from 35% to 47% over that period.
- Blogs are predicted to rise from 30% to 47% over that period.
- Mobile devices: 33% to 45%.
- Video conferencing: 38% to 42%.
- Content syndication: 21% to 33%.
- Wikis: 12% to 28%.

(EIU, 2008)

Podcast

a digital video or audio recording made available over the Internet for downloading to a PC or portable media player

Webcast

use of the Internet to broadcast messages and material to large audiences simultaneously

Intranet

an Internet-based network available only to members within a particular company or organization

Microsite

a smaller, separate website acting as a supplement to a larger, primary site

Developing an Integrated Customer Approach

Thus the technological arena will change and become more sophisticated, as companies will have more control over how they deploy their marketing expenditure for maximum impacts and returns. The key focus is on the relationship element, with the use of customer experiences and ideas being highly valued by firms. This is mainly because the basis for competitive advantage in product and service attributes will reduce, and the overall value of the relationship experience will become a key part of the organizational value proposition. Change will be ongoing in this scenario, and customers will expect companies to give them maximum control of the relationship, and even pre-empt their requirements. Relationship marketing is not only a suitable approach for traditional companies marketing goods and services, however, many different applications are possible.

Minicase 1

Liverpool Capital of Culture 2008: Relationship Marketing at the Heart of Marketing a City and the Region

Liverpool, a city on the river Mersey in the north-west of England, has been the winner of the European Capital of Culture competition for the year 2008. This is a highly valuable award that allows a city to showcase itself to the world for a year, and develop various revenue streams from increased visitor numbers, inward investment of all kinds, and economic regeneration. It will allow Liverpool to reposition itself for the twenty-first century as a knowledge-led, culturally diverse city with a great future as well as a fascinating past.

Liverpool was founded in 1207 when King John awarded it a Royal Charter, so it is 800 years old in 2007. It made its reputation as a trading port, until the economic shift of trade to Europe in the later twentieth century meant that it was not as well-situated as it had been for transatlantic trade in the previous centuries. Liverpool had been very prosperous indeed, and its relative decline in the late twentieth century seemed to spell the end for its golden years.

However, the city and its people are resilient, and Liverpool has plenty to attract visitors and investment. Two cathedrals, a Philharmonic orchestra, Liverpool and Everton are Premiership football clubs, the Beatles and their musical legacy which has led to many groups following them, some famous universities, and a host of science and technology parks with large and small employers keen to employ its many graduates.

The waterfront area of Liverpool has been awarded world heritage status, and the nostalgia of its famous ferries across the Mersey creates a backdrop for its growing movie industry. The old docklands warehouses are now high-priced luxury flats, and Liverpool has one of the youngest age profiles of any city in the UK. Liverpool has a terrific nightlife scene, and is highly popular with students from all over the world. The Merseyside region has some superb wildlife, areas of natural beauty, and affordable housing. There are still some areas in need of regeneration and investment, and there are the usual problems found in any large city.

The feeling is that Liverpool is on the rise again, and that Capital of Culture status is at the heart of this.

Liverpool has strong brand recognition as a city. On average 19 million people a year visit Liverpool, contributing £381.5 million to the local economy, and Liverpool is the sixth most visited UK city for international visitors. Liverpool expects up to 1.7 million extra visitors in 2008, which will create 14,000 more jobs. It is expected that there will be a total of £3 billion of investment in the city in 2008. Naturally, the aim is that the revenue will pour in for many years as Liverpool presents itself as a vibrant, culturally diverse city that is great both to live and work in. It aims to be a city with a fascinating past and a really great future. Companies could decide to use Liverpool to locate themselves due to the provision of a large body of graduates, excellent social and cultural facilities, and a good range of affordable housing. Combined with quick access routes by sea, air rail, and road, this provides a basis for the marketing of the Merseyside region to a range of key decision-makers. This includes local and national media, as Liverpool still has areas of deprivation, and the historical images of the Toxteth riots, union unrest, and the 'Liverpool Scally' appear on press and television quite regularly. Negative perceptions take a long time to overcome, and setting realistic targets is a very important aspect of the Capital of Culture marketing campaign. Glasgow is still benefiting from its repositioning following its 1990 award, and the Liverpool decision-makers must think in both the short and long term about their objectives in 2008 and beyond.

Liverpool will probably be the last UK city to win the European Capital of Culture award for the next 15–20 years as Europe has expanded to over 500 million people, and many East European countries are keen to showcase themselves. The marketing of the city is absolutely crucial to the success of the city in 2008 and beyond. Cities that have done very well since being awarded the honour include Glasgow in Scotland in 1990, Paris in 1989, and Dublin in 1991. Tourists return to these destinations again and again, and this retention of loyal visitors is a central requirement for success. Liverpool has to be seen as a friendly city, and its inhabitants pride themselves on their unique brand of humour based on quick wit. They are known as 'scousers' after a famous kind of stew that is very popular in the City.

Liverpool has had to work hard in the areas of services marketing, and the provision of excellent customer service, and the Capital of Culture Company with the full support of the city council set up an ambassador campaign, and customer services training sessions for its workers in key customer-focused companies. These included taxi firms, bus companies, restaurants, hotels, city guides, nightclub security and bar staff, and people working in art galleries, museums, and other attractions. First impressions count, and people remember the service interactions they had when they form an overall impression of a city. Making the city safe, tidy, and easy to move around by public transport has taken up major amounts of time and investment. Presenting the architecture, and places of interest such as the beautifully restored Albert Dock area, with its combination of shopping, restaurants, and museums, is another key aspect of the exercise.

The city had a spectacular programme of events for 2008. There were about 350 main events and literally thousands of smaller ones. The events bring a diverse range of tourists and media interest, and provide the gloss which helped to promote the city, as well as helping the local community to share the pride of being involved in the future heritage of their city.

For example, the two surviving members of the famous 1960s pop group 'The Beatles' (Sir Paul McCartney and Ringo Starr) appeared in musical events in 2008. Sir Paul was the headline act in 'The Liverpool Sound' concert at Anfield Stadium on 1 June 2008. Anfield stadium is the home of Liverpool Football Club. His presence will ensure a global audience for this event. Music is a truly universal language.

Ringo was the lead act in 'Liverpool the Musical' at the opening of the brand new Liverpool Echo Arena on 12 January 2008. The total cultural programme for 2008 saw activities to suit all tastes from fine art, to boxing, chess, and comedy. Many of the events were free, which enabled local people to sample them.

As a marketing opportunity 2008 represented a not-to-be-repeated opportunity for Liverpool to reposition itself, by defining its strengths and minimizing its weaknesses. With a full year to showcase the city, and the diverse talents of its people, every opportunity was taken to build national and global relationships, to enhance positive public relations coverage, and regenerate local communities both economically and spiritually. Internal and external stakeholder relationships are crucially important in developing the necessary good-will amongst local people on Merseyside, as well as ensuring that overseas visitors derive maximum pleasure from their short visits or longer term holidays. For example, Liverpool is working in collaboration with Chester and Manchester to develop integrated tours for visitors to show the wider region to visitors as well as just Merseyside. This is an example of competitor locations working with each other to share in the benefits of maximizing the potential for customer expenditure during their visit to the region. Internally, Liverpool City Council and the Capital of Culture Company need to work with the North West Development Agency to showcase the region as a potential investment opportunity for firms, as well as just a Merseyside-based tourist opportunity. All of the different stakeholder approaches and relationships must be carefully developed to enhance the communication synergies and revenue opportunities. This is at the heart of a real relationship-driven approach.

The location of 08 shops, known as the 08 place in Liverpool City Centre provides a venue for tourists to receive information as well an opportunity to buy memorabilia ranging from a postcard to a genuine work of art related to the Merseyside region. The 'Superlambanana' is a giant lamb/banana shaped plastic yellow emblem for the region which has led to many smaller themed ones being placed around at key venues. The media interest in this zany idea, allied to the fact that it is proving a massive hit with tourists is one way in which thinking outside conventional approaches can really pay off in terms of developing global publicity campaigns and relationship goodwill.

Liverpool needed to ensure that it did not fall into the classical trap of marketing: that of over-promising and under-delivering. Liverpool needed to deliver what it promised in 2008, and to do it on a world stage, to truly global standards of expectation.

If it has been successful, the lives of its inhabitants will be enhanced for the better for many years to come. Failure is unthinkable.

Questions

In your role as a Marketing Management Advisor to the Liverpool Capital of Culture Group, you need to provide advice to its leaders on how Liverpool can maximize the benefits it gains from the Capital of Culture year and beyond.

1. What are the key marketing-related issues and challenges facing Liverpool in 2008?

2. How can relationship marketing theory be used to benefit Liverpool in 2008?

3. Develop a communication campaign for Liverpool 2008.

4. How can Liverpool measure the success (or failure) of 2008? What measures, both financial and other, should be used to evaluate the impact of Capital of Culture?

Sources:
Author's notes
http://www.liverpool08.com accessed 06/06/08
http://www.visitliverpool.com accessed 06/06/08

Interactivity

Customer-focused innovation will be made possible by the two-way electronic dialogue that will be possible using Web 2.0 and associated techniques. From the company side, they will carefully select the customers with whom they want to have a relationship, and will target those customers with precision communications. Trust, a key factor in relationship development, will be imperative as customers ask three crucial questions:

- Do I trust this company? (Corporate trust is hard to build but easy to destroy.)

- Do I like and associate myself with the people and values in this company? (This brings business back to a key basic requirement: people stay loyal if they like and even love the companies they deal with.)

- Do I like and associate myself with the customers that this company has? (Reference groups are becoming crucial.)

Reference groups will become even more important as electronic relationships become a key business driver. David Smith of Global Futures (EIU Conference 2008) pointed out that 1.3 billion people have signed up to the top 40 social networks on the Web, and there are key overlaps between them. Companies must understand the **social networking** phenomenon, and be aware of the possibilities afforded by advertising and sponsorship as well as direct sales and favourable word-of-mouth recommendations via such sites.

> **Reference group**
> a group used by an individual to help form attitudes, opinions, and behaviours

> **Social network**
> a web of individuals who are interconnected over the Internet

A very interesting recent journal article by Meadows-Klue (2008) evaluates how Web 2.0 has radically changed the marketing approach required for a successful relationship with digitally literate and engaged consumers. The central contention of the article is that Web 2.0 and digital marketing practice facilitates frictionless access to information and transmission using Google, RSS feeds, Amazon, and other applications and tools. The fact that consumers are in control in this more democratic environment means that conversation with customers has to replace control of the media and the message. The paradigm shift in the relationship approach is that the media of the masses replaces the mass media in a more fragmented broadcasting environment. As the author notes 'granular insights and rich data replaces generalization', and social networking sites will play a crucial role in encouraging consumers to purchase for the first time and be motivated to become supporters of organizations and their products and services. The author contends that old-fashioned awareness television campaigns are not enough on their own: they have to be strongly augmented, and even replaced, by digital approaches which encourage consumers to feel a love for the organization and its people and outputs, and a desire to be involved in a two-way exploratory dialogue with the organization (Meadows-Klue, 2008).

For example, the spread and use of scientific information is changing as the Internet has taken over from television and newspapers as the public's main source of scientific news. The percentage of news coverage devoted to science was about 5% between 1975 and 2001, but is now down to around 2% (Profile, July 2008). Matthew McKay, head of public relations at BioMed Central, argues that in a more diverse and competitive media world in the twenty-first century, sites such as Wikipedia and Google's Knol, allied to rapid growth of open access science publications, will require scientific communities to embrace all of the new Web 2.0 tools to be successful. He sees blogs, podcasts, mashups, RSS feeds, social networks, widgets, and wikis as allowing a greater reach of the message beyond conventional media. This enables a more sophisticated set of messages to be delivered in an interesting way to non-science professionals, as well as biomedical specialist journalists.

McKay argues that in an era in which a large proportion of the potential audience has been saturated with material on You Tube and Second Life and other such sites, they want fast, interesting, informative, relevant material which allows virtual communities the chance to discuss and debate key issues. 'Getting actively involved online will allow you to engage in real dialogue with your audiences, and potentially gain valuable feedback on your campaigns-all in real time' (McKay Profile, 2008.)

This issue is one which faces all kinds of organizations. Integration of ideas across all media formats is often best achieved with a powerful story backed by a compelling visual brand image. For example, Felix cat food massively increased its sales by having a website focusing on stories and user generated content based on their online blogs and animations of Felix, the cheeky animated cat that people loved. The makers realized that the way to sell more cat food was to find a way to connect with the love that people feel for their cat, and then spread this across all of their communication platforms.

One organization that has been very successful over nearly 20 years is Carphone Warehouse (CPW). This has been achieved partly as a result of a well-conceived business strategy, and an understanding of the role of changes in relationships and technology over that time.

Minicase 2

Carphone Warehouse: The Changing Nature of Business Relationships

The rise of the Carphone Warehouse Company (CWC) has been one of the classic UK business success stories of the late twentieth century. It has led to its founder, Charles Dunstone, being a much celebrated and carefully studied entrepreneurial role model. In the twenty-first century, however, the business faces a much more competitive and challenging business environment and it will be fascinating to see how the company performs in the next few years.

The business was founded in 1989 by Charles Dunstone and his partner David Ross. From a small mobile-phone shop on London's Marylebone Road, they created a business that turned over around £4 billion in 2007.

Dunstone saw that people would want to make telephone calls away from the home phone or public telephone box, and set up his business to be differentiated in the market, and create real value for both customers and his staff. He set up his company with a clear set of aims and objectives, and five key rules that would drive the company forward.

1. 'If we don't look after the customer . . . somebody else will.
2. Nothing is gained by winning an argument, but losing a customer.
3. Always deliver what we promise. If in doubt, under-promise and over-deliver.
4. Always treat customers as we ourselves would like to be treated.
5. The reputation of the company is in the hands of every individual.'

(Charles Dunstone)

These fundamental rules showed that he had a customer obsession, and he wanted his staff to be able to serve customers in a way which competitors would find impossible or at least very difficult, to follow. The mission statement he developed supports this approach. 'Our mission is to become the store people unquestionably visit when they have need for mobile communication equipment' (Charles Dunstone).

Essentially he wanted to develop a clear proposition in an existing market. This proposition was based on the expertise and impartiality of the advice given by his trained staff in his High Street shops. He would stock products from all of the major network providers, and his staff would provide advice to each individual customer on the best product and payment tariff for them, not for the staff of CPW.

By developing key relationships with his suppliers (the mobile phone network suppliers), a strong internal marketing approach with his staff (using more training than competitors, and recruiting young people and promoting them based on merit), and developing very clear customer warranties and a 'total freedom guarantee', he developed loyalty and trust with all of the key stakeholders.

Delighted customers told friends, and customer numbers grew, and revenues rose. He became a multi-millionaire at a young age. Phones became smaller, slimmer, and fitted into the pocket, not the car. Far from being ashamed of the name CPW, Dunstone even used its strong brand recognition to provide a formidable obstacle to competitors in the market. The company expanded into Europe and profits soared.

In the last five years the market has matured, many more competitors have tried to fill the positioning space of CPW, and customers are demanding much better deals for them. The pressure on margins has led to network providers wanting to 'own' customers themselves by either setting up their own retailing operations, or driving very tough deals with intermediaries such as CPW.

Events in 2006–7 showed how volatile the market was. Charles Dunstone acquired AOL UK for £370 million, and this gave them one of the UK's biggest Internet service providers. This is crucial in an area where broadband, the ability to bundle mobile technology and its services, is the key to keeping customers loyal. CPW has entered into the landline market with its Talk Talk service. Dunstone has formed various strategic alliances, including one with Sir Richard Branson at Virgin Mobile.

Vodafone, the world's biggest mobile network operator, pulled out of its relationship with CPW, who are the UK's leading independent retailer of phones. The relationship with Vodafone had been a key factor in the growth and success of CPW. How could CPW claim to be offering impartial, independent advice now?

Vodafone had entered into an agreement with a major rival of CPW's, Phones 4U, which would lead to customer defections from CPW to Phones 4U. Other network providers such as Orange threatened to quit its deal with CPW if it did not receive better margins.

The early growth of CPW had been relatively untroubled, but there was now massive competition, and incredible changes, both business and technical, taking place in the market. Investors became concerned about the future and the share price of CPW fell.

The central tension between the network providers and CPW is customer 'churn'. As a retailer, CPW does not have to worry about the eventual profitability of the customers they sign up, as they receive money when a customer upgrades a handset, switches to a new tariff on a different network, or 'churns', as it is known in the trade.

For the mobile network companies, the key strategic emphasis is on long-term revenues from the best customers, so they are really keen to have their own retail outlets to 'own' their customers rather than use an intermediary.

In this environment Dunstone is attempting to turn CPW from a mobile phone retailer, into an Internet services provider. This runs the risk of him losing his big network customers such as Orange, O_2, and T-Mobile who increasingly see CPW as a dangerous competitor, rather than a friendly partner.

Despite this, Dunstone remains confident that CPW can overcome its problems and survive, and even thrive, in the changed world of mobile telecommunications. New devices such as iPods and increased functionality of the technology provide customers with an almost limitless choice of products and services, but it is much harder to be different. Most developed markets are saturated in terms of demand, whilst developing markets such as India and China are fought over hard. Aggressive selling via the company website is crucial now, as well as the High Street presence.

The telecommunications division now contributes about 50% of the Carphone Group revenue, and this is expected to rise significantly over the next five years. In 2008 the company launched Best Buy Mobile, an independent mobile retail format in the USA, and the Geek Squad, a home technology support business in the UK. Up to March the company had opened 267 new stores, to bring its total to over 2,400 in Europe.

> The future is harder to predict, but most people believe in the astute business brain of Charles Dunstone.
>
> ## Questions
>
> 1. Examine the factors that led to the success of CPW.
> 2. Why are changes in the business environment so important for a company such as CPW?
> 3. What do you understand by the term 'value proposition'?
> 4. What marketing tools and techniques can CPW use to continue to be successful in the future?
>
> Sources:
> Carphone Warehouse, an overview document to support a presentation made by Charles Dunstone to the Strategic Planning society in London, September 1997 accessed 26/05/08
> http://www.carphonewarehouse.co.uk
> http://www.timesonline.co.uk accessed 26/05/08

Fujifilm stressed usability in a digital world in their story of the brand. They set off a series of 'whispers' in their blogs that featured interesting uploads and input from key people in sport, fashion, and celebrity. This was picked up by the national media, and an online and off-line community began to discuss the campaign and its approach. Fuji sold approximately 100,000 Fuji Z10 cameras on the back of this experiential brand endorsement backed up with technology-assisted story-telling. Hellman's, the mayonnaise brand, has increased its sales by 5% by making recipe suggestions on its website and its packaging, suggesting that the product is an excellent cooking ingredient as well as a mere salad cream. The aim was to cajole each customer into using 'one cup more'. The integration of the communication media was a key factor in the spread of the information via word of Web as well as word of mouth (*The Marketer*, June 2008).

Implications for Marketers

Financial Implications

In terms of measurement, customer-related metrics such as **customer lifetime value (CLV)**, allied to customer retention approaches, have been positively received by academics, and widely employed by companies. Writers such as Gupta and Lehmann (2003) and Venkatsan and Kumar (2004) have stressed how the quantitative measurement behind the CLV approach bridges the marketing and financial metrics required at Board level, and helps a company to value its key asset, its customers, based on the main elements of CLV. They see the three main elements of the CLV approach as customer acquisition cost analysis, customer retention costs and approaches, and the potential for margin expansion via cross-selling initiatives.

For example, Harrah's, the American casino and hotel group has massively increased its profitability since it began to manage its businesses by using CRM

Customer lifetime value

the potential net worth of a customer to an organization over the period that he/she remains in the market

systems, database mining, CLV analysis, and customer retention approaches. The company based its approach on building value-based offers to cross-sell gambling opportunities and hotel-stays to people looking for lifestyle breaks incorporating their favourite activities. As the company understood its customers more, it could fine-tune its offers to different subgroups within the customer base. This is also a feature of the massive investment made by Tesco in the underlying systems to facilitate a customer-metric-based approach to its business. This integration of fast real-time information, linked with a mixture of financial and customer-focused metrics, will be at the heart of the strategic approach by many companies in the twenty-first century.

Organizational Change

However, none of this is easy or guaranteed to work without real organizational change. Peel (2002) argued that the lifetime value of customers was a useful tool for marketers, but estimated that this is not precise, and external environmental influences are difficult to predict in advance. He decided that the best method was to define the ideal customer relationship, and then define CRM processes to nurture such customers who would wish to avail themselves of such a relationship. He argued 'They may be customers who have consistency in terms of revenue generation. They may be customers who have embraced lower cost distribution channels. They may be customers who react most well to communication campaigns.' This mirrors the points made throughout this book that understanding customers must be a prerequisite in attempting to develop relationships with them.

Collaboration has led to organizational restructuring as a survival mechanism (Zineldin, 2000), and a realization that the primary asset of the business is the customer. Rich (2000) argued that this asset should be cultivated and nurtured to reduce the effects of extreme competition leading to commoditization and downward price pressure. Companies are realizing that sophisticated twenty-first century consumers want an experience rather than just a product or a service, and they rate all elements of the experience when deciding to whom to be loyal.

Customers will be the Driving Force

Buttle (2004) suggested breaking customers into four groups in a manner very similar to the old Boston Consultancy Group product matrix:

- high profit—high potential;
- high profit—low potential;
- low profit—high potential;
- low profit—low potential.

If a customer currently generates a low margin but has a significant long-term value potential, it may be necessary to re-engineer the basis of the relationship. For example, this could involve reducing costs or increasing value for the customer. Customers that are presently profitable but offer very low future potential could require nurturing to improve potential. The causes of low potential should be investigated to see how much of this can be influenced by the organization. For example, if an organization obtains the necessary quality accreditations it could make itself far more attractive as a supplier to a customer that deals in a high-value supply chain.

Customers with high historic margins and high future lifetime value potential are the most desirable customers. The company must invest in these customers and reward them for their loyalty and the value they bring to the business. Normally, they will be the 20% of customers who bring in 80% of the revenue into the business (the Pareto rule). They could be offered quicker delivery times, be assigned a dedicated customer service adviser, or offered longer payment terms as a way of rewarding their loyalty (key account management).

However, if a relationship is not working well, and is yielding very little or no margin, Buttle (2004) argues that it should not be maintained, and that the customers in this category should be 'sacked'. This view is consistent with the view of Gummesson (1999), but both writers point out that 'sacking' a customer is a last resort, and it should be done in a sensitive manner to prevent negative word-of-mouth communications damaging the reputation of the company.

Buttle (2004) argues that it is very important for companies to be aware of how their customer base is distributed amongst the four groups, in order to develop a better strategic customer profile. He proposes the following typical breakdowns:

* invest: 5%;
* nurture: 25%;
* re-engineer: 30%;
* sack: 40%.

It is important to note that he added the caveat that the relative typical percentage in each category will vary in practice from company to company due to specific factors relevant in given competitive structures. What may come as a surprise is the high proportion of customers he suggests an organization should consider divesting.

One of the main developments in strategic marketing is the move from a transactional approach as exemplified by the 4Ps or even 7Ps, to a fully oriented customer-relationship approach. This has implications for the company in terms of how customer-focused they really are.

Many companies could still benefit from deepening their level of marketing integration and focus on the customer. Fundamentally, relationship marketing involves the development of long-term relationships, whilst transactional marketing focuses on short-term exchange-based relationships. The expert consensus of opinion is that long-term relationship development can offer better long-term prospects for an organization, but this is by no means easy to achieve.

For example, Grönroos (1997) whilst agreeing that transaction marketing is both old-fashioned and suboptimal, argues that there are always exceptions to the rule for individual companies. Vandermerwe (1995) emphasized the high degree of

Figure 11.1 Taking a customer focused approach

Source: © Hawkins (1995) 'Marketing Orientation for Firms', *Market Relations*, Wiley. Reproduced with kind permission.

connectivity between consumers and producers that was a factor in the strengthening of partnerships and collaborations in the 1990s. She argued that this was backed up by a much greater need for customer-related dialogue between supplier partners and other stakeholders.

McBernie and Clutterbuck (1988) argued that it was a combination of corporate culture, creativity and commitment to customers that gave the UK companies they deemed to be excellent the 'marking edge'. They had not fully linked this to a relationship theme, but by 1999 Day was moving down the road of relationship development as the key to delivering superior value to customers, especially those customers the company really wanted to keep. In his discussion of how Xerox fought back against overseas competition and the perception that copiers had become costly and reliable, he stressed the value of a coordinated approach to solving customer problems and delivering superior value. Salespeople, service people, and operations people took collective responsibility for customer problems, and customer-based metrics became the key focus of measurement of success, backed up by a total quality management programme. As customer satisfaction scores rose and market share losses reduced, Xerox was in a position to develop deeper relationships. It used a 'no-questions asked' guarantee which gave the customer total discretion if they wanted a copier removed. No other company did this, instead maintaining control over whether or not a customer could have a replacement. Day points out that Xerox gained 4.5 points when it introduced its performance guarantee, and this virtuous cycle consisted of:

- superior value delivery;
- increased customer satisfaction;

- increased company trustworthiness;
- tighter connections between Xerox staff and the customer;
- increased customer loyalty;
- continuous investment in hard-to-match capabilities by Xerox, making it much harder for competitors.

(Day, 1999)

Relationship Marketing—A Paradigm Shift?

In 1997 Grönroos described RM as a **paradigm shift**. This new paradigm was not necessarily seen as a panacea, but something which really does seem to offer organizations a clear approach to measuring the value of customers using relational metrics, as well as a method of ensuring profit growth through retention of key customers (Reichheld, 1996). Gummesson (1999) proposed that the paradigm shift from transaction-based marketing to a longer term relationship focus should be built around 30 key relationships as opposed to the old 4Ps (see Chapter 1). Central to his argument was the idea that companies would have to focus on relationships and the network that benefits and thrives on relationship exchanges. For example, in a less manipulative, more trustworthy relationship network, companies can reap massive cost savings by reducing the number of suppliers they deal with in order to develop more intimate relationships with those firms with whom they feel they can prosper. This is illustrated in the case of the Roy Hankinson. Here, the openness of the company extends to an open book accounting approach to collaborative working with its partners in order that fair and equable financial returns can be made to them all.

Paradigm shift
a significant change in thinking from a previously accepted view to a new one

Chapter Summary

It is clear that relationship marketing is a fascinating subject which has the potential to be a dominant approach in marketing for years to come. The only issue will be how the approach modifies and develops over the next decade. Several writers have argued that some companies have been engaged in a kind of relationship marketing in the past: for example, Tadajewski (2008) gives a very interesting case study to cite how the Wannamaker retail company used a form of relationship marketing long before even the 4P approach had been developed. The generally accepted view, however, is that a shift to relationship marketing has taken place over the last 15–20 years.

This chapter has concentrated on several key issues.

Web 2.0 and the growth of the digital business environment are considered to be crucial for organizations in a more globalized and rapidly changing world. Recent research has been used to show key global trends, and examples have illustrated how companies can both understand and react to the changed circumstances. The ability to interact with customers, and to be truly customer-focused is crucial.

The importance of customer metrics has been presented as being a highly significant factor in moving firms from a product focus to a customer orientation. The use of CLV analysis is deemed to be particularly relevant for companies when evaluating the financial impacts of loyalty and retention approaches. It is widely agreed that a company must know whom it wants to target, and within that approach it must measure the returns delivered and act accordingly. Profitable customers are more difficult to acquire in the highly competitive business environment of the twenty-first century and this makes it imperative for companies to design programmes to reward and keep them once they have 'recruited' them.

A paradigm shift from short-term transactional marketing to a longer term relationship-driven approach has been evaluated. Relationship marketing is seen by some as a paradigm shift in marketing and it is becoming increasingly accepted as the mainstream approach to marketing now. The work of Buttle (2004) in terms of customer classification and that of Day (1999) has made a significant contribution in showing companies how to integrate effective relationship-building with a customer-oriented focus. The central importance of stakeholder evaluation is stressed both in the case studies, and in the work of Payne *et al.* (2005).

End of Chapter Case with Questions

Roy Hankinson Ltd

The Roy Hankinson Company was founded in 1975, and has since grown to over 250 employees and a turnover of more than £11 million per annum. It is the largest privately owned painting and property services company in the UK. The company is based at Monks Ferry at Birkenhead on the Wirral, and Liverpool lies less than one mile away over the water.

The company is proud of its reputation for fair and honest dealing, and its proud boast is that 'We will always be straight with you', meaning that they are an open and honest company who believe in ethics and corporate social responsibility, as well as giving value for money. The key issue for the company is to maximize mutual trust between themselves and clients. They aim to excel at retaining their most valuable B2B customers by offering a combination of professional standard finished work, allied to a friendly and highly customer-focused service approach suitably tailored to the requirements of each client.

The company have become very successful, and have even done specialist painting and restoration work at Buckingham Palace, home of the Queen. In 2007, the company were featured on a UK television programme offering training opportunities at good rates of pay to local unemployed young women.

The Chief Executive Stephen Hankinson is the son of the founder of the organization, and he is both astute and innovative in his approach to business. He recognizes that the company has to keep up with leading advances in technology and business strategy if it is to stay ahead of its many competitors.

The company is structured around five key business units which have to be profitable:

1. blasting and protective coating (includes demolition by water jets, and special anti-corrosion paints);

2. commercial painting (large-scale contract painting carried out for a range of commercial, government, and other organizations);

3. specialist decoration and restoration (such as that carried out at Buckingham Palace);

4. property services (maintaining properties for housing trusts, for example).

5. high-performance coatings (the newest business unit, which provides special coatings in areas such as National Health Service operating rooms).

Stephen Hankinson realizes that the products the company offers are only a part of the overall value proposition to the customers. As the vast majority of customers are business customers (B2B marketing) after-sales service, customer service, and the professional approach of the staff matters. The customers judge the whole 'experience' of being a customer of the organization, and working in partnership with them. There is a lot of competition in the industry from both large and small firms.

With this in mind, and given his innovative approach to the business, Stephen Hankinson agreed to work with two academics from Liverpool John Moores University from 2002–4 on a KTP programme. KTP stands for Knowledge Transfer Partnership, and these schemes are sponsored by the UK government. The aim is to bring industry-experienced academics into companies to evaluate how to create commercially useful knowledge. The academics create a two-year plan, and a highly qualified graduate is then hired to implement this plan under the guidance of the company and the academics. This was one of the first programmes in this industry, and the company used this to generate a great deal of publicity via its website.

The key theme of the KTP was the creation of a relationship marketing-based business approach via systems improvements and the use of the latest academic thinking applied to the business. Specifically, the viable systems model (developed by the late systems genius, Stafford Beer) was used in parallel with a relationship marketing and CRM-driven approach to create a truly strategic organizational change. The fact that the company were prepared to embrace such a level of strategic change was crucial to both the success of the KTP, and their commercial success following the end of it in 2004. During the two years, the company made great progress. Specifically, they:

• Purchased a customer relationship management software system called 'Goldmine', which allowed them systemically to track, monitor, and analyse their customer relationships and profitability. It also enabled them to assess the effectiveness of how they obtained new customers and retained them.

• Developed a powerful and interesting Web presence as a communication and retention tool. The company monitored the ways its customers used its website, and created a very relevant and interesting site which will constantly be augmented with Web 2.0 tools to maintain maximum communication and relevance for its stakeholders. The use of Web metric analysis and search engine optimization has enabled them to maximize their URL listings and the relevance and targeting of messages. This has also been linked into the CRM software, and the overall relationship marketing approach.

• Changed the way their key employees (such as contract managers) worked, in order to maximize the time they spent working in partnership with their clients.

• Emphasized to their staff that they were all part of the marketing team even if they felt they worked in technical role. Such issues as the appearance of staff uniforms and vehicles, as well as the quality of communications become even more important than before.

The effects were very beneficial, and the academics presented a paper at the World Systems Conference in Philadelphia in 2004 to show how this was achieved. The scheme was rated as highly successful, and the company began to be seen as an innovative industry leader by leading organizations.

The company had been one of the first to win a BS5750 Quality Standards accreditation in 1991, but now it won major national awards such as the 2006 Specialist Contractor of the Year, and the 2007 Decorative Painting Contractor of the Year. They were also in the finals of Family Business of the Year in 2007. Profits are rising, and the company is seen as a great employer to work for, and a great partner to work with.

As Stephen Hankinson recently said 'We have combined traditional values with leading edge business practices in areas such as systems integration, relationship marketing, and partnering approaches. We have made ourselves a company that truly puts its customers first. This is proving to be very successful for us, as we add a lot of value where it matters most. We will not rest, as we have to stay ahead of our competitors.'

Questions

1. Analyse the reasons for the success of the company, relating this to theoretical models and concepts whenever you can.

2. What are the key features of relationship marketing in a B2B context?

3. How can the company use marketing tools and techniques to stay ahead of the competition in the next ten years?

4. Evaluate the concept of 'adding value', and say why it is so important. Give some examples other than the one in the case study to support your answer.

Sources:
Author's notes
http://www.hankinson.co.uk accessed 26/02/08

Gummesson (1999) argues that not only can long-term relationships aid financial performance, but the win–win approach can actually lead to a much better set of product and service solutions for customers, as companies spend less time on bureaucratic and legal values, and more time on delivering superior service experiences. Innovation is much more likely to flourish in a collaborative approach for example, as companies are less worried about having to guard knowledge, and are more concerned about utilizing it before someone else does. Gummesson argues that whilst many of the issues that are raised in the new relationship marketing paradigm have been practised by some companies for years, the fact that relationship marketing has both a well-directed focus, and a set of underpinning ethical values and behaviours justifies it as a new paradigm.

The key implications for marketers are that customers now recognize their power, and are increasingly demanding to be given good service and reliable products by companies behaving in an ethical way at both a corporate and an individual level. This is not a competitive advantage; it is merely an expected level of performance. To rise above this and to truly delight and retain customers companies, must focus heavily on the customers they see as crucial to them, and must make every effort both to retain them and deepen the relationship with them. Marketing metrics must be blended with purely financial ones, and the value chain, not the product unit, or the firm, is the key unit of analysis (Grönroos, 1997).

Gummeson points out that when firms implement relationship marketing, the whole organization must adopt the appropriate values to support true customer orientation. Marketing staff need to see their activities within the business strategy, and not just as a tactical support to that strategy. Marketing executives and senior management must see relationship values as a natural vantage point, otherwise there will be no positive effect of relationship marketing. Many writers, including Vollman and Cordon (1998) have stressed the need for partnerships to consist of like-minded partners and people who share the same values and implement the partnership learning. In this way the relationship acts like a marriage, whilst in an overly manipulative or tactical approach the relationship is likely to end in failure and 'divorce'.

On the subject of the stakeholder approach to relationship marketing, Payne *et al.* (2005) argue that traditional transactional marketing approaches ignored stakeholder approaches, whilst relationship marketing stresses such approaches. This led them to propose the Six Markets Model described in Chapter 1.

According to Christopher *et al.* the key implications of the Six Markets framework for managers is the way in which it facilitates thinking about how value is created, recognized, and exchanged, and how flexibility can be useful when evaluating stakeholder relationships. For them the Six Markets Model is a bridge to cross boundaries. In their view this contrasts with the limited budget-focused thinking that flows from the 4P model which the authors see as being essentially a financial allocation model for marketers.

Discussion Questions

1. Why is the continuing development of web technology empowering customers?
2. Give examples of organizations that are using new technologies to build relationships and gain competitive advantage.
3. What opportunities might social networking sites present for marketers? Could they also represent a threat?
4. What is meant by integrated customer communications? Is this a new concept?
5. Is Customer Lifetime Value (CLV) an appropriate customer-related metric for all organizations? Illustrate your answer with examples.
6. Suggest how an organization might 're-engineer' its customer relationships in order to maximize CLV.
7. What is meant by a paradigm? Do you believe that Relationship Marketing represents a paradigm shift in marketing thinking?
8. Will customer empowerment force all organizations to adopt relationship Marketing strategies in the future?

Further Reading

Gummesson, E. (1999) *Total Relationship Marketing*, Butterworth Heinemann, Oxford.

Meadows–Klue, D. (2008) 'Opinion Piece: Falling in Love 2.0: Relationship Marketing for the Facebook Generation', *Journal of Direct, Data and Digital Marketing Practice*, 9, 245–250.

Zineldin, M. (2000) 'Beyond Relationship marketing: technologicalship marketing', *Marketing Intelligence and Planning*, 18(1), 9–23.

References

Buttle, F. (2004) *Customer Relationship Management: Concepts and Tools*, Elsevier Butterworth Heinemann, Oxford.

Day, G. S. (1999) *The Market Driven Organization*, The Free Press.

Economist Intelligence Unit (2008) *Ten Megatrends in B2B Marketing* 2008, EIU.

Grönroos, C. (1997) 'From Marketing Mix to Relationship Marketing: Towards a paradigm shift in marketing', *Management Decision*, 35(4), 322–39.

Gummesson, E. (1999) *Total Relationship Marketing*, Butterworth–Heinemann, Oxford.

Gupta, S. and Lehmann D. R. (2003) 'Customers as Assets', *Journal of Interactive Marketing*, 17(1) (Winter), 9–24.

Hunt, S. (1994) 'Seven Key Elements of Relationship Marketing: Keynote MEG Conference Speech at the University of Ulster at Coleraine, July 1994.

KPMG/Economist Intelligence Unit (2006) *Rethinking the Business Model*, KPMG/EIU.

McBurnie, T. and Clutterbuck, D. (1988) *The Marketing Edge*, Penguin Business.

McKay, M. (2008) 'PR 2.0', *Profile*, 67 (July), 6.

Meadows-Klue, D. (2008) 'Opinion Piece: Falling in Love 2.0: Relationship Marketing for the Facebook Generation', *Journal of Direct, Data and Digital Marketing Practice*, 9, 245–50.

Payne, A., Ballantyne, D., and Christopher, M. (2005) 'A Stakeholder Approach to Relationship Marketing Strategy—The development and use of the six markets model', *European Journal of Marketing*, 39(78), 855–71.

Peel, J. (2002) *Redefining Customer Relationship Management*, Digital Press.

Reichheld, F. (1996) *The Loyalty Effect*, Harvard Business School Press.

Rich, M. K. (2000) 'The Direction of Marketing Relationships', *Journal of Business and Industrial Marketing*, 15(2/3), 170–91.

Tadajewski, M. (2008) 'Relationship Marketing at Wanamaker's in the Nineteenth and Early Twentieth Centuries', *Journal of Macromarketing*, 28(2), 169–82.

Vandermerwe, S. (1995) *From Tin Soldiers to Russian Dolls: Creating added value through services* (2nd edn), Butterworth–Heinemann.

Venkatesan, R. and Kumar, V. (2004) 'A Customer Lifetime Value Frame work for Customer Selection and Resource Allocation Strategy', *Journal of Marketing*, 68(4), 106–25.

Vollman, T. E. and Cordon, C. (1998) 'Building Successful Customer–Supplier Alliances', *Long Range Planning*, 31(5), 684–94.

Zineldin, M. (2000) 'Beyond Relationship Marketing: Technologicalship marketing', *Marketing Intelligence and Planning*, 18(1), 9–23.

Index

Numbers in bold indicate references in Figures.